DUN & BRADSTREET'S

Handbook of Executive

Tax Management

DUN & BRADSTREET'S

Handbook of
Executive Tax
Management

Robert S. Holzman, Ph. D.

THOMAS Y. CROWELL COMPANY
New York, Established 1834

Copyright © 1974 by Robert S. Holzman

All rights reserved. Except for use in a review, the reproduction or utilization of this work in any form or by any electronic, mechanical, or other means, now known or hereafter invented, including xerography, photocopying, and recording, and in any information storage and retrieval system is forbidden without the written permission of the publisher. Published simultaneously in Canada by Fitzhenry & Whiteside Limited, Toronto.

Designed by Abigail Moseley

Manufactured in the United States of America

ISBN 0-690-00309-9

1 2 3 4 5 6 7 8 9 10

Library of Congress Cataloging in Publication Data

Holzman, Robert S.
    Dun & Bradstreet's handbook of executive tax management.

    Includes bibliographical references.
    1. Corporations—United States—Taxation.
I. Title.
KF6465.H62   658.1'53   73-15527
ISBN 0-690-00309-9

Preface

1799224

The corporate income tax is not always a tax upon income. All too often it is a tax upon management's unawareness of the tax consequences of what it considers purely business decisions. There may be burdensome taxes upon management's failure to let professional tax advisors know what's going on *before it happens*.

A businessman who stays aloof of tax matters cannot remain competitive. Tax laws are an economic reality in the business world. A tax dollar is just as real as one derived from other sources.

While taxes must occupy a prominent place in the operation of any business, business decisions are made not only on the basis of taxation (which, of course, the company's tax specialists know), but also on the basis of *business* thinking. This latter consideration is not, of course, the primary sphere of professional tax advisors. In an accumulated earnings tax matter, for example, the question of the "reasonable" needs of the business is not primarily a tax question; it is a practical question to be determined upon the principles of sound business management.

Executives must learn that their areas of discretion are often limited by tax laws. Excessive or unreasonable "executive compensation," for example, is not tax-deductible.

Additionally, the Commissioner of Internal Revenue has the authority to reallocate items of income or expense among corporations under common control where there are intercompany transactions at less than arm's length. Management may be considered derelict in its duties if it did not consider this problem. As shown in Chapter 1, if a corporation has to pay more taxes because of managerial ignorance than otherwise would be payable, stockholders may compel the offending directors or officers to reimburse the company from their own pocketbooks.

Management cannot escape its own tax responsibilities by reliance on tax advisors, however well qualified. In many areas, the tax consequences of a transaction are determined by its motivation. And only management can know that.

Management presumably (and hopefully) knows business. The tax specialists know the tax law. Management can capitalize upon the competence and experience of its tax advisors only if it knows what types of question to ask, what can be expected from first-rate professionals, and how to get the greatest mileage out of what the tax laws require or permit. This book will help management do the job. It will help management exercise its legal right and duty to reduce taxes or avoid them altogether by legal means.

Robert S. Holzman

Professor Emeritus of Taxation
Graduate School of Business Administration
New York University

Professor of Accounting
School of Business Administration
University of Connecticut

Contents

CHAPTER 1

Management's Tax Responsibilities

Management's tax responsibility is special. Taxes are often the largest single corporate expense. Corporate profits and sometimes even corporate survival may depend upon management's ability to minimize the tax burden or to take advantage of tax-favored actions.

Management cannot avoid responsibility by delegation. For example, the failure of an accountant or lawyer to prepare the return does not excuse failure to file a timely return, and penalties may be imposed.[1]

Reliance upon the advice of counsel may sometimes be a good defense for corporate directors to a shareholder's charge of mismanagement.[2] But in tax matters, the directors must first know enough about taxes to realize what questions to refer to counsel if they are to derive any such protection.

Even though a corporation asks for and gets tax advice from competent advisors, penalties may be assessed for failure to make a full and complete disclosure of facts necessary for proper advice.[3] And there is the nub of the problem. For if management does not understand the tax problem well enough to make a full disclosure of all of the facts and circumstances to the advisors, reliance upon counsel's advice can never be a defense. Also, reliance on the advice of counsel is of no help unless the counsel is competent to advise. This, of course, imposes a further responsibility upon management. Sometimes a court seems to use 20-20 hindsight to determine the consultant's competency. Clearly, if it is judicially determined that the advice given was wrong, there is some basis for questioning the competency of the advisor and the defense of reliance on his advice is weakened.[4]

Management must consult its counsel or accountant to avoid not only charges of negligence, but also far more serious charges of fraud. Failure to do so exposes management to the risk that any improperly handled matter may be characterized as fraud.[5] Additionally, the withholding of information from the tax advisor may give rise to an implication of fraud.[6]

Responsibility to the Corporation

Everyone is presumed to know the law.[7] A corporation is bound by management's ineptitude or ignorance in the formulation of a transaction. For example, management cannot say after a transaction is entered into that it is not bound because it overlooked possible tax consequences.[8] Thus, management must consider and seek advice on the tax consequences when a transaction is being negotiated.

Management must recognize the tax dangers and pitfalls in business situations; it must know *what* questions to ask. The most competent tax advisors may be rendered impotent if the right questions are not put to them at the right time. (See chapter 26, Procedure and Practice Guide.)

Management owes the corporation the duty of seeing that its books are properly kept. Improper books and records may deprive the corporation of deductions and benefits that it might otherwise claim in its tax return.

Management must set up proper record retention machinery to assure the availability of records for deductions. Necessary workpapers in areas ordinarily beyond the jurisdiction of the corporate tax department must be retained. These include, for example, salesmen's expense vouchers, details of bad debt write-offs, depreciation adjustments, documentation of the reasonableness of salary increases for executives, and much more. (See chapter 17, The Burden of Proof.)

In closely held corporations, management may have the responsibility of providing for the continuance of the business upon the death of a major shareholder, as by providing for the orderly passage of stock from the decedent or his estate to the corporation or to the surviving major stockholders under a predetermined valuation formula.[9] (See chapter 21, What Happens When a Major Stockholder Dies.)

Management must take steps to safeguard the corporate tax deduction for payments made to the widow of an officer or other employee. The payment must be shown to have been made for some economic benefit of the corporation. Ordinarily, formal action by the board of directors authorizing the payments to a widow should be taken and made a matter of record.[10] (See chapter 25, Corporate Minutes: Their Offensive and Defensive Use.)

Management must see that decisions with tax consequences are implemented so that the tax effects sought are realized. For example, if certain supplies are written off as obsolete, the deduction will be lost if employees continue to use the items and no instructions are given to them to stop such use.[11]

Management must know enough about tax matters to avoid what might amount to blackmail attempts against the corporation. For example, a consolidated Federal income tax return may be filed only when all of the corporations that have been members of the affiliated group *at any time* during the taxable year for which the return is made consent to the regulations applicable to that year.[12] Thus, if a corporation were part of an affiliated group for even one day but no longer is, that corporation (or its officers) might refuse to consent to the filing of a consolidated return for the year in which their company was a part of the group for one day *unless* . . . . And thus the corporation is faced with a fine blackmail situation. Someone should have remembered to get that consent before the company withdrew from the consolidated group or before its stock was sold.

Management should be conscious of the fact that the verbiage upon corporate securities certificates can determine the tax consequences of such securities to the corporation. An intended interest deduction could be lost in this manner.[13] (See chapter 3, Is it Stock or are they Bonds?)

Management should know the difference between an Internal Revenue Agent and a Special Agent so that if any inquiry is made by the latter, no statements or admissions should be made without first checking with legal counsel. (See chapter 23, Dealing with the Internal Revenue Service.)

One of management's most important duties to its corporation may be to keep its mouth shut in appropriate circumstances. (See chapter 24, Unnecessary and Unwitting Disclosure.)

On the other hand, there may be circumstances in which failure to speak may damage the corporation. For example, it may be very damaging for management, when questioned by an Internal Revenue agent about nonpayment of dividends, to fail to mention that earnings are being accumulated for construction of a building or other corporate purposes and to make the assertion only later when the corporation is contesting an accumulated earnings assessment judicially.[14]

Management may think that it can discontinue its qualified pension or deferred profit-sharing plan at will. Legally, it *may* be able to do so; but if this is done without the prior approval of the Commissioner of Internal Revenue, the tax consequences will be unpleasant and expensive. (See chapter 9, Profit-sharing Plans.)

Management should know enough about tax penalties so that the corporation may avoid such nondeductible payments. (See chapter 23, Dealing with the Internal Revenue Service.)

Management has the responsibility of protecting the corporation's tax returns from attack by employing any proper means. It may, in appropriate circumstances, invoke the Fourth Amendment, which protects against illegal search and seizure of one's home and property, which includes records. Officers of a corporation should invoke this right whenever it is necessary. But books and records which are required by law to be kept are not protected by this amendment.

The Fifth Amendment, which protects against self-incrimination, does not extend to corporations; nor does an order to produce corporate books and records violate an individual's privilege against self-incrimination.[15]

On the other hand, the Sixth Amendment which gives the accused in a criminal proceeding the right to be confronted with the witnesses against him, may be invoked by a corporation. Thus, corporate officers should look after their company's interests by cross-examining or otherwise confronting its accusers. However, the Sixth Amendment does not bar the use of informers. And in absence of some compelling reason for identifying an informer, courts will generally not disclose his name.[16]

Management should realize the implications of this. A person with a real or imaginary grievance against the corporation may tell the Internal Revenue Service what he "knows." This could lead to expense and trouble even if the allegations prove untrue. The time and cost of documenting a questioned transaction (such as travel and entertainment expenses of all officers) can be tremendous. A taxpayer's vulnerability is increased by the fact that the Internal Revenue Service is empowered to pay informers. Ordinarily, payment may not exceed 10 percent of the additional taxes, penalties, and fines that are recovered as a result of the information furnished.[17]

In discussing confidential matters with legal counsel, executives should understand that their company can be hurt by what an attorney is compelled to disclose as to his "private" discussions with the corporation's executives for the attorney-client relationship is not entirely sacrosanct. The elements necessary for the assertion of the attorney-client privilege are: (1) where legal advice of any kind is sought, (2) from a professional legal advisor in his capacity as such, (3) the communication relating to that purpose, (4) made in confidence, (5) by the client, (6) is at his instance permanently protected, (7) from disclosure by himself or the legal advisor, (8) except where the protection is waived.[18] Where an individual had discussed a matter with his attorney in the presence of a bank vice-president who would be concerned with custodial aspects of the arrangement, the attorney-client privilege did not apply, for it had been waived by reason of the fact that a person other than client and attorney was present, namely, the bank employee. Even though that employee also happened to be an attorney, he was not present in that capacity, but rather as a bank officer.[19] The attorney-client privilege extends to corporations as well.[20]

Officers can save their company a considerable amount of time and expense if immediate and unmistakable objection is raised to an unnecessary examination by the Internal Revenue Service. Two prohibitions are available: (1) that against "unnecessary examination or investigation" and (2) that against reexamination of books and records without prior written notice thereof.[21] The letter of request for such a reexamination must be signed by the District Director, the Assistant Regional Commissioner (Audit), or someone delegated by one of them.[22] A Revenue agent, who after an audit, thinks of something he may have overlooked or handled incorrectly, might be reluctant to go to his superior, the District Director, to get a reexamination if there is objection to reexamination without a written request.[23] A second examination may also be avoided by a showing that it is not necessary.[24]

Responsibility to the Employees

Management can ease the tax burden of employees by doing whatever is necessary to assure them of obtaining exclusions from taxable income or of getting valid tax deductions.

Within certain limits, sick pay may be excluded from an employee's gross income if paid under a sick pay plan. But the rules of such a plan must be determinable before the employee's sickness arises.[25] If employee rights under such a plan are not enforceable, knowledge of the plan must be reasonably available to the employees.[26] The use of a plan, for tax purposes, signifies something more than merely one or more *ad hoc* benefit payments.[27] The company may unwittingly cause loss of the sick pay exclusion by giving an employee work to do at home.[28] For the company to qualify for the sick pay exclusion, the employee must be absent from "work," not merely from the place of work.

Management must notify its employees of the existence of an employee benefit plan, such as a qualified pension or deferred profit-sharing plan.[29] (See chapters 9, Profit-Sharing Plans, and 10, Pension Plans.) Failure to do so may result in the disqualification of the plan. Further, management owes its employees the duty of filing the required informational data to substantiate employee benefit plans.

When an employee is assigned to a different location and not reimbursed for moving expenses, the employer may help the employee get a deduction on his own tax return by furnishing a written statement that the move is necessary to maintain employment, if such is the situation.[30]

Similarly, an employee is likely to be granted a tax deduction for educational expenses, such as going to law school, if the employer requires that such courses be taken as a condition to maintaining his present job.

Similarly, a corporation's written statement of policy that salaries have been set at a level sufficient to permit certain business expenses may help sustain a business expense deduction for entertainment on the employee's tax return.[31]

To help key personnel deduct the travel expenses of their wives who accompany them on business trips, a company may adopt a written policy that wives are expected to accompany their husbands on business trips because of the social functions incidental to such jaunts.[32] However, where no business reasons for inviting wives to attend a company function are offered, the company's payment of their expenses for attending the function may be taxable income to their husbands.

An officer or other employee does not have to include in his income the value of company-owned housing that he occupies if it is provided in advance that he must do so (as a condition of his employment) for the company's convenience.[33]

Where an employee wishes to use part of his home as an office, a company's *requiring* him to do so as a condition of his employment will very likely facilitate his getting a business expense deduction.[34]

If a corporation awards scholarships or fellowships to certain employees, the payments should not be shown on the books as compensation, nor should withholding tax be deducted. To do so would make it very difficult, although not impossible, for the employee to exclude the amounts from gross income, under the scholarship rules.[35]

Where a corporation in financial trouble requires officers or key people to lend money to the company as a condition of keeping their jobs, if the loans cannot be repaid, the lenders will be entitled to a business bad debt deduction.[36]

Life insurance proceeds are tax-exempt to the beneficiaries under most circumstances. Employee death benefits are excluded only to the extent of $5000. Thus, the taxpayer will get a far better tax break on amounts passing to beneficiaries of employees who die if the payments can qualify as life insurance proceeds than if they are characterized as employee death benefits. If the employer plans carefully, he can have life insurance proceeds treatment applied to the benefits even if a life insurance company is not used and there is no life insurance contract.[37]

Care must be exercised in handling payments to the widow of an officer or employee. If the minutes authorizing payment refer to the deceased's long and faithful service to the company, the payment may be taxed as compensation for services rendered.[38] But payment made because the widow is in financial need may be viewed as a tax-free gift.[39] So, charging disbursements on the company's books to the "Miscellaneous Expense" account and not the "Payroll" account may indicate a tax-free gift.[40]

The corporation can arrange to provide preferential tax treatment to employees in adopting tax-favored compensation arrangements (such as deferred compensation, stock options, and various fringe benefits). (See chapter 8, Compensation, Fringe Benefits.)

Management can take affirmative steps to see that employee expenses are deductible by the employees. Where employees are reminded to seek reimbursement from the company where appropriate, they are not apt to lose the deductions when claimed on their own tax returns.

Management can provide employees with information as to the filing of their own tax returns with the minimum permissible impact: access may be provided to the company's tax department or advisors; employees may be given instructional material prepared by commercial publishers or services; arrangements may be made to have a representative of the Internal Revenue Service available to assist in tax return preparation.

Responsibility to the Government

The rendering of a proper tax return is regarded by the courts as a vital part of life, equal in importance to attention to one's business.[41] The president of a corporation has a statutory obligation to file or cause to be filed proper tax returns.

A corporation has specific tax responsibilities, among which are the following: filing of timely returns, withholding income and Social Security taxes, and filing salary and other information returns. If the corporate records are subpoenaed by the Internal Revenue Service, a duty of care is imposed upon the officer in charge of these records to safeguard them so that they will be available on the effective date of the subpoena. A violation of that duty renders the officer subject to appropriate penalties for civil contempt.[42]

Responsibility to Management Itself

If directors do not know what the corporation's earnings and profits really are, a dividend in excess of that amount may be paid, perhaps to avoid accumulated earnings tax liability. Under state law, the directors might then be subject to jail terms for impairing surplus by an excessive dividend.

Directors violate their fiduciary duties when they avail themselves of a corporation in order to avoid their personal taxes. The accumulated earnings penalty tax is imposed upon a corporation which retains earnings in excess of its credit beyond the reasonable needs of the business for the purpose of avoiding shareholder income taxes.[43] If the refusal of the directors to pay dividends results in an imposition of such penalty taxes, the directors themselves may be liable for the resulting damages to the corporation and its shareholders.[44]

In setting fees on transactions between parties under common control, a corporation should keep memoranda of factors that determined the methods or figures arrived at. At the very least, this will help protect against a charge of fraud. Adjustments made by the Internal Revenue Service will not cause personal repercussions when the matter can be shown to be one where reasonable persons might differ in their interpretations.[45]

Where stockholders of a corporation make withdrawals from the company at a time when there are accumulated earnings and profits, these withdrawals will be treated as dividends, absent a showing that a debtor-creditor relationship exists. If such a relationship does exist, the corporate records and financial statements should reflect that fact.[46]

If a director objects to a course of action voted upon by the majority recorded in the minutes, he may be able to avoid personal involvement with the tax consequences of this action.[47]

A corporate officer may be held personally liable where the company fails to collect, account for, and pay over to the Government specified payroll taxes.[48] Any officer or employee of a corporation (as well as various other designated parties) who, as such, is under a duty to perform the required withholding and transmitting may be held liable. Any person required to collect and pay taxes and who fails to do so is subject to a penalty of 100 percent of the withholding tax evaded or not collected. The question is whether the person had the final word as to what bills would or would not be paid and when.[49] Corporate office in itself does not impose the duty to collect, account for, and pay over withheld taxes. On the other hand, an officer may have such a duty even though he is not the disbursing officer.[50]

Intent to defraud or to deprive the United States of the taxes collected is not required in order that penalties may be imposed upon the responsible officer personally;[51] the acts or omissions that subject an officer to penalty, must be intentional, knowing, and voluntary rather than inadvertent and unintended.[52]

The chief executive officer or the treasurer may be held liable for failure to pay over withheld taxes.[53] But personal liability may not attach to individuals who hold office solely for the purpose of protecting their investments in a company,[54] nor does it attach to a vice-president in charge of sales and sales promotion.[55]

The Government need not even seek to reach existing corporate assets, but may proceed directly against the officers.[56] It is not essential that the corporation involved be closely held.[57]

Inasmuch as management may be personally liable for taxes that should have been withheld, the officers should know upon *what* to withhold. Free vacations to employees were deemed to be compensation in one case, and management was penalized for its failure to withhold upon these.[58] Similarly, personal liability attaches for failure to deduct for nonresident alien withholding tax.[59]

Since individuals may be responsible for legal and other fees arising out of their acts while corporate officers or directors, the corporation may provide reimbursement. Such reimbursement may be tax-deductible by the corporation if necessary to induce officers and directors to serve.[60] Reimbursement may cover payments made by directors because of accumulated earnings tax imposed, personal liability for withholding taxes, and the like.

Management can also become personally involved with other Federal tax penalties. The Internal Revenue Code provides that any person who willfully makes and subscribes to a return, statement, or other document that contains or is verified by a written declaration that it is made in violation of the perjury laws and that he does not believe to be true will, upon conviction, be fined not more than $5000, or imprisoned not more than three years, or both.[61] Such also is the case if any person willfully aids or assists in the preparation or presentation of any matter arising under the Federal tax laws and which is fraudulent, whether or not the fraud is within the knowledge of or has been consented to by the person authorized to present the return or document.

Any person who willfully delivers or discloses to the Secretary of the Treasury or his delegate, the Commissioner of Internal Revenue, any list, return, account, statement, or other document known by that person to be fraudulent as to any material matter is subject to a fine of not more than $1000, or imprisonment of not more than one year, or both.[62] There are also penalties applicable to false statements relating to tax, which statements are made to purchasers or lessees.[63]

Any attempt to interfere with the administration of Internal Revenue laws constitutes an offense, punishable upon conviction by a fine of not more than $5000, or imprisonment of not more than three years, or both. If the offense is committed only by *threats* of force,[64] the maximum penalties will be a fine of not more than $3000, or imprisonment of not more than one year, or both.

Any person, who having been duly summoned to appear or to appear and to produce books, accounts, records, memoranda, or other papers, fails to comply with the terms of the summons will be subject to a fine of not more than $1000 upon conviction, or imprisonment for not more than one year, or both.[65]

Responsibility to Investors

Management may make decisions that involve the financial welfare of investors. For example, if securities are labeled correctly, the investor may not have his tax treatment of corporate distributions reopened by the Internal Revenue Service.

If the "insiders" of a corporation buy or sell company securities in interstate commerce, misrepresentation or failure to disclose material facts about the company not known to the public violates the Securities Exchange Act of 1934.[66] Insider knowledge could involve taxes. For example, management may have knowledge of substantial Federal income tax assessments or refunds; or there might be "advance" knowledge of Federal tax treatment of items of such magnitude that the price of the stock could be affected.

NOTES

1. *Logan Lumber Company v. Commissioner*, 365 F.2d 846 (5th Cir., 1966).
2. *Blaustein v. Pan American Petroleum & Transport Co.*, 293 N.Y. 281 (Ct. App., 1944).
3. *Fabacher et al. v. United States*, D.C., S.D. Miss., 1966.
4. *Sanford Refett et al.*, 39 T.C. 869 (1963).
5. *Burrell et al. v. Commissioner*, 400 F.2d 682 (10th Cir., 1968).
6. *United States v. Pepe*, 360 F.2d 1015 (3d Cir., 1966).
7. *Barnett Investment Company v. Nee*, 72 F. Supp. 81 (D.C., W.D. Mo., 1947).
8. *Clarence Clark Hamlin Trust et al. v. Commissioner*, 209 F.2d 765 (10th Cir., 1954).
9. *Mountain State Steel Foundries, Inc. et al. v. Commissioner*, 284 F.2d 737 (4th Cir., 1960).
10. *Greentree's, Incorporated v. United States*, D.C., E.D. Va., 1965.
11. *Becker v. Anheuser, Busch, Inc. et al.*, 120 F.2d 403 (8th Cir., 1941).
12. I.R.C. Section 1501.
13. *The Rappold Co.*, T.C. Memo., Docket No. 23393 (entered November 8, 1950).
14. *See Goodman et al. v. United States*, 285 F. Supp. 245 (D.C., C.D. Cal., 1968).
15. *United States et al. v. Giordano*, 419 F.2d 564 (8th Cir., 1969).
16. *Rugendorf v. United States*, 376 U.S. 528 (1964).
17. Regulations Section 301.7623-1(c).
18. *Radiant Burners, Inc. v. American Gas Association*, 320 F.2d 314 (7th Cir., 1963).
19. *In the Matter of Joseph T. Bretto et al. v. Northern City National Bank et al.*, 231 F. Supp. 529 (D.C., Minn., 1964).
20. *Radiant Burners, Inc. v. American Gas Association*, 320 F.2d 314 (7th Cir., 1963).
21. I.R.C. Section 7605(b).
22. Revenue Procedure 64-40, 1964-2 CB 971.
23. *Service Electric Company, Inc. et al.*, T.C. Memo. 1965-176 (filed June 28, 1965).
24. *DeMasters et al. v. Arend et al.*, 313 F.2d 79 (9th Cir., 1963).
25. *John C. Lang et al.*, 41 T.C. 352 (1963).
26. Regulations Section 1.105-5.
27. *Leo P. Kaufman Estate*, 35 T.C. 663 (1961), *aff'd*, 300 F.2d 128 (6th Cir., 1962).
28. *Frank A. Thomas et al.*, T.C. Memo. 1969-108 (filed May 26, 1969).
29. Regulations Section 1.401-1(a)(2).
30. *Edward N. Wilson et al.*, 49 T.C. 406 (1967), *rev'd on another issue*, 412 F.2d 314 (6th Cir., 1969).
31. *Herman E. Bischoff et al.*, T.C. Memo. 1966-102 (filed May 19, 1966).
32. *United States v. Disney et al.*, 413 F.2d 783 (9th Cir., 1969).
33. *See Adolph Coors Co. et al.*, T.C. Memo. 1968-256 (filed November 7, 1968).
34. *See George H. Newi et al.*, T.C. Memo. 1969-131 (filed June 26, 1969), *aff'd*, 432 F.2d 998 (2d Cir., 1970).
35. *Johnson et al. v. Bingler*, 394 U.S. 741 (1969).
36. *Eugene H. Rietske et al.*, 40 T.C. 443 (1963).
37. *Ross v. Ogden*, 401 F.2d 464 (5th Cir., 1968).
38. *Frances C. Cross Estate*, T.C. Memo. 1964-255 (filed September 28, 1964).
39. *Corasaniti et al. v. United States*, 212 F. Supp. 229 (D.C., Md., 1962).
40. *Fanning v. Conley, Jr.*, 357 F.2d 37 (2d Cir., 1966).
41. *Ned Wayburn*, 32 B.T.A. 813 (1935).
42. *In the Matter of D. I. Operating Company*, 240 F. Supp. 672 (D.C., Nev., 1965).
43. I.R.C. Section 532(a).
44. *United States v. Gates, Jr. et al.*, D.C., Colo., 1965, *aff'd*, 376 F.2d 65 (10th Cir., 1967).
45. *Union Packing Co. et al.*, T.C. Memo. 1955-308 (filed November 22, 1955).
46. *Gurtman et al. v. United States*, 237 F. Supp. 533 (D.C., N.J., 1965).
47. *See Southwest Properties, Inc. et al.*, 38 T.C. 97 (1962).
48. I.R.C. Section 6671(b).
49. *Wilson v. United States*, 250 F.2d 312 (9th Cir., 1957).

50. *Monday et al. v. United States et al.*, 421 F.2d 1210 (7th Cir., 1970).

51. *In re Haynes*, 88 F. Supp. 379 (D.C., Kansas, 1949).

52. *Messina v. Scanlon*, D.C., E.D.N.Y., 1965.

53. *Wilson et al. v. United States*, 250 F.2d 312 (9th Cir., 1957).

54. *Last et al. v. United States*, D.C., E.D.N.Y., 1965.

55. *Grossberg v. United States*, D.C., E.D. Va., 1968.

56. *Cash v. Campbell*, D.C., W.D. Wash., 1965.

57. *Tozier et al. v. United States*, D.C., W.D. Wash., 1965.

58. *ABC Freight Forwarding Corporation v. United States* (D.C., S.D. N.Y., 1968).

59. T.I.R.-706, March 11, 1965.

60. *Central Coat, Apron & Linen Service, Inc. v. United States*, 298 F. Supp. 1201 (D.C., S.D. N.Y., 1969).

61. I.R.C. Section 7206.

62. I.R.C. Section 7207.

63. I.R.C. Section 7211.

64. I.R.C. Section 7212.

65. I.R.C. Section 7210.

66. I.R.C. Section 16(b). *See Securities Exchange Commission v. Texas Gulf Sulphur Co. et al.*, 401 F.2d 833 (2d Cir., 1968).

CHAPTER 2

Corporations and Other Forms of Conducting Business

Significance of the Business Form

The form in which a person does business is his own choice. The choice may be made deliberately so as to get the best tax results, provided the arrangement is a real one. That the motive for adopting a particular form of business was tax avoidance is not sufficient, in and of itself, to be a basis for tax liability unless the transaction first established such liability without it. But to be afforded recognition for tax purposes, the form that a taxpayer chooses must be a viable business entity; that is, it must have been selected for a substantial business purpose or a substantive business activity must be conducted.[1] (See chapter 20, Intention and Purpose.) If, however, the form employed is so evanescent as to lack economic reality, recognition as a separate taxable entity will be denied.[2]

The form, if genuinely adopted and realistically followed, will prevail and that form adopted is customarily recognized and upheld by the courts except where it is a patent distortion of normal business practice.[3]

Selection of a business form to which Congress has specifically granted preferential tax treatment (such as the Subchapter S corporation to be discussed later in this chapter) is not regarded as tax avoidance.[4] Similarly, the general purpose of Congress in sanctioning (subject to certain ground rules) tax-free spin-offs was to rearrange corporate entities and evidences of ownership to comport with management's idea of how best to carry on its businesses.[5] The whole theory of the tax-free corporate reorganization is to allow a tax-free change in business form when undertaken for business reasons.[6]

Significance of State Law

The classes into which organizations are placed for Federal income tax purposes are determined under the Internal Revenue Code. Thus, a particular organization might be classified as a "trust" under the law of one state and as a "corporation" under the law of another. But for the purposes of the Federal tax law, the organization would be classed uniformly as one type of entity. This area is not without its jurisdictional disputes. Although it is the Internal Revenue Code rather than local law that establishes the tests or standards which will be applied in determining the classification in which an organization belongs, local law governs in determining whether the legal relationships which have been established in the formation of an organization are such that the standards are met. Thus, it is local law that must be complied with in determining such matters as the legal relationships of the members of the organization to each other and to the public at large and the interests of the members of the organization in its assets.[7]

Where a state law describes the prerequisites of a corporation, United States Treasury regulations cannot call the organization that complies with those prerequisites a "partnership" if in fact the entity comports with the definition of a "corporation" as contained in the Internal Revenue Code.[8]

Sole Proprietorship

A *sole proprietorship* has the advantages of simplicity and independence. From the tax point of view, the characteristics of this form are virtually all unfavorable— except for the fact that there are no specialized penalties (such as in the case of the personal holding company, the accumulated earnings tax, or the collapsible corporation) and in start-up situations where losses are anticipated. The losses may be available against other income.

Where business is conducted as a sole proprietorship, contacts and contracts with other businesses may be terminated upon the death of the proprietor.[9] At that time, income is accelerated to the year in which he died in the case of all obligations still due as a result of installment sales.[10]

A sole proprietor is not an employee for purposes of the sick pay exclusion.[11] That applies also to the tax-favored treatment given to qualified employee benefit plans (such as pension and deferred profit-sharing plans). Retirement plans for the self-employed are not treated as advantageously for tax purposes as are those corporate plans.

All of an individual's assets may be subject to creditors' claims. A Federal tax lien can reach even the cash surrender value of a life insurance policy that the debtor owns on his life.[12]

A tax-free changeover from proprietorship to corporate form is possible when a proprietorship transfers property to a corporation solely in return for the latter's stock or securities if immediately after the exchange the proprietor owns at least 80 percent of the voting stock and at least 80 percent of the total number of shares of all other classes of stock of the corporation.[13]

Partnership

For Federal income tax purposes, the term *partnership* includes a syndicate, group, pool, joint venture, and other unincorporated organizations through or by means of which any business, financial operation, or venture is carried on and which is not a corporation, a trust, or an estate within the meaning of the Internal Revenue Code.[14] The term may include groups not commonly called partnerships.[15]

The basic concept of a partnership is a group of persons having a common business interest and working together in their respective spheres toward the successful operation and conduct of that business interest.[16]

A partnership differs from mere co-ownership. An important distinction between mere co-owners and co-owner partners lies in the degree of business activity of the co-owners or their agents. If these activities are minimal, mere co-ownership is indicated.[17] However, the most important ingredient in determining whether a partnership exists is *intent* to conduct business as a partnership.[18] The language of an agreement does not determine whether a partnership exists for tax purposes. Even though an agreement may state specifically that the arrangement is not a partnership, that statement is not controlling for tax purposes. It is the *substance* of an agreement, not the mere written words, that determine the tax character of the agreement.[19]

A partnership as such is not taxable for Federal income tax purposes.[20] Rather, the partners individually reflect upon their own tax returns their *pro rata* share of each type of partnership income and deductions or expense.[21] The partnership agreement will determine the proportionate income or expense items of each type for the several partners; but if the principal purpose of any provision in the partnership agreement is the avoidance of tax, this provision will be disregarded for tax purposes.[22]

A *family* partnership is the same as any other partnership, except that its genuineness is more critically appraised. In finding that a *bona fide* family partnership did not exist in one case, the court noted that there were no written articles of partnership and no formal or written acts of donation by the alleged partners. There was no breakdown or separation of accounts in the partnership records to show individual accounts, drawings, net earnings, and contributions to capital. The so-called partner whose tax returns were under audit had no specific duties to perform for the partnership, exercised no control over partnership funds, and presented no evidence whatsoever that any interested persons regarded her as a partner.[23]

For some purposes, a partner may be an employee.[24] But *bona fide* members of a partnership are not employees of the partnership within the meaning of the Social Security Act or for purposes of Federal income tax withholding. A partner is regarded as a self-employed person, not an employee.[25]

There is nothing to prevent a trustee from being a partner, as in a family partnership.[26] And the laws of a good many states permit a corporation to be a partner.[27]

A partnership's principal tax utility is the splitting of income among plural parties. A partnership is a better vehicle for obtaining a business bad debt deduction than is a proprietorship (for it is often difficult to determine whether a proprietor is acting in a personal or a business role) or a corporation. The business of a partnership is considered to be the business of each partner;[28] but the business of a corporation is not that of its stockholders or officers.[29] The sole owner of the stock of a corporation is covered by this rule.[30]

A principal tax disadvantage of the partnership form is that each partner is taxed upon his distributive share of partnership earnings, whether actually distributed or not.

A partnership has the same tax disabilities as a proprietorship in the case of bunching of installment obligations that are not yet due at such time as the entity is terminated. Also absent are the tax-favored treatment of benefits available to corporate employees.

Association

An *association* may be treated for tax purposes as though it were either a partnership or a corporation, depending on the presence or absence of five corporate characteristics:

(1) Continuity of existence.
(2) Transferability of interests.
(3) Title in a single entity.
(4) Limited liability.
(5) Centralized management.

If corporate characteristics predominate, the organization will be taxed as a corporation. And of the five factors, the fifth is perhaps the most important single factor.[31]

Corporation

The corporation offers the greatest tax advantages. For that reason, the Internal Revenue Service may seek to deny corporate status where the primary motive for formation is tax avoidance. The term *corporation* is interpreted to mean a corporation that does some business in the ordinary meaning—escaping taxation is not business in the ordinary meaning.[32] Thus, the separate tax existence of a corporation will not be recognized where it serves no independence function and is merely a corporate extension of the shareholders' personalities.[33] The fact that a state, in conferring a charter, has placed the label of "corporation" on a business organization does not control its status for Federal tax purposes.[34]

However, in one case in which Internal Revenue Service sought unsuccessfully to deny corporate tax status to an enterprise that had been incorporated solely to avoid taxes, the court observed that the test is not the personal purpose of a taxpayer in creating a corporation; rather, it is whether the taxpayer intends that that purpose be accomplished through a corporation carrying out substantive business functions. If the purpose of the corporation is to carry out substantive business functions—or if it in fact engages in substantive business activity—it will not be disregarded for Federal tax purposes.[35]

A corporation and its shareholders are, of course, treated as separate taxpayers. This is normally true of one-man corporations as well.[36] Generally, whatever the purpose of organizing a corporation, so long as that purpose is pursued by the corporation, it remains a separate taxable entity.[37] However, in special circumstances, a corporation's separate existence may not be recognized. Thus, where a corporation was formed solely to liquidate real estate and had no right, power, or discretion to dispose of income, it was regarded as a mere conduit and was therefore not taxable.[38] Where a partnership created two corporations and gave real estate to each to fend off the creditors of one partner and the partners later claimed that the corporations were but dummies, it was held that entity would be disregarded as to the one corporation that did nothing but hold title to property, whereas entity would be recognized in the case of the other corporation, which had engaged in some business; namely, negotiating a loan upon its property.[39]

A stockholder (even the 100 percent stockholder) must distinguish between himself as an individual and the corporation. Thus, a 100 percent stockholder may not, for example, claim a deduction on his own tax return for the services his wife performs for the corporation and not for him.[40]

The following are the principal tax advantages available if the corporate form is used:

(1) The corporate income tax rates (22 percent on the first $25,000 and 48 percent on excess) are lower than the maximum individual tax rates. The 50 percent ceiling tax upon earned income of individuals (see chapter 8, Compensation Fringe Benefits.) tends to equalize the rates; but unearned income of an individual is still fixed at the maximum rate of 70 percent.

(2) While the corporation is taxed on its earnings, whether distributed to the shareholders or not, the shareholders are not taxed upon corporate earnings until distributed. If there are sound business reasons for retention of earnings, dividends need never be paid despite the company's prosperity. (See chapter 11, Dividends and the Tax on Accumulated Earnings.)

(3) Corporations may provide a wide variety of tax-favored compensation arrangements and benefits furthering the interests of both company and employee. These arrangements and benefits are usually not available to sole proprietors or partners. (See chapter 8, Compensation, Fringe Benefits.) But these benefits are available to shareholder-officers, even though they may be the only corporate employees.

(4) Corporate stock is readily transferable, generally without the consent of other parties, and is a useful tool in estate planning.

(5) Inasmuch as a corporation may have a permanent existence, the risk of having unmatured installment obligations taxed as income in the year in which the enterprise terminates is minimal. If a corporation is liquidated on a tax-free basis into its parent corporation, there is no taxable income with respect to these unmatured installment obligations.[41]

(6) Corporations, by means of a tax-free reorganization, may be changed relatively easily to adapt to new needs and circumstances. There may be mergers, consolidations, liquidations, division into plural companies, recapitalizations, etc.

(7) Because of tax-favored financial instruments available to a corporation, it enjoys a far greater potential for interesting investors than do other business forms.

(8) Federal tax liens and other claims against the corporation cannot involve the shareholders personally unless there is a distribution of corporate assets when the corporation is insolvent (or is made insolvent by the transfer). Only then is transferee liability created.[42] (See chapter 23, Dealing with the Internal Revenue Service.)

But there are also certain tax disadvantages:

(1) There is a double income tax—or at least a second set of income taxes—upon the same corporate earnings: when the corporation derives its profits and when the shareholders receive dividends reflecting these profits. But as will be shown later in this chapter, in certain situations this doubling up of taxes can be avoided.

(2) Even though a corporation's income may have been tax-exempt or tax-favored (e.g., interest on municipal bonds) in the corporation's hands, this preferential character is lost when dividends are received by the shareholders. Thus, a corporation is not an effective conduit for tax-favored income.[43]

(3) A corporation may be subjected to tax treatment not imposed in other areas. For example, the tax on unreasonable accumulations of earnings effectuates a Congressional intent to deter the use of a corporate entity to avoid personal income taxes.[44] There is also the personal holding company tax. At various times, Congress has seen fit to impose an excess profits tax. And this tax has been imposed only upon corporations.

(4) Corporate shareholders may face adverse tax consequences if the corporation fails to meet certain requirements of the Internal Revenue Code. For example, if a corporation meets the characterization of "collapsible corporation" because it is liquidated while it has unrealized "paper profits" under certain circumstances, the shareholders may be taxed on ordinary income rather than on capital gain.[45]

(5) The Fifth Amendment's protection against self-incrimination is not available generally or in a tax matter where a corporation is the taxpayer.[46]

There are, of course, numerous non-tax advantages and disadvantages of using the corporate form. These are detailed in the standard works on corporations and on finance.

Election Not to Be Taxed as a Corporation

Certain corporations, under appropriate circumstances, may elect not to be taxed as corporations. Instead, shareholders are taxed directly upon their proportionate parts of the corporate earnings.[47] These companies are familiarly known as Subchapter S corporations, or "pseudo-corporations."

The basic purpose of Subchapter S of the Internal Revenue Code is to permit a qualified corporation and its shareholders to avoid the double tax normally paid when a corporation distributes its earnings and profits as dividends. The corporate entity is not ignored. Corporate taxable income is computed in the same manner as in the case of any other corporation. The only difference is with respect to the net operating loss deduction and certain other specified deductions.[48]

This treatment is available to a *small business corporation,* which, for this purpose, means a domestic corporation that is not a member of an affiliated group. A corporation will not be considered a member of an affiliated group for this purpose if it owns stock of a subsidiary corporation that: (1) has not begun business at any time on or after the date of its incorporation and before the close of the parent corporation's taxable year to which the election applies and (2) does not have taxable income during the parent corporation's taxable year. A Subchapter S corporation election may not be made by a member of an affiliated group unless, in fact, only one of the corporations is an active one.[49]

Subject to this qualification, a small business corporation may elect not to be taxed as a corporation if it meets these tests:

(1) There are not more than ten shareholders.

(2) There is no shareholder who is not an individual or an estate. But the fact that a shareholder has the formal status of an estate may be insufficient if he is in reality a trustee. Thus, where shares were held in the name of an estate, but the duties of the executors as such had long since been completed, the executors were found in fact to have been functioning as trustees and, hence, this test was not satisfied.[50] An estate may step into the shoes of a deceased individual who has made the election, but cannot by itself make the election.[51]

(3) No shareholder is a nonresident alien.

(4) The corporation does not have more than one class of stock.[52] If an instrument purporting to be a debt obligation is actually stock, it will be considered as a second class of stock for this purpose.[53] But where notes constituted a *bona fide* debt, the Internal Revenue Service could not disqualify the characterization of small business corporation by alleging a second class of stock.[54] If, however, stockholder advances to a corporation are held to be equivalent to payments for stock, the "stock" represented by these advances may be regarded as a second class of stock, which would preclude Subchapter S treatment.[55] Stock warrants, options, and convertible bonds do not constitute a second class of stock for Subchapter S purposes.[56]

The election may be made by a qualified corporation at any time within the first month of the taxable year to which it applies or at any time within the month preceding the start of that year. No extension of time for making this election will be granted. The election, on *Form 2553,* is filed with the District Director of Internal Revenue.[57] For the election to be valid, all persons who are shareholders of the corporation on the first day of its taxable year or on the date of election, whichever is later, must consent to the election. The consents may be included in one statement for all shareholders. Consents are required not only of shareholders of record, but also of those who are beneficial owners.[58] Proof of delivery may be required to show that the consent was filed on time.[59]

A new shareholder ordinarily must file his consent within 30 days after he becomes a shareholder. But if he becomes a shareholder between the day of the election and the first day of the taxable year for which it is effective, his consent must be filed by the end of the first month of the corporation's taxable year.

Under certain conditions, an extension may be obtained for filing a consent by a new shareholder or a husband and wife who have failed to file a timely consent. This applies to a husband and wife where the stock was community property or where the husband and wife held the property as joint tenants, tenants by the entirety, or tenants in common.[60]

An election not to be taxed as a corporation remains in effect for the year of election and all subsequent years unless revoked or terminated. The election is revoked or terminated in the year in which any one of the following events occurs:

(1) a new shareholder does not timely consent to the election;

(2) after the first taxable year to which an election applies, all stockholders, on the day it is so decided, consent to have it revoked;

(3) the corporation ceases to qualify to elect not to be taxed;

(4) more than 80 percent of the corporation's gross receipts for a taxable year are from sources outside of the United States; or

(5) more than 20 percent of the corporation's gross receipts for a taxable year are from royalties, rents, dividends, interest, annuities, and sales or exchanges of stock or securities (to the extent of gains from such sales or exchanges). "Rent" in this sense does not include payment for the use or occupancy of rooms or other space if significant services also are rendered.

An election may be revoked by filing a statement to this effect with the District Director of Internal Revenue. This revocation will be effective for the taxable year in which it is made and for all succeeding taxable years if made in the first month of the corporation's taxable year. If made at any other time during the taxable year, it will become effective for the next taxable year and for the succeeding ones. An election must have been in effect for at least one taxable year before a revocation can become effective.

Subsequent election is not permitted without the consent of the Internal Revenue Service for five years after the taxable year for which the revocation or termination is effective. This rule also applies to a successor corporation if: (1) the stockholders directly or indirectly owning 50 percent or more of the stock of the successor corporation also own 50 percent or more of the stock of the old corporation at any time during the first taxable year the termination was effective and (2) the new corporation acquires a substantial portion of the assets of the old corporation, or a substantial portion of the new corporation's assets were assets of the old corporation.

If the election is properly made and continues in effect, the corporation will not be subject to tax. But a capital gains tax will apply if:

(1) the corporation's net long-term capital gain exceeds its net short-term capital loss by more than $25,000;

(2) the excess of its net long-term capital gain over its net short-term capital loss is more than 50 percent of its taxable income; and

(3) its taxable income for the year exceeds $25,000.

Capital gains tax will not apply if: (1) the corporation has been an electing corporation for at least the three immediately preceding years or (2) it has been an electing corporation for the entire period of its existence. Tax will apply, however, to gains and losses from the disposition of certain property by an electing corporation if:

(1) the property was acquired in the year in question or within the preceding 36 months;

(2) the property was acquired from a corporation that was not itself an electing corporation during all of this period up to the time of acquisition; and

(3) the property has a substituted basis in the hands of the electing corporation.

Thus, the capital gains tax will apply if the property in question was acquired in a tax-free transaction (such as corporation reorganizations) and the transferor was not an electing corporation during this entire period up to the time of acquisition. If the transferor itself acquired the property in a tax-free reorganization, then the test also would apply to the corporation from which that corporation acquired the property.[61]

Each shareholder of an electing corporation must report actual dividend distributions from the corporation in his gross income for the year in which he received them. If the corporation does not distribute all of its taxable income, at the close of the corporation's taxable year, shareholders must include as gross income their *pro rata* shares of the corporation's undistributed taxable income.[62]

Cash distributions made within two and a half months after the close of an electing corporation's taxable year will be considered distributions of the corporation's undistributed taxable income for the year just ended to the extent that they do not exceed the undistributed taxable income of the proceding taxable year.[63]

These distributions reduce the shareholder's net share of previously taxed income of the preceding year, are not dividends, and do not usually represent taxable income to the shareholder. Cash distributions made by an electing corporation in excess of its undistributed income are treated in the same manner as those made after the two and a half month period.

Cash distributions that exceed the corporation's earnings and profits for the year of distribution are considered distributions from previously taxed income to the extent of the recipient's net share of previously taxed income and are not usually taxable in the year they were received, inasmuch as the recipient was taxed on them in the year the corporation earned them. Any remainder is taxed to the recipient as a dividend to the extent of the accumulated earnings and profits of the corporation.

The excess of net long-term capital gain over the net short-term capital loss of the corporation, after reduction by any capital gains tax imposed on the corporation, is reported as long-term capital gain by the shareholder to the extent of the corporation's taxable income for the year, computed without regard for net operating loss, dividends received, and certain dividends paid. Under such circumstances, the *pro rata* share of the corporate taxable income will be reduced by the amount of such capital gain. The excess of net short-term capital gain over net short-term capital loss, if any, is not treated as capital gain to the shareholders, but rather, as ordinary income. The excess of capital loss over capital gain (whether long- or short-term) is not passed on to the shareholders. This excess may be used by the corporation only as a capital loss carry-over.

A corporate net operating loss is treated by the shareholder in the same manner as a loss from his trade or business. A shareholder's *pro rata* share of the loss may not exceed the adjusted basis of his stock plus the adjusted basis of any debts owed to him by the corporation.[64]

The basis of a shareholder's stock must be increased for any of the corporate earnings included in his return if these earnings are not distributed. This basis is later reduced if those earnings are distributed. A shareholder's basis of stock must also be reduced for any corporate losses included in his return, but in no case may his basis be reduced below zero. If corporate losses includable in a shareholder's return exceed the basis of his stock, that excess reduces the basis of any indebtedness of the corporation to the shareholder.

A penalty assessed against the corporation, as for claiming obviously improper deductions, must be paid by the shareholders on a *pro rata* basis.[65]

For taxable years beginning after 1970, contributions to qualified pension, profit-sharing, stock bonus, and certain other employee benefit plans by Subchapter S corporations are limited in the same way as plans for self-employed persons; that is, the contributions for shareholder-employees are limited to $2500 or 10 percent of earned income for the year, whichever is lower.[66]

A Subchapter S corporation may be formed even though the primary motivation is the saving of Federal income taxes.[67] But to be recognized as such, the Subchapter S corporation actually must operate and hold itself out to the public as a corporation.[68]

Cushioning Losses of Small Business Corporations

An individual's loss on the stock of a small business corporation (referred to, in accordance with its Code number, as Section 1244 stock) issued to that individual or to a partnership is treated as an ordinary loss attributable to a trade or business of this individual. This section was enacted to encourage *bona fide* investments in small businesses, not to create ordinary loss bail-out deductions for creditors of an insolvent company.[69]

Section 1244 stock is common stock of a domestic corporation that meets the prescribed definition of a *small business corporation*. This must be distinguished from the use of that same term, "small business corporation," in connection with a Subchapter S corporation.

For stock to qualify as Section 1244 stock, a plan must be in effect and have the following elements:

(1) The amount of stock to be offered thereunder plus the amounts previously contributed to capital or paid-in surplus of the corporation after July 1, 1958, cannot exceed $500,000. Where property is contributed in exchange for stock, the amount attributable to the stock is the adjusted basis of the property as of the date received, reduced by any liabilities assumed or to which the property is subject.

(2) The value of the stock to be offered under the plan plus the equity capital of the corporation must not exceed $1,000,000. The term *equity capital* means the corporate net worth computed without regard to any corporate indebtedness to shareholders.

(3) During its five most recent taxable years or during the whole of its existence if less than five years, the corporation cannot have received more than 50 percent of its aggregate gross receipts from royalties, rents, dividends, annuities, and sales or exchanges of stock or securities.

The stock of the small business corporation may be issued for money or other property, but not for stock or securities. Consequently, stock issued in a corporate reorganization does not qualify as 1244 stock unless received as a stock dividend (or possibly as a result of a stock split or spin-off) or in a reorganization.[70]

The special loss provision for Section 1244 stock is available only to individuals—not to partnerships, trusts, estates, or corporations. Only the individual to whom the stock was issued qualifies for ordinary loss treatment. The maximum loss in any one taxable year is limited to $25,000 in the case of one individual or $50,000 in the case of a husband and wife filing joint returns.[71]

Section 1244 stock thus affords an individual the opportunity of having an ordinary loss where the investment is unprofitable and a capital gain if the project succeeds.

Small Business Investment Company

The Small Business Investment Company Act of 1958 was designed to make equity capital and long-term credit more readily available for small business corporations. Small business investment companies are authorized to provide equity capital to small business concerns through the purchase of convertible debentures. A small business investment company must have paid-in capital and surplus of at least $300,000. The Small Business Administration is authorized to make loans to these companies of up to $150,000 through the purchase of subordinated debentures.[72]

Small business investment companies are allowed an ordinary loss deduction, rather than a capital loss, on losses realized on the convertible debentures (including stock received pursuant to the conversion privilege) acquired in connection with the supplying of long-term equity-type capital for small businesses. This loss deduction includes losses due to worthlessness as well as those arising out of the sale or exchange of the security.

Effective for taxable years beginning after July 11, 1969, a new small business investment company may, during the first ten years of its existence, base its bad debt reserves upon the industry average. After the first ten-year period of its existence, a small business investment company must then base additions to its bad debt reserve upon its own experience.[73]

Taxpayers investing in the stock of these investment companies are also allowed an ordinary loss deduction, rather than a capital loss, on losses arising from the stock's becoming worthless or from its sale.

A corporation licensed to operate as a small business investment company will ordinarily be deemed to be a "mere holding or investment company" for purposes of the accumulated earnings tax. (See chapter 11, Dividends and the Tax on Accumulated Earnings.) Such will not be the case, however, if the corporation meets all the provisions of the Small Business Investment Company Act and is actively engaged in providing funds to small businesses through investments or loans.[74]

Personal holding company status (see the discussion below) will not be imposed if a small business investment company is licensed as such and is actively engaged in providing funds to small businesses under the Small Business Investment Company Act, provided no shareholder owns a five percent or greater interest in a borrowing company.[75]

Personal Holding Company

A *personal holding company* is any corporation not specifically exempted from the small business investment company classification and which meets requirements related to: (1) gross income and (2) stock ownership.[76]

A corporation meets the gross income requirement if at least 60 percent of its total gross income for the taxable year is "personal holding company income." This includes dividends; interest; royalties (other than mineral, oil, gas, or certain copyright royalties); annuities; gains from the sale or exchange of stock or securities, gains from futures transactions in commodities; income from an estate or trust (or gain from the disposition of an interest in an estate or trust); income from personal service contracts under specified conditions; rents (unless they constitute 50 percent or more of the corporation's gross income); mineral, oil, or gas royalties (unless they constitute 50 percent or more of gross income and unless allowable business expenses equal 15 percent or more of gross income); and copyright royalties subject to certain conditions.

A corporation meets the stock ownership requirement if at any time during the last half of the taxable year more than 50 percent in value of the outstanding stock is owned, directly or indirectly, by or for not more than five individuals. Constructive ownership rules are applied; that is, a person is presumed to own stock belonging to certain other parties. Stock possessed, directly or indirectly, by or for a corporation, partnership, estate, or trust is considered to be owned proportionately by its shareholders, partners, or beneficiaries. An individual is considered as owning the stock held by or for his family or partner. "Family" *for this purpose* includes only one's spouse, brothers and sisters, ancestors, and lineal descendants. If a person has an option to acquire stock, he is considered to own this stock.[77]

When tax is due, it is imposed upon *undistributed personal holding company income*. This is taxable income reduced by income taxes paid or accrued during the taxable year. A deduction is allowed for amounts used or irrevocably set aside (to the extent reasonable with reference to the size and terms of the indebtedness) to pay off or to retire qualified indebtedness incurred prior to 1934.

The tax, at the rate of 70 percent, is payable if there is undistributed personal holding company income. Unlike the accumulated earnings tax, there is no such thing as justifiable retention of earnings for the needs of the business. The personal holding company tax is dangerous because it is automatic—without reference to business needs or purpose.

Inasmuch as the tax is based upon undistributed personal holding company income, the obvious solution is to pay dividends—and that is what this tax is all about. For this purpose, a corporation may elect to take a deduction for dividends paid on or before the fifteenth day of the third month following the close of its taxable year, provided that the dividend deduction does not exceed 20 percent of the dividends paid by the corporation during the year.[78]

A corporation otherwise subject to the personal holding company tax can avoid it by paying a "deficiency dividend" within 90 days of the assessment by the Internal Revenue Service. Or there may be a *consent dividend,* which is a hypothetical distribution that the shareholders as of the end of the taxable year agree to report on their own tax returns even though no payment was made to them.[79]

If a consolidated Federal income tax return is filed, personal holding company liability will be determined upon the basis of that return. But a consolidated return cannot be filed where one or more corporations in the group are exempted from personal holding company characterization.

The personal holding company tax does not apply to:

(1) Tax-exempt corporations.
(2) Banks or domestic building and loan associations.
(3) Life insurance companies.
(4) Surety companies.
(5) Foreign personal holding companies.
(6) Lending or finance companies meeting certain conditions, the most important of which is that 60 percent or more of ordinary gross income is derived from the active and regular conduct of a lending or finance business.[80]

The original purpose of the personal holding company tax was to force "incorporated pocketbooks" to disgorge; that is, to pay this high penalty tax. But the tax reaches small companies, including some that had no intention of avoiding shareholder taxes. In one case, a taxpayer attempted to avoid the personal holding company tax by arguing that in enacting the law, Congress intended to reach wealthy men who were "incorporating their own pocketbooks" to reduce taxes. However, it was held that Congress' original motivation does not exempt a corporation from this tax even though the company's principal shareholder might be anything but wealthy.[81] Whether or not a corporation qualifies as a personal holding company is not dependent upon the finding of a tax avoidance motive.[82]

The greatest danger is that a corporation may become a personal holding company for one or more years—without the intention of doing so and without realizing it—because of changing circumstances or stockholdings. In one case, a manufacturing corporation was taken over by a partnership comprised of three of the five shareholders. In the following two years (the taxable years), the corporation's only income was rent from the partnership, interest on United States obligations, and income derived from the recovery of a debt previously written off. The officers of the corporation had intended that their company should handle sales and distribution of the partnership products, but there was no income from such sources during the taxable years. The corporation argued that the personal holding company tax did not apply to its situation: that is, one in which a corporation, in recasting its business from manufacturing to distribution, found itself temporarily in a position of deriving most of its income from a personal holding company rather than from operational sources. The court held that the statute covered this situation regardless of whether that was what Congress had in mind.[83] The tax has been imposed where a corporation was in process of dissolution, for the declining years of a corporation are a part of its life.[84]

Amounts received by a corporation to furnish personal services represent personal holding company income where the individual who is to perform the services is designated by name in a contract. But for this provision to apply, the person designated in the contract must own 25 percent or more of the value of the corporation's outstanding stock.[85] For example, where a contract of an actors' representative corporation named the chief stockholder as the person the clients could call for by name, this resulted in personal holding company income.[86] But there was no personal service corporation in the absence of an agreement that a client could specify by name or description the person who would perform services; a probable understanding was not enough.[87]

The one tax advantage of a personal holding company is that charitable contributions are not limited to five percent of corporate income (as in the case of other corporations), but can be deductible up to the limits available to individuals.[88] (See chapter 16, What Can Be Done with Contributions.)

Regulated Investment Company

A *regulated investment company* is a mutual fund. More specifically, it is a corporation which has elected to be so treated. Additionally, it is registered under the Investment Company Act of 1940; it derives its income principally from dividends, interest, and capital gains; and it has diversified investments. The law regulates its investments. For example, it cannot invest more than five percent of the value of its assets in any one company, nor can it own more than ten percent of the voting securities of a company.[89]

Exceptions are made to the general investment diversification rules in the case of investment companies principally engaged in financing so-called *development companies*. These are defined as companies principally engaged in the development or exploitation of inventions, technological improvements, new processes, or products not hitherto generally available.

A regulated investment company that distributes at least 90 percent of its ordinary income is taxed only upon its undistributed income. Dividends paid by such a company generally are taxed in the usual manner to shareholders, except that dividends arising from capital gains realized by the company receive capital gain treatment in the hands of the recipients. In addition, dividends attributable to interest or other non-dividend income are ineligible for the dividends received credit, exclusion, or deduction.

The result of this manner of taxation is that the ordinary double taxation of corporate income is eliminated. Non-tax advantages of regulated investment companies lie in the fact that they provide for diversification of investments, expert investment counsel, and a means of collectively financing projects that the investors could not undertake singly.

Real Estate Investment Trust

A *real estate investment trust* (REIT) resembles a mutual fund. It may be either an unincorporated trust or an unincorporated association. It must meet certain qualifications and satisfy certain gross income and asset diversification requirements.

To qualify as an REIT, an unincorporated organization must have 100 or more shareholders, and certain other formal conditions must be met:

(1) At least 90 percent of its gross income must derive from dividends; interest; rents from real property; gains from the sale or other disposition of stock, securities, and real property (including interests in real property and in mortgages on real property); and abatements and refunds of taxes on real property.

(2) At least 75 percent of the organization's gross income must derive from rents from real property; interest on obligations secured by mortgages on real property or on interests in real property; gain from the sale or other disposition of real property (including interests in real property and in mortgages on real property); dividends or other distributions on, and gain from the sale or other disposition of, transferable shares or certificates of beneficial interest in other real estate investment trusts that meet these same requirements; and abatements and refunds of taxes on real property.

(3) Less than 30 percent of the organization's gross income may be derived from the sale or other disposition of stock or securities held for less than six months; and real property (including interests in real property), not compulsorily or involuntarily converted, held for less than four years.[90]

Taxation of a Real Estate Investment Trust. The trust must distribute annually to its shareholders at least 90 percent of its ordinary taxable income. The REIT then pays a tax only on the income it retains. If all such income is distributed, none is taxed to the trust. To the extent it distributes capital gains to its shareholders, the REIT pays no tax.

Method of Taxation of Holders of Shares or Certificates of Beneficial Interest. In the case of ordinary income, holders of a beneficial interest in shares or certificates would include these dividends in gross income for the taxable year in which they are received. In the case of capital gains dividends, the trust's beneficiaries would treat these as gains from the sale or exchange of long-term capital assets that were realized during the taxable year of the beneficiary in which the dividend was received.

If a person holds a share of a real estate investment trust for less than 31 days, but is required to include in gross income as long-term capital gain the amount of a capital gains dividend, he may, to the extent of this amount, treat any loss on the sale or exchange of this share as a loss from the sale or exchange of a long-term capital asset.[91]

A *capital gains dividend* is any dividend designated by a real estate investment trust as such in a written notice mailed to its shareholders not later than 30 days after the close of its taxable year. If the aggregate amount so designated with respect to the taxable year (including capital gains dividends paid after the close of the taxable year pursuant to a valid election) is greater than the excess of the net long-term capital gain over the net short-term capital loss of the taxable year, the portion of each distribution that will be a capital gains dividend will be only that proportion of the amount so designated which the excess of the net long-term capital gain over the net short-term capital loss bears to the aggregate amount so designated.[92]

Western Hemisphere Trade Corporation

A *Western Hemisphere Trade Corporation* is entitled to a special deduction against taxable income, which deduction takes the form of a fraction. The numerator is 14, and the denominator is the sum of the normal and surtax rates for that taxable year.[93.]

A Western Hemisphere Trade Corporation is a domestic corporation, all of whose business (other than incidental purchases) is done in any country or countries in North, Central, or South America or in the West Indies and which satisfies the following conditions:

(1) At least 95 percent of its gross income for the three-year period immediately preceding the close of the taxable year (or for such shorter periods as the corporation was in existence) was derived from sources without the United States.

(2) At least 90 percent of its gross income for that period or portion thereof was derived from the active conduct of a trade or business[94] as distinguished from investment income.

A Western Hemisphere Trade Corporation must be incorporated in any of the states or the District of Columbia.

A domestic corporation meeting the requirements of the legislation relating to Western Hemisphere Trade Corporations and also to possessions of the United States (see the following section) is not considered by the Internal Revenue Service to be an *includable corporation*; that is, one which may be a participant in the consolidated Federal income tax return of an affiliated group, regardless of whether it chooses to take advantage of the special tax treatment afforded taxpayers doing business with possessions of the United States.[95] But where a "possessions" corporation, without regard to the special tax benefit treatment, had incurred a net operating loss, the subsidiary was properly includable in the consolidated return.[96]

Under the Revenue Act of 1971, the Western Hemisphere Trade Corporation special deduction is not available to a Domestic International Sales Corporation (DISC), which will be discussed later in this chapter.[97]

Possessions of the United States

For citizens of the United States or domestic corporations, *gross income* means only income derived from sources within the United States if the following two conditions are met:

(1) if 80 percent or more of the gross income for the three-year period immediately preceding the close of the taxable year (or for such shorter periods immediately preceding the close of the taxable year as may be applicable) was derived from sources within a possession of the United States.

(2) If 50 percent or more of the gross income for that period or part thereof was derived from the active conduct of a trade or business within the United States.[98]

For the purposes of these conditions, "possession of the United States" does not include the Virgin Islands. It does include Puerto Rico as regards corporations, but not citizens.[99]

The special possessions' corporation treatment is not available to a corporation for any year in which it owns stock in a DISC or former DISC.[100]

If a corporation qualifies for the special treatment afforded to taxpayers doing business with possessions of the United States, it is subject to Federal income tax only upon its income from sources within the United States. And, inasmuch as it is a domestic—as opposed to a foreign corporation—it may participate in a tax-free liquidation or other form of tax-free reorganization without the approval of the Secretary of the Treasury, which is required in the case of foreign corporations and which will not be given if it appears that the original arrangement had been set up for tax reasons.[101]

China Trade Act Corporation

A *China Trade Act Corporation*, which requires the certification of the Secretary of Commerce, is allowed an additional deduction in computing taxable income, the deduction being equal in amount to the proportion of the taxable income derived from sources within Formosa and Hong Kong which the par value of the shares of the stock of the corporation owned by: (1) residents of Formosa, Hong Kong, and the United States or its possessions and (2) individual citizens of the United States wherever resident bears to the par value of the whole number of shares of stock of the corporation outstanding.[102]

Controlled Foreign Corporation

United States shareholders, as defined by statute, are taxed upon certain income of *controlled foreign corporations,* whether this income is distributed or not. This includes situations wherein the shareholder is a domestic corporation.[103]

A controlled foreign corporation is a foreign corporation of which more than 50 percent of the total voting stock is owned by United States shareholders, each of whom in turn is defined as United States persons owning at least ten percent of the stock.[104]

Domestic International Sales Corporation

The Revenue Act of 1971 created the *Domestic International Sales Corporation*, mercifully abbreviated as DISC.

In general, a DISC is not subject to Federal income tax, although its shareholders are taxed on an amount representing 50 percent of the DISC's income. The remaining 50 percent of the profits of a DISC is fully free of tax in the hands of the DISC until it is distributed or deemed distributed. Both the determination of whether a corporation qualifies as a DISC and the tax deferral apply on a year-by-year basis. The taxes foregone in the case of a DISC include not only the regular corporate income tax, but also the minimum tax on tax preferences and the accumulated earnings tax. Inasmuch as a personal holding company does not qualify as a DISC, the act does not relieve such a corporation from this tax.[105]

A corporation will qualify as a DISC if the following four requirements are satisfied with respect to any taxable year:

(1) At least 95 percent of a corporation's gross receipts for the taxable year must be composed of qualified export receipts; that is, receipts arising from the sale or lease of export products as well as receipts from other specified export-related activities.

(2) At least 95 percent of the assets of a corporation at the close of its taxable year must be qualified export assets, the determination being with reference to the adjusted basis of the assets.

(3) The corporation must have at least $2500 of capital on each day of the taxable year as measured by the par or stated value of its outstanding stock. The DISC cannot have more than one class of stock.

(4) The corporation must have elected to be treated as a DISC, and this election must be made during the 90-day period immediately prior to the beginning of its taxable year. Likewise, all of the persons who are shareholders on the first day of the initial election year must consent to the election. Once made, an election continues in effect for subsequent years, whether or not the corporation actually qualifies as a DISC in any subsequent year, until such time as the election is either revoked or terminated by reason of a continued failure of the corporation to qualify as a DISC over a five-year period. An election may be revoked at any time after the first year it is in effect. For a revocation to be effective for a given year, however, it must be made within the first 90 days of that year. A revocation made after the expiration of the 90-day period will not take effect until the following year.

Shareholders are taxed on the income of the DISC when it is actually distributed. There are also three situations where taxability does not relate to actual distribution:

(1) When certain amounts are deemed distributed in qualified years. This involves situations where a DISC receives income that does not arise from export activities, where income has the effect of being distributed to shareholders, and where there is foreign investment attributable to producers' loans of a DISC.

(2) Where a corporation no longer qualifies as a DISC because the corporation terminates its election or fails to meet the qualification requirements with respect to any year.

(3) When a shareholder disposes of stock in a corporation that has tax-deferred income. Gain on the sale of stock is classified as ordinary income to the extent that the tax-deferred DISC income is attributed to the stock. Similarly, where the existence of a DISC is terminated, gain is recognized (even though it otherwise would be tax-free) and the gain is treated as ordinary income to the extent that the tax-deferred DISC income is attributable to the stock.[106]

A corporation that is a DISC for a taxable year and that also qualifies as a Western Hemisphere Trade Corporation for the same year is not allowed the special Western Hemisphere Trade Corporation deduction (which is equivalent to a 14 percentage point reduction) for that year. The special treatment available to corporations doing business in possessions of the United States is not available to a corporation for any year in which it owns stock in a DISC or former DISC. A DISC or former DISC may not be included in a consolidated Federal income tax return.

Trust

In general, the term *trust* for Federal tax purposes means an arrangement created either by will or by declaration whereby trustees take title to property for the purpose of protecting or conserving it for the beneficiaries.[107] Trusts have many tax and non-tax functions, most of which do not involve carrying on a business. The use of the word "trust" is not determinative for tax purposes.[108] For example, what purports to be a trust may be treated as an association taxable as a corporation.[109]

A trust may be valid under the laws of the state in which it was created, but that does not necessarily mean that it will be so recognized for Federal tax purposes.[110]

One important tax advantage of a trust is that income retains the same character in the hands of a beneficiary as it had in the hands of the trustee.[111] Thus if a trust received tax-exempt municipal bond interest, the income also will be tax-exempt when distributed to the beneficiary.

Other Forms of Doing Business

There are other forms of doing business; however, they are so specialized that they cannot be regarded as forms of organization subject to any significant choice.

NOTES

1. *Perry R. Bass et al.*, 50 T.C. 595 (1968).
2. *Britt et al. v. United States*, 431 F.2d 227 (5th Cir., 1970).
3. *Nassau Lens Co., Inc. v. Commissioner*, 308 F.2d 39 (2d Cir., 1962).
4. *Modern Home Fire and Casualty Insurance Company et al.*, 54 T.C. 935 (1970).
5. *Commissioner v. Wilson et al.*, 353 F.2d 184 (9th Cir., 1965).
6. *See* Robert S. Holzman, *Tax-Free Reorganizations After the Tax Reform Act of 1969*, Lynbrook, N.Y.: Farnsworth Publishing Company, 1970. Chapter 1.
7. Regulations Section 301.7701-1.
8. *United States v. Empey*, 406 F.2d 157 (10th Cir., 1969).
9. *See V. H. Monette and Company, Incorporated*, 45 T.C. 15 (1965), *aff'd*, 374 F.2d 116 (4th Cir., 1967).
10. I.R.C. Section 453(d)(1).
11. Regulations Section 1.105-1(a).
12. *United States v. Gefen et al.*, D.C., M.D. Fla., 1966, *aff'd*, 400 F.2d 476 (5th Cir., 1968).
13. I.R.C. Section 351.
14. I.R.C. Section 761.
15. Regulations Section 1.761-1.
16. *Ramos et al. v. United States*, 260 F. Supp. 479 (D.C., N.D. Cal., 1966), *rev'd and rem'd'd on another issue*, 393 F.2d 618 (9th Cir., 1968).
17. *Lulu Lung Powell*, T.C. Memo. 1967-32 (filed February 20, 1967).
18. *Gilford v. Commissioner*, 201 F.2d 735 (2d Cir., 1955).
19. *Fishback, Jr. et al. v. United States*, 215 F. Supp. 621 (D.C., S.D., 1963).
20. I.R.C. Section 701.
21. I.R.C. Section 702.
22. Regulations Section 1.704-1(b)(2).
23. *Aldrich v. United States*, 346 F.2d 37 (5th Cir., 1964).
24. *Armstrong et al. v. Phinney*, 394 F.2d 661 (5th Cir., 1968).
25. Revenue Ruling 69-184, 1969-1 CB 256.
26. *Jensen et al. v. United States*, D.C., M.D. Ga., 1964.
27. *See Charles Turner*, T.C. Memo. 1965-101 (filed April 15, 1965).
28. *Arthur Bernstein*, T.C. Memo. 1960-213 (filed October 7, 1960).
29. *Burnet v. Clark*, 287 U.S. 410 (1932).
30. *Commissioner v. Schaefer*, 240 F.2d 381 (2d Cir., 1957).
31. *National Savings & Trust Company v. United States*, 285 F. Supp. 325 (D.C., D.C., 1968).
32. *National Investors Corporation v. Hoey*, 144 F.2d 466 (2d Cir., 1944).
33. *Apschnikat et al. v. United States*, 421 F.2d 910 (6th Cir., 1970).
34. *Britt et al. v. United States*, 431 F.2d 227 (5th Cir., 1970).
35. *Perry H. Bass*, 50 T.C. 595 (1968).
36. *Watson v. Commissioner*, 124 F.2d 437 (2d Cir., 1942).
37. *Moline Properties, Inc. v. Commissioner*, 319 U.S. 436 (1943).
38. *Silver Bluff Estates*, T.C. Memo., Docket No. 12303 (entered June 24, 1947).
39. *Paymer v. Commissioner*, 150 F.2d 334 (2d Cir., 1945).

40. *Nat Tully Semel,* T.C. Memo. 1965-232 (filed August 27, 1965).
41. I.R.C. Section 453(d)(4).
42. I.R.C. Section 6901.
43. *See James v. Commissioner,* 49 F.2d 707 (2d Cir., 1931).
44. *United States v. The Donruss Company,* 393 U.S. 297 (1969).
45. I.R.C. Section 341.
46. *Caro et al. v. Bingler et al.,* 242 F. Supp. 418 (D.C., W.D. Pa., 1965).
47. I.R.C. Section 1371.
48. *John E. Byrne,* 45 T.C. 151 (1965).
49. *The Coca-Cola Bottling Company of Gallup et al. v. United States,* 443 F.2d 1253 (10th Cir., 1971).
50. *Old Virginia Brick Company,* 44 T.C. 724 (1965), *aff'd,* 367 F.2d 276 (4th Cir., 1966).
51. Revenue Ruling 66-90, 1966-1 CB 27.
52. I.R.C. Section 1371(a).
53. Regulations Section 1.1371-1(g).
54. *Seven Sixty Ranch Co. v. Kennedy,* D.C., Wyo., 1966.
55. *Henderson et al. v. United States,* 245 F. Supp. 782 (D.C., M.D. Ala., 1965).
56. Revenue Ruling 67-269, 1967-2 CB 298.
57. I.R.C. Section 1372.
58. *Harold C. Kean et al.,* 51 T.C. 337 (1968).
59. *In re The Round Table, Inc.,* D.C., S.D. N.Y., 1965.
60. Revenue Procedure 61-30, 1961-2 CB 568, as modified by Revenue Procedure 64-20, 1964-1 CB (Part 1) 685.
61. I.R.C. Section 1378.
62. I.R.C. Section 1373.
63. I.R.C. Section 1375(f).
64. I.R.C. Section 1374.
65. *Leonhart et al. v. Commissioner,* 414 F.2d 749 (4th Cir., 1969).
66. I.R.C. Section 1379(b).
67. *Modern Home Fire and Casualty Insurance Company et al.,* 54 T.C. 935 (1970).
68. *Michael F. Beirne et al.,* 52 T.C. 210 (1969).
69. *Bruce, Jr. et al. v. United States,* 254 F. Supp. 816 (D.C., Texas, 1967).
70. Pursuant to I.R.C. Section 368(a)(1)(F).
71. I.R.C. Section 1244(b).
72. I.R.C. Section 1243.
73. I.R.C. Section 586.
74. Regulations Section 1.533-1(d).
75. I.R.C. Section 542(b)(8).
76. I.R.C. Section 542.
77. I.R.C. Section 544(a).
78. I.R.C. Section 563(b).
79. I.R.C. Section 564.
80. I.R.C. Section 542(c).
81. *Olean Times Publishing Company,* 42 B.T.A. 1277 (1940).
82. *American Packing Corporation v. Commissioner,* 125 F.2d 413 (4th Cir., 1942).
83. *Electroline Sales Company,* T.C. Memo., Docket No. 24639 (entered January 30, 1951).
84. *O'Sullivan Rubber Company v. Commissioner,* 120 F.2d 845 (2d Cir., 1941).
85. I.R.C. Section 543(a)(5).
86. *Kurt Frings Agency, Inc.,* 42 T.C. 472 (1964).
87. *S. O. Clagett,* 44 T.C. 503 (1965).
88. I.R.C. Section 545(b)(2).
89. I.R.C. Section 851.
90. I.R.C. Section 856(a).
91. I.R.C. Section 857(b).

92. I.R.C. Section 857(b)(3)(C).

93. I.R.C. Section 922.

94. I.R.C. Section 921.

95. Revenue Ruling 65-293, 1965-2 CB 323.

96. *Burke Concrete Accessories, Inc. et al.,* 56 T.C. 588 (1971).

97. I.R.C. Section 246(d).

98. I.R.C. Section 931(a), (b).

99. I.R.C. Section 931(c).

100. I.R.C. Section 246(d).

101. I.R.C. Section 367.

102. I.R.C. Section 941.

103. I.R.C. Section 7701(a)(30).

104. I.R.C. Section 951.

105. I.R.C. Section 991.

106. I.R.C. Section 995.

107. Regulations Section 301.7701-4(a).

108. *Morris M. Messing et al.,* 48 T.C. 502 (1967).

109. *Abraham et al. v. United States,* 272 F. Supp. 807 (D.C., E.D. Tenn., 1967), *aff'd,* 406 F.2d 1259 (6th Cir., 1969).

110. *Irvine K. Furman et al.,* 45 T.C. 360 (1966), *aff'd,* 381 F.2d 22 (5th Cir., 1967).

111. I.R.C. Section 652(b).

CHAPTER 3

Is It Stock or Are They Bonds?—
Interest Versus Dividends

The issuance, terms, and conditions of a corporation's stocks and bonds must be considered with a view to tax consequences both to the corporation and to the stockholders or bondholders. Careful tax planning of capital structure may well permit the corporation to get money upon more favorable terms.

Tax Distinction Between Stocks and Bonds

Whether an issue is a stock or a bond is significant for Federal income tax purposes in such areas as the following:

(1) Whether payment for the use of money advanced to the corporation is deductible by the corporation as interest.[1]

(2) Whether redemption of the issue is treated as that of a stock (ordinarily this would be treated as a dividend[2] if the corporation had earnings and profits at the time) or of a bond (return of capital).

(3) Whether the corporation has more than one class of *stock*, which would prevent the tax advantages available to a Subchapter S corporation.[3]

(4) Whether unrepaid "advances" by a stockholder to a corporation are capital losses,[4] business bad debts,[5] or nonbusiness bad debts.[6]

(5) Whether a corporation qualifies for tax exemption.[7] Some state laws provide that an exempt organization may not issue stock. Thus, if a particular issue is deemed to be stock, tax exemption is lost.[8]

(6) Whether a corporation is subject to the accumulated earnings tax. If securities are deemed bonds, interest is deductible by the corporation and there may be no remaining income to be subjected to the accumulated earnings tax.[9]

(7) Whether what is transferred to a controlled corporation is free of tax on the transfer because it is in return for *stock*.[10]

(8) Whether what is received in many types of tax-free reorganization is taxed because it represents a larger principal amount of *bonds* than what has been relinquished.[11]

The basic test of a security's classification as "debt" or "equity" is whether the form used has substantial economic reality.[12]

In theory, at least, the individuals involved are free to decide the extent to which corporate capitalization is to be through the medium of stocks or bonds. The mere fact that a more favorable tax treatment may result from the capital structure used does not entitle the Internal Revenue Service or a court to characterize as capital what had always been intended as a loan or indebtedness.[13] If the structure used has substantial economic reality, it will be upheld for tax purposes. The key word here is "if."

The essential difference between a stockholder and a creditor lies in the right to share in profits and the degree of risk assumed. It is the stockholder, and not the creditor, who is the adventurer—who bears the prime risk of loss and hope of gain.

The Nature of Interest

Interest paid on corporate debts, with a few exceptions that will be discussed later in this chapter, is, of course, deductible for tax purposes.[14] *Interest* has been defined as the compensation allowed by law or fixed by the parties for the use, or detention of money[15] or the forebearance of collection of a debt.

In most situations, interest is considered to be the cost of the use of the amounts owing a creditor and an incentive to prompt repayment, thus constituting an integral part of a continuing debt. Interest on a tax debt is an example.[16]

There are four requirements for the allowance of an interest deduction on the Federal income tax return:

(1) It must be established that there was a *bona fide* indebtedness.[17]

(2) The indebtedness must have been that of the taxpayer.[18]

(3) There must have been a liability to pay interest.[19]

(4) The particular form of interest must not have been excluded by other sections of the Internal Revenue Code as a deduction. (In certain instances, courts have broadened the disallowance areas.)

Unlike most other types of tax deductions, interest need not serve a business purpose, be ordinary and necessary, or be reasonable in order to be deductible. But deduction will be denied where there is no reality in the arrangement.[20] Interest may lose its deductible character if an indebtedness, contracted as such, subsequently ceases to represent a debtor-creditor relationship.[21]

As has already been indicated, certain types of interest are not deductible. These are:

(1) Certain amounts paid in connection with insurance, endowment, or annuity contracts.[22] An interest deduction is not allowed in the case of indebtedness incurred or continued to purchase or carry a single-premium life insurance, endowment, or annuity contract. No deduction is allowed for any amount paid or incurred on indebtedness incurred or continued to purchase or to carry insurance of the types named above pursuant to a plan

of purchase that contemplates systematic direct or indirect borrowing of part or all of the increases in the cash value of the contract. There are four exceptions to this rule:

(a) If four of the first seven annual premiums are paid without borrowing.

(b) If the interest otherwise subject to the rules does not exceed $100.

(c) If the debt was incurred because of an unforeseen substantial loss of income or an unforeseen substantial increase in financial obligations.

(d) If the indebtedness was incurred in connection with the taxpayer's trade or business.

(2) Interest on indebtedness incurred to purchase or to carry tax-exempt securities.[23] Whenever tax-exempt securities are held and money is borrowed for any purpose, consideration must be given to the possible loss of part of the interest deduction.[24] However, it does not follow automatically that some part of the interest expense must be disallowed on the theory that the borrowed money *could* have been used to carry the tax-exempt bonds. Thus, where tax-exempt bonds were held as an investment and money was borrowed for a variety of business purposes, none of the interest deduction was lost. A reasonable person in that taxpayer's position would not necessarily have sacrificed the liquidity and security provided by his tax-exempt holdings by liquidating these holdings instead of incurring indebtedness to finance his ventures.[25]

(3) Amounts paid or accrued for such taxes and carrying charges as are chargeable to capital accounts with respect to property if the taxpayer elects to treat these taxes or carrying charges as capital expenditures.[26]

(4) Certain interest in transactions between related taxpayers.[27] (See chapter 26, Tax Pitfalls.)

(5) Intercompany interest, the genuineness of which cannot be established by the taxpayer.

(6) Prepaid interest. If a taxpayer uses the cash receipts and disbursements method of accounting, interest paid in advance for a period in excess of 12 months following the taxable year in which the prepayment is made is deemed by the IRS to materially distort income. Whether or not prepayment for lesser periods distorts income will be considered by the IRS on a case-by-case basis. Some of the factors considered are the amount of income in the current and prior years, the amount prepaid, the time of payment, the reason for prepayment, and the existence of a varying rate of interest over the period of the loan. Where a material distortion of income is found, the Service will require an allocation of interest payments over the taxable years involved.[28]

(7) Unrealistic "interest." Deduction of interest will be denied in the absence of a showing that the payment was really made for the forebearance of the use of money.[29] Amounts paid to a "lender" will not be deductible as interest if made only to provide a facade for a loan transaction. Likewise, synthetic interest charges have been disallowed in a variety of situations where interest was merely a book entry or a disguised

payment, which was an incident to the manufacture of a deduction without any real indebtedness.[30]

(8) Interest on investment indebtedness. For taxable years beginning after December 31, 1971, individuals are limited in their deduction for interest borrowed for investment purposes (*investment interest*), but not for interest incurred in a trade or business. The interest deduction is limited, in the following order, to

(a) $25,000 ($12,500 in the case of a separate return by a married individual) plus

(b) the amount of the net investment income plus

(c) the excess of net long-term capital gain over the net short-term capital loss for the taxable year plus

(d) one-half of the amount by which investment interest exceeds the amounts described in (a), (b), and (c).[31] (There is a limited carry-over rule.)

(9) Interest on indebtedness incurred by a corporation to acquire stock or assets of another corporation. If a corporation issues bonds to acquire stock in another corporation or to acquire at least two-thirds of that corporation's assets, interest is disallowed on these bonds provided the issuing corporation has interest expenses of more than $5,000,000 for that taxable year. This does not refer to tax-free acquisitions of stock in a subsidiary corporation or to the acquisition of stock or assets of certain foreign corporations.[32]

The Interest-Dividend Debt Equity Guidelines

An analysis of the cases reveals at least 38 factors which have been used by the courts to decide whether a security is debt and payments made to the holder are interest or whether the security is equity and the payments made are dividends.

(1) *Formal Authorization.* Is there formal authorization for the "indebtedness" of the corporation? [33]

(2) *Ascertainable Principal Amount.* Debt is not recognized for tax purposes where there is no principal amount ascertainable and payable in any event.[34]

(3) *Time of Maturity.* A security was not recognized as a bond where the maturity date was too far off.[35] Lack of a realistic maturity date suggests a stock issue.

The fact that a note is payable on demand argues strongly against its constituting corporate indebtedness.[36] If demand notes issued are never the subject of a demand, one might obviate this danger by replacing the notes to avoid the statute of limitations barring collection of the old notes.[37]

(4) *Postponement of Maturity.* Frequent postponement of the stated maturity date suggests that there was no intention of paying off the "indebtedness." [38]

A reasonable extension of time for payment of a bond is not fatal to the recognition of a debt.[39] But an extension for an inordinate period tends to rebut the contention of the presence of a debt.[40]

(5) *Default Provision.* A *bona fide* indebtedness includes provision for debtor rights upon default. Such a provision was not found where the indenture required action by 75 percent of the debenture holders to accelerate maturity upon default.[41]

(6) *Default Was not Contested.* A default provision is effectively nonexistent if it is not invoked by the "creditors" when there is a default.[42] Where the alleged creditors fail to make claims for unpaid "interest," this will be regarded as "scarcely the attitude of a money lender . . . ."[43]

The court will want to know what steps were taken to foreclose when there was a default.[44] In the case of alleged debt obligations where the "creditors" waived their rights to periodic payments, this was found to be stock.[45] Failure of either the bondholder or the corporation to act can be fatal.[46]

(7) *Spelling out of Interest Provision.* Income bonds may be accepted as such where the fact that interest is payable only from earnings is stated in the indenture.[47] But indebtedness was not found where there was no written provision for interest.[48] (It is not essential that interest be computed at a stated rate.[49])

(8) *Source of Interest.* Indebtedness was not recognized where interest was payable out of general corporate funds with no obligation to pay the same out of other funds.[50]

(9) *Interest Payments Leave no Discretion to the Obligor.* There was no recognized indebtedness where interest was not due for the first five years of a note and would be waived if the corporation paid off the note within five years. This was only a contingent liability.[51]

(10) *Lack of "Understanding" as to Nonobservance of Terms.* Indebtedness was not recognized where the payment schedule as to the debtors was ignored.[52] A debtor-creditor relationship was not found where other creditors were paid, but an affiliate was not.[53]

Interest was allowed where two payments had not been made to bondholders, but the plausible reason for this nonpayment was oversight.[54]

(11) *Cumulativeness of Interest.* Where interest is not paid, in the case of income bonds or otherwise, the liability should be cumulative.[55]

(12) *Unilateral Modification Must Not Be Possible.* Indebtedness was not recognized where the conditions of a bond issue were subject to unilateral modification.[56]

(13) *Rights upon Dissolution Must Be Spelled Out.* The indenture must provide for what happens to the bondholders upon liquidation of the corporation.[57] Indebtedness was not recognized where rights of debenture holders were subordinated to those of bank creditors in liquidation.[58]

(14) *Subordination.* Subordination of the indebtedness to the rights of other creditors is not in itself enough to convert debt into equity; but it is a factor to be considered.[59]

Bonds were not recognized as such where, upon liquidation, not the preference of this security over the stock but its inferiority to the claims of other creditors was spelled out.[60] Indebtedness was not recognized in the case of a security that could be subordinated to future bank indebtedness.[61]

(15) *Dependency of Repayment upon Success of an Untried Business Venture.* Indebtedness was not found where the so-called bondholders had to look to

the prosperity of a completely untested business for their money.[62] The essence of an equity interest is a participation in the pot luck of an enterprise.[63]

(16) *Identity of Interests of Stockholders and Bondholders.* An issue was deemed to be stock where stockholders and bondholders owned the same proportions of all securities, whether they were denominated stocks or bonds.[64] The opposite result was held where the holdings were not proportionate.[65] Proportionality of bondholdings and stockholdings may not by itself void an otherwise valid debt, but it will render the relationship suspect.[66]

(17) *To Whom Is the Debt Owed?* A loan to a bank unrelated to the parties is far less likely to create unallowable interest than is a loan to stockholders.[67]

(18) *Dependency of Interest upon Director Action.* If interest payments depend upon affirmative action by the board of directors, it is difficult for a corporation to meet its burden of showing that the payment was not a dividend.[68]

(19) *Participation of Bonds in the Profits.* Securities of a corporation that participates in the profits of an enterprise are likely to be regarded as stock, having one of the essential ingredients of stock.[69]

(20) *Participation in Management.* If creditors participate in the management of a corporation, the creditors' securities are likely to be regarded as stock.[70] It is pertinent to inquire whether the bondholders possess control over management.[71]

(21) *Package Financing of the Corporation.* Were the corporation's stocks and bonds issued as a unit? [72] Could a stockholder ever buy stock in the corporation without buying a debenture? If he could, this may indicate a true loan. But if he had to buy a debenture in order to buy stock, this may indicate a risk-capital investment.[73]

(22) *Did the Bonds Represent New Money?* Conversion of equity interests into debt does not necessarily defeat tax treatment as *bona fide* indebtedness. But lack of new money can be an important factor in holding a purported indebtedness to be a capital transaction.[74]

(23) *Was the Original Capital Adequate?* One important test is whether the initial capital was adequate to begin the corporate life.[75]

(24) *Timing of Creation of the Indebtedness.* The time of the advances to a corporation is significant, especially where shareholders supplied money one month *after* the formation of the corporation.[76]

(25) *Thinness of Capital.* In order to justify its so-called debt, a corporation must prove that its capital structure was not top-heavy with debt.[77] The adequacy of capitalization depends to some extent upon the nature of the business, but there must be a reasonable relationship between the capital of a corporation and the assets it needs to carry on its operations.[78]

There exists no rule that permits the Internal Revenue Service to dictate what portion of a corporation's operations must be provided for by equity financing rather than by debt.[79] Yet the thin corporation has a greater burden of proof to meet, that burden being in direct proportion to its thinness.

(26) *Form of the Instrument.* It is safest to follow a standard bond format. But substance, not form, is the final arbiter.[80]

(27) *Uncertainty of the Obligor as to What the Security Is.* Where alleged indebtedness was carried on the corporate books of account as stock or in a suspense account, it was not recognized as debt.[81]

(28) *Ability of the Corporation to Obtain Funds from Nonstockholders.* Would the "bonds" have been acceptable to an outside investor? [82] But a stockholder doesn't have to be so "hard-nosed" as a banker, to have an advance treated as a loan.[83]

(29) *Creditors' Expectation of Repayment.* The creditors' attitude toward money advanced is highly significant.[84] A debt will not be recognized if the "debtor" does not expect to be repaid until the corporation is running on a profitable basis.[85]

(30) *How the Obligor Carried the "Debt" on its Books.* Corporate accounting treatment of alleged indebtedness is very revealing.[86] Book entries may indicate the nature of stockholder advances.[87]

(31) *Corroborative Evidence.* Where a corporation's charter described the characteristics of a security issue, it was recognized as indebtedness.[88]

Proof as to the true nature of the "indebtedness" may be gleaned from tax returns, records, and financial statements.[89] It should be asked if the mortgage bonds were recorded in a county clerk's office.[90]

(32) *Convertability of Indebtedness.* Did the notes or other evidences of indebtedness have any rights of conversion into the corporation's stock? A so-called indebtedness was deemed to be stock where the issuing corporation had an absolute option for ten years to convert these "bonds" into stock.[91]

(33) *Nomenclature.* Where a security bears positive characteristics of a stock or a bond, the label may be unimportant; but where the issue has characteristics of both stock and bond, the presence of a label on such hybrid securities has assumed great significance.[92]

(34) *Industry Practice.* Was the form and method of capitalization of a corporation the standard practice in the industry? [93]

(35) *Security of the Indebtedness.* Debentures may be regarded as debt even though unsecured. But if the so-called bonds are adequately secured, there is a presumption that they are not stock.[94]

(36) *Existence of a Sinking Fund.* A sinking fund is not an absolute necessity for *bona fide* indebtedness. But the case for indebtedness is much stronger if there is a sinking fund requirement.[95]

(37) *Pattern of Stockholder Borrowing.* Stockholder advances are not likely to be characterized as indebtedness where there is a regular repayment of such advances, even though this repayment may be just before the end of the year when there are new stockholder loans at the start of each new year.[96]

(38) *Intent.* Of all of the yardsticks for determining whether an issue represents stock or bonds, the most important is the *intent* of the parties.[97]

Stock or Bonds—Reversal of Roles of the Parties

Occasionally, the parties reverse their traditional roles, the taxpayer claiming that a particular "security" was a stock and the Internal Revenue Service that it was a bond. Such may be the case where the payee desires the dividends received deduction or credit for amounts received from the payer. Of course, this twist in no way alters the customary yardsticks.[98]

Advance Rulings Are Not Available

The Internal Revenue Service has announced that it will no longer issue prior rulings or determination letters as to whether advances to thin corporations are loans or equity investments.[99]

Guidelines Authorized by the 1969 Tax Reform Act

The Tax Reform Act of 1969 gave the Treasury Department a statutory authorization to issue regulatory guidelines distinguishing between debt and equity. The factors that may be taken into account in these guidelines, according to the specific language of the statute, include the following:

(1) Whether there is a written unconditional promise to pay on demand or on a specified date a sum certain in money for an adequate consideration in money or money's worth, and a promise to pay a fixed rate of interest.

(2) Whether there is a subordination to, or preference over, any indebtedness of the corporation.

(3) The ratio of debt to equity of the corporation.

(4) Whether the debt is convertible into the stock of the corporation.

(5) The relationship between the holdings of stock in the corporation and the holdings of the interest in question.[100]

But as noted previously in this chapter, at least 38 yardsticks have been furnished by the courts for making the debt–equity determination. In comparison, these five suggested guidelines are very modest indeed.

Stock Dividends

A corporation's distribution of its own shares to its shareholders with respect to its stock is not taxable, with these exceptions:

(1) Distributions in lieu of money, including a distribution where any shareholder may elect to receive his dividend in stock, property, or cash.

(2) One or more disproportionate distributions that result in the

receipt of cash or other property by some shareholders and an increase in the proportionate interests of other shareholders in the corporation's assets or its earnings and profits.

(3) Distributions of common and preferred stock, with some common shareholders receiving preferred and others receiving common.

(4) Distributions on preferred stock other than an increase in the conversion ratio of convertible preferred stock made solely to take account of a stock dividend or stock split with respect to the stock into which the convertible preferred can be exchanged. Thus, antidilution distributions are not taxable.

(5) Distributions of convertible preferred stock, unless it is established to the satisfaction of the Secretary of the Treasury or the Commissioner of Internal Revenue that this distribution will not have the result described in (2).

The Treasury is authorized to issue regulations under which certain transactions will be treated as distributions: a change in conversion ratio, a change in redemption price, a difference between redemption price and issue price, a redemption that is treated as a dividend, and any transaction (including a recapitalization) that has a similar effect on the interest of any shareholder.[101]

In general, these stock dividend rules apply to distributions made after January 10, 1969. But there are some highly complex exceptions as to the effective date in the case of disproportionate distributions and distributions on preferred stock. In specified instances, the effective date is 1991.

NOTES

1. I.R.C. Section 163(a).
2. Under I.R.C. Section 301.
3. *W. C. Gamman*, 46 T.C. 1 (1966).
4. Under I.R.C. Section 166(g).
5. Under I.R.C. Section 166(a).
6. Under I.R.C. Section 166(d).
7. *See United States v. Henderson*, 375 F.2d 36 (5th Cir., 1967).
8. *Knollwood Memorial Gardens*, 46 T.C. 764 (1966).
9. *Gazette Telegraph Co.*, 19 T.C. 692 (1953), *aff'd*, 209 F.2d 926 (10th Cir., 1954).
10. *Gooding Amusement Company v. Commissioner*, 236 F.2d 159 (6th Cir., 1956).
11. I.R.C. Section 356(d)(2).
12. *Edwin C. Hollenbeck et al.*, 50 T.C. 740 (1968).
13. *Daytona Marine Supply Co. v. United States*, D.C., N.D. Fla., 1961.
14. I.R.C. Section 265.
15. *Fall River Electric Light Co.*, 23 B.T.A. 168 (1931).
16. *Bruning v. United States*, 376 U.S. 358 (1964).
17. *Joseph H. Bridges*, 39 T.C. 1064 (1963), *aff'd*, 325 F.2d 180 (4th Cir., 1964).
18. *George D. Nann*, 33 B.T.A. 281 (1935).
19. *Howell Turpentine Co.*, 6 T.C. 364 (1946), *rev'd on another issue*, 162 F.2d 316 (5th Cir., 1947).
20. *Goldstein et al. v. Commissioner*, 364 F.2d 734 (2d Cir., 1966).
21. *Cuyuna Realty Company v. United States*, 382 F.2d 298 (Ct. Cl., 1967).
22. I.R.C. Section 264.

23. I.R.C. Section 265(2).

24. *Wynn, Jr. et al. v. United States*, 288 F. Supp. 797 (D.C., E.D. Pa., 1968), *aff'd*, 411 F.2d 614 (3d Cir., 1969).

25. *Edmund F. Ball et al.*, 54 T.C. 1200 (1970).

26. I.R.C. Section 266.

27. I.R.C. Section 267(a)(2).

28. Revenue Ruling 68-643, 1968-2 CB 76.

29. *Cahn et al. v. Commissioner*, 358 F.2d 492 (9th Cir., 1966).

30. *Knetsch v. Commissioner*, 364 U.S. 361 (1960).

31. I.R.C. Section 163(d).

32. I.R.C. Section 279.

33. *In the Matter of W. T. Ray et al. v. United States* (D.C., M.D. Tenn., 1968), *aff'd*, 409 F.2d 1322 (6th Cir., 1969).

34. *Sherwood Memorial Gardens, Inc. v. Commissioner*, 350 F.2d 225 (7th Cir., 1965).

35. *John W. Walter, Inc.*, 23 T.C. 550 (1954).

36. *Peter Raich et al.*, 46 T.C. 604 (1966).

37. *W. C. Gamman et al.*, 46 T.C. 1 (1966).

38. *Sayles Finishing Plants, Inc. v. United States*, 399 F.2d 214 (Ct. Cl., 1968).

39. *Wilshire & Western Sandwiches, Inc. v. Commissioner*, 175 F.2d 718 (9th Cir., 1949).

40. *J. S. Biritz Construction Co. et al.*, T.C. Memo. 1966-227, filed October 18, 1966, *rev'd on another issue*, 387 F.2d 451 (8th Cir., 1968).

41. *R. C. Owen Co. v. Commissioner*, 351 F.2d 410 (6th Cir., 1965).

42. *Gooding Amusement Co., Inc. v. Commissioner*, 236 F.2d 159 (6th Cir., 1956).

43. *Jewell Ridge Coal Corp. v. Commissioner*, 318 F.2d 695 (4th Cir., 1963).

44. *Motel Co.*, T.C. Memo. 1963-174 (filed June 26, 1963), *aff'd*, 340 F.2d 445 (2d Cir., 1965).

45. *W. C. Gamman et al.*, 46 T.C. 1 (1966).

46. *Foresun, Inc.*, 41 T.C. 706 (1964), *aff'd*, 348 F.2d 1006 (6th Cir., 1965).

47. *S. Glaser & Sons, Inc.*, T.C. Memo., Docket No. 2897 (entered May 22, 1944).

48. *Donald J. Peterson et al.*, T.C. Memo. 1957-96, filed June 18, 1957.

49. *Kena, Inc.*, 44 B.T.A. 217 (1941).

50. *1661 Corporation v. Tomlinson*, 247 F. Supp. 936 (D.C., M.D. Fla., 1965).

51. *1220 Realty Co. et al. v. Commissioner*, 322 F.2d 495 (6th Cir., 1963).

52. *Aronov Construction Co., Inc. v. United States*, 223 F. Supp. 175 (D.C., M.D. Ala., 1963), *aff'd*, 338 F.2d 337 (5th Cir., 1965).

53. *Ludwig Baumann & Co. v. Commissioner*, 321 F.2d 557 (2d Cir., 1963).

54. *Air-Vent Aluminum Awning Manufacturing Company v. United States*, D.C., S.D. Cal., 1966.

55. *Gregg Company of Delaware v. Commissioner*, 239 F.2d 498 (2d Cir., 1957).

56. *Motel Co.*, T.C. Memo. 1963-174, filed June 26, 1963, *aff'd*, 340 F.2d 445 (2d Cir., 1965).

57. *S. Glaser & Sons, Inc.*, T.C. Memo., Docket No. 2897 (entered May 22, 1944).

58. *Commissioner v. Schmoll Fils Associated, Inc.*, 110 F.2d 611 (2d Cir., 1940).

59. *Foresun, Inc.*, 41 T.C. 706 (1964), *aff'd*, 348 F.2d 1006 (6th Cir., 1965).

60. *S. Glaser & Sons, Inc.*, T.C. Memo., Docket No. 2897 (entered May 22, 1944).

61. *P. M. Finance Corporation v. Commissioner*, 302 F.2d 786 (3d Cir., 1962).

62. *Burr Oaks Corporation v. Commissioner*, 365 F.2d 24 (7th Cir., 1966).

63. *Aqualane Shores, Inc. v. Commissioner*, 351 F.2d 116 (5th Cir., 1959).

64. *W. C. Gamman et al.*, 46 T.C. 1 (1966).

65. *Turner Advertising of Kentucky, Inc.*, T.C. Memo. 1966-101, filed May 17, 1966.

66. *George E. Warren Corporation v. United States*, 141 F. Supp. 935 (Ct. Cl., 1956).

67. *Fors Farms, Inc. et al. v. United States*, D.C., W.D. Wash., 1966.

68. *Hoguet Real Estate Corporation*, 30 T.C. 580 (1958).

69. *Wilbur Security Company v. Commissioner*, 279 F.2d 657 (9th Cir., 1960).

70. *Fors Farms, Inc. et al. v. United States*, D.C., W.D. Wash., 1966.

71. *R. C. Owens Company v. United States*, 180 F. Supp. 369 (Ct. Cl., 1960).

72. *Fellinger v. United States*, 363 F.2d 826 (6th Cir., 1966).

73. *815 Riverside Company v. United States*, D.C., M.D. Ga., 1965.

74. *Sayles Finishing Plants, Inc. v. United States*, 399 F.2d 214 (Ct. Cl., 1968).

75. *Byerlite Corporation v. Williams*, 170 F. Supp. 48 (D.C., N.D. Ohio, 1959), *rev'd on another issue*, 286 F.2d 285 (6th Cir., 1961).

76. *Henderson et al. v. United States*, 245 F. Supp. 782 (D.C., M.D. Ala., 1965).

77. *Oak Hill Finance Company*, 40 T.C. 419 (1963).

78. *Murphy Logging Co. et al. v. United States*, 239 F. Supp. 794 (D.C., Ore., 1965), *rev'd on another issue*, 378 F.2d 222 (9th Cir., 1967).

79. *Herbert B. Miller Estate v. Commissioner*, 239 F.2d 729 (9th Cir., 1957).

80. *Sherry Park, Inc. v. United States* (D.C., S.D. Fla., 1964).

81. *Crown Iron Works Co.*, T.C. Memo. 1956-199 (filed August 29, 1956), *aff'd*, 245 F.2d 357 (8th Cir., 1957).

82. *John Town, Inc.*, 46 T.C. 107 (1966), *aff'd*, (7th Cir., 1967).

83. *Motel Company*, T.C. Memo. 1963-174 (filed June 26, 1963), *aff'd*, 340 F.2d 445 (2d Cir., 1965).

84. *Phil Kalech et al.*, 23 T.C. 672 (1955).

85. *Wood Preserving Corporation of Baltimore, Inc. v. United States*, D.C. Md., 1964, *aff'd*, 347 F.2d 111 (4th Cir., 1965).

86. *Mullin Building Corporation*, 9 T.C. 350 (1947), *aff'd*, 167 F.2d 1001 (3d Cir., 1948).

87. *Ortmayer et al. v. Commissioner*, 265 F.2d 848 (7th Cir., 1959).

88. *Choctaw, Inc.*, T.C. Memo., Docket No. 36173 (entered December 9, 1953).

89. *Intermountain Furniture Manufacturing Company, Inc. v. United States*, D.C., Utah, 1967, *rev'd on another issue*, 363 F.2d 554 (10th Cir., 1966); *Golden Belt Lumber Company*, T.C. 741 (1943); *Kennickel Printing Company v. United States* (D.C., S.D. Ga., 1966).

90. *Plastic Toys, Inc. et al.*, T.C. Memo. 1968-143 (filed July 8, 1968).

91. *Covey Investment Company v. United States*, 377 F.2d 403 (10th Cir., 1967).

92. *Jordan Company v. Allen*, 85 F. Supp. 437 (D.C., M.D. Ga., 1949).

93. *Sherwood Memorial Gardens, Inc. v. Commissioner*, 350 F.2d 225 (7th Cir., 1965).

94. *Henderson et al. v. United States*, 245 F. Supp. 782 (D.C., M.D. Ala., 1965).

95. *Fellinger v. United States*, 363 F.2d 826 (6th Cir., 1966).

96. *Atlanta Biltmore Hotel Corporation v. Commissioner*, 349 F.2d 677 (5th Cir., 1965).

97. *Wilshire & Western Sandwiches, Inc. v. Commissioner*, 175 F.2d 718 (9th Cir., 1949).

98. *Ragland Investment Company et al.*, 52 T.C. 867 (1969).

99. Revenue Procedure 69-6, 1969-1 CB 396.

100. I.R.C. Section 385.

101. I.R.C. Section 305(b).

CHAPTER 4

What Can Be Done
Through Subsidiary Corporations

Reasons for Having Subsidiaries

Subsidiary corporations may be created for such reasons as these:

(1) To spread tort and other liability.[1]

(2) To have separate companies run by individuals or family groups to reduce personal conflicts.[2]

(3) To satisfy the demands of an important supplier[3] or customer.

(4) To dispose of part of a corporation's business in order to comply with a Federal antitrust action.[4]

(5) To circumvent a state law restricting the amount of land one corporation can own.[5]

(6) To get around ceilings imposed by some banks upon the size of a loan that can be made to one borrower.[6]

(7) To avoid loss of state unemployment insurance merit ratings by concentration of high-turnover employees in a single company.[7]

(8) To avoid identifying the sales of cheap, inferior products with the quality line of an established, highly-regarded company.[8]

(9) To overcome local prejudice against large national companies.[9]

(10) To reduce the possibility of state or local tax discrimination against out-of-state corporations.

(11) To carry out specialized functions.[10]

(12) To comply with the specialization that is accepted practice in the industry.[11]

(13) To provide broader compensation arrangements for key employees related to the subsidiary's earnings.[12]

(14) To avoid loss of business if a regulated-industry company is suspended because of violation of technical requirements.

(15) To be able to adopt inconsistent accounting, inventory, and other elections.

(16) To permit tailoring of employee benefit plans to match contributions of different groups to the success of the enterprise while reducing vulnerability to charges of discrimination.

(17) To keep a union from seeing the corporate books for the entire enterprise.

(18) To avoid union jurisdictional disputes where several activities are carried on or operations are in different geographical areas.

(19) To have separate boards of directors drawn from different areas served by the enterprise.[13]

(20) To get around the restrictions of a franchise.[14]

(21) To take advantage of different types of permissible tax-favored business forms—DISCs, Western Hemisphere Trade Corporations, non-resident foreign corporations, etc.

Disadvantages of Subsidiary Corporations

If plural corporations are used and a consolidated Federal income tax return is not filed for any reason, there could be intercompany income that is not eliminated or losses that cannot be utilized.

If state or local gross receipts or sales taxes are involved and consolidated returns are not permitted, there could be overlapping or duplicate taxes upon gross receipts or sales.

Where two or more corporations are under common control, the Internal Revenue Service may seek to reallocate items of income or expense among the corporations.[15] (See chapter 5, Arm's Length Transactions.)

Parent-Subsidiary Relationship

In order for a parent to establish that a subsidiary is its mere instrumentality, three elements must be proved: (1) control by the parent to such a degree that the subsidiary has become a mere instrumentality; (2) fraud or wrong by the parent through its subsidiary (such as violations of a statute or stripping the subsidiary of its assets); and (3) unjust loss or injury to a claimant (such as might occur in the insolvency of the subsidiary[16]).

Even if parent and subsidiary are separate corporations, for tax purposes they may be treated as a single corporation, as where there is a reallocation of income or expenses because of less than arm's length transactions. (This will be discussed in chapter 5.)

Creation of Subsidiary Corporations

No gain or loss is recognized if property is transferred to a corporation by one or more persons (this can include a corporation) solely in exchange for stock provided that, immediately after the exchange, the transferors collectively own at least 80 percent of the total combined voting power of all classes of the corporation's voting stock and at least 80 percent of the total number of shares of all other classes of stock.[17]

A corporation may separate its business into two or more corporate entities without accounting for gain or loss to itself or to the shareholders if the business has been in active operation for at least five years and was owned for at least five years by the corporation that is "separating." But to be tax-free, the transaction must not be principally a device for the distribution of corporate earnings. Where a corporation "separates" by distributing stock or securities of controlled corporations, all of the shares, etc., that it owns must be distributed.[18] It is immaterial whether distributing corporation's shareholders get *pro rata* shares or not, and it does not matter whether the recipient shareholders surrender any of their stock in return for the shares that are given to them.[19]

Multiple Corporations

Starting in 1975, a group of controlled corporations is to have only one $25,000 surtax exemption and one $100,000 accumulated earnings credit.

A controlled group may be any one of the following:

(1) *Parent-subsidiary controlled group,* where a common parent corporation owns at least 80 percent of either the total combined voting power or the total value of the stock of each other company in a chain connected through stock ownership.

(2) *Brother-sister controlled group,* where there are two or more corporations, 80 percent or more of whose stock (by voting power or value) is owned by five or fewer persons. A "person" in this sense can be an individual, an estate, or a trust. Each of these five or fewer persons must own more than 50 percent of each corporation identically. For example, a person who owns 70 percent of one corporation and 30 percent of another corporation is treated as owning only 30 percent of each corporation. It is only this amount that is taken into account in applying the 50 percent test.

(3) *Combined group,* where each of three or more corporations is a member of a group of corporations described in (1) or (2) and one of the corporations is a common parent corporation included in (1) and also is included in a group of corporations described in (2).[20]

This law was part of the Tax Reform Act of 1969 and provided a six-year transition period, reducing the additional surtax exemptions and accumulated earnings credits by one-sixth in each of the years 1970 through 1975.

Taxable years including December 31	Surtax exemptions	Minimum accumulated earnings credits
1970	$20,833	$83,333
1971	16,667	66,667
1972	12,500	50,000
1973	8,333	33,333
1974	4,167	16,667
1975	None	None

Where members of a controlled group had elected to use multiple $25,000 surtax exemptions, a 6 percent penalty tax was imposed for this privilege upon the first $25,000 of taxable income of each corporation. For years beginning after 1974, the election no longer exists nor does the 6 percent penalty.

Dividends Received Deduction

The dividends received deduction allowed to members of a controlled group was increased by the Tax Reform Act of 1969 from 85 to 100 percent.

Dividends from earnings for taxable years including December 31	Dividends received deduction percentage
1970	$87\frac{1}{2}$
1971	90
1972	$92\frac{1}{2}$
1973	95
1974	$97\frac{1}{2}$
1975	100

Consolidated Income Tax Returns

An *affiliated group* of corporations has the privilege of making a consolidated Federal income tax return in lieu of separate or individual returns. However, this privilege is conditional upon all corporations' having been members of the affiliated group at any time during the taxable year for which the return is made consenting to the regulations applicable to that year. The making of the consolidated return is considered consent.[21]

The term *affiliated group* means one or more chains of *includable corporations* connected through stock ownership with a common parent corporation which is an includable corporation if

(1) One or more of the other includable corporations directly owns stock possessing at least 80 percent of the voting power of all classes of stock and at least 80 percent of each class of the nonvoting stock of each of the includable corporations (except the common parent corporation); and

(2) The common parent corporation directly owns stock possessing at least 80 percent of the voting power of all classes of stock and at least 80 percent of each class of the nonvoting stock of at least one of the other includable corporations.[22]

The term *includable corporation* means any corporation except a tax-exempt corporation, an insurance company, a foreign corporation (except those incorporated in Canada and Mexico), a Western Hemisphere Trade Corporation, a company doing business within a possession of the United States,[23] a China Trade Act Corporation, a regulated investment company, a real estate investment trust (REIT), a Subchapter S corporation, and a Domestic International Sales Corporation (DISC).[24]

Brother-sister corporations may not file consolidated returns even if the corporations are a business unit with the same executive officer owning all of the stock in both corporations.[25]

The consolidated Federal income tax return must comprise every includable corporation that is a member of the affiliated group. The filing of *separate* returns does not constitute a binding election for future years. But if a consolidated return is filed, a consolidated return must also be filed for each subsequent taxable year during which the affiliated group remains in existence unless the IRS grants permission to switch back to separate returns or unless certain changes take place.

The principal advantages to be obtained through filing a consolidated return are:

(1) Losses of one or more of the corporations may offset income of the other companies.

(2) Intercompany dividends are eliminated in the same manner as any other intercompany item and not limited by the dividends received deduction.

(3) All intercompany transactions are eliminated.

(4) One or more corporations in an affiliated group might be vulnerable to the accumulated earnings tax or to the personal holding company tax. But the filing of a consolidated return might eliminate this hazard, for the tax (if any) would be asserted upon the tax return as actually filed. *Consolidated* reasons for retention might eliminate the danger of the first tax; *consolidated* gross income might mean that the personal holding company tax would not be applicable.

(5) Corporations are not entitled to any deduction for net capital losses. But on a consolidated return, capital losses of one corporation can be set against capital gains of other corporations.

The disadvantages of filing a consolidated Federal income tax return are:

(1) There has been an election that is usually regarded as binding for subsequent years, absent permission from the Service to switch back.

(2) If a consolidated return is filed in order to absorb the loss of one or more corporations, the possibility of such corporations' using the net operating loss carry-back or carry-over is lost. It should be determined mathematically whether it is better to file a consolidated return or make use of the net operating loss technique.

(3) On a consolidated return, there is but one surtax exemption and one minimum accumulated earnings credit. But as has been mentioned previously in this chapter, multiple exemptions and credits are now being phased out for multiple corporations.

(4) If a consolidated Federal income tax return is filed, a state in which one of the corporations files its return might require the submission of a copy of the Federal return. The state might then assess its own tax upon a

consolidated basis, which might bring into the state the far greater income of the parent or other companies. If a consolidated return were filed in a particular state, the net state tax cost would usually be increased dramatically.

The Internal Revenue Service might not permit a consolidated Federal income tax return if a corporation has been acquired for reasons having nothing to do with the carrying on of business through plural companies. This could cover an acquisition of a deficit company for a low price, the losses of which would reduce consolidated income. Even though proper connection through stock ownership is shown, a business purpose must also be shown for an affiliation before the acquired corporation can be treated as a member of the affiliated group.[26]

NOTES

1. *Alcorn Wholesale Company et al.,* 16 T.C. 75 (1951).
2. *Albert W. Badanes et al.,* 39 T.C. 410 (1962).
3. *Rena B. Farr,* 24 T.C. 350 (1955).
4. *Continental Can Company, Inc. v. United States,* 422 F.2d 405 (Ct. Cl., 1970).
5. *Cuyuna Realty Company v. United States,* 382 F.2d 298 (Ct. Cl., 1967).
6. *Bernstein et al. v. United States,* 345 F.2d 558 (Ct. Cl., 1965).
7. *Commissioner v. Chelsea Products, Inc.,* 197 F.2d 620 (3d Cir., 1950).
8. *Standard Fruit Products Co.,* T.C. Memo., Docket No. 17628 (entered August 22, 1949).
9. *The Coca-Cola Bottling Company of Gallup et al. v. United States,* 443 F.2d 1253 (10th Cir., 1971).
10. *Grenada Industries, Inc. v. Commissioner,* 202 F.2d 873 (5th Cir., 1953).
11. *Miles-Conley Company, Inc.,* 10 T.C. 754 (1948), *aff'd,* 173 F.2d 958 (4th Cir., 1949).
12. *Epsen Lithographers, Inc. v. O'Malley,* 67 F. Supp. 181 (D.C., Neb., 1946). *Fair Price Stations, Inc.,* T.C. Memo., Docket No. 6102 (entered May 23, 1944).
13. *Commissioner et al. v. Gordon et al.,* 391 U.S. 83 (1968).
14. *Barq's Bottling Company,* T.C. Memo., Docket No. 6758 (entered June 21, 1946).
15. I.R.C. Section 482.
16. *Steven v. Roscoe Turner Aeronautical Corporation,* 324 F.2d 157 (7th Cir., 1963).
17. I.R.C. Section 351.
18. I.R.C. Section 355.
19. I.R.C. Section 355. (For an extended discussion of this subject, see Robert S. Holzman, *Tax-Free Reorganizations after the Tax Reform Act of 1969.* Lynbrook, N.Y., 1970.)
20. I.R.C. Section 1563(a).
21. I.R.C. Section 1501.
22. I.R.C. Section 1504(a).
23. In accordance with I.R.C. Section 931.
24. I.R.C. Section 246(d).
25. *Ray Engineering Co., Inc. v. Commissioner,* 347 F.2d 716 (3d Cir., 1965).
26. *Naeter Brothers Publishing Co.,* 42 T.C. 1 (1964).

CHAPTER 5

Arm's Length Transactions

The Theory

Top management must be concerned with Section 482 of the Internal Revenue Code which provides: "In any case of two or more organizations, trades, or businesses (whether or not incorporated, whether or not organized in the United States, and whether or not affiliated) owned or controlled directly or indirectly by the same interests, the Secretary [of the Treasury] or his delegate may distribute, apportion, or allocate gross income, deductions, credits, or allowances between or among such organizations, trades, or businesses, if he determines that such distribution, apportionment, or allocation is necessary in order to prevent evasion of taxes or clearly to reflect the income of any such organizations, trades, or businesses."

The purpose of the reallocation is to reflect the true income of related companies.[1] Reallocation need not be on an item-by-item basis; the *total* income and expenses of one related party may be reallocated to another.[2] In certain instances, the Commissioner of Internal Revenue may reallocate *net* income as a shortcut to allocating gross income and deductions.[3]

Through reallocation under Section 482, the Commissioner can make sure that the consequences of a transaction between parties under common control are what an independent individual bargaining at *arm's length* and in his own economic interest would have accepted.[4] The Commissioner may step in where one of the parties under common control would not have entered into the contract with a party not so related.[5]

Section 482 has remained virtually unchanged for more than 40 years. It was designed to prevent the shifting of income or deductions arbitrarily between controlled companies.[6] The Commissioner can rectify abnormalities and distortions in income of separate tax-paying entities under common control.[7] If such entities under common control deal with each other at less than arm's length, the Internal Revenue Service can "unscramble" the situation.[8]

Section 482 may be invoked to prevent evasion of taxes. Any kind of intercompany diversion of income or expenses may be involved. One such example is converting what would be a dividend taxable at ordinary rates into a capital gain by merely passing it through another corporate shell.[9]

The idea is to attribute income or deductions to the entity that has earned or sustained them.[10] If there has been no shifting of income or deductions, there should be nothing to be concerned about. But an intercompany transaction may in substance involve such a shifting even if the parties neither recognized this fact nor intended it.

While a taxpayer may legitimately do what he can to minimize his taxes, he cannot reduce his income tax by transferring his money from one pocket to another even though he uses different pairs of trousers, for that would enable a party with a large wardrobe to gain a tax advantage not available to those in more modest circumstances.[11]

That the company to which income is reallocated under Section 482 did not actually receive it does not prevent its being taxed according to the reallocation if the use of this income was available at the pleasure of the company to which reallocation was made.[12]

Power to Shift Income Does Not Trigger the Statute

Common control is not *prima facie* evidence of less than arm's length dealing.[13] Undoubtedly, the great majority of corporations owned by sole stockholders (whether individuals or parent corporations) are "dummies" in the sense that their policies and day-to-day activities are determined not as decisions of the controlled corporations, but by their owners acting individually.[14] However, that by itself does not mean that the corporations are dealing at less than arm's length or are being utilized to reduce some other company's taxes. Section 482 does not permit the Commissioner to reallocate income or deductions between controlled parties merely because the common owners have the *power* to shift income. Reallocation must be based upon the *actual shifting* of income or deductions between commonly controlled businesses and not on what *might* have been done.[15]

Although transactions between taxpayers owned and controlled by the same interests are carefully scrutinized by the Commissioner, they cannot be disturbed solely for that reason if they in fact conform to acceptable business requirements.[16]

What Is Required for a Reallocation?

The two primary elements that must exist if the IRS is to sustain a reallocation of income or deductions under Section 482 are: (1) the existence of commonly controlled companies and (2) the presence of income earned by some of these companies which, unless the reallocation was made, would not otherwise have been reported for Federal income tax purposes.[17] Sometimes, the courts rely upon a third element—namely, the use of separate entities for the conduct of a business or businesses where the separate entities serve a tax avoidance or tax minimization purpose rather than a business purpose.[18]

Where the Commissioner has made a reallocation under Section 482, a court may reallocate income in a manner that the evidence demonstrates to be correct. The Commissioner's reallocation need not be approved or disapproved in its entirety.[19] Neither the taxpayer's nor the Commissioner's method of allocation or reallocation is final. It is for the court to determine which method is the more appropriate under the circumstances.[20]

The fact that the parties are satisfied with an arrangement is not enough. The Commissioner must see that one party does not earn the income and then escape the payment of taxes by apportioning the income to a related party.[21] Even if a transaction creates an enforceable liability between the parties, the court has the responsibility of discovering whether the payments are required *for tax purposes.*[22]

For the Commissioner to make a reallocation, there must be collusive or improper conduct between the controlled taxpayers.[23] But this need not involve intent to avoid taxes. Inquiries into subjective intent, especially in intra-family transfers, are particularly perilous.[24] Thus, Section 482 may be applicable where there is no suspicion of fraud or deliberate tax avoidance.[25] Reallocation may be required even where the Commissioner does not question the good faith of a transaction.[26]

Even the existence of a sound business purpose for a transaction does not mean that Section 482 is inapplicable.[27] The only question is whether income actually earned by one company has been artificially deflected to another company under common control.[28] But the lack of any purpose for a transaction other than tax avoidance strongly indicates that the overall plan was an arbitrary shifting of income among controlled businesses primarily to evade taxes. This justifies a reallocation.[29]

The Commissioner "May" Reallocate

The statute provides that the Commissioner "may" reallocate items of income or expense; he does not have to do so. The fact that he permitted the filing of income tax returns of controlled companies in a certain manner for one or more years does not mean that he has to do so in a subsequent year.[30]

Even though the Commissioner required an enterprise to make a reallocation under Section 482 in one year, he is not bound to this method in subsequent years.[31] The Commissioner has broad discretion to make a reallocation under appropriate circumstances. A court cannot substitute its judgment for the Commissioner's unless the taxpayer can show that the Commissioner has abused his discretion.[32] But the Commissioner's determination will stand if the court finds that it was neither arbitrary nor capricious.[33] If the taxpayer appeals the Commissioner's action in a court, the taxpayer bears a heavier than normal burden of proving arbitrariness. Thus, the Commissioner must give the taxpayer fair notice in advance of trial that he is acting pursuant to Section 482.[34]

The Commissioner must do more than merely state that a reallocation is being made. He must show a factual basis upon which a more proper reallocation should be made.[35] The Commissioner will not prevail if he does not direct a reviewing court to a single entry or account that he contends is improper or inaccurate or that he seeks to correct.[36] Accordingly, the taxpayer must be advised of the basis for the reallocation. No particular form of notice is required. Sufficient notice was deemed to have been furnished where a Revenue Agent's report declared: "It has been determined that the income reported by this corporation was earned by the parent . . . and is reportable by it, under Section 45 [the forerunner of Section 482] . . . ."[37]

Limitation on the Commissioner's Authority

Where parties under common control are found to be dealing at less than arm's length, it does not follow that the Commissioner may reallocate *all* of the income. In one such situation, assuming that it could arrive at its own arithmetical determination where the taxpayer's figures were incomplete, the court[38] reallocated 70 percent of the income instead of the 100 percent sought by the Commissioner.[39]

The Commissioner does not have untrammeled discretion as to reallocation techniques even where a reallocation is indicated. Thus, where a number of bus companies was under common control, he was required to reallocate on the basis of the bus mileage of each company, not on the basis of the total number of buses.[40] Likewise, the Commissioner could not reallocate bonuses in the case of four corporations under common control where only two of the corporations paid bonuses; bonuses were based upon earnings, and only two of the corporations had earnings.[41]

Section 482 provides for a reallocation, not a disallowance. Of course, in certain instances, a deduction or loss may be transferred to a company that cannot use it. A proper reallocation has thus taken place—even if the effect is that of a disallowance.[42]

Conflict of Section 482 and Other Code Sections

Section 482 is stated in general terms and may come in conflict with some other section of the Internal Revenue Code that provides for the specific tax treatment of a given transaction. In any such situation, Section 482 prevails over another section with which it comes into conflict.

If this were not the case, Section 482 would be wholly superfluous. The application of the section will not be denied because it runs afoul of the literal provisions or specific language of other sections of the Code. If the Commissioner's action in reallocating was a proper exercise of his discretion, it will prevail.[43]

Control

Under Section 482, reallocation is permitted only in the case of transactions at less than arm's length between parties under common *control*. Congress has not defined "control" within the meaning of Section 482. However, a broad definition of the term has been adopted in the Treasury Regulations.[44] The regulations declare: "The term 'controlled' includes any kind of control, direct or indirect, whether legally enforceable, and however exercisable or exercised. It is the reality of the control which is decisive, not its form or the mode of its exercise. A presumption of control arises if income or deductions have been arbitrarily shifted." [45]

Where four families each owned one-fourth of the stock of a corporation and a partnership was formed with each family holding a one-fourth interest, common control existed even though within one of the family units certain persons who owned stock in the corporation did not own interests in the partnership, having given these interests to their children. The court concluded that the purpose of Section 482 would be frustrated if a short-term diversion of income were sufficient to defeat a finding of control where the shift is among related family members and that no change has taken place in the actual ownership of the underlying properties or interests.[46]

Even if no stock is owned, the beneficial owner of a corporation may be deemed to be in *control* of it. It is not record ownership, but actual control, that counts in the application of the statute. Factually, a corporation may be controlled by a person despite what appears upon stock certificates or ownership tables.[47] While actual, practical control rather than any particular percentage of stock ownership is the criterion, courts have, in some instances, held that in the case of a corporation, "control" means ownership of *more* than 50 percent of the stock.[48] Thus, where a corporation was owned by each of two unrelated corporations, each of which held 50 percent of the stock, reallocation was denied to the Commissioner, since neither of the two shareholders controlled the company that they owned together. Where two or more corporations owned by different sets of stockholders controlled a third corporation, the court ruled that it could not be said that the third corporation was controlled by the same interests.[49] Originally, the Internal Revenue Service acquiesced in that decision. But this acquiescence was withdrawn 20 years later. Since then, it has been held that there is common control where two unrelated groups each own 50 percent of the stock of a corporation.

The Measure of Arm's Length

The best proof of the arm's length character of a transaction is a showing of comparable rates or prices elsewhere.[50] Thus, discounts given to affiliates could not be reshuffled by the Commissioner where they were the standard discounts given by those in the industry to wholesale jobbers.[51] Similarly, discounts and agents' commissions used by businesses under common control could not be disturbed where the terms were shown to be similar to those ordinarily employed by these businesses in transactions with unrelated parties.[52]

Amounts paid to an affiliate as freight charges were reasonable where they were based on rates used by the Pacific Conference, represented uniform rates established by an association of steamship companies operating in the Pacific Ocean, and all major companies in the industry belonged to this conference.[53] Where a sale of automobiles was made by one affiliate to another, the transaction was deemed to be at arm's length inasmuch as the price reflected the wholesale discount basis authorized by the company's contract with General Motors Corporation and the same terms could have been obtained from other dealers.[54] Intercompany rates also could not be reallocated where they were the same as the rates charged by an independent agency.[55]

If an intercompany transaction cannot be related to terms used in transactions with outside parties, the arm's length price may be established by an independent appraiser.[56] A computation made by an independent certified public accountant may be accepted by the court.[57] But the terms of an intercompany transaction may be subjected to especially sharp scrutiny if made upon the recommendation of a tax specialist.[58]

An arm's length price or fee may be justified by reference to actual market prices or quotations;[59] or there may be a showing of a *bona fide* offer from an outsider.[60]

Intercompany charges may be justified by a rule of reason if no other criteria exist. Thus, broadcasting costs of a radio station were allocated in part to its selling company affiliate upon the basis of their respective sales volumes.[61] Undistinguishable administrative and overhead expenses were allocated at the end of each year in proportion to the respective sales of the two related corporations involved.[62] Rent allocated between affiliates should be in accordance with the space used by the respective participants in the premises.[63]

Testimony of a bank officer that he would have lent money on the same terms as were used in an intercompany transaction that had already taken place is apt to be accepted by the court—although sometimes with suspicious reluctance. In one case, a reluctant court accepted such testimony, but observed that the bank officer stretched the truth for a good customer on circumstances which did not exist and probably would not occur. The banker was lucky, concluded the court, that he did not have to defend the loan before a bank examiner.[64] Obviously, a friendly witness acts at his own peril.

The Commissioner's reallocation was sustained where a company president sought no outside advice as to the mathematics of a transaction.[65]

Sometimes, the Commissioner bases his reallocation upon the fact that no bargaining between the affiliated companies has taken place. But arm's length bargaining between affiliates is not required so long as the transaction actually is carried out under terms which would have been acceptable to unrelated parties.[66]

Intercompany transactions are likely to be subjected to reallocation if the parties grossly defy any rule of reason. Thus, the fact that commissions charged to a company under common control were almost double those paid to unrelated parties was regarded as evidence that the intercompany charges were not fair and reasonable.[67] A transaction between parties under common control was deemed not to have been carried on at arm's length where a brand-new facility was leased to an affiliate for a sum not sufficient to cover its fixed book expenses.[68]

May the Commissioner Reallocate Nonexistent Income?

In 1968, the Treasury Regulations were amended to allow for reallocation by the Commissioner in certain instances where the related parties had not provided for any income that could be reallocated. In six specified situations, it was stipulated that income could be reallocated even where there was no income at all in the transaction as cast by the parties.

Loans or Advances. Where one member of a group of controlled corporations directly or indirectly makes a loan or advance to, or otherwise becomes a creditor of, another member of this group and charges no interest or charges interest at a rate which is not an arm's length one, the Commissioner may make appropriate reallocations to reflect an arm's length interest rate for the use of such a loan or advance. For this purpose, the arm's length interest rate will be the rate of interest that would have been charged had the indebtedness arisen in an independent transaction between unrelated parties under similar circumstances. If the creditor is not regularly engaged in the business of making loans or advances of the same general type as the loan or advance in question to unrelated parties, the Treasury Regulations specify that the arm's length rate will be:

(1) the rate of interest actually charged if at least four percent, but not in excess of six percent per annum simple interest; or

(2) five percent per annum simple interest if no interest was charged or if the rate of interest charged was less than four percent or in excess of six percent per annum simple interest.

However, the above rates will not be given effect if the taxpayer establishes a more appropriate rate under the standards previously mentioned.[69]

This regulation is directly contrary to decisions reached by the courts under the same law before the adoption of the regulation where no interest had been charged in transactions between parties under common control.[70] In those cases, it was emphasized that Section 482 was predicated on the existence of income and did not authorize the Commissioner to reallocate income where none had existed. But nonexistent intercompany interest was found to be subject to reallocation in a case heard after the adoption of the regulation.[71]

Performance of Services for Another. Where one group of controlled entities performs marketing, managerial, administrative, technical, or other services for the benefit of, or on behalf of, another member of the group without charge or at a charge that does not constitute an arm's length charge, the Commissioner may make appropriate reallocations to reflect an arm's length charge for such services.

Allocations may be made to reflect arm's length charges with respect to services undertaken for the mutual benefit of the members of a group of controlled entities as well as with respect to services performed by one member of the group exclusively for the benefit of another member of the group. In general, reallocations may be made if the service, at the time it was performed, related to the carrying on of an activity by another member or was intended to benefit another member either in the member's overall operations or in its day-to-day activities. Costs to be taken into account are direct costs or deductions that are identified separately with a particular service. Indirect costs or deductions may also be taken into account if they are not specifically identified with a particular activity or service, but relate to the direct costs referred to in the preceding sentence.[72]

Use of Tangible Property. Where one member of a controlled group permits the use of its tangible property by another member, the Treasury Regulations provide a safe haven which may be used by the taxpayers in determining an appropriate rental. The rental charge is expressed in terms of a formula that takes into account depreciation, a factor somewhat equivalent to interest, and certain expenses incurred in connection with the property.[73]

Transfer or Use of Intangible Property. In connection with the transfer of intangible property by one member of a controlled group to another member, the regulations require an arm's length charge be made. Determination of the arm's length charge may be avoided if the parties using the property enter into a *bona fide* cost-sharing arrangement in connection with the development of the intangible property. Detailed rules with respect to the establishment of a *bona fide* cost-sharing arrangement have not been supplied; instead, there is a concise statement of general rules based upon arm's length standards.[74]

Sales of Tangible Property. An *arm's length price* is the price that an unrelated party would have paid for the property under the same circumstances. Inasmuch as unrelated parties normally sell products at a profit, an arm's length price normally involves a profit to the seller.[75]

Three methods of determining an arm's length price are described.

(1) The taxpayer should use the comparable uncontrolled price method if possible.

(2) If not, he should use the resale price method where the standards for its application are met because it is the method that is most likely to result in the next most accurate estimate in such instances.

Suppose that a manufacturer sells products to a related distributor, who, without further processing, resells the products in uncontrolled transactions.

(3) If all the standards for the mandatory application of the resale price method are not satisfied, either that method or the cost-plus method may be used, depending upon which method is more feasible and which is likely to yield a more accurate estimate of an arm's length price. The cost-plus method may be appropriate where a manufacturer sells products to a related entity which performs substantial manufacturing, assembly, or other processing on the product or adds significant value by reason of its utilization of its intangible property prior to resale in uncontrolled transactions.

The taxpayer also has the opportunity of showing that some other method is more appropriate. Additionally, less than arm's length figures may be used if there are differences in quality, terms of sale, geographic market, time of sale, or level of the market.

Where there is a *bona fide* cost-sharing arrangement in the case of an interest in intangibles, there will be no reallocation.[76]

Intercompany Services. Where tangible or intangible property is transferred, sold, assigned, loaned, leased, or otherwise made available by one member of a controlled group to another member and services are rendered by the transferor to the transferee in connection with the transfer, the Commissioner may make a reallocation under the rules applicable to intercompany use of tangible property, transfer or use of intangible property, or sale of tangible property (whichever is applicable). Services are deemed to be rendered in connection with the transfer of property where they are merely ancillary and subsdiary to the transfer or to the commencement of effective use of the property by the transferee.[77]

Reimbursement Arrangement

In making a reallocation, the Internal Revenue Service will consider whether the controlled parties had an arrangement that would have provided for reimbursement within a reasonable period before or after the taxable year if that arrangement would have rectified a transaction which seemingly was at less than arm's length.

For example, a parent corporation, P, performed services in 1969 for the benefit of its subsidiary corporation, S, in connection with S's manufacture and sale of a product. S did not pay P for these services in 1969, but agreed in that year to pay P a percentage of the proceeds from the sales of the product in the years 1969 through 1973. In 1969, it appeared that this arrangement would provide adequate consideration for the services. No reallocation would be made with respect to the services performed by P.[78]

Claimed Setoff

If the Internal Revenue Service makes a reallocation, the parties under common control have an opportunity to bring to the Service's attention any other transactions at less than arm's length that might be setoffs of an appropriate nature.[79] The Service must be notified of previously unnoticed transactions at less than arm's length in sufficient detail to permit verification within 30 days of the proposed reallocation.[80]

Mitigation

Where the Internal Revenue Service has made a reallocation under Section 482, taxpayers whose incomes have been increased may be permitted to make certain adjustments so that their accounts may reflect this reallocation. If the reallocation was not made because of an arrangement one of whose principal purposes was the avoidance of Federal income tax, the taxpayer will be eligible for special treatment. Under this circumstance, dividends received from a corporation under common control may be reduced or excluded from income.

Detailed instructions have been provided for related taxpayers who desire this treatment.[81]

Foreign Corporations

A United States controlling taxpayer is granted relief from economic double taxation that occurs as a result of reallocations under Section 482. The taxpayer is allowed to offset against the United States tax attributable to the reallocation a sum equal to (1) the amount by which the controlled foreign entity's foreign income tax liability, as actually determined, exceeded (2) the amount that would have been determined if the controlled foreign entity had originally treated the transactions giving rise to the reallocation in a manner consistent with the reallocation. The amount of the relief is limited to that portion of the United States controlling taxpayer's tax liability attributable to the reallocation.

For this purpose, economic double taxation is deemed to exist if, as a consequence of the reallocation, the total income tax payable to the United States and another nation by the United States controlling taxpayer and its controlled foreign entity is greater than that which would have resulted if these parties originally had treated the transactions giving rise to the reallocation in a manner consistent with the reallocation. Detailed ground rules have been provided for this treatment.[82]

Treatment of Controlled Companies as One Entity

Sometimes, the Internal Revenue Service claims that several companies are, in effect, a single corporation and that all income and expenses must be reallocated to the single company. Take the case of a construction company that formed 88 corporations to build residences for ultimate sale to war veterans. Most of the stock of the 88 corporations was owned by stockholders of the original construction company. The multiple corporations borrowed construction funds from outsiders, but the original company guaranteed the loans. The multiple corporations had no employees, payroll, independent offices, or capital beyond the nominal amounts set up by the incorporators. It was held that the Commissioner could deny the existence for tax purposes, of the multiple corporations and could reallocate all of the income to the original construction company.[83]

In another case, a corporation was without funds to make required payments on a Federal Housing Administration mortgage. The stockholders, fearful lest a default should sour the FHA on other projects which the enterprise contemplated, decided that the corporation should lease the property to the stockholders. Actually, this arrangement was advantageous to them taxwise, for under it, the corporation apparently would have losses that could not be utilized, whereas the shareholders had income from other sources that could be offset by operating losses of the property. The Internal Revenue Service was permitted to reallocate the losses to the corporation since the stockholders had agreed to pay a substantial fixed rent to their corporation when occupancy was low and the shareholders assumed all renovation and operating costs of the property.[84]

But reallocation will not be required if there are non-tax reasons for the existence of separate companies and the companies are in fact operated as separate entities, assuming all transactions are carried on at arm's length. For example, a primary purpose for forming an additional corporation may be to disassociate cheaper products from a corporation's regular line.[85] Separate companies may be formed, upon the advice of counsel, for the purpose of dividing operations along state lines.[86] Income from sales made by a taxpayer's Philippine subsidiary, but diverted to the taxpayer's Panamanian subsidiary because of Philippine currency restrictions, did not have to be included in the taxpayer's income.[87]

Consequences of a Reallocation

A reallocation of income or expenses by the Internal Revenue Service may involve far more than a reshuffling of taxable income. Here are some potential consequences:

(1) A deduction might be transferred from a corporation which can use it to a deficit company which cannot.

(2) A deduction might be reallocated from a company whose tax returns are still open under the statute of limitations to a company whose tax returns are now closed.

(3) A reallocation might be made to a corporation which is forbidden by state law to receive that type of income. The resultant penalties prescribed by state law will accompany the reallocation.[88]

(4) Reallocation of some of one corporation's income to a supposedly inactive affiliate can cause loss of Subchapter S status for the former. (See chapter 2, Corporations and Other Forms of Conducting Business.) Subchapter S corporation election is not available to a corporation that is a member of an affiilated group. The making of the supposedly inactive affiliate into an active company would create affiliated group status unless the affiliate were brand-new and had little income.[89]

(5) Reallocation of income could assign earnings to a corporation in excess of its business needs for retention. It would then be impossible to declare dividends or develop reasons for retention after the close of the taxable year. The probable result would be an accumulated earnings tax.

(6) Reallocation of earnings *from* a corporation which already had paid a dividend could retroactively cause a situation where the corporation had declared a dividend in excess of its earnings and profits. This might conceivably result in the imposition of criminal penalties against the directors.

(7) Deduction of corporate contributions under a qualified deferred profit-sharing plan is limited to payments made not later than the last day for filing the income tax return.[90] If reallocation of profits is made from an

affiliate to the corporation after that date, payments must be made to the implementing fund under the profit-sharing plan, but no tax deduction is allowed for these additional payments in any year.

(8) To the extent that income of an individual is reallocated to a corporation that he controls, a constructive dividend may be taxable to him.[91]

(9) Any corporate distribution to a shareholder may be taxed as a dividend even though informally authorized and distributed disproportionately to actual stockholdings. Situations of this kind occur most often in closely-held corporations that are controlled by members of one family and are the result of transactions that have not been carried out at arm's length.[92]

(10) Where the income of two brother-sister corporations was reallocated by the Internal Revenue Service from one corporation to the other, the income which had been "omitted" was taxed as a dividend to the shareholders.[93]

(11) If 95 percent or more of a corporation's gross income is from non-United States sources in the Western Hemisphere and if 90 percent or more of its gross income is from the active conduct of a trade or business, that corporation may qualify for the preferential tax treatment as a Western Hemisphere Trade Corporation.[94] (See chapter 4, What Can Be Done Through Subsidiary Corporations.) A reallocation could prevent the corporation's obtaining this preferential tax treatment.

(12) A situation such as that in (11) exists in the case of income from United States possessions, except that the specified percentages are 80 and 50 percent, respectively.[95]

(13) One of the requirements for personal holding company status is that at least 60 percent of a closely-held corporation's adjusted ordinary gross income be of the nonoperating type.[96] (See chapter 2, Corporations and Other Forms of Conducting Business.) Thus, a reallocation could make a closely-held company a personal holding company.

(14) There could be reallocation of income to a corporation which is subject to state taxation far more onerous than that to which the original company was subject.

(15) The minimum tax upon tax preferences is imposed after the application of a $30,000 exemption.[97] A reallocation could concentrate income of smaller entities so that the minimum tax would then be triggered.

NOTES

1. *Young & Rubicam, Inc. v. United States*, 410 F.2d 1233 (Ct. Cl., 1969).
2. *J. R. Land Company v. United States*, 361 F.2d 607 (4th Cir., 1966).
3. *Ballentine Motor Co.*, 39 T.C. 348 (1962), *aff'd*, 321 F.2d 796 (4th Cir., 1963). *Nat Harrison Associates, Inc. et al.*, 42 T.C. 601 (1964).
4. *Baldwin Brothers, Inc. et al. v. Commissioner*, 361 F.2d 668 (3d. Cir., 1966).
5. *Borge et al. v. Commissioner*, 405 F.2d 673 (2d Cir., 1968).
6. *Central Cuba Sugar Company v. Commissioner*, 198 F.2d 214 (2d Cir., 1952).

7. *L. E. Shunk Latex Products, Inc. et al.*, 18 T.C. 940 (1952).

8. *Griffin & Company, Inc. et al. v. United States*, 389 F.2d 802 (Ct. Cl., 1968).

9. *Davant et al. v. Commissioner*, 366 F.2d 874 (5th Cir., 1966).

10. *Granada Industries, Inc.*, 17 T.C. 231 (1951), *aff'd*, 202 F.2d 873 (5th Cir., 1953).

11. *Alpha Tank & Sheet Metal Mfg. Co. v. United States*, 116 F. Supp. 721 (Ct. Cl., 1953).

12. *Local Finance Corporation v. Commissioner*, 407 F.2d 629 (7th Cir., 1969).

13. *George E. Warren Corporation v. United States*, 141 F. Supp. 935 (Ct. Cl., 1956).

14. *National Carbide Corporation et al. v. Commissioner*, 336 U.S. 422 (1949).

15. *V. H. Monette and Company, Incorporated et al.*, 45 T.C. 15 (1965), *aff'd*, 374 F.2d 116 (4th Cir., 1967).

16. *Little Carnegie Realty Corporation*, T.C. Memo. 1970-150 (filed June 10, 1970).

17. *Local Finance Corporation et al. v. Commissioner*, 407 F.2d 629 (7th Cir., 1969).

18. *Pacific Northwest Food Club*, T.C. Memo. 1964-8 (filed January 20, 1964).

19. *Pauline W. Ach et al.*, 42 T.C. 114 (1964), *aff'd*, 358 F.2d 342 (6th Cir., 1966).

20. *Standard Paving Company v. Commissioner*, 190 F.2d 330 (10th Cir., 1951).

21. *Birmingham Ice & Cold Storage Co. v. Davis*, 112 F.2d 453 (5th Cir., 1940).

22. *Utter-McKinley Mortuaries v. Commissioner*, 225 F.2d 878 (9th Cir., 1955).

23. *Simon J. Murphy Company et al. v. Commissioner*, 231 F.2d 639 (6th Cir., 1956).

24. *United States v. Joseph P. Grace Estate et al.*, 395 U.S. 316 (1969).

25. *United States Gypsum Company et al. v. United States*, 304 F. Supp. 627 (D.C., N.D. Ill., 1969).

26. *Central Cuba Sugar Company v. Commissioner*, 198 F.2d 214 (2d Cir., 1952).

27. *Eli Lilly and Company v. United States*, 372 F.2d 990 (Ct. Cl., 1967).

28. *Philipp Brothers Chemicals, Inc. (Md.)*, 52 T.C. 240 (1969), *aff'd*, 435 F.2d 53 (2d Cir., 1970).

29. *Spicer Theatres, Inc. et al.*, T.C. Memo. 1964-79 (filed March 26, 1964).

30. *Lassoine et al. v. United States*, D.C., N.D. Cal., 1943.

31. *Interstate Fire Insurance Company v. United States*, 215 F. Supp. 586 (D.C., E.D. Tenn., 1963), *aff'd*, 339 F.2d 603 (6th Cir., 1964).

32. *G. U. R., Inc. v. Commissioner*, 117 F.2d 187 (7th Cir., 1941).

33. *National Securities Corporation v. Commissioner*, 137 F.2d 600 (3d Cir., 1943).

34. *Young & Rubicam, Inc. v. United States*, 410 F.2d 1253 (Ct. Cl., 1969).

35. *The Friedlander Corporation*, 25 T.C. 70 (1955).

36. *Seminole Flavor Company*, 4 T.C. 1215 (1945).

37. *Baldwin-Lima-Hamilton Corporation v. United States*, D.C., N.D. Ill., 1967.

38. *Cohan v. Commissioner*, 39 F.2d 540 (2d Cir., 1930). (For a discussion of the *Cohan* rule, see chapter 17, The Burden of Proof.)

39. *Pauline W. Ach et al.*, 42 T.C. 114 (1964), *aff'd*, 358 F.2d 342 (6th Cir., 1966).

40. *Oklahoma Transportation Company v. United States*, 272 F. Supp. 729 (D.C., W.D. Okla., 1966).

41. *Ibid.*

42. *National Securities Corporation v. Commissioner*, 137 F.2d 600 (3d Cir., 1943).

43. *Ibid.*

44. *Maxwell Hardware Company v. Commissioner*, 343 F.2d 713 (9th Cir., 1965).

45. Regulations Section 1.482-1(a)(3).

46. *South Texas Rice Warehouse Co. v. United States*, 366 F.2d 890 (5th Cir., 1966).

47. *Pauline W. Ach et al.*, 42 T.C. 114 (1964), *aff'd*, 358 F.2d 342 (6th Cir., 1966).

48. *B. Forman Company, Inc. et al.*, 54 T.C. 912 (1970), *aff'd on this issue*, 453 F.2d 1144 (2d Cir., 1972).

49. *Lake Erie and Pittsburgh Railroad Company*, 5 T.C. 558 (1945).

50. *Roy J. Champayne et al.*, 26 T.C. 634 (1956).

51. *Commissioner v. Chelsea Products, Incorporated*, 197 F.2d 620 (3d Cir., 1952).

52. *Joseph Morgenstern et al.*, T.C. Memo. 1955-86 (filed April 14, 1955).

53. *Elizalde & Co., Ltd.*, T.C. Memo., Docket No. 68 (entered September 30, 1948).

54. *Q. I. Roberts et al.*, T.C. Memo., Docket Nos. 15773-5 (entered January 19, 1949).

55. *Sterno, Inc. et al.*, T.C. Memo. 1965-23 (filed February 9, 1965).

56. *Burrell Groves, Inc.*, 16 T.C. 1163 (1951).

57. *Robert Gage Coal Company et al.*, 2 T.C. 488 (1943).

58. *Spicer Theatre, Inc. et al. v. Commissioner*, 346 F.2d 704 (6th Cir., 1965).

59. *Grenada Industries, Inc. v. Commissioner*, 202 F.2d 873 (5th Cir., 1953).

60. *Ray's Clothes, Inc.*, 22 T.C. 1332 (1954).

61. *Essex Broadcasters, Incorporated*, 2 T.C. 523 (1943).

62. *J. E. Dilworth Co. v. Henslee*, 98 F. Supp. 957 (D.C., M.D. Tenn., 1951).

63. *Southern College of Optometry, Inc.*, T.C. Memo., Docket No. 10556 (entered March 31, 1947).

64. *Murphy Logging Co. et al. v. United States*, 239 F. Supp. 794 (D.C., Ore., 1965).

65. *Differential Steel Car Company et al.*, T.C. Memo. 1966-65 (filed March 28, 1966).

66. *United States Gypsum Company et al. v. United States*, 304 Supp. 627 (D.C., N.D. Ill., 1969).

67. *Oil Base, Inc.*, T.C. Memo. 1964-298 (filed November 17, 1964), *aff'd*, 362 F.2d 212 (9th Cir., 1966).

68. *South Texas Rice Warehouse Co. v. Commissioner*, 366 F.2d 890 (5th Cir., 1966).

69. Regulations Section 1.482-2(a)(2).

70. *Tennessee-Arkansas Gravel Company v. Commissioner*, 112 F.2d 508 (6th Cir., 1940); *Smith-Bridgman & Company*, 16 T.C. 287 (1951).

71. *B. Forman Company, Inc. et al. v. Commissioner*, 453 F.2d 1144 (2d Cir., 1972).

72. Regulations Section 1.482-2(b)(1)-(7).

73. Regulations Section 1.482-2(c).

74. Regulations Section 1.482-2(d).

75. Regulations Section 1.482-2(e)(1).

76. Regulations Section 1.482-2(e).

77. Regulations Section 1.482-2(b)(8).

78. Regulations Section 1.482-1(d)(3).

79. Regulations Section 1.482-1(d)(3).

80. Revenue Procedure 70-8, I.R.B. 1970-13, 36. (That same Revenue Procedure also contains the ground rules to be followed in the case of a reimbursement arrangement, as discussed immediately above.)

81. Revenue Procedure 65-17, 1965-1 CB 833.

82. Revenue Procedure 64-54, 1964-2 CB 1008.

83. *Shaw-Construction Company v. Commissioner*, 323 F.2d 316 (9th Cir., 1963).

84. *Baldwin Brothers, Inc. et al.*, T.C. Memo. 1965-173 (filed June 28, 1965), *aff'd*, 361 F.2d 668 (3d Cir., 1966).

85. *Fawn Fashions, Inc.*, 41 T.C 205 (1963).

86. *Lanteen Medical Laboratories, Inc.*, 10 T.C. 279 (1948).

87. *Columbian Rope Company*, 42 T.C. 800 (1964).

88. *Local Hardware Corporation et al. v. Commissioner*, 407 F.2d 629 (7th Cir., 1969).

89. *The Coca-Cola Bottling Company of Gallup et al. v. United States*, 443 F. Supp. 1253 (D.C., N.M., 1969), *aff'd*, 443 F.2d 1197 (5th Cir., 1971).

90. I.R.C. Section 402(a)(6).

91. *Q. I. Roberts et al.*, T.C. Memo., Docket Nos. 15773-5 (entered January 19, 1949).

92. *Gibbs et al. v. Tomlinson*, D.C., M.D. Fla., 1964.

93. *George W. Knipe*, T.C. Memo. 1965-131 (filed May 17, 1965).

94. I.R.C. Section 921.

95. I.R.C. Section 931.

96. I.R.C. Section 542(a)(1).

97. I.R.C. Section 57.

CHAPTER 6

Capital Assets, Capital Gains and Losses

Significance of Capital Asset Treatment

It has been said on good authority: "[T]here are no provisions in the Internal Revenue Code more difficult to understand and to apply than those which relate to capital gains and losses," [1] and, we might add, none more important. The importance of "capital asset" characterization stems from the preferential tax treatment afforded to such assets. The full impact of the Federal income tax falls upon ordinary income. Capital gains and certain other gains are less severely treated, and capital losses are specially treated.

In the case of individuals, 50 percent of the net long-term capital losses are deducted from ordinary income. Net capital losses are deductible to the extent of $1000 from ordinary income in any one year, any unused capital losses being carried forward indefinitely. But because of this 50 percent rule, $2000 of the long-term capital losses are required to offset $1000 of ordinary income. Deduction of capital losses against ordinary income for married persons filing separate returns is limited to $500 for each spouse.[2]

Corporations are able to use capital losses only to offset capital gains. However, there is a three-year capital loss carryback. But the carryback is not available for foreign expropriation capital losses, nor is it available for a net capital loss arising in a year for which a corporation is treated as a Subchapter S corporation.[3] (See chapter 2, Corporations and Other Forms of Conducting Business.)

Alternative Capital Gains Tax. Under the Tax Reform Act of 1969, up to $50,000 in long-term capital gains ($25,000 for a married person filing a separate return) qualifies for the maximum alternative capital gains rate 25 percent without regard to the taxpayer's tax preference items. The rate of tax on long-term capital gains in excess of $50,000 is half that of the ordinary income rates.

For corporations, an alternative capital gains procedure is available in lieu of the regular method of income tax computation. The excess of net long-term capital gains over net short-term capital losses is excluded from the regular tax base and subject to a 30 percent tax. But corporations with taxable incomes of less than $25,000 (including capital gains) pay a tax at the rate of 22 percent (the normal tax rates applicable to all corporate taxable income under $25,000) on such capital gains.[4]

What Is a Capital Asset?

Congress intended to afford capital gains treatment in situations typically involving the realization of appreciation in values accrued over a substantial period of time, wanting to ameliorate the hardship of taxation of the entire gain in one year.[5] Thus, a *capital asset* involves the appreciation or depreciation of property held over a period of time in a risk situation.[6] An asset is not a capital asset if the owner sells it in the ordinary course of his business.

The tax-favored capital asset is commonly associated with a "going concern." Favored treatment is given for the purpose of facilitating ready transfer of going enterprises by reducing the incidence of taxation on increments in value built up over a long period.[7] It was not intended that this policy should apply to a situation where one of the essential purposes of holding property is *sale.*[8]

A capital asset is defined by the Internal Revenue Code Section 1221 as property held by the taxpayer, whether or not connected with his trade or business, with the following exceptions:

(1) Inventory.

(2) Property used in the trade or business, which property is subject to depreciation, or real property used in the trade or business.

(3) A copyright or a literary, musical, or other such artistic composition if held by a person whose personal efforts created this property or whose basis is the same as the creator's (such as a person who received the property as a gift from the creator). Letters, memoranda, and similar property (or collections thereof) are not treated as capital assets if they are held by the person whose personal efforts created the property or for whom the property was prepared or produced (or by a person who had the same basis as the creator's).

(4) Accounts or notes receivable acquired in the ordinary course of trade or business for services rendered or from the sale of inventory.

(5) Certain governmental obligations issued on a discount basis, without interest and with a fixed maturity not exceeding one year.[9]

Although franchises, trademarks, and trade names are capital assets, a franchisor or licensor is not entitled to capital gains treatment on a transfer if he retains any "significant power, right, or continuous interest" with respect to the interest transferred. The quoted phrase includes, but is not limited to: a right to disapprove any assignment; a right to terminate at will; a right to prescribe standards of quality; a right to require exclusive sale or advertising of products or services of the transferor; a right to require exclusive purchase of supplies and equipment from the transferor; and a right to payments contingent on productivity if such payments constitute a substantial element under the transfer agreement. The transfer of a franchise to engage in professional sports is not covered by this rule.[10]

What is looked upon as a capital asset in the hands of one taxpayer might not be viewed as such in the hands of another, nor need the same asset be characterized as capital in the hands of the same taxpayer in successive years. In a case involving payments received by José Ferrer for portraying the dwarf Toulouse-Lautrec in the moving picture *Moulin Rouge*, the court observed: "The difficulties Mr. Ferrer must have had in fitting himself into the shape of the artist can hardly have been greater than ours in determining whether the transaction here at issue fits the rubric 'gain from the sale or exchange of a capital asset held for more than 6 months' . . . or constitutes ordinary income. . . ."[11]

Perhaps the most common form of capital asset is corporate stock. But such stock is not to be classified as a capital asset where it has been bought and kept only as an incident to the conduct of the taxpayer's business. All of the surrounding circumstances must be considered in making such a determination. The substance, as distinguished from the form, of the taxpayer's actions determines whether the sale of the stock is ordinary gain or loss in a particular case.[12]

"Held . . . Primarily for Sale"

Most of the cases dealing with capital asset characterization involve the question of whether property is held primarily for sale to customers in the ordinary course of a trade or business; an affirmative answer would mean that the asset is not capital and hence disposition would beget ordinary gain or loss. Frequently, the question involves situations where the taxpayer is engaged in some activity apart from his usual occupation, and the focus is upon whether this activity amounts to a trade or business. The term "trade or business" is subject to varying interpretations,[13] as is the term "ordinary course."[14]

The character of property can be changed by someone other than the taxpayer. Thus, condemnation of property held by a real estate developer for improvement and sale may convert the property into a capital asset; for, upon condemnation, the property ceased to be an asset held primarily for sale in the ordinary course of the trade or business.[15] "Primarily" in this sense means "essential" or "substantial" rather than "principal" or "chief."[16]

If a taxpayer holds property for the dual purpose of renting or sale, whichever proves to be more profitable, capital gain treatment is not allowed, for it cannot be said that the property was not being held for sale in the ordinary course of the business.[17]

Section 1231 Assets

Section 1231 assets are depreciable property used in the trade or business, with certain exceptions, and real property so used if held for more than six months.

Although a Section 1231 asset sometimes receives capital gains treatment, it is not a capital asset. Section 1231 assets produce the best of both possible tax worlds upon disposition: tax on gain is limited in the manner of capital assets, while loss is fully deductible in the manner of noncapital assets. Excepted from the category of Section 1231 assets are:

(1) Inventory.

(2) Property held primarily for sale to customers in the ordinary course of the trade or business.

(3) A copyright, a literary, musical or other artistic composition, a letter or memorandum, or a similar property held by the person whose personal efforts created it or by a person (such as a donee) with the creator's basis for the property.[18]

Explicitly included within the Code's definition of Section 1231 assets are:

(1) Timber, coal, or domestic iron ore.[19]

(2) Livestock. To qualify, cattle and horses must be held by the taxpayer for draft, breeding, dairy, or sporting purposes and must be held by him for 24 months or more from the date of acquisition. Other livestock held for similar purposes must be held for 12 months or more.

(3) Unharvested crops or land used in the trade or business and held for more than six months if the crops and the land are sold or exchanged (or compulsorily or involuntarily converted) at the same time and to the same person.[20]

Capital assets subject to Section 1231 treatment include only capital assets involuntarily converted.[21]

Recognized gains from sales or exchanges of Section 1231 assets are added to recognized gains from the compulsory or involuntary conversion of: (1) property used in the trade or business and (2) capital assets held for more than six months. Such losses are similarly aggregated. Then, a *net* gain is treated as long-term capital gain. A *net* loss is fully deductible as an ordinary loss.

Where property that is a capital asset or a Section 1231 property is sold on an installment basis and part of the payments is due more than one year from the date of the sale or exchange and where no interest payments are specified or the interest is below a rate provided by Treasury regulations, a part of each payment due after the first six months is to be treated as an interest payment rather than as part of the sales price.[22]

Depreciation Recapture

When depreciable personal property and certain other tangible property— buildings and their structural components excluded—are sold at a gain, the proceeds are taxed as ordinary income under Section 1245 of the Code. The underlying theory is that this represents merely a recapture of the previously excessive depreciation. For had the proper depreciation been taken, there would not have been a gain at the time of disposition.[23] The depreciation recapture rules override any conflicting language in Section 1231.[24]

When depreciable real property is sold, except in the case of residential property, gains from the sale of such property after 1969 are subject to depreciation recapture to the extent of the accelerated depreciation taken after 1969 in excess of what straight-line depreciation would have produced.[25]

When Is a Disposition of Assets "Capital"?

A capital gain or loss requires the disposition of capital assets or, under circumstances previously mentioned, of Section 1231 assets. Everyday operations of a business are directed to ordinary income rather than to capital gain and loss.[26] Some of the factors or tests that the courts have set up to determine when capital treatment is applicable are: (1) the purpose for which the property was acquired; (2) the purpose for which it was held at the time of disposition; (3) the frequency, number, and continuity of sales; (4) the extent and substantiality of the transactions; (5) the nature and extent of the taxpayer's business; and (6) whether the taxpayer had been making efforts to sell the property.[27]

The effect of a taxpayer's effort, or lack of effort, in selling may be significant. So, where sales were made to persons who initially contacted the taxpayer and who were previously unknown to him, capital gain resulted as the court felt that the facts indicated the property was not being held for sale.[28]

Sale, Exchange, or Other Disposition Is Necessary

To get capital treatment, a taxpayer must establish that the gain or loss resulted from a "sale or exchange" or "from the compulsory or involuntary conversion" of property used in the trade or business.[29] Capital loss is not deductible if not the result of a transaction entered into for profit.[30]

In this context, the terms "sale" and "exchange" are given their ordinary meaning.[31] A "sale" in the ordinary sense of the word is a transfer of property for consideration.[32]

Loss attributable to failure to exercise a privilege or option to buy or to sell property is deemed to be loss from the sale or exchange of property.[33]

Holding Period

Short-term capital gain results from the sale or exchange of capital assets held for not more than six months. Assets held for more than six months produce *long-term capital gains*.[34]

For holding period purposes, the date the property is acquired is excluded and the date the property is disposed of is included.[35] The fact that holidays or short business days intervene is irrelevant.[36]

If a corporate reorganization is tax-free, there is a *tacking on* of the periods during which the capital asset was held by the original or transferor corporation and the successor or transferee corporation. But such is not the case where the reorganization is not tax-free.[37]

Where assets are distributed by a partnership to a partner, the latter may tack onto his own holding period the holding period of the partnership.[38]

Where property was inherited from someone who died after December 31, 1970, if the characterization of this property in the legatee's hands is the same as that on the estate tax return, long-term capital treatment is provided even though the property is sold within six months of the decedent's death.[39]

In the case of a gift where the donee takes on the same basis as the donor, the holding period in the donee's hands includes the holding period of the donor.[40] Where the donee does not use the donor's basis (such as in the case of a gift deemed to have been in contemplation of death), the holding period of the donee begins with the date of the gift.[41]

The date of destruction of a capital asset is the significant date in fixing the termination of the holding period.[42]

Capital Expenditures

A taxpayer cannot deduct as a current business expense the full cost of acquiring an asset, tangible or intangible, if the expenditure benefits him for more than one year.[43] The expenditure is regarded as being in the nature of a capital outlay if it provides an advantage with a life of more than one year.[44] Where an expenditure is made only once, while the benefits continue, the possibility arises that the outlay was for a capital asset.[45]

The rule for all taxpayers, whether they use the cash or the accrual method of accounting, is that costs incurred in the acquisition, production, and development of capital assets, inventory, and other property used in the trade or business may not be deducted currently, but must be deferred until the year of sale, at which time the accumulated costs may be set off against the proceeds of the sale.[46] Thus, a commission paid a broker for obtaining a long-term property lease is a capital expenditure which must be amortized over the life of the lease, regardless of the taxpayer's accounting method.[47] So a bonus paid for delivery of capital assets before the contract date is a capital expenditure.[48]

As a general rule, the costs of acquiring a franchise or license to do business, if it has a useful life of more than one year, are treated as capital expenditures which can be amortized over the period of its useful life.[49] If the useful life cannot be determined, deduction for amortization is not available.[50] The cost of a five-year franchise, renewable indefinitely by mutual consent, has been held amortizable over a five-year period.[51]

The cost of revising existing accounting methods and of installing an up-to-date system has been held to be a currently deductible operating expense and not a capital expenditure.[52] A current deduction was held proper for the cost of a management survey of a taxpayer's business.[53]

The cost of a catalog with a useful life of several years in the taxpayer's business is not currently deductible.[54] The amount paid a competitor to discontinue copying the taxpayer's product could not be deducted for tax purposes, for the benefits of the disbursements were to be enjoyed over a period of years that could not be measured.[55]

Where doctors who had difficulty in getting hospital affiliations paid a hospital a "staff fee" with knowledge that the hospital would be replaced after a few years, the fee could be amortized over the estimated number of years remaining for the hospital.[56] It has also been held that a fee paid by a physician for lifetime hospital privileges could be amortized over a useful life equal to his life expectancy.[57]

Medical Expenses

Certain capital expenditures may be deducted as medical expenses; an elevator in the home of a taxpayer with a heart condition is an example. The cost is allowed as medical expense to the extent that the total cost exceeds the increase in the value of the property.[58] The expenditures for medical expense must be capitalized when they add to the value of a building or land.[59]

Legal Expenses

Expenses of litigation for the purpose of defending or perfecting title to capital assets are capital expenditures constituting a part of the cost of the property and are not deductible.[60]

Legal expenses incurred by a seller in avoiding a sale induced by the buyer's fraud and in obtaining a higher price were characterized as a kind of selling expense that must be capitalized, inasmuch as the problem still was to reach mutually satisfactory or binding terms of sale.[61]

Where property was seized by a state and the condemnation award was treated as long-term capital gain, legal and associated litigation expenses related to seeking a higher award were not deductible, but instead were classified as capital expenditures.[62]

Legal expenses connected with the acquisition of real estate must be capitalized. Where such an expense covered the cost of land and depreciable improvements, an allocation had to be made in a manner that reasonably represented the portion of the expenses attributable to the land and to the improvements (such as an allocation of the expenses according to the respective fair market values of the land and the improvements at the time of purchase).[63]

Protection of Earnings

Payments to protect earnings are capital expenditures.[64] However, expenditures for the purpose of eliminating competition are generally not deductible.[65] Nevertheless, where the elimination of competition is for a definite and limited term, the cost may be deducted over that term.[66] But where the benefits of restraint or elimination of competition are permanent or of indefinite duration, no expense deduction is allowed.[67]

Ordinary and Necessary Expenses Related to Capital Transaction

Expenses of a type customarily deductible as ordinary business or investment expenses are capital when related to capital assets. Thus, where stockholders of a dissolved corporation were obliged as transferees to pay a subsequently imposed corporate tax deficiency (the corporation, of course, was no longer there to be taxed), the payment represented a capital loss to the stockholders inasmuch as it related to a capital transaction—namely, gain or loss on stock upon corporate liquidation.[68] This principle applies to gain as well as to loss.[69] Where one stands to achieve capital gains through an investment, any losses incurred in connection with the investment are capital.[70] Where whiskey was being held for capital gain appreciation, storage and insurance costs had to be capitalized and not expensed.[71]

Labor and transportation costs in connection with moving certain of a taxpayer's capitalized physical assets to another location were deductible, for the relocation did not add to the value of these assets, nor did it appreciably prolong their useful lives.[72]

Acquisition of Stock for Business Purposes

If stock is purchased as an integral and necessary act in the conduct of one's business, there may be ordinary gain or loss. Thus, where a wholesaler of petroleum products purchased the stock of a refinery so as to have a source of supply in a time of acute shortages, loss on the subsequent sale of these shares was categorized as an ordinary loss.[73] (This subject will be considered in more detail in chapter 7, Ordinary, Necessary, and Reasonable.)

Loss of Capital Treatment

Under certain circumstances, capital treatment may be denied on the disposition of capital assets. (This subject will be considered in chapter 26, Tax Pitfalls.)

Corporate Redemptions and Liquidations

When something is exchanged for something else or is changed in form, there is often some element of gain or loss. What is its character for tax purposes? [74]

A corporation's redemption of its stock when it has earnings and profits large enough to support a dividend is customarily taxed as though it were a dividend. Such will not be the case, however, if a shareholder can establish that the redemption is not essentially equivalent to a dividend, that there is a substantially disproportionate redemption of stock, or that his interest had been completely terminated.[75] Similarly, a redemption of stock to pay death taxes will beget capital treatment if the necessary ground rules are met.[76]

Complete liquidation of a corporation, subject to statutory limitations, results in capital gain to the shareholders regardless of the size of the corporation's accumulated earnings and profits.[77]

If a corporation is deemed to be "collapsible," gains from sales or liquidations of its stock are treated as ordinary income rather than as capital gain; it is the shareholders who receive this treatment, not the corporation itself. Briefly, a *collapsible corporation* is one formed or availed of principally for the manufacture, construction, or production of property with a view to the stockholders' selling the stock or receiving a liquidating distribution before the corporation realizes a substantial part of the income to be derived from the property.[78]

If a distribution meets the tests for a partial liquidation, it will be treated on a capital basis despite the existence of corporate earnings and profits at the time.[79]

Minimum Tax on Tax Preference Income

The Tax Reform Act of 1969 provides for a tax of ten percent on certain defined tax preference income in excess of $30,000 plus the amount of the taxpayer's regular Federal income tax. Several of the preferences relate to capital transactions. The following are the tax preference items covered:

(1) Accelerated depreciation on personal property subject to a net lease in excess of straight-line depreciation (see chapter 12, Depreciation).

(2) Accelerated depreciation on real property in excess of straight-line depreciation.

(3) Amortization of rehabilitation expenditures, the excess of the amortization deduction over straight-line depreciation.

(4) Amortization of certified pollution control facilities in excess of accelerated depreciation.

(5) Amortization of railroad rolling stock, the excess of the amortization deduction over accelerated depreciation.

(6) The bargain element in stock options. In the case of qualified stock options, this is the excess of the fair market value of the stock at the time of exercise of the option over the option price of the stock. (See chapter 8, Compensation, Fringe Benefits.)

(7) Bad debt deductions of financial institutions under certain circumstances.

(8) Depletion costs to the extent they exceed the cost or other basis of the property involved.

(9) Capital gains for individuals to the extent of one-half of the gains. For corporations, the tax preference is the excess of the net long-term capital gain over the net short-term capital loss multiplied by a ratio whose denominator is the sum of the regular corporate normal and surtax rates and whose numerator is the regular corporate rate minus the rate applicable to capital gains. In other words, the corporate capital gains are included among the tax preference items in the ratio of the difference between their special tax rate and the general corporate rate to the general corporate tax rate.[80]

Income Averaging

Income averaging for individuals now extends to long-term capital gains.[81]

NOTES

1. L. Wayne Dobson, "The Taxation of Capital Gains and Losses and Commercial Bank Portfolio Management," *TAXES—The Tax Magazine*, May 1963, Volume XLI, Number 5, page 285.
2. I.R.C. Section 1211.
3. I.R.C. Section 1212(a)(1).
4. I.R.C. Section 1201.
5. *Commissioner v. Gillette Motor Co.*, 364 U.S. 130 (1960).
6. *Silverstein et al. v. United States*, 293 F. Supp. 1106 (D.C., N.D. Ill., 1968).
7. *Haggard, Jr. et al. v. Wood*, 298 F.2d 94 (9th Cir., 1961).
8. *Rollingwood Corp. v. Commissioner*, 190 F.2d 263 (9th Cir., 1951).
9. I.R.C. Section 1221.
10. I.R.C. Section 1253.
11. *Commissioner v. Ferrer*, 304 F.2d 125 (2d Cir., 1962).
12. *John J. Grier Co. v. United States*, 328 F.2d 163 (7th Cir., 1964).
13. *Fackler v. Commissioner*, 133 F.2d 509 (6th Cir., 1943).
14. *Thompson Lumber Co.*, 43 B.T.A. 726 (1941).
15. *Tri-S Corporation*, 48 T.C. 316 (1967), *aff'd*, 400 F.2d 862 (10th Cir., 1968).
16. *Rollingwood Corp. et al. v. Commissioner*, 190 F.2d 263 (9th Cir., 1951).
17. *Desilu Productions, Inc.*, T.C. Memo. 1965-307 (filed November 20, 1965).
18. I.R.C. Section 1221.
19. Under certain conditions set forth in I.R.C. Section 631.
20. I.R.C. Sections 1231 (b)(3), (4).
21. Regulations Section 1.1231-1(a).
22. I.R.C. Section 483.
23. I.R.C. Section 1245.
24. Regulations Section 1.1245-6(a).
25. I.R.C. Section 1250.
26. *Corn Products Refining Co. v. Commissioner*, 350 U.S. 46 (1955).
27. *Fishback, Jr. et al. v. United States*, 215 F. Supp. 621 (D.C., S.D., 1963).
28. *Goldberg et al. v. United States*, D.C., N.D. Ill., 1963.
29. *Kurlan et al. v. Commissioner et al.*, 343 F.2d 625 (2d Cir., 1965).
30. *Brown et al. v. United States*, 396 F.2d 459 (Ct. Cl., 1968).

31. *Pounds v. United States*, 372 F.2d 342 (5th Cir., 1967).

32. *Grinnell Corporation v. United States*, 390 F.2d 932 (Ct. Cl., 1968).

33. I.R.C. Section 1234(a).

34. I.R.C. Section 1222.

35. I.T. 3287, 1939-1 CB (Part 1) 138.

36. I.T. 3705, 1945 CB 174.

37. I.T. 3721, 1945 CB 164.

38. I.R.C. Section 735(b).

39. I.R.C. Section 1223(11).

40. I.R.C. Section 1223(2).

41. Revenue Ruling 59-86, 1959-1 CB 209.

42. *Rose v. United States*, 229 F. Supp. 298 (D.C., S.D. Cal., 1964).

43. *Richmond Television Corporation v. United States*, 345 F.2d 901 (4th Cir., 1965).

44. *United States v. Akin*, 248 F.2d 742 (10th Cir., 1957).

45. *Wells-Lee et al. v. Commissioner*, 360 F.2d 665 (8th Cir., 1966).

46. *United States v. Catto, Jr. et al.*, 384 U.S. 102 (1966).

47. Revenue Ruling 70-408, 1970-2 CB 52.

48. *Sears Oil Co., Inc. v. Commissioner*, 359 F.2d 191 (2d Cir., 1966).

49. *Riss & Company, Inc. et al.*, T. C. Memo. 1964-190 (filed July 14, 1964).

50. *Nachman v. Commissioner*, 191 F.2d 934 (5th Cir., 1951).

51. *Hampton Pontiac, Inc. v. United States*, 294 F. Supp. 1073 (D.C., S.C., 1969).

52. *Schlosser Bros., Inc.*, 2 B.T.A. 137 (1925).

53. *Goodwyn Crockery Company*, 37 T.C. 355 (1961), *aff'd on another issue*, 315 F.2d 110 (6th Cir., 1963).

54. Revenue Ruling 68-360, 1968-2 CB 197.

55. *American Dispenser Co., Inc. v. Commissioner*, 396 F.2d 137 (2d Cir., 1968).

56. *Wells-Lee et al. v. Commissioner*, 360 F.2d 665 (8th Cir., 1966).

57. Revenue Ruling 70-171, 1970-1 CB 55.

58. Regulations Section 1213-(e)(1) (iii).

59. *Oliver et al. v. Commissioner*, 364 F.2d 575 (8th Cir., 1966).

60. *Addison v. Commissioner*, 177 F.2d 521 (8th Cir., 1949).

61. *Munson v. McGinnes*, 283 F.2d 333 (3d Cir., 1960).

62. *Stickles v. United States*, D.C., N.D. N.Y., 1970.

63. Revenue Ruling 68-528, 1968-2 CB 331.

64. *Dodge Brothers v. United States*, 118 F.2d 95 (4th Cir., 1941).

65. *Clark Thread Co. v. Commissioner*, 100 F.2d 257 (3d Cir., 1939).

66. *Farmers Feed Co.*, 17 B.T.A. 507 (1938).

67. *Press Publishing Co.*, 17 B.T.A. 452 (1928), *aff'd sub nomine Newspaper Printing Co. v. Commissioner*, 56 F.2d 125 (3d Cir., 1932).

68. *Arrowsmith v. Commissioner*, 344 U.S. 6 (1952).

69. *Alvin B. Lowe et al.*, 44 T.C. 363 (1965).

70. *Borge et al. v. Commissioner*, 405 F.2d 673 (2d Cir., 1968).

71. *Schultz et al. v. Commissioner*, 420 F.2d 490 (3d Cir., 1970).

72. Revenue Ruling 70-392, 1970-2 CB 33.

73. *FS Services, Inc. v. United States*, 413 F.2d 548 (Ct. Cl., 1969).

74. For a complete discussion of this subject, see Robert S. Holzman, *Tax-Free Reorganizations After the Tax Reform Act of 1969*, Lynbrook, N.Y.: The Farnsworth Publishing Company, 1970.

75. I.R.C. Section 302(b)(1), (2), and (3).

76. I.R.C. Section 303.

77. *Pridemark, Inc.*, 42 T.C. 510 (1964), *aff'd on this issue.* 345 F.2d 35 (4th Cir., 1965).

78. I.R.C. Section 341.

79. I.R.C. Section 346(a).

80. I.R.C. Section 57.

81. I.R.C. Section 1302.

CHAPTER 7

Ordinary, Necessary, and Reasonable

What Is "Ordinary"?

For Federal income tax purposes, deductions are allowed for business expenditures that are both "ordinary and necessary." There is not, and probably cannot be, any exact definition of the terms "ordinary" and "necessary." Each situation must be evaluated largely upon its own facts and circumstances.[1]

A first requirement is that there be a *business expense,* something related to the carrying on of a trade or business.[2]

A principal function of the term "ordinary" is to clarify the distinction between those expenditures which are currently deductible and those which are in the nature of capital expenditures; the latter, if deductible at all, must be amortized over the useful life of the asset.[3]

"Ordinary" means, in a broad sense, customary, usual, regular, normal, common, and unexceptional.[4] However, ordinary expenses need not be habitual or normal expenses in the sense that the same taxpayer makes them frequently, but may include an expense incurred only once in a taxpayer's lifetime. What is ordinary is affected by the time, place, and circumstances of the expense, but there must be a degree of consistency about it. A pertinent question is: Was the transaction giving rise to the payments one that is common or frequent in the type of business in which the taxpayer is engaged?[5]

What Is "Necessary"?

The word "necessary" does not, for Federal income tax purposes, mean "absolutely necessary." It is a relative term. It has been variously defined as "appropriate" or "substantially necessary," or qualified in some other way.[6] The United States Supreme Court has ruled that it is sufficient if the expense is appropriate and helpful for the development of the taxpayer's business.[7] But it must be established that there are both business ends to be served and that there is an intention to serve those business needs by means of these particular expenditures.[8] The voluntary nature of a payment alone will not preclude its deductibility as an ordinary and necessary business expense.[9]

One court equated the concept of "ordinary and necessary" with the common sense test of whether a hard-headed businessman would have been expected to have incurred the expense under like circumstances.[10] The concept of the phrase cannot be static or immutable; it must be flexible. As the nature, form, and scope of business activity changes, it is inevitable that notions of what constitutes "ordinary and necessary" business expenses will likewise change.[11]

A payment may be ordinary and necessary in one year, while a similar payment in a subsequent year will not be so deductible. The tax consequences must be viewed as of the years in question. Payments may be ordinary and necessary business expenses at the inception of a contract; for example, as those necessary to enable the business to stay alive, but not ordinary and necessary when the business necessity ends.[12]

Expenditure Cannot Be of a Capital Nature

Even if a payment meets the "ordinary and necessary" test, it is not deductible if it is of a capital nature.[13]

Purpose is an important criterion in distinguishing between capital outlays and ordinary and necessary expenses;[14] and there is a *judgment* involved. In the ordinary course of a manufacturing business, the differentiation of capital expenditures and operating expense disbursements is largely a matter of sound discretion and experienced business judgment.[15]

Construction costs must be capitalized, even for temporary buildings used during the course of construction, for these costs relate to the acquisition of a capital asset.[16] Similarly, costs incurred by a corporation in connection with the issuance of its capital stock in payment of a stock dividend is not deductible as an ordinary and necessary expense, for this cost is a capital expenditure.[17] Just because no meaningful or valuable asset is being built up by the expenses incurred in paying a stock dividend does not make such expenditures deductible. Certain expenditures that are capital in nature but do not cause any increase in the value of an asset are not deductible as ordinary and necessary business expenses.[18] Payments to a competitor to withdraw its application for licenses also sought by the taxpayer have been ruled to be capital in nature.[19]

The Expenditure Must Be Business-Oriented

A basic restriction placed upon the deduction of any business expense is that the item involved be business-oriented.[20] Thus, expenses incurred when the taxpayer is not able to be in the business allegedly involved cannot be deducted.[21]

Where a suit or action against a taxpayer is directly connected with, or proximately results from, his business, the expense incurred is a business expense.[22] A taxpayer's business need not be one which he owns. For example, a corporate officer is engaged in the business of being a corporate officer, and expenses in connection with this business may be deducted if they are ordinary and necessary.[23]

Going Business and Pre-business Expenses

The business must be one in which the taxpayer is presently engaged.[24] Thus, the term "trade or business" is used in the practical sense of a going trade or business.[25]

Expenses incurred prior to and for the purpose of reaching a decision as to whether to establish a business are capital expenditures.[26] So, expenses incurred by a company in anticipation of getting a TV license were ruled not deductible.[27]

No deduction was allowed a taxpayer for a trip abroad to study marketing *in preparation* for starting his own business.[28] Expenditures incurred in investigating a potential new trade or business or in preparation for possible entrance into a new trade or business were held not to have been incurred in connection with a trade or business so as to be deductible in computing taxable income.[29]

Even such ordinarily deductible items as salaries, travel expense, telephone and telegraph, and office supplies were classified as capital expenditures when they were incurred in establishing a new and additional business.[30]

Fines, Penalties, and Kickbacks

In business, fines and penalties sometimes must be paid. In addition, just getting business sometimes seems to depend on buying the friendly interest of persons who place purchase orders. It is often necessary to make such expenditures if one is to stay in business, and the practice is common enough to be characterized as ordinary. But the tax law has provided specific rules in this area. No deduction is allowed for any of the following:

(1) Fines or similar penalties paid to a government for violation of any law; for example, as a result of conviction of a felony or misdemeanor.

(2) On amounts paid on any judgment for damages in a civil suit under the Clayton Antitrust Act, no deduction is allowed for two-thirds of the damages where intent has been clearly proved in a criminal proceeding.[31] Payments to the government are not deductible at all.

(3) Bribes to government officials.

(4) Illegal bribes or kickbacks to other than government officials and employees are non-deductible if in a criminal proceeding the taxpayer is convicted of an illegal bribe or kickback or if he enters a plea of "guilty" or "no contest." [32]

(5) Under the Revenue Act of 1971, deduction is denied for any payment that constitutes an illegal bribe, an illegal kickback, or any other illegal payment under any law of the United States or any state law that is generally enforced if the applicable law subjects the payor to a criminal penalty or the loss of license or privilege to engage in a trade or business. For this purpose, the term "kickback" includes a payment in consideration of the referral of a client, patient, or customer.

(6) Deduction is disallowed for any kickback, rebate, or bribe made by a provider of services, supplier, physician, or other person related to items

or services for which payment is or may be made under the Social Security Act, or, in whole or in part, out of Federal funds under a state plan approved under that Act.[33]

Requirement of Reasonableness

By its very nature, an expenditure may be ordinary and necessary, but at the same time it may be unreasonable in amount.[34] Thus, however helpful the program may have been in the taxpayer's opinion, it was ruled to be neither ordinary nor appropriate as a business practice for a corporation to entertain the responsible officers of a customer so frequently and so lavishly as is often the case.[35]

Determination of allowable deductions by reference to a standard of reasonableness is not unusual under the Federal income tax laws.[36] The term "reasonable" brings a relative, as opposed to a definite, determination into the law.[37]

The Internal Revenue Service will carefully examine any excessive business expenditures, particularly those relating to lavish travel and entertainment expenses, executive expense allowances, business gratuities, and disguised remuneration of corporate officials in the form of personal living expenses. Expenditures for advertising, research and development, and repairs and maintenance will also be examined with an eye to reasonableness in the light of existing circumstances in each case.[38] Thus, a bond redemption premium may be disallowed to the extent that it is unreasonable.[39] Rentals or other payments for the use of property which are excessive in amount, considering all the facts of a particular situation, may be higher than could be recognized as ordinary and necessary expenses.[40]

It is especially important that selling and servicing expenses charged to a corporation under common control be reasonable.[41]

The deductibility of interest is not subject to the ordinary and necessary requirement and generally need not be reasonable.[42] Interest in the case of parties under common control, however, may be subject to reallocation by the Internal Revenue Service under the "arm's length transaction" doctrine.[43] (See chapter 5, Arm's Length Transactions.)

Personal Expenses Are Not Covered

It has been pointed out that, in order to be deducted, ordinary and necessary expenses must be business as opposed to personal. The characterization of "personal" may apply to corporations as well as to individuals. Not every payment by a corporation is an expense of *its* business. A corporation, for example, is not permitted to deduct legal fees of its principal stockholder in connection with divorce proceedings even though defeat in the divorce proceedings might adversely affect the business.[44]

In the absence of special circumstances sustaining a business need, a corporation is not permitted to deduct expenses in connection with providing a home for an executive.[45] Nor can a corporation deduct wedding expenses of a key officer's daughter even though important customers are invited.[46]

On the other hand, a corporation was permitted to deduct the cost of union dues of a corporate officer where the corporation benefitted by his membership.[47]

Legal Fees

The controlling test of the deductibility of legal fees as business expenses is whether the claim has a business origin and character. The crucial factor is the kind of transaction out of which the obligation arises.[48] The expenditure cannot relate to matters purely personal.[49]

Legal fees are deductible even though incurred in the unsuccessful defense of an action arising from the carrying on of a trade or business.[50] A broker's expenses in defending a lawsuit charging him with "churning" an account to increase his commissions have been held to be deductible.[51]

However, legal expenses incurred in lawsuits that involve only the transfer of capital assets must be capitalized and, for tax purposes, merely constitute an adjustment to the basis of the assets.[52] But the cost of recovering taxes relating to capital assets assessed under a law subsequently held to be unconstitutional were deductible.[53]

Even though a corporate officer in the performance of his corporate responsibilities commits criminal acts, his legal expenses may be deductible as ordinary and necessary expenses on his own return.[54] Payment of an officer's legal fees under an indemnification bylaw has been characterized as a fringe benefit necessary to induce officers and directors to serve. Thus, it was held deductible by the corporation.[55]

Advertising

To be deductible, an advertising expense must be ordinary, necessary, and reasonably related to the nature of the business.[56] Expenditures for institutional or good will advertising that keeps the taxpayer's name before the public generally are deductible as ordinary and necessary expenses provided the expenditures are related to the patronage the taxpayer might reasonably expect in the future. For example, a deduction ordinarily will be allowed for the cost of advertising if it keeps the taxpayer's name highly visible in connection with encouraging contributions to such organizations as the Red Cross or with the purchase of United States Treasury Bonds. In like fashion, expenditures for advertising that present views on economic, financial, social, or other subjects of a general nature but do not involve lobbying are deductible if they otherwise meet the requirements of ordinary and necessary expenses.[57]

However, deduction is not allowed for advertising which it is "politic" to make if a business benefit is not anticipated. Thus, a gambling organization was not permitted to deduct the cost of an anonymous advertisement in the publication of a state police association.[58] No deduction was allowed for advertising a product in a state which forbade the sale of that product.[59]

If the advertising is of an unusual nature the taxpayer must be prepared to show results. An attorney and accountant was not permitted to deduct the expenses of a yacht flying a red, white, and blue pennant that displayed the numerals "1040" where he could not prove that this device had attracted any new clients.[60] No deduction was allowed the L & F Machine Company for expenses of a fishing vessel named "Ellen-F." The court found the pun too subtle and remote to publicize the company.[61]

Advertising is one of the items which the Internal Revenue Service may seek to reallocate where two corporations are under common control. But if each of the two or more corporations has its own brands or products, there is no basis for a reallocation of general advertising expense.[62]

Advertising costs must be capitalized if there are expenditures for items such as signs that have a life of several years.[63]

Lobbying and Political Contributions

Expenditures for lobbying purposes, for the promotion or defeat of legislation, for political campaign purposes (including the support or opposition to any candidate for public office except within narrow limits provided by law) or for propaganda campaigns (including advertising) related to any of these items are not deductible. For example, the cost of advertising to promote or to defeat legislation or to influence the public with respect to the desirability or undesirability of proposed legislation is not deductible as a business expense even though the legislation may directly affect the taxpayer's business.[64]

Deductions are now allowed for certain types of activity related to legislative matters: (1) appearances before, or communications with, committees or individual members of Federal, state, or local legislative bodies; (2) communication of information on legislative matters to business or trade organizations; and (3) the portion of membership dues in such an organization attributable to the activities in (1) and (2).[65]

Charitable Contributions Versus Business Expenses

There are limitations upon the amount of allowable charitable contributions. (See chapter 16, What Can Be Done with Contributions.) Thus, it is desirable to get a deduction as an ordinary and necessary business expense, if possible, rather than as a contribution.

An expenditure is not precluded from being an ordinary and necessary business expense merely because the recipient is a charitable organization.[66] A corporation was permitted to deduct payments made to the school board in the community where its plant was located as consideration for the upgrading of the local educational facilities so that employees would not move to communities providing better schools. The payments made were treated as ordinary and necessary business expenses.[67]

A corporation in a small community could deduct as ordinary and necessary business expenses the costs incurred by its president in contributing his time and talents to civic and community activities. This was regarded as a legitimate expenditure for the purpose of keeping the company's name before the public.[68]

Repairs

Certain repairs represent deductible expenses. A deductible repair is an expenditure whose purpose is to keep the property in an ordinarily efficient operating condition. It does not add to the value of the property, nor does it appreciably prolong the property's life. Deductible repairs are distinguished from replacements, alterations, improvements, or additions, which prolong the life of the property, increase its value, or make it adaptable to a different use. The latter are additions to capital investment and not deductible against current earnings.[69]

A repair of the type ordinarily recognized as deductible will not be allowed if the objective of the expenditure is anything other than the continued use of the asset by the taxpayer. Thus, when repairs were made so that the assets would be acceptable to a buyer, this was not deemed an ordinary and necessary expense to the seller.[70]

Frequently, it is stated that, to be deductible, a repair must be made with the same materials as those being replaced. But that is not necessarily the case. Thus, costs were deductible where a roof was repaired with materials different from the original ones when the new materials neither added to the value of nor prolonged the use of the property.[71] Thus, a repair is deductible if the purpose is merely a restoration of the *status quo*.[72] Where part of a roof collapsed because of faulty construction, deduction was allowed for the cost of replacement. However, the cost of strengthening the balance of the roof so that it too would not collapse was a capital expenditure.[73]

The sum of a series of expenditures may amount to a capital expenditure even though the items taken separately would not. So, where a taxpayer purchased an office building for rental purposes and a potential tenant demanded that substantial work be done (amounting to about 50 percent of the building's cost) to adapt the building to its needs, *all* of the costs had to be capitalized even though, standing alone, many of the items could have been deducted as repairs.[74]

Frequently, the Internal Revenue Service takes the position that expenditures for the repair of used equipment in the year of its purchase must be capitalized, inasmuch as the equipment was presumably purchased with the realization that the "repairs" would have to be performed to make the assets serviceable.[75]

Travel

Three conditions must be satisfied before a traveling expense deduction may be made:

(1) The expense must be a reasonable and necessary traveling expense as that term generally is understood. This includes such items as transportation fares and food as well as lodging expenses incurred while traveling.

(2) The expenses must be incurred "while away from home."

(3) The expenses must be incurred in pursuit of business.[76]

The focus of the inquiry is the dominant purpose of the trip, and the mere presence of some pleasurable features will not negate the finding of an overall business purpose.[77]

A travel expenditure requires proof of actual or potential business benefit.[78] *Proof* is the essence of a travel expense deduction. There must be evidence of where the taxpayer went on business trips, the costs for the various categories of expenditures, and the business purpose. Canceled checks charged to a selling or travel expense account prove nothing.[79]

Wife's Travel

Ordinarily, a businessman cannot deduct the expenses of taking his wife on a business trip.[80] However, the wife's travel expenses are deductible if it can be demonstrated that her presence helps her husband perform his business functions better or that her presence helps the corporate image.[81] Deductibility of a wife's expenses requires a finding that she performed services that were *necessary* to her husband's trade or business, not merely *helpful*.[82]

Commuting Expenses

Generally, commuting expenses are personal and nondeductible.[83] It does not matter that the commuter is not *permitted* to live at his place of work (such as a high-security governmental base).[84]

Entertainment

No deduction is allowed for entertainment unless the taxpayer establishes:

(1) that the expenditure was directly related to the active conduct of his trade or business; or

(2) in the case of an expenditure directly preceding or following a substantial and *bona fide* business discussion (including business meetings at

conventions or otherwise), that the expenditure was associated with the active conduct of his trade or business.[85]

An expenditure is deemed to be directly related to the taxpayer's trade or business if it meets all four of the following tests:

(1) At the time of the expenditure, the taxpayer had more than a general expectation of deriving income or a business benefit other than good will at some indefinite future time.

(2) During the entertainment period, the taxpayer actively engaged in a business meeting, negotiation, discussion, or other *bona fide* transaction, other than entertainment, for the purpose of obtaining a business benefit.

(3) In the light of all the facts and circumstances, the principal character or aspect of the combined business and entertainment to which the expenditure related was the active conduct of the taxpayer's trade or business. It is not necessary that more time be devoted to business than to entertainment to meet this requirement.

(4) The expenditure was allocable to the taxpayer and a person or persons with whom he engaged in the active conduct of a trade or business during the entertainment or with whom he would have been so engaged if it were not for circumstances beyond the taxpayer's control.

The expenditures must be in a "clear business setting." Expenditures are not allowable as deductions:

(1) where the distractions were substantial; for example, at meetings or discussions held at nightclubs, theatres, sporting events, cocktail parties; and

(2) where the taxpayer was not present.

But expenditures for food and drink will be allowed without reference to the above limitations where the circumstances are conducive to business discussions.[86]

The costs of business entertainment at an athletic club may be denied as a deduction where persons other than the host and his customers are present. While the circumstances may not make business discussion impossible, a court is likely to doubt whether more than social conversations would result.[87]

That entertainment is ordinary and necessary may not be difficult for a businessman to establish, particularly in an industry or at a time where there is a high degree of competition.[88] Yet the mere fact that customers or clients must be entertained from time to time is not proof that any particular expenditures are business-oriented deductions.[89]

Gifts

No deduction is allowed for the cost of gifts made directly or indirectly to an individual to the extent that the expense, when added to prior expenses for gifts made to the same person during the same taxable year, exceeds $25. This does not apply to:

(1) An item costing the taxpayer not more than $4 on which the taxpayer's name is clearly and permanently imprinted and is one of a number of similar items generally distributed.

(2) A sign, display rack, or other promotional material to be used on a recipient's business premises.

(3) An item of tangible personal property having a cost to the taxpayer not in excess of $100 that is awarded to an employee by reason of length of service or for safety achievement.[90]

(4) Payments to a widow or other beneficiary of a deceased employee to the amount of $5000 are tax-free to the recipient and deductible by the company.

Over and above the $5000 exception, a corporate payment to the widow of an officer or other employee has occasionally been treated as a nontaxable gift to her provided the payment was gratuitous, was clearly not given for services, and was made for a reason such as consideration of her own financial need.[91] Although court decisions have not been completely consistent, the weight of authority seems to be that the corporation may deduct the payment to the widow when it serves a business purpose. Such was the finding where a corporation could show that it regularly had made such payments to widows (14 in all) of employees who had died in the past 15 years.[92]

Where the facts indicate that corporate payments are not gifts, but are made solely for corporate purposes (for example, to increase employee morale) and with no primary intent to make a gift, the $25 limit may be inapplicable.

Medical Reimbursement Plan

An employer may deduct as an ordinary and necessary business expense any expenditures for sickness, accident, hospitalization, and medical or similar benefit plans.[93] Payments made under such a plan are not taxable to the employee. This includes payments, if the plan so provides, that are made to the employee's spouse and/or major dependents.[94]

Life Insurance Premiums

A corporation cannot deduct premiums upon the life of an officer, employee, or any other person financially interested in the business if the corporation is directly or indirectly a beneficiary under the policy.[95]

The Internal Revenue Service has ruled that where, as a condition to receiving a loan, a corporation takes out insurance on the lives of each officer in a stipulated amount and makes the lender the beneficiary, the premiums are not deductible since the corporation is an indirect beneficiary of the insurance proceeds.[96]

Directors' and Officers' Liability Insurance

A corporation can deduct premiums on liability insurance covering wrongful acts of its officers and directors in the line of their duties. Such an expenditure is regarded as ordinary and necessary to the corporation; for, in the absence of such an arrangement, it might be impossible to obtain persons who would be willing to undertake the making of decisions on behalf of the company. Although the officers concerned receive an economic benefit from the company (protection against a suit), premiums paid by the corporation are not taxable to them as compensation.[97]

Unreimbursed Expenses

If a corporation is entitled to claim reimbursement from some party for casualty or other losses, but fails to do so, no tax deduction is permitted. For example, where a generator was partially destroyed because of a defect and the owner did not wish to sue the machine's manufacturer lest future purchases of equipment on favorable terms be jeopardized, and did not wish to make a claim against its insurance company out of fear of jeopardizing his obtaining further insurance, the loss suffered was not deductible because the corporation had not exhausted its means of claiming reimbursement.[98]

This same rule applies to corporate officers who seek to deduct entertainment or other expenses for which reimbursement could have been obtained from the company. By not seeking reimbursement through other means, an individual cannot change an ordinary and necessary business expense of his employer's into an ordinary and necessary expense of his own.[99] An employee is not entitled to such a deduction even if he absorbed it because of the company's financial condition.[100] At most, the company has gone into a debt to him which he could deduct only if the company defaulted.[101]

But an officer may deduct expenses of entertaining corporate customers if he is required to do such entertaining and the corporation has specifically provided that no reimbursement will be made.[102]

NOTES

1. *Jones et al. v. Commissioner*, 242 F.2d 616 (5th Cir., 1957).
2. *The Jefferson Mills, Inc. v. United States*, 259 F. Supp. 305 (D.C., N.D. Ga., 1965), *aff'd*, 367 F.2d 392 (5th Cir., 1966).
3. *Commissioner v. Tellier et al.*, 383 U.S. 687 (1966).
4. *Francis M. Ellis et al.*, T.C. Memo. 1967-94 (filed May 1, 1967).
5. *Pizitz, Inc. et al. v. Patterson*, 183 F. Supp. 901 (D.C., N.D. Ala., 1964).
6. *Warwick et al. v. United States*, 236 F. Supp. 761 (D.C., E.D. Va., 1964).
7. *Commissioner v. Tellier et al.*, 383 U.S. 687 (1966).
8. *Loewy Drug Company of Baltimore City v. United States*, 232 F. Supp. 143 (D.C., Md., 1964), *aff'd*, 356 F.2d 928 (4th Cir., 1966).
9. *Waring Products Corporation*, 27 T.C. 921 (1957).

10. *First National Bank of Omaha v. United States*, 276 F. Supp. 905 (D.C., Neb., 1967).
11. *Edward N. Wilson et al.*, 49 T.C. 406 (1968).
12. *Swed Distributing Company v. Commissioner*, 323 F.2d 480 (5th Cir., 1963).
13. *Wells-Lee et al. v. Commissioner*, 360 F.2d 665 (8th Cir., 1966).
14. *Kennecott Copper Corporation v. United States*, 347 F.2d 275 (Ct. Cl., 1965).
15. *American Seating Co.*, 4 B.T.A. 649 (1926).
16. *E. F. Simms*, 28 B.T.A. 988 (1933).
17. Revenue Ruling 60-254, 1960-2 CB 42.
18. *General Bancshares Corporation*, 39 T.C. 423 (1962), *aff'd*, 326 F.2d 712 (8th Cir., 1964).
19. *KWTX Broadcasting Company, Inc.*, 33 T.C. 952 (1959).
20. *United States v. Gilmore et al.*, 372 U.S. 39 (1963).
21. *Munroe v. United States*, D.C., S.D. N.Y., 1965.
22. *Kornhauser v. United States*, 276 U.S. 145 (1928).
23. *Mitchell et al. v. United States*, 408 F.2d 435 (Ct. Cl., 1969).
24. *John F. Koons*, 35 T.C. 1092 (1961).
25. *Martin Mayrath*, 41 T.C. 582 (1964), *aff'd*, 357 F.2d 209 (5th Cir., 1966).
26. *Morton Frank et al.*, 20 T.C. 511 (1953).
27. *Richmond Television Corporation v. United States*, 345 F.2d 901 (4th Cir., 1965), *rev'd and rem'd'd on another issue*, 382 U.S. 68 (1965).
28. *Harold V. Bell, Jr. et al.*, T.C. Memo. 1958-33 (filed February 28, 1958).
29. *Stanton et al. v. Commissioner*, 399 F.2d 326 (5th Cir., 1968).
30. *Mid-State Products Co.*, 21 T.C. 696 (1954).
31. *Senate Finance Committee Report*, to accompany P.L. 91-172, page 274.
32. I.R.C. Section 162(c).
33. I.R.C. Section 162(c).
34. *United States v. Haskel Engineering & Supply Company*, 380 F.2d 786 (9th Cir., 1967).
35. *Walker et al. v. Commissioner*, 362 F.2d 140 (7th Cir., 1966).
36. *E.g., United States v. Ragen et al.*, 374 U.S. 513 (1942).
37. *Foster Frosty Foods, Inc.*, 39 T.C. 772 (1963).
38. Press Release S-2979 (February 26, 1952).
39. *United States v. Haskel Engineering & Supply Company*, 380 F.2d 786 (9th Cir., 1967).
40. *Limericks, Inc. v. Commissioner*, 165 F.2d 483 (5th Cir., 1948).
41. *Hall v. Commissioner*, 294 F.2d 82 (5th Cir., 1961).
42. *Goldstein et al. v. Commissioner*, 364 F.2d 734 (2d Cir., 1966).
43. Under I.R.C. Section 482.
44. *Clay Hartwell et al.*, T.C. Memo. 1965-49 (filed March 8, 1965).
45. *Robert R Walker, Inc. et al.*, T.C. Memo. 1965-28 (filed February 16, 1965), *aff'd*, 362 F.2d 140 (7th Cir., 1966).
46. *Haverill Shoe Novelty Co.*, 15 T.C. 517 (1950).
47. *Boyd Construction Company, Inc. v. United States*, 339 F.2d 620 (Ct. Cl., 1964).
48. *United States v. Gilmore et al.*, 372 U.S. 39 (1963).
49. *David B. Trott Estate*, T.C. Memo. 1969-18 (filed January 29, 1969).
50. *Commissioner v. Tellier et al.*, 383 U.S. 687 (1966).
51. *Ditmars v. Commissioner*, 302 F.2d 481 (2d Cir., 1962).
52. *Mitchell et al. v. United States*, 408 F.2d 435 (Ct. Cl., 1969).
53. *California & Hawaiian Sugar Refining Corporation v. United States*, 311 F.2d 235 (Ct. Cl., 1962).
54. Revenue Ruling 68-662, 1968-2 CB 69.
55. *Larchfield Corporation v. United States*, 373 F.2d 159 (2d Cir., 1966).
56. I.T. 3564, 1942-2 CB 87.
57. Regulations Section 1.162-15.
58. *George C. Ebner et al.*, T.C. Memo. 1958-108 (filed June 9, 1958).
59. *Fred N. Newman*, T.C. Memo., Docket No. 28955 (entered August 29, 1952).
60. *Robert Lee Henry et al.*, 36 T.C. 879 (1961).

61. *Larrabee et al. v. United States*, D.C., C.D. Cal., 1968.
62. *Glenmore Distilleries Company, Inc.*, 47 B.T.A. 213 (1942).
63. *Alabama Coca-Cola Bottling Company et al.*, T.C. Memo. 1969-123 (filed June 18, 1969).
64. Regulations Section 1.162-15(c).
65. I.R.C. Section 162(e).
66. "Ways and Means Committee Report to Accompany the Revenue Bill of 1938," *H. Report No. 1860*, 75th Congress, 3d Session, 1939-1 CB (Part 2) 740.
67. *The Jefferson Mills, Inc. v. United States*, 259 F. Supp. 305 (D.C., N.D. Ga., 1965), *aff'd*, 367 F.2d 392 (5th Cir., 1966).
68. *Leo Daly Company v. Vinal*, D.C., Neb., 1968.
69. *Illinois Merchants Trust Co.*, 4 B.T.A. 103 (1926).
70. *Ritner K. Walling Estate et al.*, 45 T.C. 111 (1965).
71. *Munroe Land Company*, T.C. Memo. 1966-2 (filed January 4, 1966).
72. *Oberman Manufacturing Company*, 47 T.C. 471 (1967).
73. *The Wellston Company*, T.C. Memo. 1965-55 (filed March 18, 1965).
74. *United States v. Wehrli et al.*, 400 F.2d 686 (10th Cir., 1968).
75. *Lanz v. United States*, 258 F. Supp. 796 (D.C., N.D. N.Y., 1968).
76. *Commissioner v. Flowers*, 326 U.S. 465 (1946).
77. *United States v. Gotcher et al.*, 401 F.2d 118 (5th Cir., 1968).
78. *Alexander P. Reed et al.*, 35 T.C. 199 (1960).
79. *A. C. Engineering Corporation*, T.C. Memo. 1958-147 (filed July 30, 1958).
80. *Cornelius Vanderbilt, Jr.*, T.C. Memo. 1957-235 (filed December 23, 1957).
81. *United States v. Disney et al.*, 413 F.2d 783 (9th Cir., 1969).
82. *L. L. Moorsman*, 26 T.C. 666 (1956).
83. *United States v. Tauferner et al.*, 407 F.2d 243 (10th Cir., 1969).
84. *Raymond A. Sanders et al.*, 52 T.C. 964 (1969).
85. I.R.C. Section 274.
86. Regulations Section 1.274-2.
87. *Thomas C. St. John et al.*, T.C. Memo. 1970-238 (filed August 24, 1970).
88. *James J. Glenn et al.*, T.C. Memo. 1970-184 (filed June 30, 1970).
89. *Eugene H. Lorenz*, T.C. Memo., Docket No. 17811 (entered August 25, 1949).
90. I.R.C. Section 274(b).
91. *Corasaniti et al. v. United States*, 212 F. Supp. 229 (D.C., Md., 1962).
92. *Weyenberg Shoe Manufacturing Company*, T.C. Memo. 1964-322 (filed December 17, 1964).
93. Regulations Section 1.162-10(a).
94. I.R.C. Section 105(b).
95. I.R.C. Section 264(a)(1).
96. Revenue Ruling 68-5, 1968-1 CB 99.
97. Revenue Ruling 69-491, 1969-2 CB 22.
98. *Kentucky Utilities Company et al. v. Glenn et al.*, 394 F.2d 631 (6th Cir., 1968).
99. *Robert C. McGuire*, T.C. Memo. 1965-231 (filed August 26, 1965).
100. *Milford C. Beiner et al.*, T.C. Memo. 1961-23 (filed January 31, 1961).
101. *William Ockrant et al.*, T.C. Memo. 1966-60 (filed March 22, 1966).
102. *Holland et al. v. United States*, 311 F. Supp. 422 (D.C., C.D. Cal., 1970).

CHAPTER 8

Compensation, Fringe Benefits

Nature of Compensation

"[E]xecutive compensation today is a financial smorgasbord made up of a combination of salary, deferred compensation, stock options, bonuses, pensions, hospital care along with lagniappe ranging from limousines to life insurance." [1]

It is true that the 50 percent ceiling rate on earned income makes cash more attractive than ever. It is also true that higher capital gains rates plus the minimum tax on tax preference income as well as stock market weakness at any given time make stock options less attractive. Still, cash plus some form of stock options, profit sharing, medical care, and life insurance, along with a variety of fringe benefits ranging from company cars to country-club membership are part of many executive compensation packages.

The statutory definition of gross income is, for tax purposes, broad enough to include any economic or financial benefit conferred on the employee as compensation, whatever the form or mode by which it is effected. [2]

Payment for services is taxable to the person who rendered those services. Assignments or other contracts will not serve to transfer income for tax purposes to lower-bracketed persons who did not earn this income. A metaphor frequently used by the courts is that the fruit must be attributed to the tree on which it grew. [3] Thus, a person cannot escape tax upon compensation which is paid to a relative or other nominee. Even if the payment is made directly by the beneficiary of services to a charitable organization, the one performing the services is taxed. [4]

Payments made on behalf of an executive by his employer may be regarded as compensation (such as corporate payment of an individual's legal fees). [5] Free vacations to employees are compensation. [6] An employer's payment of an employee's income taxes is regarded as additional compensation. [7] However, an employer's interest-free loan to an employee was held not to be compensation. [8]

Normally, anything of value that flows from the employer to the employee will be regarded by the Internal Revenue Service as compensation for services. In the absence of a statutory exemption, it will be taxable to the employee in the year received and, subject to the requirement of reasonable compensation, will be deductible by the employer.

Requirement of Reasonableness

An employer can deduct compensation he has paid only to the extent that it may be considered reasonable. There is a rather naive presumption that if the directors of a corporation have considered the amount of compensation, it is reasonable. This is based upon the theory that the management of a business is presumed to be familiar with the amount and value of services rendered.[9] But there is no *de minimis* rule as to the amount of compensation which must be justified as reasonable. In one case, a director's compensation of $2400 for the year was halved by the court for purposes of the tax deduction for reasonable compensation.[10]

The burden of proof is on the corporate payor to show that the salary claimed as a deduction is reasonable and commensurate with the services actually rendered by the officer or other employee. Once the corporation has established what it considers to be a reasonable salary and supports this with acceptable evidence, the burden shifts to the Internal Revenue Service to refute such proof.

There can be no overall standard as to what *reasonable compensation* is. "Reasonableness" is a relative standard which may be used to measure an absolute such as an amount of compensation only after observation of surrounding facts which place the absolute in perspective. As a result, many criteria have been set forth by the courts as guides in determining the reasonableness of compensation in particular cases.[11] The reasonableness of compensation is in the end largely controlled by the human element involved; that is, by the capacity, judgment, and diligence of the employee under specific conditions.[12] But, in assaying this subjective determination, one is furnished with the following objective standards that should stand as practical and acceptable guidelines.

Tests as to Reasonableness

Here are the leading criteria which have been developed by the courts in appraising the reasonableness of compensation for purposes of the taxpayer's deduction:

(1) The value of a particular employee's services to a particular employer.[13]

(2) The amount paid to similar employees engaged in similar industries.[14]

(3) The extent to which the employee's services contribute to the success of the business.[15]

(4) Contributions made by the employee not only as an employee, but in some other capacity (such as that of an inventor).[16]

(5) Testimony of expert witnesses as to the value of an employee.[17]

(6) Testimony of a competitor, who presumably is thoroughly familiar with services of this type;[18] testimony of a competitor that a certain executive was worth all that he was paid favorably impressed one court.[19]

(7) The amount of time the employee devoted to his work, including overtime.[20]

(8) The portion of his time that the executive or other employee devoted to his work. An individual may have had time-consuming interests or activities which were not related to company business.[21] But an employee's contributions to the business may be so considerable that the time he spends in his office is irrelevant. In one case compensation was held to be reasonable on the facts even though two officer-stockholders spent only six weeks in the office.[22] Compensation was found to be reasonable in another case where an executive never went to the office. He gave counsel, arranged for new products, and performed other services without being physically present at the corporation's place of work.[23]

(9) The actual performance of the enterprise under the executive's direction. A corporation could not justify the reasonableness of the compensation of its president where, under his direction, sales and net earnings steadily decreased.[24]

(10) The prior earning capacity of an officer.[25]

(11) The salary policy of the corporation as to all employees.[26]

(12) Reasonableness of compensation for the current year was justified by the demonstrated inadequacy of compensation for a prior period.[27]

(13) The conditions under which the employee was required to live.[28] Thus, services in a crude undeveloped area might call for higher than normal compensation in order to attract a person willing to live in such circumstances.

(14) The extent of control which the recipient of the purported salary had over the corporation in setting the amount of his own compensation.[29]

(15) The relationship if any between the employee and the principal stockholders or officers.[30]

(16) Consideration of any physical hazards in the work.[31]

(17) Whether the amount of the purported salary was set at a time when the profits for each of the years were known.[32] (This test is particularly important in the case of a closely-held corporation.)

(18) The amount of fringe benefits that were paid in addition to the stated salary.[33] Thus, pension contributions by the employer are taken into account in assaying the reasonableness of compensation;[34] so are company insurance payments.[35]

(19) The relationship of compensation to the percentage of shares of company stock held.[36]

(20) Highly specialized talents which are necessary.[37]

(21) Whether the amounts were approved by unrelated stockholders and directors who were not on the payroll.[38]

(22) The availability of others to fill the job.[39]

(23) The ultimate responsibility for those policy decisions which are critical to the success or failure of an enterprise.[40]

The fact that a corporation's salary payments to officers are made pursuant to valid contracts does not in any way tend to prove that these payments are reasonable.[41] Also, of slight significance is an officer's title.[42] Where one of four equal shareholders held the title of president, a court stated that for organizational purposes, it was necessary that one of the equal shareholders be designated president. That, in itself, did not render his services of significantly greater value to the corporation.[43] Job descriptions and titles are no substitute for evidence of services actually rendered.[44]

A corporation's own listing of desirable executive qualities may differ considerably from the yardsticks the courts set to determine reasonable compensation. Thus, United States Steel Corporation listed 12 personal qualities for a successful executive.[45] The first was "attitude," which is scarcely a quality to which the Internal Revenue Service would assign a sizable dollar valuation on the corporate income tax return. Other qualities of more interest to the corporation than to the Service, one would assume, were "adaptability" and "expression."

Closely Held Corporations

Understandably, an aura of suspicion surrounds the amount of compensation paid to employees who are also stockholders of the corporation. Dividends are nondeductible to the corporate payor. Thus, salaries could conceivably be, at least to some extent, disguised dividends.

The same weight does not attach to salary allowances voted by the directors of a closely held corporation as attaches in instances where officers have little or no financial interest in the corporation. Thus, where a closely held corporation is involved, payments made to stockholder-officers as compensation will be scrutinized carefully by the Internal Revenue Service to determine whether the payments in fact constitute a distribution of profits.[46]

Reasonableness of compensation in a closely-held corporation cannot be judged by the same standards that apply to a widely held corporation; for with the former, the compensation cannot be said to have been arrived at pursuant to a free bargain between the corporation and the officers involved.[47] A controlling shareholder-executive is entitled to be paid as generously as is a comparable executive of a publicly held corporation. But this is not to say that, where the controlling shareholder sets his own compensation as an executive, the reasonableness of such compensation does not warrant a second look by the Commissioner due to the obvious lack of arm's length bargaining.[48]

Where a majority shareholder is also an officer, a factual showing of the exact nature of his duties may be required to justify a salary deduction.[49]

A bonus-type contract that is reasonable in the case of a non-stockholder may be adjudged unreasonable if made with a large stockholder, inasmuch as the incentive of the bonus presumably would not be needed to call forth the stockholder's best efforts.[50] A court is not likely to be impressed with the argument that a sole shareholder can pay himself incentive compensation.[51]

"Compensation" as Dividends

Where a corporation makes payments to shareholders in proportion to their stock, the amounts involved may not be deductible as salaries despite their being labeled as such. They may be regarded as dividends.[52] Even where a payment to an officer-shareholder is reasonable in amount, it may not be deductible in full if part of it is characterized as a distribution of corporate earnings as contrasted with compensation for services rendered.[53]

An officer-stockholder may be found to have received a dividend where salaries paid to persons other than himself are deemed to be unreasonable. Such was the situation where a corporation paid salaries to six young ladies. Inasmuch as the corporation could not prove that the alleged secretarial and stenographic services actually had been performed, the court found that the amounts paid to these persons were expended for the personal nonbusiness benefit of the chief stockholder. So he was taxed on the theory that he had derived an economic benefit from amounts paid by the corporation.[54]

The income tax liability of the recipient with respect to an amount ostensibly paid to him as compensation, but not allowed as a deduction as such by the corporate payor, depends upon the circumstances of each case. Thus, where a corporation makes excessive payments, which correspond to or bear a close relationship to stockholdings and are found by the Commissioner to be a distribution of corporate earnings and profits, they will be treated as a dividend. If the corporate payments constitute remuneration for property that the individual made available to the corporation, they should be treated by the corporation as a capital expenditure and by the recipient as part of the purchase price. In the absence of evidence to justify other treatment, excessive payments for salaries or other compensation for personal services must be included in the gross income of the recipient.[55]

Fraud penalties have been imposed in cases where the recipient performed no services, or even relatively minor services, and the payments were continued over a period of years.[56]

Repayments of Excessive Compensation

If an employee voluntarily repays amounts he had received as compensation, his income for the year of original receipt is not reduced. The transaction is regarded as a gift or contribution of income already received.[57] Even the discovery of accounting errors several years later, as where commissions never should have been paid in the first place, will not form the basis for adjusting income and tax of the earlier years.[58]

However, an individual will be allowed a deduction for amounts that he repaid to his employer after the Internal Revenue Service disallowed a portion of the deduction for the employee's compensation as unreasonable where the employee was *required* to make this repayment because of a corporate bylaw calling for an officer's reimbursing an amount of his compensation which had been disallowed as a corporate tax deduction.[59]

If a corporation has a contract or other written agreement with an officer to the effect that the latter will reimburse the company for any portion of his salary which is disallowed as unreasonable, it may be anticipated that this will trigger a salary disallowance. An Internal Revenue agent may well feel that if both employer and employee have doubts as to the reasonableness of compensation, a disallowance is at least partially expected. But if all executives are covered by such an arrangement, without mention of specific names, the dubious character of one person's compensation seems less likely to invite scrutiny.

Treasury Ruling as to Reasonableness

Although the Internal Revenue Service will supply taxpayers with advance rulings in many areas as to the tax consequences of a particular transaction, no ruling will be issued as to whether compensation is reasonable in amount.[60]

Earned Income Ceiling Rate

An individual's maximum Federal income tax rate on earned income is now 50 percent. This, of course, makes cash more attractive than when it was subject to a 70 percent top rate.

Earned taxable income is that proportion of total taxable income which is in the same ratio (but not in excess of 100 percent) as the ratio of earned income to adjusted gross income. Thus, if 40 percent of an individual's adjusted gross income is earned income, then 40 percent of this taxable income is considered earned taxable income.

Earned income generally includes wages, salaries, professional fees, or compensation for personal services, and, in the case of an individual engaged in a trade or business where both personal services and capital are material income-producing factors, a reasonable amount, but not in excess of, 30 percent of his share of the net profits of the business. Earned income does not include lump-sum distributions from employee benefit plans where long-term capital gains treatment is afforded to the employer's contribution, nor does it include the employer's contribution where that is eligible for the special seven-year averaging rules applicable if the total distribution occurs in one year. In addition, deferred compensation is not considered to be earned income; nor is the earned income limit available to taxpayers who use income averaging on their tax returns or to married couples who file separate returns.

The ceiling is applicable to earned income reduced by tax preferences in excess of $30,000 in the current year or the average tax preferences in excess of $30,000 over the current and the previous four years, whichever is greater.[61]

Contingent Compensation

A contingent salary agreement that could result in a low salary under unfavorable circumstances may serve as a justification for an unusually high payment in favorable years.[62] Generally speaking, if contingent compensation is paid pursuant to a free bargain between the employer and the individual before the services are rendered, and is not influenced by any consideration on the part of the employer other than that of securing on fair and advantageous terms the services of the individual, it is allowed as a deduction even though in the actual execution of the contract it proves to be greater than the amount which ordinarily would have been paid.[63]

Thus, where there is a contingent compensation arrangement, an important factor is whether the arrangement is the result of a free bargain. Special care must be taken in closely-held family corporations to guard against domination by senior shareholders. In the case of such domination, free bargaining may be absent even where competent adults are involved.[64]

Where a contingent compensation arrangement results in very high payments, but the contingency was actually unrelated to the employee's work, as in the case of an industry's wartime prosperity after some unspectacular earnings' years, a court may feel the result to be unreasonable, at least in part.[65]

Bonuses

Bonus payments are governed by the rules that generally apply to other compensation payments. They are deductible to the extent the entire compensation, including the bonus, represents reasonable payment for services actually rendered.[66] A bonus may be called in question when paid to major stockholders. The sole owner of an enterprise paying himself a bonus as incentive to do his best in managing his own business has been characterized as "nonsense."

In the case of an employee-stockholder, a bonus may appear to be a disguised dividend, particularly if this bonus is set up after there is strong evidence of what profits would be. But this presumption may be refuted as where the corporate minutes state that the bonuses were authorized after consideration of the services performed by the individual concerned.[67] (Stock bonuses are treated later in this chapter.)

Stock Options

Once an employee gets an option, he's not just an employee any more. He's a potential part owner.[68] At any rate, getting "a piece of the action" is a valued compensation device. Qualified stock options constitute a special form of bonus.[69]

The general rule is that no tax is imposed either at the time the qualified stock option is granted or exercised. If the stock is held for three years, the difference between the selling price and the purchase price is treated as a capital gain or loss. If the stock is not held for that long, the difference between the option price and the value of the shares at the time the option is exercised must be reported as ordinary income in the year the stock is sold. The amount cannot exceed the taxpayer's gain on the sale of his stock. But the excess of the amount realized over the amount reported as ordinary income is capital gain. In the case of a non-statutory option, the employee has ordinary income to the extent that the option's value exceeds any amount he paid for it.[70]

In the case of a qualified stock option, the option may be exercised during the optionee's lifetime only by the optionee himself. There is more leeway in the exercise of the option after he dies. For example, it may be provided that the option is to be exercised by a person so named in the employee's will. Any change in an option after it is set up may be treated as the grant of a new option. In that event, the option price would have to be adjusted so that it equals or exceeds the fair market value of the stock on the date of modification. But it has been ruled that an amendment to a plan to provide the optionee an alternative method to designate a person who may exercise his option in the event of his death is not such a "modification" resulting in a new option.[71]

A corporation does not get a deduction for income tax purposes when a qualified stock option is used as a compensatory device. Of course, stock issued operates to dilute earnings per share and, to the extent that the value of the stock received by an employee exceeds the amount the stock cost him, there is also dilution of the value of the shareholder's equity.[72]

Where an employee was advised by his employer-corporation that if he tendered his stock option for cancellation, he would receive a certain price "as additional compensation for his services," long-term capital gain treatment was not permitted upon his acceptance of the offer. This was ordinary income as it did not result from the exercise of a qualified stock option.[73] Such also was the finding where an employee relinquished all rights in and from his employer-corporation in return for a sum that was referred to in the agreement as "compensation." [74] Valuable potentialities from the use of a qualified stock option are lost if the option is used in any manner other than that which the Internal Revenue Code defines as "exercise."

Nonstatutory Stock Options

If an employee receives a non-qualified (that is, nonstatutory) option to purchase stock from his employer-corporation, he realizes taxable income by way of compensation on the date he receives the stock to the extent of the difference between the fair market value of the stock when it is received and the price paid therefor. If he transfers the option for consideration in an arm's length transaction, he realizes taxable income by way of compensation on the date he receives the consideration to the extent of the value of the consideration.[75]

Use of a nonstatutory option permits a company's favoring certain employees. The company gets a tax deduction when the employee is required to report income equal to the amount the employee is required to report.[76]

If a nonstatutory stock option has a readily ascertainable fair market value at the time it is granted (which is normally the case with publicly traded stock), the employee realizes compensation income at the time of the grant in an amount equal to the excess, if any, of the fair market value over the amount paid for the option, and the company gets a deduction for that amount. Where there is no readily ascertainable fair market value at the time of the grant, taxation is delayed until the exercise or transfer of the option.[77] An option has no readily ascertainable fair market value if: (1) it is not exercisable in full immediately; (2) it is subject to the employee's continued employment; (3) it is not traded on any established market; and (4) it is not freely transferable.[78]

Stock Bonus Plan

A *stock bonus plan* is a plan established and maintained by an employer to provide benefits similar to those of a profit-sharing plan, except that in the former, the employer's contributions are not necessarily dependent upon profits and the benefits are distributable in the stock of the employer-corporation.

Deferred Compensation

Deferred compensation arrangements are designed to postpone the receipt of income until a later year, usually after retirement when the income can be taxed at lower rates under most circumstances. A deferred compensation plan includes pension, profit-sharing, and stock bonus plans which, if they meet the Internal Revenue Service requirements,[79] can assure employees of relatively favorable tax treatment when they receive payments. Such a plan may also include nonstatutory devices or arrangements outside the confines of qualified employee benefit plans. These nonstatutory plans can be molded to fit the particular circumstances of a single individual or of a particular group of persons.

A mere promise to pay—not represented by notes or secured in any way—is not regarded as a receipt of income by a person using the cash basis, as virtually all individuals do.[80] Taxpayers on a receipts and disbursements basis are required to report only income actually received despite their having entered into any binding contracts to receive more.[81]

But, under the doctrine known as *constructive receipt,* an individual may not deliberately turn his back upon income and thereby select the year for which he will report it.[82] Nor may a taxpayer postpone receipt of income from one taxable year to another by private agreements.[83] Unpaid amounts due from a corporation are not to be included in the income of a cash-basis individual unless it appears that the money was available to him, that the corporation was able and ready to pay him, and that his failure to receive the money was due to his own choosing.[84]

The following is an example of a deferred compensation plan that passed IRS muster: Under an employment contract, a corporation paid to a cash-basis officer a flat salary and a designated additional amount which would be deferred, accumulated, and paid in annual installments equal to one-fifth of the amount in the reserve at the end of each year after the first. Payments would be made to him only upon: (1) termination of his employment, (2) his becoming a part-time employee, or (3) his becoming incapacitated. The contract provided that if he failed or refused to perform his duties, the corporation would be relieved of its obligation to make further payments into the reserve, but still would have to pay out prior accumulations. If he died, payments of whatever remained in the account would be made to his estate, one-fifth for each of five successive years.[85]

Deferment was also achieved where corporation set up a supplementary retirement plan under which a committee of directors (none of whom was an officer or employee) could award incentive bonuses to selected employees for payment at future dates to be designated by the employee. Employees thus tapped had no right to any money until the date named by the committee, and no payment could be made more than ten years after an employee's normal retirement date. The awards were not funded, nor could they be assigned, although they would be paid to the employee's beneficiary at the time of his death.[86]

Another corporation made contracts with all full-time employees providing that any one of 40 or more persons who earned a specified amount could irrevocably elect to defer either five or ten percent of his salary for a particular year. Amounts thus deferred would be paid on January 1 of each of the ten years following the termination of full-time eployment, with immediate payment to beneficiaries in case of death. Here too, it was ruled that the amounts thus deferred were taxable when received or otherwise made available.[87]

If an individual performs personal services in return for a percentage of the proceeds of an undertaking, he may defer reporting income which the contract provides is to be paid in subsequent years. Such treatment is not allowed, however, if he arranges to share in both profits and losses, for this is regarded as a joint venture, profits from which must be reported in the joint venture's taxable year.[88]

The Internal Revenue Service will not issue advance rulings in specific cases involving deferred compensation arrangements.[89]

Profit-Sharing Plans

The tax aspects of deferred profit-sharing plans will be discussed in chapter 9.

Pension Plans

The tax aspects of pension plans will be discussed in chapter 10.

Group Insurance

An employee must include in his gross income an amount equal to the cost of group-term life insurance on his life under policies carried by his employer, but only to the extent that this cost exceeds the sum of: (1) the cost of $50,000 of such insurance and (2) the amount, if any, paid by the employee for the purchase of insurance. There are three exceptions: (1) where the employee is retired or disabled; (2) where the employer or a charity is the beneficiary; (3) and where the insurance is provided by a qualified employee trust.[90]

If the state which licensed the insurance company to sell the policy in question has imposed a lower maximum coverage per individual than $50,000, the $50,000 figure established for Federal tax purposes will be reduced to that amount.[91]

Other Life Insurance

Ordinarily, where an employer pays regular life insurance premiums upon the life of an employee and the benefits are payable to the employee's beneficiary, the premiums are taxable income to the employee because he is receiving an economic benefit. This is so even if the employee has no right to change the beneficiary, to assign the policy, or to exercise any other incidents of ownership of the policy.[92]

Split-Dollar Insurance

Where the *split-dollar* technique is used, an employer and employee join in purchasing an insurance policy, in which there is a substantial investment element, on the life of the employee. The employer provides the funds to pay part of the annual premiums to the extent of the increase in the cash surrender value each year, and the employee pays the balance of the premium. Although the employee must pay a substantial part of the first premium, the practical effect is that after the first year his share of the premiums decreases rapidly and, in some cases, it even becomes zero after a relatively short time. The employee thus obtains valuable insurance protection (decreasing each year, but still substantial for a long time) with a relatively small outlay for premiums in the early years and at little or no cost to him in later years. The employee is taxed each year on the value of the insurance protection in excess of the portion, if any, of the premiums provided by him.

The employer is entitled to receive, out of the proceeds of the policy, an amount equal to the cash surrender value of the policy or at least a sufficient part thereof to equal the funds provided by the employer for the premium payments. The employee has the right to name the beneficiary of the balance of any proceeds payable on his death. The employer is not entitled to any tax deduction for the premium payments that he makes.[93]

An advantage to the employee is that insurance may be taken out before he is able to pay the full premiums, thus enabling purchase of the insurance at lower cost because of his youth. If he waits until he can afford the insurance, he may become uninsurable. Proceeds payable upon death are highest in the earlier years of the policy, which usually is the time of an employee's greatest need as he has not had time to build up an estate, children still must be supported, etc. In effect, the split-dollar arrangement amounts to an employer making annual loans to his employee without interest and of an amount equivalent to the annual increase in the cash surrender value of the policy.

Health Insurance Plans

The health insurance benefits provided by some employers do not provide great amounts of money, but they are one of the most desirable of all fringe benefits in the security provided for employees. If the plan meets certain statutory requirements,[94] the expenditures are deductible by the employer and the benefits provided thereby are not taxable to the employees. Generally, any arrangement, written or informal, for payments to employees will be considered a *plan* as required by the statute. Intermittent, irregular payments, however, may not qualify.[95]

An employee may exclude from gross income any amounts received, directly or indirectly, by himself, his spouse, or his dependents under an accident and health plan as reimbursement for medical expenses if these amounts are attributable to payments made by his employer.[96] This includes payments made directly to physicians or hospitals.[97] Such an arrangement provides tax-free income to offset nondeductible medical expenses; that is, medical expenses which do not exceed three percent of adjusted gross income.

Unlike employee benefit plans in general, the plan may be discriminatory in favor of executives, employee-stockholders, or other privileged persons.[98] However, the Internal Revenue Service may attack a health insurance plan as being, in effect, a preferential dividend in the case of employee-stockholders.[99]

The plan must be "communicated" to the employees. Such was not the case where no employee was ever shown a copy of any resolution, minutes, or other writing which set forth the benefits.[100]

Officers' Liability Insurance

Where a corporation pays premiums upon indemnity policies covering wrongful acts of officers and directors during the course of their employment, the premiums are deductible. They do not constitute constructive income to the individuals involved.[101]

Bargain Sale

Where an employee is sold property at bargain prices, there is compensation to the extent of the differential.[102] Nothing is apt to be done by the Internal Revenue Service about modest sales by employer to employee. The employee expects to be able to get his employer's product for personal use at a discount—unless he works in a bank.

However, the bargain element in more substantial sales is taxable as ordinary income. This is true of an officer's purchase of stock in his own corporation where the transaction is simply a means by which his services are secured and paid for.[103] The same rule applies to any employee. In computing the gain or loss from the subsequent sale of this stock, one takes its basis as the amount paid for the property, increased by the amount of this difference included in his gross income.[104]

However, a bargain sale of stock is not regarded as compensation to an employee if he does not know that he is getting a bargain.[105]

Payment in Payor's Stock

A corporation's discharge of its salary obligations to shareholder-employees through the issuance of the corporation's stock to them equal in value to the salary obligations is compensation for services and taxable to the employees in an amount equal to the fair market value of the stock received.[106] The employees must report this as income even though their proportionate interest in the corporation has not changed as a result of the issuance of the stock.[107]

Where a corporation distributes shares of its treasury stock to employees as compensation and the cost basis of the stock to the corporation is less than its fair market value at the date of distribution, the fair market value is deductible as business expense.[108]

Restricted Property

If a person receives compensation for services in the form of property (as stock) which is subject to a restriction, the person who performed the services is taxed as of the time of receipt of the property unless his interest is subject to a substantial risk of forfeiture. The restrictions on the property are not taken into account in determining its value unless the restriction, by its own terms, will never lapse.

One who performs services may elect within 30 days of the transfer of property, subject to substantial risk of forfeiture to include the value of this property in his income for the year of receipt. If this election is made and his right to this property is subsequently forfeited, he will neither recover the tax nor receive any deduction for the amount forfeited. Election might be made if it appeared that the stock or other property would increase in value. It is better to pick up ordinary income when the value is low, in which event the increment will be taxed (if at all) as capital gain.

If restricted property is involved in a tax-free exchange for other property subject to substantially the same restrictions, no tax applies to the exchange, and the property received is treated as restricted property.[109]

The employer is allowed a deduction for the amount reported as income by the employee.

Compensation in Other Forms

Compensation for services is taxable regardless of the form of payment—it need not be in cash. Where property is given for services, the valuation is the fair market price at the time of the distribution. Christmas gifts of nominal value given to employees as merchandise (chickens, hams, and the like) are not taxable even though the employer gets a tax deduction. But this exception does not apply to cash, gift certificates, or similar items readily convertible into cash, regardless of the amount involved.[110]

Payments for Not Working

Payments made by a company to employees for "idle time," during which the employees perform no services for the company, are wages for tax purposes.[111]

Strike Benefits

Where a union paid strike benefits to persons out on strike, regardless of whether these persons were members of the union, and the amounts were nominal and not contingent upon participation in strike activities, they were treated as gifts.[112] But strike benefits are not gifts when they are based upon a percentage of the salaries of members of the union, the payments not being grounded upon the personal needs of the union members nor upon employment benefits which might be available.[113] Lockout benefits are taxable.[114]

In holding that certain strike benefits were taxable, one court stated that perhaps the strongest (though it was not held to be conclusive in itself) support establishing compensation was the fact that the union had made no inquiry into the personal financial situations and needs of its individual striking members. Although the union's officers may well have been aware of financial hardships, this awareness was not determinative of the amount received as strike benefits.[115]

Suggestion Awards

Even if a corporation has no agreement that it will pay for employee suggestions which are accepted, payments that are in fact made are considered to be for work or ideas intended to increase the company's efficiency; they are remuneration for employment. That means that they are taxable compensation.[116]

Meals and Lodgings

The value of meals or lodgings furnished to an employee by his employer for the employer's convenience is excluded from the gross income of the former. In the case of lodgings, this exclusion applies only if the employee is required to accept such lodgings on the business premises of his employer as a condition of his employment.[117] Three tests are necessary if the value of lodgings is to be thus excluded:

(1) The lodgings are furnished on the business premises of the employer.

(2) The lodgings are furnished for the convenience of the employer.

(3) The employer is required to accept such lodgings as a condition of his employment.[118]

"Required" in this context means required in order for an employee to properly perform the duties of his employment. Thus, exclusion was not permitted where company policy specified full-time availability, for the duties of the job did not call for this and the officers who benefitted from the policy were the persons who had framed it.[119]

The lodging must be provided either at a place where the employee performs a significant portion of his duties or on the premises where the employer conducts a significant portion of his business. An employee's merely being "on call" is not enough to satisfy the statute, as where the manager of a motel was furnished with rent-free quarters at rented facilities two blocks from the motel.[120]

Correspondence, job descriptions, advertisements, and company manuals could spell out the fact that in order to meet the employer's needs or to be ready for emergencies, the holder of a stipulated position would be required to live on the employer's premises or to eat there.[121]

The vice-president of a corporation was not required to include as income the value of meals furnished to executives at daily luncheons held in a hotel suite rented by the company. Business was discussed and company affairs were conducted there.[122]

Reimbursement of Moving Expenses

An employer's reimbursement of an employee's moving expenses are includable as compensation for services. But the employee is entitled to offset this by a deduction on his own return within the limits provided by the Internal Revenue Code and Treasury Regulations.[123]

Use of a Trust in Compensation Arrangements

A corporation may set up a revocable trust for compensation arrangements for one of its officers. The corporation could deposit some of its shares with a trustee, the dividends going to the officer. The amount of trust income thus paid to the officer each year would be deducted by the corporation as compensation, provided that the dividends plus the officer's regular salary did not constitute unreasonable compensation.[124] When the officer's employment ceased, the trust would be terminated and the corporation would get its shares back. Thus, where it was desired that stock of a closely-held corporation should remain solely in the hands of a certain group, an officer not part of this group could gain the advantage of sharing in the profits via dividends that his services created without actually owning the stock.

Gifts

If a benefit flowing from the employer to an employee is intended to be a gift, this should be spelled out in the minutes or elsewhere. In providing the questioned payment, the employer should indicate unequivocally whether the payment was intended as an expression of philanthropic attitude, as a bid for employee good will, or as some other kind of noncompensating payment.[125] A voluntarily executed transfer of his property by one to another without any consideration or compensation is not necessarily a "gift" for Federal income tax purposes. If the transfer or payment arises from a sense of moral or legal duty, it is not a gift.[126] Where the payment is in return for services rendered, it is irrelevant that the donor derives no economic benefit from it.[127] A gift in the income tax sense must proceed from generosity that is detached and disinterested.[128] The most critical consideration is the donor's intention.[129]

Payments to Employees' Widows. Where a corporation gratuitously and without contractual or other obligation makes payments to the widow of an officer or other employee who dies in service, the question arises as to whether this is a nontaxable gift or a taxable compensation. Where the payment to the widow was in return for services performed by her deceased husband, it is taxable compensation as far as the widow is concerned. But the payment could be characterized as a gift if the employer had habitually made such payments to widows, even in the absence of a formal plan.[130] Usually, the payment is treated as compensation because somewhere along the line it was referred to in corporate minutes or correspondence as in grateful recognition for services performed by the decedent.

Whether the payment to the widow actually is a gift to her for Federal income tax purposes depends upon these yardsticks:

(1) Was there any employer obligation to make payments beyond those the deceased employee already had received?[131]

(2) Had the recipient ever rendered services for the payor?[132]

(3) Did benefits accrue to the payor from the payment?[133]

(4) Was the payment to the widow the same amount as the deceased employee's salary for a specified period (such as a year)?[134]

(5) Was the financial condition of the widow taken into consideration?[135]

(6) Was the payment treated as salary on the payor's books? It is difficult to argue that the payment had been intended as a gift if it was reflected in a compensation account on the corporation's books.[136]

(7) Was such payment a customary practice of the corporation?[137]

Compensation Capital in Nature

Salaries are not deductible by the payor if they are deemed to be of a capital nature. Thus, no compensation deduction was allowed for overtime wages incurred in the construction of a commercial building so as to speed up the completion time. The cost of the building was a capital expenditure, and the wages were a part of that cost.[138] A corporation which was engaged in the distribution and sale of gas also leased automatic hot water heaters to customers on a five-year basis. Bonuses and commissions paid to its own salesmen and to contractors for securing customers for the taxpayer's heaters for rental were not deductible as compensation. The payments related to the acquisition of leases and should properly have been recovered over the five-year term of the leases.[139]

Salaries and bonuses related directly to production are included as part of the cost of inventory and are thus not deductible as compensation.[140]

Time of Deduction

Compensation for the following year is not deductible for tax purposes. The deduction is for services "actually rendered" and those that will not be rendered, as where an officer under contract is paid the required amount even though his disenchanted employer has requested that he do nothing further.[141]

Where an employee directly or indirectly owns more than 50 percent of the stock of a corporation and is on the cash basis while the corporation is on the accrual basis, the corporation is entitled to the deduction only if the amount is paid within two and a half months after the close of the taxable year. This payment may be actual or constructive.[142]

Allocation

Where an individual has served as an officer of several related corporations, it is necessary to establish the value of his services to *each* corporation. Part of the compensation claimed by one corporation was disallowed where it could not be shown what his services to that company actually were. The officer himself had testified that it was difficult for him to distinguish which particular company he was working for at any given time. (See chapter 5, Arm's Length Transactions, in connection with the Commissioner's authority to reallocate salaries in the case of corporations under common control.)

NOTES

1. Patricia Korenvozs, "Wanted: $50,000-a-Year Men," *Dun's* Review, February 1966, Volume 85, No. 2; page 41.
2. *Commissioner v. LoBue*, 351 U.S. 243 (1956).
3. *Lucas v. Earl*, 281 U.S. 111 (1930).
4. T.D. 5141, 1942-1 CB 34.
5. *Sam Goldstein et al.*, T.C. Memo. 1965-233 (filed August 17, 1965).
6. *ABC Freight Forwarding Corporation v. United States*, D.C., S.D. N.Y., 1968.
7. *Levey v. Helvering*, 68 F.2d 401 (C.A., D.C., 1933).
8. Revenue Ruling 55-713, 1955-2 CB 23.
9. *Indiatlantic, Inc. v. Commissioner*, 216 F.2d 203 (6th Cir., 1954).
10. *George L. Blanton et al.*, 46 T.C. 527 (1966).
11. *Hammond Lead Products, Inc.*, T.C. Memo. 1969-14 (filed January 16, 1969).
12. *First National Bank of Hale Center, Texas v. United States*, D.C., N.D. Texas, 1968.
13. *F. J. Bass, Inc.*, 7 B.T.A. 196 (1927).
14. *Griffin & Company, Inc. et al. v. United States*, 389 F.2d 802 (Ct. Cl., 1968).
15. *Lakewood Manufacturing Co.*, T.C. Memo. 1970-133 (filed May 28, 1970).
16. *Appleton Electric Company*, T.C. Memo. 1967-211 (filed October 27, 1967).
17. *Griswold Rubber Company, Inc.*, T.C. Memo. 1965-33 (filed February 18, 1965).
18. *Wright-Bernet, Inc. v. Commissioner*, 172 F.2d 343 (6th Cir., 1949).
19. *Harolds Club v. Commissioner*, 340 F.2d 861 (9th Cir., 1965).
20. *L. R. Schmaus Co., Inc. et al.*, T.C. Memo. 1967-197 (filed October 11, 1967).
21. *Coca-Cola Bottling Company of Mitchell, South Dakota v. United States*, D.C., S.D., 1958.
22. *W. Braun Co., Inc.*, T.C. Memo. 1967-66 (filed April 5, 1967).
23. *Dr. Pepper Bottling Co., Inc.*, T.C. Memo 1968-13 (filed January 22, 1968).
24. *Herbert G. Hatt et al.*, T.C. Memo. 1969-229 (filed October 28, 1969), *aff'd*, 457 F.2d 499 (7th Cir., 1972).
25. *Ibid.*
26. *Mayson Manufacturing Company v. Commissioner*, 178 F.2d 115 (6th Cir., 1949).
27. *Weiss-Winkler Binding, Inc.*, T.C. Memo. 1967-259 (filed December 28, 1967).
28. T.B.M. 44, 1 CB 220.
29. *First National Bank of Hale Center, Texas v. United States*, D.C., N.D. Texas, 1968.
30. *Riss & Company, Inc. et al.*, T.C. Memo. 1964-190 (filed July 14, 1964).
31. *Coastal Stevedoring Corporation*, T.C. Memo., Docket No. 638 (entered May 12, 1944).
32. *First National Bank of Hale Center, Texas v. United States*, D.C., N.D. Texas, 1968.
33. *Gilles Frozen Custard, Inc. et al.*, T.C. Memo. 1970-73 (filed March 26, 1970).
34. I.R.C. Section 404(a).
35. *Draper & Company*, 5 T.C. 822 (1945).
36. *Northlich, Stolley Inc. v. United States*, 368 F.2d 272 (Ct. Cl., 1966).
37. *W. R. Vermillion Company, Inc. v. United States*, 283 F. Supp. 350 (D.C., W.D. Mo., 1968).
38. *Savoy Brass Manufacturing Co.*, T.C. Memo., Docket No. 20176 (entered April 21, 1950).
39. *Harry Suffrin, Inc.*, T.C. Memo., Docket No. 17203 (entered May 12, 1949).
40. *Hammond Lead Products, Inc.*, T.C. Memo. 1969-14 (filed January 16, 1969).
41. *Craigs Drug Store, Inc.*, T.C. Memo. 1969-208 (filed October 8, 1969).

42. *Herbert G. Hatt et al.*, T.C. Memo. 1969-229 (filed October 28, 1969), *aff'd*, 457 F.2d 499 (7th Cir., 1972).

43. *Doyle Fuel Company et al.*, 53 T.C. 162 (1969).

44. *Lakewood Manufacturing Company*, T.C. Memo. 1970-133 (filed May 28, 1970).

45. *Sports Illustrated*, September 5, 1966, page 15.

46. *Builders Steel Co.*, T.C. Memo., Docket No. 17796 (entered May 7, 1951), *rev'd on another issue*, 179 F.2d 377 (8th Cir., 1950).

47. *Hammond Lead Products, Inc.*, T.C. Memo. 1969-14 (filed January 16, 1969).

48. *The Barton-Gillet Company*, T.C. Memo. 1970-157 (filed June 17, 1970).

49. *Bromley Plating Company*, T.C. Memo. 1958-217 (filed December 31, 1958).

50. *Irby Construction Co. v. United States*, 290 F.2d 824 (Ct. Cl., 1961).

51. *The Barton-Gillet Company*, T.C. Memo. 1970-157 (filed June 17, 1970).

52. *Medical and Professional Services, Inc.*, T.C. Memo. 1965-238 (filed August 31, 1965).

53. *Irby Construction Company v. United States*, 290 F.2d 824 (Ct. Cl., 1961).

54. *Miles Production Company et al.*, T.C. Memo. 1969-274 (filed December 16, 1969).

55. Regulations Section 1.162-8.

56. *United States v. Ragen et al.*, 314 U.S. 513 (1952). *J. L. Norie*, 3 T.C. 676 (1944), *aff'd sub nomine Coast Carton Co. v. Commissioner*, 149 F.2D 739 (9th Cir., 1945).

57. *Leicht v. Commissioner*, 137 F.2d 433 (8th Cir., 1943).

58. *Haberkorn v. United States*, 173 F.2d 587 (6th Cir., 1949).

59. *Vincent E. Oswald et al.*, 49 T.C. 645 (1968).

60. Revenue Procedure 69-6, 1969-1 CB 396.

61. I.R.C. Section 1348.

62. *Madison Silo Company*, T.C. Memo., Docket No. 21480 (entered January 23, 1947).

63. Regulations Section 1.162-7(b)(2).

64. *Harolds Club v. Commissioner*, 340 F.2d 861 (9th Cir., 1965).

65. *The Charles E. Smith & Sons Company et al. v. Commissioner*, 184 F.2d 1011 (6th Cir., 1950).

66. *James J. Glenn et al.*, T.C. Memo. 1970-184 (filed June 30, 1970).

67. *Ibid.*

68. Vartanig G. Vartan in the *New York Times* account of the annual stockholders' meeting of General Aniline & Film. Quoted in *Twenty-Sixth Annual Report of Stockholder Activities at Corporation Meetings During 1965*, New York: Lewis D. and John J. Gilbert, 1966, page 143.

69. *Luckman et al. v. Commissioner*, 418 F.2d 381 (7th Cir., 1969).

70. I.R.C. Section 422(a).

71. Revenue Ruling 69-648, 1969-2 CB 103.

72. *Luckman et al. v. Commissioner*, 418 F.2d 381 (7th Cir., 1969).

73. *Dugan et al. v. United States*, 234 F. Supp. 7 (D.C., S.D. N.Y., 1964).

74. *Nathan Putchat et al.*, 52 T.C. 470 (1969), *aff'd*, 425 F.2d 737 (3d Cir., 1970).

75. I.T. 3795, 1946-1 CB 15.

76. I.R.C. Section 404(a)(5).

77. Regulations Section 1.421-6.

78. *Wanvig, Jr. et al. v. United States*, 295 F. Supp. 882 (D.C., E.D. Wis., 1969).

79. As set forth in I.R.C. Section 401.

80. *United States v. Christine Oil & Gas Company*, 269 F. 458 (D.C., W.D. La., 1920).

81. *C. Florian Zittel*, 12 B.T.A. 675 (1928).

82. *The Hamilton National Bank of Chattanooga*, 29 B.T.A. 63 (1933).

83. *James E. Lewis*, 30 B.T.A. 318 (1934).

84. *C. E. Gullett et al.*, 31 B.T.A. 1067 (1935).

85. Revenue Ruling 60-31, 1960-1 CB 174.

86. Revenue Ruling 69-649, 1969-2 CB 106.
87. Revenue Ruling 69-650, 1969-2 CB 106.
88. Revenue Ruling 70-435, 1970-2 CB 100.
89. Revenue Ruling 60-31, 1960-1 CB 174.
90. I.R.C. Section 79.
91. Revenue Ruling 69-423, 1969-2 CB 12.
92. *Paul L. Frost et al.*, 52 T.C. 89 (1969).
93. Revenue Ruling 64-328, 1964-2 CB 11.
94. As set forth in I.R.C. Section 105.
95. Regulations Section 1.105-5.
96. I.R.C. Section 105(b).
97. Regulations Section 1.105-2.
98. *Bogene, Inc.*, T.C. Memo. 1968-147 (filed July 11, 1968).
99. *Larkin v. Commissioner*, 394 F.2d 494 (1st Cir., 1968).
100. *Samuel Levine*, 50 T.C. 422 (1968).
101. Revenue Ruling 69-491, 1969-2 CB 22.
102. *Hudson Motor Car Co. v. United States*, 3 F. Supp. 834 (Ct. Cl., 1933).
103. *James H. Knowles et al.*, T.C. Memo. 1965-27 (filed February 15, 1965), *aff'd*, 355 F.2d 931 (3d Cir., 1966).
104. T.D. 5507, 1946-1 CB 18.
105. *James M. Hunley et al.*, T.C. Memo. 1966-66 (filed March 30, 1966).
106. *Commissioner v. Fender Sales, Inc. et al.*, 338 F.2d 924 (9th Cir., 1964).
107. Revenue Ruling 67-402, 1967-2 CB 135.
108. Revenue Ruling 62-217, 1962-2 CB 59.
109. I.R.C. Section 83.
110. Revenue Ruling 59-58, 1959-1 CB 17.
111. Revenue Ruling 70-235, 1970-1 CB 193.
112. *United States v. Kaiser*, 363 U.S. 299 (1960).
113. *Godwin et al. v. United States*, D.C., W.D. Tenn., 1964.
114. Revenue Ruling 58-139, 1958-1 CB 14.
115. *Woody v. United States*, 368 F.2d 668 (9th Cir., 1966).
116. Revenue Ruling 70-471, 1970-2 CB 199.
117. I.R.C. Section 119.
118. Regulations Section 1.119-1(b).
119. *M. Caratan et al.*, 52 T.C. 960 (1969).
120. *Commissioner v. Anderson et al.*, 371 F.2d 59 (6th Cir., 1966).
121. *See Arthur Benaglia*, 36 B.T.A. 838 (1937).
122. *Carlton R. Mabley, Jr. et al.*, T.C. Memo. 1965-323 (filed December 27, 1965).
123. I.R.C. Section 82.
124. Revenue Ruling 69-559, 1969-2 CB 25.
125. *Peters v. Smith*, 221 F.2d 721 (3d Cir., 1955).
126. *Bogardus v. Commissioner*, 302 U.S. 34 (1937).
127. *Robertson v. United States*, 343 U.S. 711 (1959).
128. *Commissioner v. LoBue*, 351 U.S. 243 (1956).
129. *Commissioner v. Duberstein et al.*, 363 U.S. 278 (1960).
130. *Schleyer v. United States*, D.C., E.D. Mo., 1963.
131. *Bounds v. United States*, 262 F.2d 876 (4th Cir., 1958).
132. *Martin Kunz, Sr. Estate v. Commissioner*, 300 F.2d 849 (6th Cir., 1962).
133. *Gaugler v. United States*, 312 F.2d 681 (2d Cir., 1963).
134. *Cronheim v. Commissioner*, 323 F.2d 706 (8th Cir., 1963).
135. *Smith v. Commissioner*, 305 F.2d 778 (3d Cir., 1962).
136. *Simpson v. United States*, 261 F.2d 497 (7th Cir., 1958).
137. *Spear et al. v. Vinal*, 240 F. Supp. 33 (D.C., Neb., 1965).

138. *W. P. Brown & Sons Lumber Company*, 26 B.T.A. 1192 (1932).

139. Revenue Ruling 69-331 1969-1 CB 87.

140. *See Lincoln Electric Company*, 54 T.C. 926 (1970).

141. *D. K. McColl*, B.T.A. Memo., Docket No. 95834 (entered January 11, 1941).

142. I.R.C. Section 267(a)(2).

CHAPTER 9

Profit-Sharing Plans

Advantages

Qualified profit-sharing plans offer important tax benefits. They are not taxable to the employee for whom contributions are made at the time they are made, irrespective of whether he has vested or forfeitable rights to the contributions. An employee is taxable when he receives a distribution from the fund, but there are a number of provisions that mitigate the burden at that time. Income earned by the trust that administers most such plans can accumulate tax-free.[1]

Under certain circumstances to be detailed later in this chapter employer contributions under the plan through 1969 may be entitled to long-term capital gain treatment by the recipient employee or his beneficiary or, even if this does not apply, the recipient may be benefitted by a special seven-year averaging formula.[2] Where distributions are made in the form of the employer corporation's securities, tax on the unrealized appreciation may be deferred until the securities are disposed of by the employee.[3] The $5000 exclusion from gross income for death benefits includes payments from a qualified profit-sharing plan.[4] Employer contributions that are paid to beneficiaries (other than the executor) in the form of annuities after the employee's death may be exempted from the Federal tax on his estate.[5] Certain annuities may be transferred to an employee's beneficiaries without Federal gift tax liability.[6]

Apart from their tax aspects, profit-sharing plans may help in the recruitment and retention of employees. Lower merit ratings for state unemployment insurance purposes may result, and employees may be given an incentive to work more effectively and to cut down on unnecessary costs.

A major advantage to the employer is that he gets an immediate tax deduction for amounts paid into the profit-sharing fund, within limits set forth later in this chapter, even though the money does not go to those employees who thereupon decide to work elsewhere.

What a Profit-Sharing Plan Is

A *profit-sharing plan* is a plan established and maintained by an employer to provide for his employees' (or their beneficiaries') participation in his profits to a stated degree. The plan must provide a definite formula for allocating the distributions made to the plan among the participants and for distributing the funds accumulated under the plan after a fixed number of years, upon the attainment of a stated age, or upon the occurrence of some event (such as layoff, illness, disability, retirement, death, or severance of employment). A formula for allocating the contributions among the participants is definite if it provides for example, for an allocation in proportion to the basic compensation of each participant. A plan (whether or not it contains a definite predetermined formula for ascertaining the profits to be shared with the employees) does not qualify for this purpose if contributions are made at such times or in such amounts that the plan in operation discriminates in favor of officers, shareholders, persons whose principal duties consist in supervising the work of other employees, or highly compensated employees.[7]

Qualified Plans

While any plan to share profits is a profit-sharing plan, the tax advantages discussed in this chapter inhere to qualified profit-sharing plans; that is, those which qualify by conforming to the Internal Revenue Code requirements.

The plan must be based upon employer profits.[8] There is no requirement as to how the term "profits" is defined. Thus, the yardstick may be profits per the books, per the tax returns, per an accountant's report, or profits according to any agreed upon method for the inclusion or exclusion of certain items.

The plan must be in the form of a definite written program which is communicated to the employees and approved by the Service.[9]

A qualified plan must be a funded plan. Contributions can be made to a trust or under a custodial account to pay premiums on insurance contracts, to pay for the purchase of face-amount certificates, to buy retirement bonds, or to accumulate funds in some other manner to pay to employees or their beneficiaries under the conditions of eligibility.

Employer contributions to or under a recognized funding medium may, under appropriate circumstances, be delayed pursuant to an established funding method.[10]

A profit-sharing plan will be considered qualified if, by the 15th day of the third month following the close of the taxable year in which the plan has been put into effect, it conforms to the statutory requirements.[11] It is not necessary that there be a plan and trust instrument fully reduced to writing and executed as such within the taxable year in order for it to qualify for the deduction claimed. Where a valid trust comes into existence on or before the last day of the taxpayer's fiscal year, the contributions to that trust are deductible in that year if the formal requirements of the tax law are met within the next two months and 15 days.[12]

A plan may provide that no participant has any vested right in any asset of the trust fund prior to the approval of the plan by the Internal Revenue Service.[13]

A domestic corporation may include in its qualified plan, and make contributions on behalf of, employees of a foreign subsidiary who are citizens of the United States and covered by Social Security benefits in the United States.[14] Similarly, a domestic parent corporation may include in its qualified plan employees of a domestic subsidiary who are citizens of the United States and are engaged in foreign service. Contributions by others, however, are not precluded.[15]

A profit-sharing plan may cover the employees of several employers. In the case of a plan of an affiliated group, the companies having profits may make up a contribution for a member suffering losses.[16] A single trust or plan may be used by a group of corporations, regardless of the degree of affiliation, but each corporation within the group must satisfy the requirements for qualification and deduction.[17] Where, under specified conditions, separate qualified and exempt trusts pool their funds in a group trust created to provide diversification of investments, the group trust may also be exempt, and the status for exemption of the separate trusts will not be adversely affected.[18]

Discrimination

In a qualified plan, there may be no discrimination in favor of officers, stockholders who own ten percent or more of the shares, supervising employees, or highly compensated employees.[19]

The term "highly compensated" is relative; this characterization depends upon the facts and circumstances of each case. Thus for example, while persons earning $9000 a year might not be deemed "highly compensated," they may be so regarded by persons earning $6000. Thus, where a plan covered persons whose average salary was $9000, but the salary of persons not covered was an average of $6000, the plan was held to be discriminatory.[20] But larger employer contributions on the basis of higher salaries do not by themselves make a plan discriminatory.[21] However, a plan is discriminatory if contributions and benefits provided thereunder for rank-and-file employees are based solely upon compensation, whereas the contributions and benefits for certain officer-employees are based upon compensation plus credits made to their accounts under an unfunded arrangement to pay them at a later date for services being currently rendered.[22] Employer contributions on behalf of officers may not be based upon imputed compensation (such as non-cash fringe benefits) if such coverage is not available to other employees.[23]

Whether a person is a "supervisory employee" and thus one in whose favor discrimination cannot exist is ordinarily a question of fact, dependent upon whether his principal duties consist of supervising the work of other employees.[24]

A plan which is limited to salaried employees of a corporation is not for this reason discriminatory.[25] But where an employer of 20 persons limited its plan to salaried or clerical workers aged 30 or older who had at least six months of service and only two persons met the eligibility requirements (17 persons were paid at an hourly rate), and these two were of the type in whose favor there can be no discrimination, the plan was deemed discriminatory.[26] So was another plan limited to full-time salaried employees, of which, out of 60 employees, there were only six, five of whom were officer-shareholders earning $26,000 per annum.[27]

Variations in contributions or benefits may be provided as long as the plan, viewed as a whole for the benefit of employees with all of its attendant circumstances, does not discriminate in favor of officers, etc. In some cases, benefits under a profit-sharing plan may vary by reasons of a contribution formula which takes into account years of service.[28]

There is no discrimination in a plan where only the profits in excess of a plainly stated formula are to be shared with the employees—and only with those employees whose efforts made possible such excess profits.[29] However, a plan was held to have been discriminatory where the distribution of benefits was left solely to the corporation's discretion.[30] Where an employee's participation in a plan depends upon his making contributions which are so large as to be burdensome to low-income employees, the plan is discriminatory. As a general rule, employee contributions of six percent of compensation or less are not regarded as burdensome.[31]

The provisions against discrimination are applied to *de facto* discrimination as well as to discrimination written into the plan.[32] Usually, the former occurs in a plan which apparently covers all employees who have worked for a specified length of time, but where rank-and-file employees are in fact not covered because they are not employed for a long enough time.

A profit-sharing plan was held to be discriminatory even though, in addition to officers and other highly compensated employees, it covered one employee whose compensation was commensurate with that of employees paid at an hourly rate who were excluded from the plan. The inclusion of this one employee did not save the plan from being characterized as discriminatory.[33] A little window dressing may not be enough.

In profit-sharing plans (but not in pension plans), provision may be made for accelerated distribution because of "hardship," provided that this term is defined and the rules are uniformly and consistently applied to all employees in similar circumstances and provided further that the distribution does not exceed the employee's vested interest.[34]

Rule of 70 and 80 Percent Coverage

A qualified employee benefit plan (such as a profit-sharing plan) will not be regarded as discriminatory because of exclusions if: (1) 70 percent or more of the remaining employees are covered *or* (2) 70 percent or more of the remaining employees are eligible to participate in the plan *and* 80 percent or more of these actually decide to participate in the plan where the choice is theirs.[35]

Permissible (nondiscriminatory) exclusions are for:

(1) persons who have not worked a sufficiently long period of time, which may not exceed five years;

(2) persons who have not worked a sufficiently long work week, which may not be more than 20 hours; and

(3) persons who have not worked for a sufficiently long period of employment, which may not be more than five months in the calendar year.[36]

The coverage requirements must be met on at least one day in each quarter of the calendar year.[37]

In lieu of meeting the percentage requirements, an employer may set up a classification of employees which, if found by the Internal Revenue Service not to discriminate in favor of officers, shareholders, etc., will satisfy the requirements that the plan not be discriminatory. Plans may qualify which are limited to employees who are within a prescribed age group, who have been employed for a stated number of years, who have been employed in designated departments, or are in other classifications, provided that the effect of covering only these employees does not amount to discrimination where discrimination is prohibited.[38]

An employee benefit plan for a Subchapter S corporation (where election has been made to be taxed only at the shareholder level) may be approved even though only shareholder-employees are eligible for coverage.[39]

In the case of a plan which provides contributions or benefits for an owner-employee who owns more than ten percent of the business, the trust can be qualified only if the plan provides benefits for each employee who has been employed for three years or more.[40]

No Requirement for Fixed Formula

No fixed formula is required of a qualified profit-sharing plan. But the employer's contributions must be both "substantial" and "recurring." [41] However, a plan will not lose qualification even though no payments are made into the fund for a period of years where there is a fixed formula that did not become operative during these years inasmuch as income was too small.[42]

A definite formula may contain a variable factor if the value of this factor cannot vary at the discretion of the employer. If the employer can vary the percentage of profits to be contributed from year to year at his pleasure, the formula is not definite and the plan will not qualify.[43]

A profit-sharing plan will not fail to qualify merely because it provides that contributions are to be made from current profits and accumulated earned surplus determined without regard to whether they are current or accumulated earnings and profits for dividend purposes.[44]

Past Service Credit

Many pension plans have past service credits as will be seen in the next chapter, but this is rather unusual for profit-sharing plans. However, credit for years of service may be given if a prohibited discrimination does not result. For example, credit for service performed after the adoption of the plan may be given.[45] So, if there is no discrimination, past service years may be taken into account in a plan's distribution formula.[46]

Distribution Formula

Although a profit-sharing plan need not have a fixed formula for employer contributions, the plan must have a formula for allocating distributions to the participants who qualify.[47]

To be eligible for qualification, a deferred profit-sharing plan must provide a definite predetermined formula for allocation of contributions among the participants and for distribution of the accumulated funds after a fixed number of years, the attainment of a stated age, or upon the occurrence of some event (such as severance of employment, illness, disability, etc.). The term "fixed number of years" is considered to mean at least two years.[48]

Distribution may be in accordance with the number of *units* that a participant accumulates. An employee's share of the employer's contribution may be defined as the proportion of the contribution arrived at by dividing his total units into the aggregate of the units assigned to all of the employees. In one case, the court rejected as discriminatory a formula wherein no employee was entitled to share in the plan until after completion of three years of service. At the end of three years, the employee was given one point for the three years' service; upon the completion of three years of continuous service beyond the eligibility date, one additional point was given; and upon completion of ten years of continuous service beyond the eligibility date, three more points were given. In addition to the points awarded for years of service, points also were assigned for training and experience.[49]

In the case of one company, compensation was multiplied by years of service to arrive at a weighted compensation. Allocations were made to the weighted compensation for all participants. Inasmuch as the more highly compensated employees had the greater number of years of service, the multiplication factor resulted in proportionately higher allocations to these employees. This plan was ruled to be discriminatory.[50]

Vesting

To be eligible for qualification, an employee benefit plan must contain an appropriate provision for the granting of fully vested rights to participants upon discontinuance of contributions by the employer—this is similar to a case in which actual termination takes place.[51] *Vesting* is an important benefit in any plan and one which must be considered in deciding whether a plan is discriminatory as to benefits.[52]

There is no requirement for immediate vesting, except in the case of one who is self-employed. However, vesting must take place by the time an individual ceases employment. It may take place, as provided by the plan, at any intermediate point.

Permanency of the Plan

A qualified plan is a permanent and continuing program. A plan which is set up during years of high tax rates and abandoned when profits drop does not satisfy this requirement.[53]

Inasmuch as a corporation with declining profits is not likely to be disturbed about the "fixed-charge" aspect of the plan in poor years in the case of a profit-sharing plan, the subject will be considered with reference to pension plans in chapter 10.

Prototype Plans

Instead of a corporation's drafting its own profit-sharing plan and then submitting it to the Internal Revenue Service for approval, that corporation may utilize a master or prototype plan prepared by a trade association, professional society, insurance company, or the like, of which the Service already has approved.[54]

The following forms may be used for this purpose:

Form 4461, "Sponsor Application. Approval of Master or Prototype Plan." To be filed by trade or professional associations, banks, insurance companies, or regulated investment companies.

Form 4462, "Employer Application. Determination as to Qualification of Pension, Annuity, or Profit-sharing Plan and Trust."

Form 3672 must be used for plans covering self-employed persons.

Permissible Beneficiaries

The plan may restrict an employee's beneficiaries to his estate, his dependents, or persons who are the natural objects of his bounty.[55]

Implementing Trust

While it is not essential that a qualified deferred profit-sharing plan have an implementing trust, a trust is customarily used. Sometimes, the employer's contributions go directly to a third party, as in the case of an insured plan.

The trust must be created exclusively for the benefit of the employees or their beneficiaries and must meet further requirements as to source of contributions, nondiversion of funds, nondiscrimination in contributions or bene-fits, nonforfeitable rights upon termination, and application of any forfeitures.[56]

A trust forming part of a qualified employee benefit plan is normally exempt from federal income tax. But this exempt status may be lost if the trust engages in any "prohibited transactions," which, in general, are less than arm's length dealings with the employer (such as lending money without adequate security).[57]

A qualified trust may contain a spendthrift clause putting trust funds beyond the reach of a participant's creditors and preventing a sale, transfer, or assignment of a participant's interest. Such a prohibition may, however, be limited so as not to be applicable to indebtedness to the employer. The mere fact that the employer is the only one who has that right does not change the result.[58]

Custodial Account

A custodial account is treated as a qualified trust and is subject to the requirements that apply to trusts.[59]

Transfers to the Trust

A corporation's gain on its transfer of securities to the trust is a sale or exchange and as such subject to Federal income tax.[60] But losses on the transfer are not recognized for tax purposes under Section 267 of the Internal Revenue Code.[61]

Loss of Qualification

An approved plan will lose its qualification, despite a favorable letter from the Internal Revenue Service, if there has been a drastic change in the facts which had been the basis for the granting of qualification.[62] Administration and operation of the plan in a discriminatory way or otherwise in violation of the law will result in disqualification.

A plan will not be disqualified merely because, in the normal course of the employer's business, the number of participants is reduced to one.[63] But a one-employee plan in which the beneficiary falls within one of the four categories in whose favor the plan may not discriminate may be a wholly different matter.[64]

Employee benefit plans may be amended without voiding a previously issued favorable determination letter if the amendment is solely for the purpose of conforming to changes in other legislation.[65]

What Happens upon Termination of the Plan?

A qualified plan must expressly provide that upon its termination or complete discontinuance of contributions thereunder, the rights of each employee to benefits accrued to the date of such termination or discontinuance to the extent then funded or the rights of each employee to the amounts credited to his account at that time are nonforfeitable.[66] Provision must also be made for the allocation of any previously unallocated funds to participating employees upon termination of the plan or complete discontinuance of contributions. Any provision for allocation is acceptable if it specifies the method to be used and does not discriminate in favor of highly compensated or otherwise favored employees.[67]

The moneys contributed may not under any circumstances revert to the employer.[68] Specifically, it must be impossible at any time prior to the satisfaction of all liabilities with respect to employees and their beneficiaries under the plan for any part of the corpus or income to be used for or diverted to other purposes.

The plan should provide for what will happen in the case of various contingencies. One such plan, for example, provided that in the event of a merger, the successor corporation could either adopt the plan as its own or, by inaction, allow it to lapse after 90 days.[69] It may be provided that the plan or trust will terminate automatically if the corporation is dissolved or merged into or with another corporation which does not assume the obligations of the plan.[70]

Time of Deduction

An employer is entitled to a tax deduction for proper contributions into the employee benefit plan by the filing date of the Federal income tax return for that year. No deduction is allowed for a belated payment unless an extension of time for filing the income tax return has been obtained.[71]

A deduction for a contribution to the plan cannot be taken before the year in which the plan was created. There is a distinction between a resolution by the directors to create a plan and the actual establishment of an approved plan.[72] No deduction was allowed for amounts set aside for an employee benefit plan when the plan was not adopted until after the close of the taxable year.[73]

Where a corporation delivers its own demand notes to the trustee of its employee benefit plan, payment is deemed to have been made *if* it is proven that the corporation is solvent and the note is worth its face amount at the time of delivery.[74] Timely payment was deemed to have been made into a profit-sharing plan when delivery was made by a solvent corporation of a secured, interest-bearing, negotiable note payable on or before a certain date and with a fair market value at all times equal to its face value.[75]

A contribution to an employee benefit plan may be made by a conveyance of real estate.[76]

Book entries are not enough to constitute payment. An accrual-basis taxpayer must deliver something of value to the plan's trustee. The accrual of an obligation on a corporation's books is not enough.[77]

Amount of Deduction

The employer is entitled to an income tax deduction for contributions under the profit-sharing plan not in excess of 15 percent of the compensation of persons covered by the plan.[78] Amounts paid into the fund in excess of that figure may be carried forward without limitation to subsequent years to be aggregated with contributions of those years for the 15 percent purpose at that time.[79] But no carry-over of contributions to a qualified profit-sharing plan is permitted when such contributions are disallowed by virtue of an employee's total compensation being unreasonable.[80]

Contributions by Subchapter S corporations to qualified plans on behalf of shareholder-employees are limited to ten percent of each employee's salary or $2500, whichever is smaller. For this purpose, a shareholder-employee is an officer or other employee who at any time during the taxable year owns more than five percent of the shares of the corporation's stock, including stock actually owned by his spouse, parents, children, and grandchildren.[81]

A shareholder-employee must include in his gross income the contributions made by the corporation under a qualified plan to the extent the contributions exceed ten percent of his salary or $2500, whichever is smaller. This amount is treated as his contribution to the plan. At the time of the employee's retirement or other separation from employment entitling him to receive benefits under the plan, his contribution will be recovered tax-free according to the rules for the tax treatment of annuities.[82]

Lump-Sum Distributions

Prior to the Tax Reform Act of 1969, amounts received by an individual as a lump-sum distribution from a qualified employee benefit plan in one of his taxable years by reason of his separation from employment were treated as long-term capital gain. That provision has been changed, but not retroactively. The employee still is entitled to long-term capital gain treatment, but only to the extent of the employer's contributions under the plan through December 31, 1969.[83] This includes any part of the payment which consists of earnings or appreciation in the fund which is based upon the employer's contributions.[84]

Any portion of a lump-sum payment which represents employer contributions after 1969 is ordinary income to the employee. But his tax liability on this ordinary income is limited by a special seven-year averaging rule (five years in the case of the self-employed) to seven times the increase in tax which would result from including one-seventh of the ordinary income portion of the net lump-sum distribution in gross income in the taxable year in which the total distribution is received. This special averaging method is not available to an employee unless: (1) he has been a participant in the plan for at least five years before the taxable year in which the lump-sum distribution is made and is at least $59\frac{1}{2}$ years old or (2) the payment is made because of his death or disability.[85]

Even if earlier distributions had been made, a final payment still may be characterized as a lump-sum payment.[86]

If an employee receives a lump-sum payment and subsequently goes back to work for the same corporation, the preferential tax treatment afforded the lump-sum payment will not be disturbed if it can be proven that the employee had intended the original "separation" to be permanent.[87]

The Internal Revenue Service has ruled that an employee is considered to have separated from the service of his employer in the following situations:

(1) Corporation A in a tax-free reorganization transfers for stock all of its assets and liabilities to Corporation B, which in turn transfers the assets and liabilities to its wholly-owned subsidiary, Corporation C, the taxpayer becoming an employee of Corporation C.[88]

(2) Corporation A sells all of its stock for cash to Corporation B, which completely liquidates Corporation A and takes over A's assets.[89]

(3) Corporation A, incident to complete liquidation, sells all of its assets to Corporation B.[90]

(4) Corporation A, incident to complete liquidation, sells all of the assets used in carrying on one of its divisions to unrelated Corporation B, the division employees going to work for Corporation B.[91]

(5) Corporation A, incident to liquidation and dissolution, sells all of its assets to a partnership composed of two former stockholder-employees.[92]

(6) Corporation A, incident to a tax-free merger, sells all of its assets to unrelated Corporation B.[93]

A qualified profit-sharing plan may *require* mandatory lump-sum distributions.[94]

Accumulated Earnings Tax

It has been held that the requirements of a profit-sharing plan constituted a valid reason for nonpayment of dividends so that the accumulated earnings tax was not assessed.[95]

Unreasonable Compensation

Where an employee's total compensation for a taxable year is held to be unreasonable or excessive, contributions to a qualified profit-sharing plan will be affected. Thus, for the purpose of determining the allowable deduction for employee benefit expenses, the contribution paid must be adjusted for any amount that has been disallowed. Where the plan requires or permits reallocation of the disallowed contribution among the employees covered by the plan and the reallocation when made does not cause the contributions made on behalf of the other employees to exceed the allowable amount, the employer would be able to deduct the amount of the reallocated contributions in the taxable year in which his contribution was paid to the trust.[96]

Gross Estate

A decedent's gross estate does not include amounts receivable by a beneficiary (except his executor) under a qualified profit-sharing plan to the extent these payments are attributable to employer contributions or any other amounts not provided by the decedent himself.[97]

Gift Tax

Federal gift tax does not apply to the value of certain annuities for the benefit of the employees' surviving beneficiaries. Under the general rule, where an employee has an unqualified right to an annuity, but takes a lesser annuity with the provision that upon his death a survivorship annuity or other payment will be given to his designated beneficiary, the employee will be deemed to have made a gift to the beneficiary when he gives up his right to the full payment.[98] But gift tax does not apply to that portion of the value of the annuities or other payments which otherwise would be considered gifts by the employees to their beneficiaries. This refers only to qualified plans.[99]

NOTES

1. *Bernard McMenamy, Contractor, Inc. et al.*, 54 T.C. 1057 (1970), *aff'd*, 442 F.2d 359 (8th Cir., 1971).
2. I.R.C. Section 402(a)(5).
3. I.R.C Section 402(a)(2).
4. I.R.C. Section 101(b)(2)(i).
5. I.R.C. Section 2039(c).
6. I.R.C. Section 2517(b).
7. Regulations Section 1.401-1(b)(1)(ii).
8. Revenue Ruling 70-182, 1970-1 CB 88.
9. Regulations Section 1.401-1(a)(2).
10. Revenue Ruling 65-178, 1965-2 CB 94.
11. I.R.C. Section 401(b).
12. *Hill York Corporation et al. v. United States*, D.C., S.D. Fla., 1964.
13. *Meldrum & Fewsmith, Inc.*, 20 T.C. 790 (1953).
14. I.R.C. Section 406.
15. I.R.C. Section 407.
16. I.R.C. Section 404(a)(3)(B).
17. Revenue Ruling 69-250, 1969-1 CB 116.
18. Revenue Ruling 56-267, 1956-1 CB 206.
19. I.R.C. Section 401(a)(3)(B).
20. *Commissioner v. Pepsi-Cola Niagara Bottling Corporation*, 399 F.2d 390 (2d Cir., 1968).
21. *Betty C. Steekvis*, T.C. Memo., Docket No. 20316 (entered January 25, 1951).
22. Revenue Ruling 68-454, 1968-2 CB 164.
23. Revenue Ruling 62-206, 1962-2 CB 129.
24. *Marjorie F. Birnie et al.*, T.C. Memo., Docket Nos. 23764-5 (entered July 31, 1953).
25. I.R.C. Section 401(a)(5).

26. Revenue Ruling 66-13, 1966-1 CB 73.
27. Revenue Ruling 66-14, 1966-1 CB 75.
28. I.T. 3685, 1944 CB 324.
29. *Ryan School Retirement Trust*, 24 T.C. 127 (1955).
30. *Bank of Sheridan et al. v. United States*, D.C., Mont., 1963.
31. Revenue Ruling 57-163, 1957-1 CB 128.
32. Regulations Section 1.401-1(b)(3).
33. *Peter Mitchell Corp.*, T.C. Memo. 1968-209 (filed September 23, 1968).
34. Revenue Ruling 65-178, 1965-2 CB 94.
35. I.R.C. Section 401(a)(3).
36. I.R.C. Section 401(a)(3)(A).
37. I.R.C. Section 401(a)(6).
38. Revenue Ruling 65-178, 1965-2 CB 94.
39. Revenue Ruling 66-218, 1966-2 CB 120.
40. I.R.C. Section 401(d)(3).
41. Regulations Section 1.401-1(b)(2).
42. *Commissioner v. Sherwood Swan and Company, Ltd. et al.*, 352 F.2d 306 (9th Cir., 1965).
43. Revenue Ruling 68-115, 1968-1 CB 166.
44. Revenue Ruling 66-174, 1966-1 CB 81.
45. *Bernard McMenamy, Contractor, Inc.*, 54 T.C. 1057 (1970), *aff'd*, 442 F.2d 359 (8th Cir., 1971).
46. I.T. 3685, 1944 CB 324.
47. Regulations Section 1.401-1(b)(1)(ii).
48. Revenue Ruling 54-231, 1954-1 CB 150.
49. *Auner et al. v. United States*, 440 F.2d 516 (7th Cir., 1971).
50. I.T. 3686, 1944 CB 326.
51. Revenue Ruling 55-186, 1955-1 CB 39.
52. *Hall v. United States*, 398 F.2d 383 (8th Cir., 1968).
53. Revenue Ruling 65-178, 1965-2 CB 94.
54. Revenue Procedure 68-45, 1968-2 CB 957.
55. Revenue Ruling 54-398, 1954-2 CB 239.
56. Revenue Ruling 65-178, 1965-2 CB 94.
57. I.R.C. Sections 502 and 503.
58. Revenue Ruling 56-432, 1956-2 CB 284.
59. Revenue Ruling 65-178, 1965-2 CB 94. [A custodial account is defined in I.R.C. Section 401(f).]
60. Revenue Ruling 61-163, 1961-2 CB 58.
61. *Dillard Paper Company v. Commissioner*, 341 F.2d 897 (4th Cir., 1965). The statutory authority is I.R.C. Section 267.
62. *Harold D. Greenwald et al.*, 44 T.C. 137 (1965), *aff'd on this issue*, 366 F.2d 538 (2d Cir., 1966).
63. *Marjorie F. Birnie et al.*, T.C. Memo., Docket Nos. 23674-5 (entered July 31, 1953).
64. Revenue Ruling 55-81, 1955-1 CB 392.
65. Revenue Procedure 67-26, 1967-1 CB 629.
66. Regulations Section 1.401-6(a)(1).
67. Revenue Ruling 65-178, 1965-2 CB 94.
68. I.R.C. Section 401(a)(2).
69. *Rybacki et al. v. Conley*, 340 F.2d 944 (2d Cir., 1965).
70. *E. N. Funkhouser et al.*, 40 T.C. 178 (1965).
71. Revenue Ruling 56-674, 1956-2 CB 293.
72. *C. Arthur Weaver Company*, T.C. Memo. 1963-279 (filed October 10, 1963).
73. *Arlington Realty Company, Incorporated*, T.C. Memo. 1962-125 (filed May 24, 1962).
74. *Sachs v. Commissioner*, 208 F.2d 313 (3d Cir., 1953).

75. *Steele Wholesale Builders Supply Company et al. v. United States*, 222 F. Supp. 82 (D.C., N.D. Texas, 1963).

76. *Colorado National Bank of Denver*, 30 T.C. 933 (1958).

77. *F. & D. Rentals, Inc.*, 44 T.C. 335 (1965), *aff'd*, 365 F.2d 34 (7th Cir., 1966).

78. I.R.C. Section 404(a)(3)(A).

79. I.R.C. Section 404(a)(1)(D).

80. Revenue Ruling 67-341, 1967-2 CB 156.

81. I.R.C. Section 1379(b)(1).

82. I.R.C. Section 1379(b)(2).

83. I.R.C. Section 402(a)(5).

84. I.R.C. Section 403(a)(2).

85. I.R.C. Section 72(n).

86. Revenue Ruling 69-495, 1969-2 CB 100.

87. *Barrus et al. v. Commissioner*, D.C., E.D. N.C., 1969.

88. Revenue Ruling 58-94, 1958-1 CB 194.

89. Revenue Ruling 58-95, 1958-1 CB 197.

90. Revenue Ruling 58-96, 1958-1 CB 200.

91. Revenue Ruling 58-97, 1958-1 CB 201.

92. Revenue Ruling 58-98, 1958-1 CB 202.

93. Revenue Ruling 58-383, 1958-2 CB 149.

94. Revenue Ruling 62-195, 1962-2 CB 125.

95. *Bremerton Sun Publishing Company*, 44 T.C. 566 (1965).

96. Revenue Ruling 67-341, 1967-2 CB 156.

97. I.R.C. Section 2039.

98. I.R.C. Section 2511.

99. Regulations Section 25.2517-1.

CHAPTER 10

Pension Plans

Nature of a Pension Plan

This chapter deals principally with the tax aspects of pension plans. For this purpose, the term *pension* is defined in the Internal Revenue Code and in the Treasury Regulations. It is a plan established and maintained by an employer primarily to provide for the systematic payment of definitely determinable benefits to his employees over a period of years, usually for life, after retirement. Retirement benefits generally are measured by and based on such factors as years of service and amount of compensation received by the employees. The determination of the amount of retirement benefits and the contributions to provide such benefits are not dependent upon profits. Benefits are not definitely determinable if funds arising from forfeiture on termination or other reasons may be used to provide increased benefits for the remaining participants.

A plan designed to provide benefits for employees or their beneficiaries to be paid upon retirement or over a period of years after retirement will be considered a pension plan if the employer's contributions under the plan can be determined actuarially on the basis of definitely determinable benefits or, as in the case of money purchase pension plans, if such contributions are fixed without being geared to profits. A pension plan may provide for the payment of a pension due to disability and also for the payment of incidental death benefits through insurance or otherwise. But a plan is not regarded as a pension plan for tax purposes if it provides for the payment of benefits not customarily included in a pension plan (such as layoff benefits, benefits for sickness, accident, hospitalization, or medical expenses for retired employees, their spouses, and their dependents).[1] Such benefits are allowed only where they are subordinate to the retirement benefits provided by the pension plan.[2]

A pension plan which provides benefits that vary with the increase or decrease in the market value of the assets from which the benefits are payable or which vary with the fluctuations of a specified and generally recognized cost of living index will be recognized as a plan providing for "definitely determinable" benefits.[3] Such a plan is known as a *variable annuity.*

In general, the Federal income tax aspects of a pension plan are the same as those of a deferred profit-sharing plan (as discussed in the preceding chapter 9) although the amounts of contribution allowable to the employer may vary between the two.

Comparison of Profit-Sharing and Pension Plans

Here, in tabular form, are the salient tax and non-tax characteristics of each type of plan.

Factor	Deferred Profit-sharing Plan	Pension Plan
1. Dependency upon corporation's prosperity.	Direct	Indirect. But if company cannot afford to continue the plan in the long run, the employees will lose out.
2. Cost.	Up to 15 percent of compensation of covered employees.	Up to five percent of compensation or actuarial cost of funding the plan.
3. Is there a fixed charge upon employer?	No.	Yes.
4. Past service credit.	Customarily none. But "units" could be added for past service.	Readily available.
5. Amount of benefits.	Indeterminable.	Definitely determinable.
6. Use of forfeitures.	Available for the benefit of remaining employees.	Available only to reduce employer's cost.
7. Incentive to employees to work hard and to cut costs.	Direct.	Extremely indirect. (But see commentary under 1.)
8. Age group to which plan generally is most attractive.	Younger employees.	Older employees.
9. Employee reaction.	Employees are apt to become dissatisfied with and critical of management if profits drop.	Indirect.
10. Union reaction.	Generally unfavorable.	Favorable. Often the subject of collective bargaining.
11. Possibility of manipulation by officers.	Profits could be "increased" by executives near retirement. This could yield a higher price for company stock that is surrendered.	Inapplicable.
12. May mandatory lump-sum distribution be provided?	Yes.	No.

Basic Requirements of Qualified Pension Plans

Tax-preferred treatment requires that the plan be *qualified* (approved) by the Internal Revenue Service, that there be no discrimination in favor of officers or other designated parties, that allowable deductions be limited to stipulated percentages of the compensation of persons covered by the plan (or actuarial cost determination in the case of a pension plan), and that the employer contributions not be returnable.

Under appropriate circumstances, there may be tax-favored treatment for lump-sum distributions in one of an employee's taxable years by reason of his separation from the company. The employer gets an immediate tax deduction for his contributions within the framework of the Code although the employee does not receive them until he fulfills the conditions of the plan so that the employer retains an economic hold over him. The employee customarily is taxed when he receives his money, which is, as a rule, after he has retired and hence is in a lower tax bracket. The trusts which administer most such plans have tax-exempt accumulations of income.

Discrimination

Tests applicable in determining whether discrimination exists in the case of pension plans are different from those taken into account in deferred profit-sharing plans. The former emphasize scrutiny of benefits; the latter, scrutiny of contributions.[4]

Pension plans may contain provisions for early retirement because of disability, provided that the term "disability" is defined and the rules with respect thereto are uniformly and consistently applied to all employees in similar circumstances.[5]

If a corporation has a profit-sharing plan covering certain employees and a pension plan covering others, the two plans may be viewed as a unit in determining whether sufficient employees are covered so as to avoid discrimination. But even if the plans meet this test collectively, there still may be discrimination because of other phases of the plans that cannot be compared—such as percentages of salary represented by employer contributions, benefits, vesting provisions, borrowing rights, benefits for employment after age 65, disability rights, death benefits, and the like.[6]

Where a corporation has both a profit-sharing and a pension plan, each covering different employees, it is often difficult to compare the two plans to ascertain whether there is discrimination. But the following situation and Internal Revenue Service ruling shows how it can be done: On the same day, a corporation established two plans. One was a pension plan for the benefit of its hourly-paid union employees pursuant to a collective bargaining agreement. The maximum annual benefit was a life annuity of $100 per year of service, payable at normal retirement age 65. The company contributed three percent of each participant's compensation. The other plan provided for contributions out of profits in amounts to be determined annually by the board of directors. It was held that the pension plan in itself was entitled to qualification. But the profit-sharing plan, standing alone, did not meet the requirements for qualification as only two 50 percent stockholders were covered. It therefore was necessary to determine whether the two plans could be considered as a single plan for qualification purposes. And the answer was negative. During the three years the plan had been in operation, contributions on behalf of the pension plan participants amounted to three percent of compensation, while contributions were 15 percent in the case of the profit-sharing plan. So there was discrimination in *contributions*. Under the pension plan, the maximum benefit worked out to one percent of contributions; under the profit-sharing plan, each participant's benefit worked out to figures ranging from three percent of compensation in one year to 8.7 percent two years later. So there was discrimination in *benefits*. The profit-sharing plan could not be qualified.[7]

A corporation may have two or more pension plans, neither (or none) of which is in itself discriminatory. If all of these plans taken as a whole result in an overall arrangement which is not discriminatory, the advantages of Internal Revenue Service qualification will be available to each plan.[8]

Contributory Plans

A qualified pension plan may be *contributory*. Employees may be required to contribute specified amounts or percentages of their salaries into the fund. This, of course, will mean that greater ultimate benefits may be anticipated. A contributory plan is eligible for qualification unless the contribution requirements are so large as to be burdensome to a substantial number of employees.[9]

The coverage requirements for pension plans are the same as those for the deferred profit-sharing plans discussed in chapter 9. If a significant number of employees is opposed to a contributory plan, it may not have sufficient coverage to permit qualification. The plan must cover 70 percent or more of all employees after permissible exclusions or 80 percent or more of those who agree to come under the plan if 70 percent or more of all the employees are eligible to participate.[10] Thus, employees who refuse to "come in" in sufficiently large numbers can prevent the plan from qualifying.

A qualified pension plan may receive voluntary contributions from covered employees of up to ten percent of their compensation.[11] These produce tax-free accumulations and potentially favorable tax treatment upon separation from service. An employee is allowed to make catch-up voluntary contributions. The total of such voluntary contributions for all years may not exceed ten percent of the aggregate basic compensation received for all years since the employee became a participant under the plan.[12]

An employee may not deduct his own contributions to a pension plan, even if the plan requires the contribution.[13]

A pension plan may be qualified where the employer makes no contributions to the fund, which fund consists only of stated contributions from employees and the income thereof, provided the employer is required to pay the full amount of the stipulated retirement benefits to each retired employee participant after the funds credited to the employee have been exhausted.[14] The mere fact that contributions to an employees' trust are only those of the employee will not, of itself, preclude the qualification of the trust so long as the trust forms part of a pension plan established and maintained by the employer and is not one established by unilateral action of the employees to which the employer merely acquiesced.[15]

A pension plan may be noncontributory except to the extent that additional costs are incurred by reason of the health or age of a particular participant. Such was the case with a plan wherein an employer was to pay all costs of a retirement plan consisting of life insurance protection plus retirement annuities at age 65, with any employee falling into a higher risk category than the group insured being required to pay the excess costs.[16]

An amendment to a qualified pension plan to eliminate its contributory feature and to return employee contributions did not adversely affect qualification of the plan merely because it also provided for the payment to the participants of an additional amount not in excess of the increments actually earned on their contributions.[17]

An employer's recognition of an employee's rights to withdraw his own contributions carries with it a right to receive any increment actually earned on his own contribution to the plan.[18]

Amount of Deduction

While the employer may make as large a pension contribution as he chooses, his tax deduction is limited by the Internal Revenue Code.

An employer can deduct his contributions under the plan in an amount up to five percent of the payroll of persons covered by the plan.[19] Alternatively, deduction is allowed for the actual cost of funding the program on a sound actuarial basis under a level method.[20] For the first taxable year following the year in which the employer claims a pension deduction not in excess of five percent of the compensation of covered employees and for every fifth year thereafter (or more frequently if the taxpayer desires), the employer is required to submit with his tax return an actuarial certification of the amount reasonably necessary to provide the remaining unfunded cost of past and current service credits of all employees covered by the plan along with a statement of the actuarial assumptions used. The Internal Revenue Service may reduce the deduction ceiling to a figure lower than five percent of the payroll on the basis of these data.[21]

Tax Treatment of Payment Made

When a contribution is made to a pension trust of a capital asset, the employer realizes a capital gain measured by the difference between the fair market value of the property (the same valuation given it by the employer for deduction purposes) and the employer's basis for that property.[22]

It makes no difference whether the deduction for the transfer to the trust is taken over one year, taken over several, or never taken at all.[23]

Deduction for Payment to Combined Plan

If the employee benefit plan is a combination of deferred profit-sharing and pension plan, the employer's contribution is limited to 25 percent of the payroll of persons covered.[24]

Where a corporation has a combined plan, the individual limitations of 15 percent of the compensation of persons covered by the profit-sharing plan and of five percent of the compensation of those covered by the pension plan still apply to the respective contributions. The 25 percent is a *further* limitation upon the total of the two.[25]

Reasonableness of Compensation

To be deductible for Federal income tax purposes, the employer contributions towards an individual's pension benefits made during the taxable year, when added to his other compensation, must be reasonable in amount.[26]

Past Service Credit

A corporation may elect to add a *past service credit* to the usual *current service credit* so as to cover years (or a specified number of them) before the plan was adopted. If a plan bases employee benefits upon years, or any portion of such years, worked before the plan was adopted, the employer is allowed an additional deduction for tax purposes for the cost of providing such benefits. This cost can be deducted in amounts not in excess of ten percent of that cost in any one taxable year.[27]

Where a corporation transferred to its subsidiary an employee whose past service was already being funded by the parent and the subsidiary was covered by the parent's pension plan, the employee's pension costs were provided for by the subsidiary after the transfer took place. But his past service had been rendered to the parent for whom he no longer worked. It was held that the parent corporation could continue to deduct its costs of completing the funding of past service credits.[28]

The Internal Revenue Service approved a plan which provided that until the entire past service cost was liquidated, the employer would be required to contribute (in addition to its current service costs) an additional amount of not less than two nor more than ten percent of the cost as of the date the plan was established; but in any event, enough to keep the unfunded past service credit cost at any time from exceeding the unfunded past service cost as of the date of establishment of the plan.[29]

Pension Contributions as Charitable Contributions

A charitable deduction cannot be taken for a bequest to an employees' pension trust even though the trust is characterized as tax-exempt.[30]

An organization created by the will of a corporate stockholder for the sole purpose of paying pension benefits to retired employees of the company does not qualify as a tax-exempt organization since it does not automatically follow that all retired corporate employees are among the needy poor.[31]

Taxability of the Employee

The employer's contribution to a qualified pension or deferred profit-sharing plan is not currently taxable to the employee. It is not taxed until an amount is distributed or made available to him, even though his right to the contribution becomes nonforfeitable at the time it is made.[32] Availability commences when the employee can withdraw the funds without substantial limitation.[33]

An employee benefit plan may, within limits, apply employer contributions to pay premiums on group permanent or individual cash value life insurance covering the employee. For tax purposes, the premium is divided into two parts: (1) the cash value and (2) the balance of the face amount, which is the current insurance protection. That part of the premium (paid out of employer contributions) that pays for the current insurance protection is treated as a current distribution by the plan and thus included in the employee's gross income for the year in which the premium is paid.[34] Of course, to the extent that an *employee's* own contributions to the plan are used to pay insurance premiums, there is no taxable income to him.

The tax treatment of distributions will depend upon when and how they are made. The general rules are:

(1) Distributions to the extent of the employee's own contributions (if any) are tax-free. To the extent that they exceed the employee's contributions, they are treated as ordinary income in the year of distribution.[35]

(2) A lump-sum distribution of the entire amount in an employee's account within a single taxable year, which distribution occurs by reason of his retirement, death, or other separation from service, is treated as long-term capital gain to the extent attributed to employer contributions through December 31, 1969. To the extent that the payment is attributed to employer contributions after that date, it is subject to a special seven-year forward averaging procedure. A special exclusion of up to $5000 is available when payments are made by reason of an employee's death.[36]

The preferential tax treatment for a lump-sum payment is available only if the payment is made by reason of the death or other separation from service of the employee *himself*. An employee of a corporation with a qualified employee benefit plan had named his wife as primary beneficiary of all of his benefits and his sons contingent beneficiaries if she died. After his death, his wife received certain payments; upon her death, the remaining credits to his account were paid to the sons in lump sums. The sons were not entitled to preferential tax treatment as what they received was not by reason of the death of the covered employee, but by reason of the death of the primary beneficiary.[37]

Where persons covered by a qualified employee benefit plan could have obtained their benefits for a year immediately, but privately agreed not to make withdrawals for a period of years, they nonetheless were taxed currently. Where the trust instrument vests a beneficiary with the right to receive benefits, his waiver or postponement of the benefits for a valid business reason or for personal tax advantage does not make the funds any less available to him for Federal income tax purposes.[38]

Lump-sum payments may be treated preferentially only when there is a separation from service because of the employee's death, retirement, resignation, or discharge. There is no such separation for this purpose when he continues on the same job for a different employer as a result of a liquidation, merger, or consolidation of his former employer.[39]

Unlike a deferred profit-sharing plan, a qualified pension plan cannot provide for a mandatory lump-sum distribution, as there must be a systematic provision for retirement benefits in order to have such distribution.[40]

Vesting

A pension plan must provide that an employee's rights to benefits vest when he has reached a stated retirement age and has met reasonable tests as to length of service or participation in the plan.[41] Whether vesting will take place before that time depends upon the language of the plan. For example, it could be provided that a covered employee will have vested rights after 20 consecutive years of employment although no benefits will be payable until the attainment of age 65, or whatever limit may be provided in the plan.

Forfeitures

An employee's rights to or derived from the employer contribution must be nonforfeitable (assuming the requirements for ultimate benefits are met) at the time the contribution is made.[42] However, forfeitures may occur where the conditions of the plan cannot be met. For example, if benefits are payable when a covered employee attains age 65 and he leaves the company before that time, his rights are forfeited at the moment of his departure unless he has vested rights.

A qualified plan may provide for discontinuance of benefits to a retired employee for a cause, which must be distinctly specified—such as, for example, taking a position with a competitor of the employer or divulging the employer's trade secrets to competitors—or for the suspension of benefits for any period of time during which primary insurance benefits under the Social Security Act are discontinued because of employment after retirement.[43] Similarly, provision may be made for the granting of less liberal rights under these circumstances.

However, whatever provisions are made must not discriminate in favor of employees who are officers, shareholders, supervisors, or highly compensated persons.[44]

Forfeitures cannot increase the pension benefits of other employees. However, they may be used to reduce future employer contributions under the plan.[45]

Leave of Absence

An employee benefit plan will not lose qualification merely because it might cover employees of three years or more service who were on leave of absence under the corporation's regular and nondiscriminatory leave policy.[46]

Right to Designate Beneficiaries

A qualified employee benefit plan must be for the exclusive benefit of employees or their beneficiaries. One pension plan provided that upon the death of a participating employee, all benefits under the plan would be paid to his spouse if she were alive or, otherwise, to his executor or administrator. Such a plan will not fail to qualify merely because employees cannot designate their own beneficiaries.[47]

Integration with Social Security

In ascertaining whether a plan is discriminatory, the Internal Revenue Service may consider the interrelationship of the corporation's plan and the Federal Social Security Act. If the combined benefits the employer provides under its plan plus Social Security benefits are not more favorable for the higher salaried employees than for the lower, the private plan is not deemed to be discriminatory from this point of view. Thus, a pension plan will not fail to meet this requirement of nondiscrimination merely because it provides no benefits on compensation covered under the Social Security Act or because it provides benefits at a lesser rate on compensation covered under that Act than on compensation not covered under it. Plans so structured in relation to the Social Security Act are known as *integrated plans*.

The IRS guidelines for such integration are subject to change with modifications in the Social Security Act. Hence, it is necessary to check the latest IRS regulations on this subject.[48]

Termination of Plan

A qualified employee benefit plan is considered permanent. Ordinarily, if such a plan is discontinued, the Internal Revenue Service will consider that this is an indication that the plan was not intended to be permanent from the start and that it was merely a strategem to get a tax deduction in a high tax year. In consequence, the plan may lose its qualification *retroactively* for all years not yet closed by the statute of limitations.[49] That would mean loss of tax advantages to all parties concerned for these years.

A plan may be terminated without adverse tax consequences if this action was taken for reasons which could not reasonably have been foreseen when the plan was adopted. A plan may legitimately be terminated if the participants are dissatisfied with it.[50] A plan could be discontinued without untoward tax consequences when it was known that the corporation would be liquidated in the following year.[51] A plan was not disqualified retroactively where employees, in accordance with their demand, were given substantial pay increases. It was proven that corporate losses would have resulted if pension contributions were continued.[52]

Acceptable reasons for termination have included bankruptcy, insolvency, a change of ownership in an arm's length transaction, a *bona fide* and substantial change in stock holdings and management, and financial inability to continue meeting the cost of the plan.[53]

Trustees of any qualified employee benefit plan which is being terminated should notify the Internal Revenue Service before the trust assets are distributed.[54]

Formal Requirements

The employees should be given full details about the plan. If they are not informed of all of the details of the plan, they must be told of the existence of the plan and such notice must clearly state that a copy of the complete plan may be inspected at a designated place on the employer's premises during reasonable times (which must be stated).[55] No specific time need be spelled out by which the requirement of writing and communication are to be met.[56]

For the first taxable year for which a deduction is claimed for qualified profit-sharing or pension plan deductions, the employer must file a large body of data with the Internal Revenue Service. This information will include copies of the plan and of all instruments pertaining to it (including amendments), copies of advice as to the plan made available to employees, details of distribution formulæ, schedules of employees ineligible for coverage and the reasons for the ineligibility, financial data as to an implementing trust, and description of actuarial assumptions made. A statement must be submitted with reference to each of the 25 highest paid employees, showing such data as name, title, percentage of stock of each class held, age, length of service, compensation according to categories, amount allocated for the benefit of each employee or his beneficiaries, etc.[57]

If the employer fails to submit the required information as to the 25 highest paid employees and the like, the plan will not be regarded as qualified.[58] Obviously, this can hurt all parties concerned.

Advance Ruling

No advance rulings will be issued by the Internal Revenue Service as to the effect of amendments to pension plans.[59]

Advice on Pension Option

If a corporation assists in advising an employee in the selection of settlement options in the light of his personal tax considerations and the advice given is incomplete or incorrect, the corporation may have a costly bill to pay. For example, a retiring employee wrote to the company president and asked for his personal "consideration and action" in electing the most appropriate settlement election. The employee stated that he was inclined to elect to receive a lump-sum cash payment, but did not feel qualified to make the proper choice. The reply came from the employer's pension consultants, who set forth the amounts which would be paid under each of the settlement options. The employee chose the method which apparently would have given him the largest settlement. Shortly thereafter, he was killed in an accident, and his executor brought suit against the employer corporation on the ground that it had negligently (although in good faith) misinformed the employee as to the consequences of the election he had made upon retirement. The court decided in favor of the estate. The employer's communication, declared the court, failed to warn the employee that, in choosing a lump sum, he would be taking a risk of some diminution in the event of his early death. The company did not have to give him advice; however, once the employer had undertaken to answer the letter, he had the obligation of explaining the risk of one option as against another in a manner that the employee could understand.[60]

Loss of Trust's Tax Exemption

The trust which administers most pension plans can lose its tax-exempt status if it engages in a *prohibited transaction* with the employer. Typical of this is a pension fund loan to the corporation that had created it without adequate security or recording.[61] The pledge of a corporation's general assets as security for a loan was regarded as a prohibited transaction even where interest was deemed to be adequate.[62]

Dividend Implications

If corporate distributions to an employee benefit plan were made where the chief stockholders were the principal beneficiaries, these payments may be regarded as dividends.[63]

NOTES

1. Regulations Section 1.401-1(b)(1)(i).
2. I.R.C. Section 401(h).
3. Revenue Ruling 185, 1953-2 CB 202.
4. *Bernard McMenany, Contractor, Inc.*, 54 T.C. 1057 (1970), *aff'd*, 442 F.2d 359 (8th Cir., 1971).
5. Revenue Ruling 65-178, 1965-2 CB 94.
6. *Loper Sheet Metal, Inc.*, 53 T.C. 385 (1969).
7. Revenue Ruling 70-183, 1970-1 CB 103.
8. Revenue Ruling 70-76, 1970-1 CB 102.
9. Revenue Ruling 57-163, 1957-1 CB 128.
10. I.R.C. Section 401(a)(3).
11. Revenue Ruling 59-185, 1959-1 CB 86.
12. Revenue Ruling 69-217, 1969-1 CB 115.
13. *Gerard J. Bruns et al.*, T.C. Memo. 1965-74 (filed April 2, 1965).
14. Revenue Ruling 54-142, 1954-1 CB 149.
15. Revenue Ruling 66-205, 1966-2 CB 119.
16. *See Joseph M. Sperzel et al.*, 52 T.C. 320 (1969).
17. Revenue Ruling 67-340, 1967-2 CB 147.
18. Revenue Ruling 60-281, 1960-2 CB 146.
19. I.R.C. Section 404(a)(1)(A).
20. I.R.C. Section 404(a)(1)(B).
21. Regulations Section 1.404(a)-4(b).
22. *A. P. Smith Manufacturing Co. v. United States*, 364 F.2d 831 (Ct. Cl., 1966).
23. *Tasty Baking Company v. United States*, 393 F.2d 992 (Ct. Cl., 1968).
24. I.R.C. Section 404(a)(2).
25. *Parker Pen Company v. O'Day et al.*, 234 F.2d 607 (7th Cir., 1956).
26. *The Charles E. Smith & Sons Company et al. v. Commissioner*, (6th Cir., 1950).
27. I.R.C. Section 404(a)(1)(C).
28. Revenue Ruling 70-316, 1970-1 CB 91.
29. Revenue Ruling 70-184, 1970-1 CB 105.
30. *Watson et al. v. United States*, 355 F.2d 269 (3d Cir., 1965).
31. Revenue Ruling 68-422, 1968-2 CB 207.
32. Regulations Section 1.402(a)-1(a).
33. Revenue Ruling 55-423, 1955-1 CB 41.
34. Regulations Section 1.72-16(b)(2).
35. I.R.C. Sections 72(e), 402(a)(1), 403(a)(1).
36. I.R.C. Section 101(b)(2).
37. *Richard N. Gunnison et al.*, 54 T.C. 1766 (1970).
38. *William B. Leavens, Jr. et al.*, 44 T.C. 623 (1965).
39. *United States v. Johnson*, 331 F.2d 943 (5th Cir., 1964).
40. Revenue Ruling 62-195, 1962-2 CB 125.
41. Revenue Ruling 65-178, 1965-2 CB [Part 5(c)(2)] 94.

42. I.R.C. Section 401(a)(7).
43. Revenue Ruling 82, 1953-1 CB 288.
44. Revenue Ruling 65-178, 1965-2 CB 94.
45. I.R.C. Section 401(a)(8).
46. Revenue Ruling 70-101, 1970-1 CB 278.
47. Revenue Ruling 70-173, 1970-1 CB 87.
48. Such guidelines are set forth in Revenue Ruling 69-4, 1969-1 CB 118. (They may be
    · modified when the Social Security Act is itself modified, as frequently happens.)
49. Regulations Section 1.401-6(b)(2).
50. *Kane Chevrolet Company, Inc.*, 32 T.C. 596 (1959).
51. *Harold S. Davis Estate et al.*, 22 T.C. 807 (1954).
52. Mimeograph 6136, 1947-1 CB 58, *modified by* Revenue Ruling 55-60, 1955-1 CB 37.
53. Revenue Ruling 69-24, 1969-1 CB 110.
54. Revenue Ruling 69-252, 1969-1 CB 128.
55. Revenue Ruling 65-178, 1965-2 CB 94.
56. *Hill York Corporation et al. v. United States*, D.C., S.D. Fla., 1964.
57. A listing of the detailed information that must be filed is contained in Regulations
    Section 1.404(a)-2.
58. *Keco Industries, Inc.,* T.C. Memo. 1957-12 (filed January 24, 1957).
59. Revenue Procedure 69-6, 1969-1 CB 396.
60. *Gediman v. Anheuser Busch, Inc.*, 299 F.2d 537 (2d Cir., 1962).
61. Revenue Ruling 66-324, 1966-2 CB 230.
62. Revenue Ruling 70-131, 1970-1 CB 135.
63. Regulations Section 1.404(a)-1(b).

CHAPTER 11

Dividends and the Tax
on Accumulated Earnings

Reason for the Tax

With taxes being so subject to change, it is comforting (from one point of view) to know that the accumulated earnings tax has been with us as long as the income tax. Congress realized in 1913 that corporations could be used as tax shelters by their shareholders. A corporation could retain its earnings until a principal stockholder was in lower tax brackets before paying dividends. Or perhaps the corporation would never pay a dividend so that when a stockholder sold his shares, he would derive a higher price by reason of the retained earnings and would thus have capital gain instead of ordinary income upon realization of his share of the corporate earnings. Or the corporation might be liquidated at some later date so that he could receive capital gain upon the full distribution. Or he could hold his shares until he died with the result that his beneficiaries would get the shares with a basis at the date of death or six months later, and no one ever would pay income tax on his share of the corporate earnings.

So the Tariff Act of 1913 provided that every shareholder would be taxed upon his distributive share of corporate profits, whether paid out as dividends or not, in the manner that partnership profits are taxed today. But doubt soon arose as to whether the stockholders could be taxed upon profits that were not yet theirs.[1] One year later, the tax structure was changed so that this tax was imposed upon the corporation instead of on the shareholders. Later, in 1924, it was provided that the fact that profits are permitted to accumulate beyond the reasonable needs of the business is *prima facie* evidence of an attempt at avoiding shareholder taxes.

The purpose of the accumulated earnings tax is to discourage individuals from abusing the corporate form for the purpose of decreasing their personal income tax liability; it is not to award the Commissioner of Internal Revenue an after-the-fact veto over the decision of the board of directors in retaining earnings for reasonable business needs.[2]

Rate of Tax

The accumulated earnings tax is $27\frac{1}{2}$ percent of the first $100,000 of *accumulated taxable income* and $38\frac{1}{2}$ percent of *accumulated taxable income* in excess of $100,000.[3]

What Is Accumulated Taxable Income?

Accumulated taxable income is taxable income less Federal income tax, foreign income taxes not allowed as foreign tax credits, charitable contributions in excess of the five percent of income which is allowable as a deduction, disallowed capital losses, and the excess of net long-term capital gain over net short-term capital loss reduced by the tax attributable to this excess. Deduction is also allowed for dividends paid and for the *accumulated earnings credit.*

The accumulated earnings credit is, in effect, an adding machine tape of the business reasons for retention of earnings with the required dollar amounts inserted. There is a *minimum accumulated earnings credit* of the amount by which $100,000 exceeds the accumulated earnings at the close of the preceding taxable year. If a corporation is a "mere holding or investment company," its accumulated earnings credit is computed in the same manner as the minimum credit.[4]

A controlled group of corporations will be limited to one $100,000 minimum accumulated earnings credit starting in 1975. Until 1975, the credits of controlled groups of corporations in excess of one are reduced as follows:

Taxable years including	Minimum accumulated earnings credit
December 31, 1970	$83,333
December 31, 1971	66,667
December 31, 1972	50,000
December 31, 1973	33,333
December 31, 1974	16,667
Thereafter	0[5]

The Internal Revenue Code nowhere defines a "mere holding or invest-ment company." The fact that a corporation is a holding or investment company does not necessarily mean that it is a *mere* holding or investment company.[6] A corporation's activities in expanding and modernizing the real property it owned were sufficient to remove the taxpayer from the "mere holding or investment company" category.[7] There is no requirement that a corporation conduct a large-scale day-to-day operation in order to fall without the "mere holding or investment company" characterization.[8]

Corporations Subject to Tax

The accumulated earnings tax may be imposed upon any corporation formed or availed of for the purpose of avoiding shareholder taxes by permitting earnings to accumulate instead of being distributed. The only corporations exempted from this are personal holding companies, foreign personal holding companies, and tax-exempt corporations.[9]

The Commissioner's Presumptions

The Commissioner of Internal Revenue is aided immeasurably in the imposition of accumulated earnings tax by two presumptions which Congress built into the tax law. The statutory presumptions, which may be rebutted by the taxpayer corporation, are: (1) that an accumulation of corporate earnings and profits beyond the reasonable needs of the business is determinative of the existence of the forbidden purpose unless the corporation proves otherwise by a preponderance of the evidence and (2) that a corporation is a "mere holding or investment company" constitutes *prima facie* evidence of its purpose to avoid taxes.[10]

A very unfavorable presumption against a corporation is also created if the Commissioner produces a compilation of the savings that would have resulted to the shareholders from the corporation's retention of earnings. Thus, in a case won by the Government, a tabulation was exhibited to the court which showed that if earnings had been distributed, the stockholders would have paid additional income taxes of $87,858, which was $49,181 more than the proposed accumulated earnings tax.[11] And the Commissioner can readily obtain such a damaging tabulation *from the corporation*. If required by the Commissioner, every corporation must supply a statement of its accumulated earnings and profits, the names and addresses of the individuals who would be entitled to such accumulated earnings if they were divided and distributed, and the amounts which would be payable to each.[12] One wonders why such a request is not made more frequently.

If earnings accumulate beyond the reasonable needs of the business, the corporation must establish by the preponderance of the evidence that tax avoidance with respect to shareholders was not one of the purposes of the accumulations.[13] A negative purpose is infinitely more difficult to establish than is an affirmative purpose; an example of the latter is the fact that retention of earnings was for the purpose of expansion of facilities. One corporation argued on appeal that the Tax Court had placed a burden upon the company to prove not only a negative purpose (that it did not accumulate its earnings and profits to avoid the tax), but also an affirmative one (that it accumulated its earnings and profits for some reason other than avoidance of shareholder tax). The appeals court did not agree that the Tax Court improperly increased the taxpayer's burden, stating that it is difficult to prove a negative without in any event advancing one or more affirmatives.[14]

A sound business purpose to utilize corporate earnings for commercial reasons is not enough. The existence of even a *bona fide* business purpose is not necessarily inconsistent with another purpose to reduce the tax burden of the shareholders.[15]

Significance of Prior Earnings

Where applicable, the accumulated earnings tax is imposed only upon the earnings of the taxable year. But determination of whether the tax *is* applicable may require examination of the availability of earnings of prior years, and in such form as to take care of current requirements without accumulation in the current year. Taxable years under review do not stand in isolation, but must be viewed as a part of the corporation's operational history from the time of its incorporation to the present.[16] Where the accumulated earnings and profits of prior years are sufficient for the reasonable needs of the business, any earnings and profits of a later year which are retained may not be considered as retained for reasonable business needs.[17] But to the extent that such accumulated surplus has been translated into plant expansion, necessary inventories, or other assets related to the business, it is not available for meeting the corporation's current or anticipated business needs. On the other hand, at least to the extent that such accumulated surplus is reflected in liquid assets, it is available to meet business needs; and if it is sufficient to meet current and reasonably anticipated business needs of the corporation, there is a strong indication that any accumulation of earnings and profits of the current year is beyond the reasonable needs of the business.[18]

Reasonable Needs of the Business

Except in two highly specialized subsections which were added by the Tax Reform Act of 1969, the Internal Revenue Code does not define the term "reasonable needs of the business." The two subsections relate to a corporation's redemptions to pay death taxes[19] and a corporation's acquisition of its shares where a private foundation must dispose of stock it owns in excess of what is defined as "permitted holdings." [20]

While the word "reasonable" is not contained in the statute, the element of reasonableness has been held to be inherent in the familiar phrase "ordinary and necessary." [21]

Treasury Regulations give these examples of reasonable accumulations:

(1) To provide for *bona fide* expansion of a business or replacement of a plant.

(2) To acquire a business enterprise through purchase of stock or assets.

(3) To provide for the retirement of *bona fide* indebtedness created in connection with the trade or business (such as the establishment of a sinking fund for the purpose of retiring bonds issued by the corporation in accordance with contractual obligations incurred at the time of issue).

(4) To provide necessary working capital for the business (such as for the procurement of inventories).

(5) To provide for investments or loans to suppliers or customers if necessary in order to maintain the corporation's business.[22]

These are examples of what the regulations regard as unreasonable accumulations of earnings and profits:

(1) Loans to shareholders or the expenditure of corporate funds for the personal benefit of the shareholders.

(2) Loans having no reasonable relation to the conduct of the business made to relatives or friends of shareholders or to other persons.

(3) Loans to another corporation, the business of which is not that of the taxpayer corporation if the capital stock of the other corporation is directly or indirectly owned by the shareholder or shareholders of the taxpayer corporation and such shareholder or shareholders are in control of both corporations.

(4) Investments in properties or securities, which properties or securities are unrelated to the activities of the taxpayer corporation.

(5) Retention of earnings and profits as protection against unrealistic hazards.[23]

The concept of "reasonable needs" cannot be construed in an absolute sense. For this purpose, reasonable needs as a measure or standard must be related to a specific enterprise at a specific time.[24] Each corporation has its own history, its own problems, its own managerial policies.[25] But the reasonable needs must not be bereft of reality. The mere possibility that retained earnings and profits will be used for a business purpose at some indeterminate time in the future is not sufficient to make the accumulations reasonable.

The controlling intention is that which existed at the time the decision to accumulate the earnings was made; subsequent intentions, which may merely be the products of afterthoughts whether of the corporate executives or their professional advisors, will not be considered. The intention must have been manifested by some course of conduct at the time of the accumulation.[26]

Expansion

The need for expansion may provide justification for retention of earnings if it can be shown expansion was essential.

Expansion may be needed to maintain a competitive position, to retain the services of promising talent, or to produce operating economies.[27] Another reason may be the presence of cramped space and inadequate room to carry inventory.[28] The acquisition of marketing facilities[29] or reasonable expectations of an increase in sales[30] may also justify retention of earnings for expansion.[31] The construction of new plants closer to important customers where competitors enjoy freight rate advantages may also afford justification.[32]

But mere plans without any attempt at implementation may be insufficient.[33]

Hazards

Sufficient earnings may be retained to serve as self-insurance against floods where such insurance is not available except at prohibitive rates.[34] Tax was not imposed where a corporation demonstrated, among other things, that it carried its own collision insurance on its equipment.[35] So retention may be justified where insurance may be inadequate in the light of risks involved in a situation.[36] Under appropriate circumstances, the accumulated earnings tax itself may be a contingency for which provision is justified.[37]

The hazard claimed must be real.[38] Management's fears must be evaluated as to reasonableness. A corporation could not accumulate earnings because of the prospect that it might be called upon to contribute additional capital to a bank in which it had an 85 percent stock interest where the bank was in sound financial condition and a demand for funds was highly speculative.[39] Earnings may not be retained to protect the corporation from competition where it has an impressive record of earnings throughout its entire history.[40]

Outside Investments— Needs of an Affiliate

Investment in properties unrelated to the activities of the business of the taxpayer corporation may indicate that earnings are being accumulated beyond the reasonable needs of the business.[41] A taxpayer's business may be regarded as including the business of a subsidiary of whose voting stock it owns at least 80 percent, but the business of one corporation does not include the business of another corporation which is not engaged in the active conduct of a trade or business.[42]

Where a parent corporation borrowed money on a note to obtain funds and secured the loan with its own real estate so that a subsidiary could enter into a business venture, the parent could with impunity retain earnings to meet the reasonably anticipated needs of the business venture. At the same time, the parent was primarily liable on the note.[43]

Redemption of a Dissident's Stock

The fact that a corporation can spare funds to buy up its own stock is a potential accumulated earnings tax hazard. If the corporation has funds for a noncorporate purpose, it might be asked why had it been obliged to retain any earnings. But retention to buy up a dissident's stock may be reasonable where it can be shown that if this stock were to get into the hands of a person with views strongly opposed to the majority shareholders, this could and probably would be most disruptive of the harmony of the corporation.[44]

Earnings were not retained unreasonably where a corporation redeemed all of the shares of one of the two family groups each of which owned 50 percent of the stock when the groups were shown to have irreconcilable differences of opinion.[45]

The promotion of harmony in the conduct of a business is a proper business purpose. If redeeming the stock of one shareholder is designed to secure the corporation against dissension among those who determine business policy, accumulation of funds for that redemption is justified as a business need.[46]

Retention to Buy Shares of an Ill Stockholder

Retention of earnings to redeem the shares of ill stockholders, serves no corporate purpose.[47] But, as mentioned earlier in this chapter, earnings may be retained to redeem the shares of a deceased stockholder in a transaction which meets the technical requirements of a redemption to pay death taxes.[48]

Reserves

The existence of reserves will not help a corporation justify the retention of earnings in an affirmative sense, for a corporation is not required to set up reserves for contingencies, and a book entry does not in itself establish need. But absence of reserves may be fatal if a corporation argues fear of natural hazards, renegotiation, and the like.[49] If the threat looked so real to management, why was not a reserve set up?

Depreciation

A corporation may not include a fund equal to its depreciation reserve escalated for the economic factor of increased replacement costs in justifying the reasonable needs of its business. But the reserve for depreciation itself may be considered and given appropriate weight in conjunction with the other facts and circumstances in each case.[50]

Diversification

Retention of earnings to permit diversification is not looked upon with favor.[51] A corporation faced with declining profits in its field of automobile engine rebuilding was subjected to tax on accumulations for the purpose of entering the field of television film production.[52] A radio broadcasting company was not sanctioned in retaining surplus for the purchase of a department store, the court pointing out that expected investment in a merchandising enterprise had no bearing on the broadcasting business in which the corporation was engaged.[53] A real estate corporation was taxed upon earnings retained to enter the automobile leasing and renting field.[54]

On the other hand, a manufacturer of automobile clutches could switch to the rebuilding of automobile engines when the Ford Motor Company, its chief customer, began the manufacture of its own transmissions.[55] A manufacturer of wooden containers could retain earnings while considering entry into the plastic can field where a substantial number of existing customers were shown to have an interest in a new type of container for their products.[56]

But the weight of authority holds that a corporation's diversion of earnings from its business and its reasonable business needs for use in activities or investments unrelated to that business usually is persuasive evidence that the diverted earnings are not reasonably needed in the business and/or that the corporation is being availed of for the purpose of avoiding shareholder taxes by nonpayment of dividends.[57]

No "Immediacy" Test

The law does not require that retained earnings and profits be invested immediately in the business so long as there is an indication that the present or future needs of the business warrant such an accumulation and that the corporation has specific, definite, and feasible plans for the disposition of the accumulation. Where future needs are uncertain, however, or plans for future use of an accumulation are indefinite, this may be considered in determining whether an accumulation went beyond the reasonable needs of the business.[58]

Plans for Utilization of Earnings

The business needs of a corporation are probably best expressed in terms of *plans*.[59] But plans in themselves do not make an accumulation reasonable. To protect corporate taxpayers from the accumulated earnings tax, the plans must have some reality related to the year under review.[60]

To succeed in justifying the retention of earnings, a plan must be definite and specific. And it must be feasible.[61] A corporation's failure to relate the amount of its retained earnings to specific business needs will lead to the issuance of a deficiency notice.[62] Tax was imposed where a corporation had no reasonable expectation of consummating its reason for retention: to operate a Cadillac franchise *if obtained*.[63]

Retention is most certainly not justified where there is merely an unarticulated plan or a desire on the part of the corporate management.[64] *Articulation* is a necessity. In general, a plan must have some specificity.[65] But the fact that a corporation's alleged plans have not been consummated is not fatal where there are reasons beyond the corporation's control for delay in implementation.[66] The minutes of directors' and stockholders' meetings should set out reasons for such a delay.[67]

A corporation may properly accumulate earnings even if there is no specific plan or commitment if it can be established by other means that management was actively engaged in efforts to acquire business properties or had agreed on the amount that could be paid for specific properties if they could be obtained.[68]

Earnings were reasonably retained for expansion purposes where there was no formal plan, but the company had been engaged in continuous expansion for a good many years.[69]

A plan for future development need not be a voluntary plan; for example, a governmental agency might order that certain acquisitions or modernization take place.[70]

Wisdom of the Directors' Plans

If the reason for the retention was not to avoid shareholder taxes by permitting earnings to pile up, it does not matter that the method employed was not the best way to cope with whatever problem the corporation was trying to solve. The fact that the corporation's method of coping with a problem was imprudent does not mean that it was unreasonable. To say that would be to place the Commissioner's business judgment in place of management's, giving him the benefit of hindsight.[71]

If the record shows that the directors focused their business judgment upon a matter, the courts seem inclined to believe that there was a business reason for the resultant action. Where there is evidence that a board of directors has given serious consideration to the actual needs of the business based on the directors' experience in the business and on known or reasonably predictable factors, a court probably would be hesitant to substitute its judgment of the reasonable needs of the business for that of the directors.[72]

The Effects of Subsequent Events

Subsequent events cannot be used to show that the retention of earnings and profits was reasonable at the time the decisions to retain the earnings were made unless the decisions to retain earnings actually were influenced by the possibility of occurrence of those subsequent events. But subsequent events may be considered as evidence in determining whether the corporation actually intended to consummate any plans it had for the earnings and profits which had accumulated.[73]

The evidence of subsequent events may be considered for certain purposes; for example, to determine whether a corporation actually consummated the plans for which it claimed the earnings had been accumulated and to support or to attack the credibility of the testimony with respect to the reasons for accumulations, but not to permit justification for such actions based upon subsequent events which were not considered by the directors during the taxable year in question.[74]

The Burden of Proof

A special rule covers the burden of proof as to accumulated earnings for tax purposes. Prior to sending out a deficiency notice, the Service must notify the corporation that the imposition of accumulated earnings tax is being considered. Upon receipt of such a letter, the corporation has 30 days to submit a statement explaining *why* the accumulation is reasonable under present circumstances.[75] A 30-day extension for this response may be applied for. If the corporation returns the statement on time with a fully documented explanation of the reasons for retention, the burden is shifted to the Service, which then must show that the retention is unreasonable. But if the corporation fails to return the statement on time or if this statement is vague and incomplete, the burden of proof remains with the corporation.

To be *adequate* to shift the burden to the Commissioner, the supporting facts submitted by the corporation must be substantial, material, definite, and clear.[76]

The taxpayer's statement may convince the Internal Revenue Service that it is useless to proceed further.[77] The Tax Court may rule prior to trial on whether the corporation has shifted the burden of proof.[78] And it is worth noting that this procedure applies only in a matter which is before the Tax Court, not one before any other tribunal.[79]

The burden may be shifted to the Commissioner on *certain* of the grounds only.[80] Of course, the fact that the burden of proof has been shifted to the Commissioner does not mean that the corporation's statement will be believed by the court.[81] And even where the burden is on the Commissioner, it may be rebutted by affirmative proof.[82]

Shifting of the burden of proof to the Commissioner does not change the fact that imposition of the tax depends upon the corporation's reasons for retention, regardless of who has to prove or to disprove them. The ultimate burden of proving that the corporation was not availed of for the purpose of avoiding shareholder taxes is and remains upon the corporation.[83]

Yardsticks for Accumulation

There are no mathematical guidelines to measure reasonable accumulation of earnings, although at one time, the Commissioner arbitrarily used a figure of 70 percent; that is, if the corporation distributed at least 70 percent of its earnings in dividends, no question would be raised as to the remainder.

Where it was argued that a corporation was entitled to accumulate earnings so that there could be at least a two to one ratio between current assets and current liabilities, the court pointed out that that was only one factor to be considered.[84] Another court announced that there was no need for it to adopt any general theory or accounting practice as a legal principle that would be applicable in all situations.[85]

Form of Surplus

Earnings that have been legitimately ploughed back into the business in past years cannot form the basis for determination of whether current earnings are reasonable for the corporation's objectives. The accumulated earnings which have been converted into brick, mortar, machinery, equipment, and inventory are not available for current expenses or expansion.[86] Thus, to the extent that earned surplus has been translated into plant expansion or other assets related to its business, a corporation may accumulate surplus with impunity.[87]

If available assets of a corporation are required to meet the reasonable needs of the business, the mere fact that some of those assets could be used for dividends without impairing current business operations is irrelevant.[88]

The absence of liquid assets is no reason for a corporation not to pay dividends if it has assets which are not being used for business purposes. Thus, cancellation of stockholder loans could have been in the form of a dividend not requiring cash.[89]

In appraising the reasonableness of earnings and profits for the purpose of the accumulated earnings tax, the Service may have to take into account the acquired earnings of a predecessor corporation. Where there has been a tax-free reorganization, the accumulated earnings and profits of a predecessor corporation are taken over by the successor corporation and thus become available for distribution by the successor.[90]

Past Dividend History

There is an inference that earnings and profits are deliberately being retained to avoid shareholder taxes if a corporation has neither declared nor paid a dividend on its stock.[91] In one case won by a corporation, the court noted that it was significant that the company had a long history of paying substantial dividends on a regular basis.[92]

Significance of Past Practice

Retention of earnings was justified upon a showing that a corporation had always financed its own needs out of earnings.[93] Similarly, a corporation won its case with evidence that it was a cardinal principle of the chief stockholder to operate without borrowed money. The court agreed that this was a valid reason to retain earnings.[94]

But past practice also can work against a corporation's alleged reasons for retention, for courts are likely to assume that past practices will be continued.[95]

The Cash Flow Theory

Earnings may legitimately be retained to provide for working capital requirements.[96] If the payment of a dividend would leave a corporation with insufficient working capital, it follows that failure to pay a dividend does not necessarily result in an unreasonable accumulation of income.[97] But management must show that such data were considered when dividends were being reviewed.

The question is primarily one of determining whether a corporation has enough liquid assets (not earnings and profits) to meet estimated needs, including demands for working capital.[98]

The cash flow doctrine had its genesis in a court finding that there was a reasonable necessity for sufficient capital to meet operating expenses for at least a year.[99] But this one-year rule must give way to a corporation's own operating cycle.[100] Corporations are not automatically entitled to one year's operating expenses as working capital. Some may be so entitled; others may not. A full year's operating cycle was not allowed to a retail store which never sold on credit and which prepaid its merchandise purchases. Rather, a single operating cycle was the permissible period for accumulation, and this involved inventory turnover. In determining the number of times the inventory turned over, the company should have used the "peak" inventory during the year rather than the "average" inventory.[101]

Under a formula devised by the Tax Court, known as the *Bardahl Formula,* a corporation's computation of its need for operating capital involves the determination of the amount of cash it reasonably expects to be sufficient to cover its operating costs for a single operating cycle. An "operating cycle" was defined as the period of time required to convert cash into raw materials, raw materials into an inventory of marketable products, the inventory into sales and accounts receivable, and the period of time required to collect its outstanding accounts. In the taxable years involved, this cycle worked out to 4.2 months. The corporation was justified in retention of liquid assets to meet operating expenses for a maximum of 4.2 months. Additional expenditures for operating costs beyond the first 4.2 months of each year would not be incurred without production of operating revenue.[102]

Operating expenses cannot be considered in a vacuum. If anticipated earnings currently offset anticipated expenses, there is no need of accumulation of earnings for operating expenses.[103] Working capital needs of businesses vary, being dependent upon the nature of the business, its credit policies, the amount of inventories and the rate of turnover, the amount of accounts receivable and the collection rate thereof, the availability of credit to the business, and similar relevant factors.[104]

In the absence of supportive evidence, it cannot be assumed that the directors considered cash flow needs as a reason for nonpayment of dividends. In one case lost by a corporate taxpayer, it was disclosed that the accountants had discussed with the company officers the business needs in general, but no reference was made to prospective needs for the next fiscal year.[105]

Advice by Outside Parties

Corporations have defended accumulated earnings tax assessments successfully by showing that earnings were retained because of the advice of outside consultants or other parties.[106]

Subchapter S Corporations

Exemption from the accumulated earnings tax is accorded to corporations where election has been made under Subchapter S to be taxed solely at the shareholder level.[107]

Accumulated Earnings Tax Dangers

A corporation with retained earnings must be able to document that business needs were considered by the directors when dividends were discussed. But in the case of a closely-held corporation, contemporaneous records may not be kept. Where the management personnel are in constant daily contact with each other, there may be a feeling that there is no need for definite written commitments, corporate resolutions, interoffice correspondence, and other material which could establish that there had indeed been a plan for the utilization of earnings in the taxable year.[108]

Any Federal income tax audit can create additional income and with it a built-in accumulated earnings tax situation.[109]

NOTES

1. *Eisner v. Macomber*, 252 U.S. 189 (1920).
2. *Electric Regulator Corporation v. Commissioner*, 336 F.2d 339 (2d Cir., 1964).
3. I.R.C. Section 531.
4. I.R.C. Section 535.
5. I.R.C. Section 1564(a).
6. *Olin Corporation*, 42 B.T.A. 1203 (1940), *aff'd*, 128 F.2d 185 (7th Cir., 1942).
7. *Battelstein Investment Company v. United States*, 302 F. Supp. 920 (D.C., S.D. Texas, 1969), *aff'd*, 442 F.2d 87 (5th Cir., 1971).
8. *The Dahlem Foundation, Inc.*, 54 T.C. 1566 (1970).
9. I.R.C. Section 532.
10. *The Dahlem Foundation, Inc.*, 54 T.C. 1566 (1970).
11. *Dickman Lumber Company v. United States*, (D.C., W.D. Wash., 1964), *aff'd*, 355 F.2d 670 (9th Cir., 1966).
12. I.R.C. Section 6042.
13. *United States v. The Donruss Company*, 390 U.S. 1023 (1969).
14. *Young Motor Company, Inc. v. Commissioner*, 339 F.2d 491 (1st Cir., 1964).
15. *Perfection Foods, Inc.*, T.C. Memo. 1965-15 (filed January 29, 1965).
16. *Mohawk Paper Mills, Inc. v. United States*, 262 F. Supp. 365 (D.C., W.D. N.Y., 1966).
17. *Robert R. Walker, Inc. et al.*, T.C. Memo. 1965-28 (filed February 16, 1965).
18. *Novelart Manufacturing Company*, 52 T.C. 794 (1969).
19. I.R.C. Section 303.
20. I.R.C. Section 537.
21. *E-Z Sew Enterprises, Inc. v. United States*, 260 F. Supp. 100 (D.C., E.D. Mich., 1966).
22. Regulations Section 1.537-2(b).
23. Regulations Section 1.537-2(c).
24. *United States v. The McNally Pittsburgh Manufacturing Corporation et al.*, 342 F.2d 198 (10th Cir., 1965).

25. *Sears Oil Co., Inc. v. Commissioner*, 359 F.2d 191 (2d Cir., 1966).
26. *Fischer Lime & Cement Company v. United States*, D.C., W.D. Tenn., 1963.
27. *Freedom Newspapers, Inc.*, T.C. Memo. 1965-248 (filed September 15, 1965).
28. *Magic Mart, Inc.*, 51 T.C. 775 (1969).
29. *Fisher & Fisher*, 32 B.T.A. 211 (1935).
30. *Universal Steel Company*, 5 T.C. 627 (1945).
31. *Shaw & Keeter Motor Company*, T.C. Memo., Docket No. 26977 (entered August 16, 1951).
32. *J. E. Baker Company*, B.T.A. Memo., Docket No. 87758 (entered June 6, 1939).
33. *Battelstein Investment Company v. United States*, 302 F. Supp. 320 (D.C., S.D. Texas, 1969), *aff'd*, 442 F.2d 87 (5th Cir., 1971).
34. *Magic Mart, Inc.*, 51 T.C. 775 (1969).
35. *Hardin's Bakeries, Inc. et al. v. Martin, Jr.*, 293 F. Supp. 1129 (D.C., S.D. Miss., 1967).
36. *Halby Chemical Company, Inc. et al. v. United States*, 180 Ct. Cl. 584 (Ct. Cl., 1967).
37. Revenue Ruling 70-301, 1970-1 CB 138.
38. *Havens & Martin v. United States*, D.C., E.D. Va., 1965.
39. *Carlen Realty Company v. Tomlinson*, 345 F.2d 998 (5th Cir., 1965).
40. *Motor Fuel Carriers, Inc. v. United States*, 244 F. Supp. 380 (D.C., N.D. Fla., 1965).
41. Regulations Section 1.537-2(c).
42. Regulations Section 1.537-3(b).
43. *The Montgomery Co.*, 54 T.C. 986 (1970).
44. *Gazette Publishing Company v. Self*, 130 F. Supp. 779 (D.C., Ark., 1952).
45. *Mountain State Steel Foundries, Inc. v. Commissioner*, 284 F.2d 737 (4th Cir., 1960).
46. *Farmers and Merchants Investment Co.*, T.C. Memo. 1970-161 (filed June 22, 1970). (In that case, the retention was proper even though there was no dissension involving the shareholder who wished to close out his investment for personal reasons.)
47. *Dickman Lumber Company v. United States*, D.C., W.D. Wash., 1964, *aff'd*, 355 F.2d 670 (9th Cir., 1966).
48. I.R.C. Section 303.
49. *Robert A. Goodall Estate et al. v. Commissioner*, 391 F.2d 775 (8th Cir., 1968).
50. Revenue Ruling 67-64, 1967-1 CB 150.
51. Regulations Section 1.537-3(a).
52. *Automotive Rebuilding Co.*, T.C. Memo, 1958-197 (filed November 28, 1958).
53. *Southland Industries, Inc.*, T.C. Memo., Docket No. 3387 (entered October 31, 1946).
54. *Fenco, Inc. v. United States*, 348 F.2d 456 (6th Cir., 1965).
55. *Alma Piston Company*, T.C. Memo. 1963-195 (filed July 23, 1963).
56. *New England Wooden Ware v. United States*, 289 F. Supp. 111 (D.C., Mass., 1968).
57. *Mead's Bakery, Inc. v. Commissioner*, 364 F.2d 101 (5th Cir., 1966).
58. *The McNally Pittsburgh Manufacturing Corporation et al. v. United States*, D.C., Kansas, 1963, *rev'd and rem'd'd on another issue*, 342 F.2d 198 (10th Cir., 1965).
59. *Duke Laboratories, Inc. v. United States*, 207 F. Supp. 746 (D.C., Conn., 1963).
60. *Chappell and Co., Inc. v. Church*, D.C., S.D. N.Y., 1965.
61. *Federal Ornamental Iron and Bronze Company*, T.C. Memo. 1969-71 (filed April 16, 1969).
62. *Ted Bates & Company, Inc.*, T. C. Memo. 1965-251 (filed September 17, 1965).
63. *Nodell Motors, Inc.*, T.C. Memo. 1967-209 (filed October 25, 1967).
64. *Carlen Realty Company v. Tomlinson*, 345 F.2d 998 (5th Cir., 1965).
65. *Othmar Real Estate Corporation*, T.C. Memo. 1965-189 (filed July 13, 1965).
66. *Magic Mart, Inc.*, 51 T.C. 775 (1969).
67. *Carolina Rubber Hose Company*, T.C. Memo. 1965-229 (filed September 3, 1965).
68. *The Dahlem Foundation, Inc. v. United States*, 405 F.2d 993 (6th Cir., 1968).
69. *John P. Scripps Newspapers*, 44 T.C. 453 (1965).
70. *Havens & Martin v. United States*, D.C., E.D. Va., 1965.
71. *The Harry A. Koch Co. v. Vinal*, 228 F. Supp. 782 (D.C., Neb., 1964).
72. *Walter C. McMinn, Jr. et al.*, T.C. Memo. 1962-165 (filed June 29, 1962).

73. *Fischer Lime & Cement Company v. United States*, D.C., W.D. Tenn., 1963.

74. *The Schneuit Rubber Company v. United States*, 293 F. Supp. 280 (D.C., Md., 1968).

75. I.R.C. Section 534.

76. *J. Gordon Turnbull, Inc.*, 41 T.C. 358 (1963), *aff'd*, 373 F.2d 87 (5th Cir., 1967).

77. *See* Revenue Procedure 56-11, 1956-1 CB 1028.

78. *Chatham Corporation*, 48 T.C. 145 (1967).

79. I.R.C. Section 534(a).

80. *The Shaw-Walker Company v. Commissioner*, 390 F.2d 205 (6th Cir., 1968), *rev'd and rem'd'd on other grounds*, 393 U.S. 478 (1969).

81. *The Factories Investment Corporation*, 39 T.C. 908 (1963), *aff'd*, 328 F.2d 781 (2d Cir., 1964).

82. *The Smoot Sand & Gravel Corporation v. Commissioner*, 274 495 (4th Cir., 1960).

83. *The Kirlin Company*, T.C. Memo. 1964-260 (filed September 30, 1964).

84. *Motor Fuel Carriers, Inc. v. United States*, 322 F.2d 576 (5th Cir., 1965).

85. *Carlen Realty Company v. Tomlinson*, 345 F.2d 998 (5th Cir., 1965).

86. *Electric Regulator Corporation v. Commissioner*, 336 F.2d 339 (2d Cir., 1964).

87. *Carolina Rubber Hose Company*, T.C. Memo. 1965-229 (filed September 3, 1965).

88. *Faber Cement Block Co., Inc.*, 50 T.C. 317 (1968).

89. *Nemours Corporation*, 38 T.C. 585-1962, *aff'd*, 325 F.2d 559 (3d Cir., 1963).

90. *Stanton Corporation*, 44 B.T.A. 56 (1941), *aff'd*, 138 F.2d 512 (2d Cir., 1943).

91. *Farmers and Merchants Investment Co.*, T.C. Memo. 1970-161 (filed June 22, 1970).

92. *Kingsbury Investments, Inc.*, T.C. Memo. 1969-205 (filed September 30, 1969).

93. *Havens & Martin v. United States*, D.C., E.D. Va., 1965.

94. *Halby Chemical Company, Inc. et al. v. United States*, 180 Ct. Cl. 584 (Ct. Cl., 1967).

95. *E.g., Wellman Operating Corporation*, 33 T.C. 162 (1959); *Motor Fuel Carriers, Inc. v. United States*, 202 F. Supp. 497 (D.C., N.D. Fla., 1962), *aff'd*, 322 F.2d 576 (5th Cir., 1963); *American Metal Products Corporation et al.*, 34 T.C. 89 (1960), *aff'd*, 287 F.2d 860 (8th Cir., 1961).

96. Regulations Section 1.537-2(b)(4).

97. *Sterling Distributors, Inc. v. United States*, 325 F.2d 236 (5th Cir., 1963).

98. *Ted Bates & Company, Inc.*, T.C. Memo. 1965-251 (filed December 3, 1965).

99. *The J. L. Goodman Furniture Co.*, 11 T.C. 630 (1948).

100. *The Shaw-Walker Company v. Commissioner*, 390 F.2d 205 (6th Cir., 1968), *rev'd and rem'd'd on other issues*, 393 U.S. 418 (1969).

101. *Magic Mart, Inc.*, 51 T.C. 725 (1969).

102. *Bardahl Manufacturing Corporation*, T.C. Memo. 1965-200 (filed July 23, 1965).

103. *Chappell and Co., Inc. v. Church*, D.C., S.D. N.Y., 1965.

104. *The Smoot Sand & Gravel Corporation v. Commissioner*, 241 F.2d 197 (4th Cir., 1957).

105. *Chappell and Co., Inc. v. Church*, D.C., S.D. N.Y., 1965.

106. *E.g., Gazette Telegraph Co.*, 19 T.C. 692 (1953), *aff'd*, 209 F.2d 926 (10th Cir., 1954); *See Davis et al. v. United States*, 408 F.2d 1139 (6th Cir., 1969), *rev'd and rem'd'd on another issue*, 397 U.S. 301 (1970); *New England Wooden Ware v. United States*, 289 F. Supp. 111 (D.C., Mass., 1968); *Metal Office Furniture Co.*, T.C. Memo., Docket Nos. 107369 and 238 (entered October 28, 1952).

107. I.R.C. Section 1372(b).

108. *Thompson v. United States*, 110 F.2d 585 (5th Cir., 1940).

109. *Oklahoma Transportation Company v. United States*, 272 F. Supp. 729 (D.C., W.D. Okla., 1966).

CHAPTER 12

Depreciation

What Is the Depreciation Allowance?

Depreciation has been defined variously by economists, engineers, accountants, and others. But for tax purposes, the United States Supreme Court has said the depreciation deduction represents the reduction in value, during the year, through the wear and tear of depreciable assets. The amount of the allowance for depreciation is the sum which should be set aside for the taxable year in order that, at the end of the useful life of the facility in the business, the aggregate of the sums set aside will (with salvage value) suffice to provide an amount equal to the original cost.[1]

Basically, the Federal income tax is a tax on net income, and the expenses of generating income are normally considered deductible from gross income. The purpose of the depreciation allowance is to enable a taxpayer to recover the net cost of a wasting asset used in his trade or business by charging the diminution in the asset's value each year against the gross income of that year. Inasmuch as the income tax system is based upon annual reporting and liability and a taxpayer normally holds wasting assets for more than a year, the proper amount of depreciation to be taken each year must depend upon estimates.[2]

In its lifetime, a depreciable asset must pay for itself before it can be said to pay anything to its owner.[3] The objective of the depreciation allowance, then, is to approximate and to reflect the financial consequences to a taxpayer of the effects of use and time on the value of depreciable assets.[4]

Essentials of the Depreciation Deduction

Depreciation is a recognition of the fact that most property deteriorates physically with use and time.[5] Obsolescence is also a factor in depreciation.[6]

The essential concept underlying the depreciation allowance is prediction or estimate.[7] By its very nature, depreciation is an estimate of future events distilled from the prologue of history. Analysis of historical evidence traditionally serves as the means of forecasting probabilities of future life.[8]

The components of the depreciation allowance are the cost, the salvage value, and the useful life of the property.[9] The second and third of these components are estimates.

The depreciation allowance should include an allowance for *normal obsolescence;* that is, recognition of the fact that in time any asset may have to be replaced solely because improved assets of the same kind become available. Obsolescence may render an asset economically useless to the taxpayer regardless of its physical condition. Obsolescence is attributable to many causes, including technological improvements and reasonably foreseeable economic changes.[10] (For a discussion of *abnormal obsolescence,* see chapter 13, Bad Debts and Other Write-Offs.)

Who Can Take Depreciation?

Depreciation is not predicated upon ownership of property, but rather upon an investment in property.[11] The test is whether the taxpayer would suffer an economic loss as the result of a decrease in the value of the property due to depreciation.[12] A taxpayer cannot recoup an investment on depreciable assets made by some other party by means of depreciation deductions.[13]

Where property must be returned by a lessee at the end of the lease in its original condition, the lessor is entitled to no depreciation deduction for he has sustained no loss by reason of wear and tear.[14]

What Can Be Depreciated?

Depreciation can be taken only upon property used in the taxpayer's trade or business or property held for the production of income.[15] The business use of property must be more than incidental.[16]

Where property is held for the production of income during the taxable year, depreciation is allowed, even though in fact the property produces no income.[17]

To the extent that property is used for business purposes, depreciation is available, even though the property is also used for personal purposes, as where a portion of one's residence is used regularly for business.[18]

Depreciation cannot be taken upon inventories or any property held for sale to customers in the ordinary course of the taxpayer's trade or business.[19] Nor is land subject to the depreciation allowance.[20] Depreciation can be taken only on property whose useful life can be fixed with reasonable certainty.[21] If the cost or some other basis of property cannot be ascertained, no depreciation can be taken on such property.[22]

Good will is not subject to depreciation because its useful life cannot be estimated.[23] Intangible assets usually will not be the proper subject of the depreciation allowance unless the useful life of the asset is definitely limited or unless the intangible asset has value in the production of income for only a limited period of time, the duration of which can be estimated with reasonable accuracy.[24]

A franchise to run for five years with provision for an indefinite succession of automatic renewals subject to a possible breach has been ruled to be for an indefinite and unlimited period and not depreciable for tax purposes.[25]

Depreciation is not generally allowed on works of art, for they do not have a determinable useful life. While the actual physical condition of the property may influence the value placed on the object, it will not ordinarily limit or determine its useful life.[26]

An individual is not subject to depreciation (in a tax sense, that is). But a personal service contract calling for an individual's services (for example, those of a baseball player) is subject to depreciation.[27]

Depreciation must be capitalized rather than expensed in the case of a building which still is under construction.[28]

If a taxpayer uses equipment in a manner which is prohibited by state law, the Internal Revenue Service may seek to deny the depreciation deduction. But the Service will not prevail if the state statute is remedial rather than punitive and if the allowance of the depreciation deduction would not frustrate a sharply defined state policy.[29]

The Service has announced that it will disallow depreciation deductions where purchases of property appear designed, in the light of all the facts and circumstances, to improperly create or inflate depreciation deductions.[30]

On What is Depreciation Taken?

Cost or other basis—that is, the taxpayer's investment—is depreciation's anchor.[31]

In most instances, the basis for the depreciation allowance is the adjusted basis for determining gain upon the sale or other disposition of the property. In the case of property which had neither been used in the trade or business nor held for the production of income, but which was subsequently converted to such use, the fair market value on the date of such conversion, if less than the adjusted basis of the property at that time, is the basis for computing depreciation.[32] The basis of property contributed to a corporation to locate in a specific place is zero.

Useful Life

Depreciation is calculated on the basis of the remaining *useful life* of an asset. Useful life, for tax purposes, may bear no relationship whatever to the inherent physical life of an asset; rather, useful life is purely subjective, depending upon the use the taxpayer intends for the asset in his business.[33] Useful life of an asset may become longer or shorter during the time it is held by the taxpayer and is subject to redetermination at the end of every taxable year.[34]

A taxpayer's past experience with a type of asset is only one of several factors to be considered. Present conditions and probable future developments must be taken into account.[35] Some of the factors to be considered in determining the estimated useful life *to the taxpayer* are: (1) wear and tear and decay or decline from natural causes; (2) the normal progress of the artistic and economic changes, invention, and current developments within the industry and the taxpayer's trade or business; (3) the climatic and other local conditions peculiar to the taxpayer's trade or business; and (4) the taxpayer's policy as to repairs, renewals, and replacements. Salvage value is not a factor for the purpose of determining useful life.

If the taxpayer's experience is inadequate, the general experience in the industry may be used until such time as the taxpayer's own experience forms an adequate basis for making the determination. The estimated remaining useful life may be subject to modification by reason of conditions known to exist at the end of the taxable year and will be determined by the Internal Revenue Service when necessary, regardless of the method of computing depreciation. But estimated remaining useful life will be redetermined by the Internal Revenue Service only when the change in the useful life is significant and the Service has a clear and convincing basis for the redetermination.[36]

The Service may not make use of hindsight in appraising the reasonableness of a taxpayer's depreciation.[37]

Yardsticks for Useful Life

What is the useful life of an asset for tax purposes? Quite simply, it is what depreciation is all about; and it is what a substantial amount of tax administration and tax litigation is about.

The Treasury Department first published a schedule of suggested lives of assets in 1931, the lives being of individual assets used by industry groups. This schedule, known as *Bulletin F,* was revised several times and ultimately included thousands of items.[38] But many claimed that the rates were too conservative, that useful lives were in fact shorter than the Treasury indicated.

In 1962, the Treasury supplied instead a series of "guidelines," which substituted about 75 broad industrial classifications for *Bulletin F*'s individualized asset "lives." [39] These guidelines shortened by approximately 30 to 40 percent the lives provided in the old bulletin. But use of the new guidelines was dependent upon the adoption of a highly complex system of proving that a taxpayer's depreciation deductions and the related reserves conformed to a presumed life cycle of replacements. This system was so complex as to be virtually incomprehensible, and a new system, known as the Asset Depreciation Range System, was adopted in 1971.[40]

Asset Depreciation Range System

The *Asset Depreciation Range* (ADR) System made five principal changes in the depreciation regulations:

(1) Machinery and equipment placed in service after December 31, 1970 may be depreciated over the useful lives selected from a range of years 20 percent below to 20 percent above the guideline lives of Revenue Procedure 62-21. The new guideline lives will be amended from time to time in the future by the newly created Office of Industrial Economics in the Internal Revenue Service.[41] Useful lives are provided in the form of 89 sets of rates for listed categories. For example, office furniture that is not a structural component of a building has a guideline period of ten years and an upper limit of 12 years. The annual asset guideline repair allowance percentage (to be discussed below) is 7.5.[42] The useful life of an asset is selected from this range in the year it is acquired. The life does not subsequently change for the asset even though the guideline life for that asset class may be changed in the future for later acquisitions. If the Treasury lengthens an asset depreciation range during a year, a taxpayer may choose a depreciation period from the old range for asset acquisitions in that year. These useful lives, or rates if expressed on an annual basis, are optional for the taxpayer. If he thinks he can meet the elaborate burden of proof of showing that he is entitled to shorter lives, if he thinks he can justify a lower depreciation rate in the early years of his business before it begins to reflect profits, or if he simply cannot be bothered by the rules of qualifying for this new treatment, he may choose to ignore the whole ADR idea.

(2) To simplify the establishment of the depreciation deduction in the year in which assets are acquired, the taxpayer may choose between two simplified procedures: (a) all property acquired during the first half of a taxable year may be deemed to have been placed in service on the first day of that taxable year or (b) all assets acquired during the second half of that year may be deemed to have been placed in service on the first day of the second half of the year. Alternatively, the taxpayer may treat all assets acquired during that year as having been placed in service at the midpoint of that year.[43]

(3) Prior to ADR, salvage had been an extremely contentious part of the depreciation deduction because what may be obtained for an asset when it is retired, either as a second-hand piece of equipment or as scrap metal, depends upon such factors as premature retirement of property or the current state of the second-hand market. Before ADR, the salvage value estimated by a taxpayer in the first instance ordinarily would not be changed by the Internal Revenue Service if the facts and circumstances known at that time did not warrant an adjustment of more than ten percent of the cost of the asset. Depreciation now will be taken upon the cost or other basis of the assets without reduction for an estimated salvage value. But depreciation of an asset will cease when estimated salvage is reached.[44]

(4) Expenditures for the repair, maintenance, rehabilitation, or improvement of property may not be deductible for tax purposes; they must be capitalized if they increase the productivity or capacity of an asset, adapt it to a substantially different use, or extend its life. The balance of expenditures for repairs, maintenance, and rehabilitation (the status of which is apt to be highly ambiguous) may be treated under ADR on an elective basis under the "repair allowance" provisions. As mentioned

previously under (1), 7.5 percent of the expenditure for machinery and equipment may be deducted under the repair allowance without meeting the burdensome requirements of showing that the amount really is an expense for tax purposes. The allowance includes repairs and maintenance expenditures with respect to assets placed in service before 1971. Most tax elections are irrevocable or changeable only with the consent of the Internal Revenue Service. But a taxpayer is allowed to determine annually whether he will use this repair rule.[45]

(5) A comprehensive system of depreciation accounting is prescribed, requiring in particular the use of "vintage accounts," under which assets are accounted for by year of acquisition. Each item of eligible property is placed in a vintage account of the taxable year of election. Any number of vintage accounts of a taxable year may be established. More than one account of the same vintage may be established for different assets of the same asset guideline class.[46] Property whose original use does not commence with the taxpayer may not be placed in a vintage account with property whose original use does commence with the taxpayer. Nor may personal property be placed in a vintage account with other property.[47] The reasonable allowance for depreciation of property for any taxable year in a vintage account may not be changed to reflect any supplement or revision of the asset guideline classes or periods or revision of asset depreciation ranges after the end of the taxable year in which the account was established.[48]

ADR may be applied only in the case of "eligible property," which means property subject to the depreciation allowance, and only if:

(1) An asset guideline class and period are in effect for such property for the taxable year of election. Conceivably, there will be types of property which simply cannot qualify.

(2) The property is tangible personal property or other tangible property (not including a building or its structural components) which: (a) is used as an integral part of manufacture, production, or extraction or is used as an integral part of furnishing transportation, communications, or utility services; or (b) constitutes research or storage facilities used in connection with any of the activities described in (a).

(3) The property is first placed in service by the taxpayer after December 31, 1970, subject to a special rule where there is a mere change in the form of conducting a trade or business.

(4) During the taxable year of election, the property is used predominantly within the United States.[49]

ADR applies to used property as well as new and includes property improvements. If the unadjusted basis of used property first placed in service by the taxpayer during the taxable year of the election exceeds ten percent of the unadjusted basis of all eligible property first placed in service during the taxable year of election, the taxpayer may exclude all (but not less than all) of the eligible used property from the ADR election. Property subject to the carry-over rules applicable to tax-free reorganizations[50] is treated as used property.[51]

An election to use ADR is made with the income tax return filed for the first taxable year in which property is first placed in service by the taxpayer.[52]

Absence of Useful Life

Not every asset has an estimated useful life. Thus, no depreciation may be allowed for radium used in business, as the life of radium is indeterminate.[53] The burden of proof on the issue of useful life is on the taxpayer.[54]

The estimated useful life must be that of the asset, not that of the owner or the owner's estimate of how long it will be useful to him.[55] Depreciation cannot be taken upon the cost of an engineer's college education since there is no basis for determining the period over which the expenditure could be useful and amortized.[56]

Economic Life

Generally, depreciation is based upon the remaining useful life of the property less (in most situations) estimated salvage. But under some circumstances, the structural integrity of the property is disregarded in favor of the remaining economic life. For example, a "taxpayer" type of building on a site that is so valuable that the building is certain to be replaced by a taller structure long before the taxpayer's normal useful life span expires may be depreciated on a basis that takes into account the building's remaining economic life.[57]

But proof that economic life is shorter than structural life is not always easy to establish.[58]

Straight-Line Depreciation

The most commonly used method of determining depreciation is *straight-line depreciation.* Under this method, the estimated salvage value of an asset at the end of its estimated useful life is subtracted from the cost (or other basis) of the property, and the remainder is deductible in equal amounts over the period of the estimated useful life of the asset. If the Internal Revenue Service determines prior to the end of the period claimed by the taxpayer as the useful life of the asset that the useful life of the property should be extended, the cost of the property less its estimated salvage value less the depreciation previously allowed (or allowable) is divided equally over the remaining years of the property, as extended by the Service.[59]

The straight-line method must be used in all cases where the taxpayer has not adopted a different *acceptable* method.[60]

Objection has been raised to the straight-line method on the ground that, regardless of the use of an asset, deductions are the same in each year. That need not be the case, for if the asset can be shown to have been subject to more rapid depreciation in a particular year or years, *accelerated straight-line depreciation* is available. A taxpayer successfully argued that abnormally long working days caused assets to wear out more rapidly, the case being won by proof of excessive use and wear and tear.[61] But a court rejected this form of argument where there was no evidence that the effective life of equipment was shortened as the result of increased use.[62] Greater wear as a result of use by inexperienced operators was allowed where facts substantiated the argument.[63]

An inadequate repair program may justify accelerated straight-line depreciation where there is solid evidence that improper repairs affected the life of assets.[64]

Clearly, an allegation of more rapid wear and tear requires more than a statement of the theory that assets wear out more rapidly if used under abnormal circumstances.

Declining Balance Depreciation

The declining balance method of computing depreciation is available for some types of property. With this method, there is no subtraction of an estimated salvage value from the cost or other basis of an asset. The useful life of the property is estimated, and a uniform rate (which cannot exceed twice the appropriate straight-line rate computed without adjustment for salvage) is applied each year to the unrecovered cost of the property. In the case of an asset with a useful life of five years, for example, the taxpayer using the double declining balance method can deduct for depreciation in the first year 40 percent of the cost of the property; he can deduct for the second year 40 percent of what remains after subtracting the allowable depreciation for the first year from the cost of the property; he can deduct for the third year 40 percent of what remains after subtracting the allowable depreciation for the first and second years; and so on. The unrecovered cost at the end of the useful life of the property is presumed to be the salvage value of the asset.[65]

Where a change in declining balance depreciation is made by the Internal Revenue Service, subsequent computations of depreciation are made as though the revised useful life had been the original estimate.[66]

Sum of the Years-Digits Depreciation

The sum of the years-digits method of computing depreciation is also available for some properties. Here, the allowable depreciation is computed by applying changing fractions to the cost or other basis of the property less the estimated salvage value of the asset at the end of its estimated useful life. The fractions to be used in this computation are derived in the following manner: Add the numbers representing the years of the useful life of the asset (for example, if the useful life of the asset is five years, the numbers to be added would be 1 plus 2 plus 3 plus 4 plus 5; the total would be 15); use the sum thus obtained (15) as a denominator; use as the numerators of the fractions the same numbers taken in inverse order for each succeeding year of useful life; and multiply the total allowable depreciation (that is, cost less salvage value) by such fractions in order to compute the amounts of depreciation allowable for the several years during the useful life of the asset. Thus, in the case of an asset having a useful life of five years, $\frac{5}{15}$ of the total allowable depreciation would be deductible in the first year, $\frac{4}{15}$ would be deductible in the second year, and so on.[67]

Other Depreciation Methods

The straight-line, declining balance, and sum of the years-digits methods are not the only ones available. A taxpayer may employ any other consistent method which, when added to all allowances for the period commencing with his first use of the property and including the taxable year, does not, during the first two-thirds of the useful life of the property, exceed the total of such allowances which would have been used had depreciation been computed under the double declining balance method.[68]

When Accelerated Depreciation May Be Used

A taxpayer may not use the so-called *accelerated depreciation* methods at will. Declining balance depreciation in excess of 150 percent of the appropriate straight-line rate and the sum of the years-digits depreciation may be used only in the case of: (1) tangible property having a useful life of three years or more (there are special rules as to real estate discussed below) where (2) the original use of the property commenced with the taxpayer. The term "original use" means the first use to which the property is put, whether or not this use corresponds to the use of this property by the taxpayer. For example, a reconditioned or rebuilt machine will not qualify. Use of this method is not available to a corporation where the property had been acquired new by an individual who subsequently transferred the asset to the corporation in a nontaxable transaction for stock.[69] Where the transfer was within three years of purchase, however, accelerated depreciation was allowed.[70] Where a subsidiary corporation is liquidated tax-free into its parent company, the parent may take accelerated depreciation on property thus acquired where the subsidiary was the original user of the property. This is so even even though the subsidiary had used the straight-line method if the parent obtains Internal Revenue Service permission to change its depreciation method.[71]

Accelerated Depreciation on Real Estate

In the case of acquisitions of real estate after July 24, 1969, double declining balance depreciation is limited to new residential rental property, at least 80 percent of the net income of which is derived from rental of residential units. Other new real property acquired after that date may be depreciated only under the straight-line method or 150 percent declining balance method. In the case of used real property acquired before July 25, 1969 and used real property acquired after July 24, 1969 where construction, acquisition, or permanent financing arrangements were entered into before July 24, 1969, depreciation is limited to the 150 percent declining balance method. All other used real property, except residential property, acquired after that date may only be depreciated under the straight-line method.[72] For used residential property with a useful life of 20 years or more, one may use the 125 percent declining balance method.

Effect upon Earnings and Profits

If accelerated depreciation wipes out a corporation's earnings and profits, distributions by the corporation may be treated as taxable dividends despite the absence of such earnings and profits. For purposes of computing the earnings and profits of a corporation for any taxable year beginning after June 30, 1972, the allowance for depreciation (and amortization, if any) is deemed to be the amount which would have been allowed for that year if the straight-line method of depreciation had been used for each taxable year after that date.[73]

Thus, even if a corporation had no taxable income because accelerated depreciation had wiped out any earnings, distributions could not be regarded as tax-free on the ground that the corporation had no earnings and profits. Earnings and profits will be imputed.

Election as to Depreciation Method

A taxpayer elects to use a depreciation method in the first instance by using that method. No permission is required and there is no formal election.[74]

Change in Depreciation Method

Internal Revenue Service approval is not required for a change from the double declining balance method to the straight-line method. Request for permission to make a change is required in all other situations.[75]

When is Depreciation Taken?

Wear and tear do not wait on net income. Nor can depreciation be accumulated for use in that year in which it will bring the taxpayer the most tax benefit. Inasmuch as the year is the unit of taxation, depreciation must be taken in that year to which it is assigned by the depreciation method the taxpayer consistently applies.[76]

A taxpayer must claim the deduction in his tax return for the year in which the depreciation occurs; he cannot take it in a later year.[77] The general rule is that the cost or other basis of the property must be decreased for depreciation by the amount *allowed* or the amount *allowable,* whichever is greater. *Allowed* means the extent of reduction of the taxpayer's income taxes. *Allowable* means the amount that should have been deducted.

When Depreciation Commences

Depreciation can be taken when depreciable property is available for use "should the occasion arise" even if the property is not in fact in use.[78]

Preparatory to engaging in the sawmill business, an individual acquired machinery and equipment to be used in that business. By the end of the taxable year, he had not completed preparations for engaging in that business and was not in fact engaged in it. No depreciation was allowed, for he was not carrying on that business during the taxable year, nor were the assets shown to have been used in any other trade or business during that time.[79]

Depreciation is not allowed on assets used in a training program prior to the taxpayer's commencing its business.[80]

Salvage

Except in the case of declining balance depreciation, salvage must be taken into account in arriving at the basis of property to be subjected to the depreciation allowance.[81] The special treatment of salvage under the new Asset Depreciation Range System (ADR) was discussed earlier in this chapter.

Salvage value is the estimated amount, determined at the time an asset is acquired, that will be realizable upon the sale or other disposition of that asset when it is no longer useful in the taxpayer's trade or business. This value should be determined from the taxpayer's experience in disposing of the particular type of asset in question, or if he has no experience, he must undertake an estimate based on the best information available to him.[82]

A taxpayer cannot ignore his own experience and practice over the years and base the salvage value on the experience of someone else who happens to be in a similar line of business.[83] The most important factor is the taxpayer's own experience in his own business.[84]

Salvage value must include estimated resale or second-hand value.[85] But a taxpayer may elect not to take salvage into consideration in the case of tangible personal property where such salvage does not amount to more than ten percent of the adjusted basis of an asset.[86] Salvage value is not to be changed at any time after the determination made when an asset is acquired merely because of changes in price levels.[87]

Without proof as to the existence or nonexistence of salvage, a taxpayer cannot determine depreciation properly. The Internal Revenue Service's determination of salvage will stand unless the taxpayer can rebut it with proof.[88]

Estimated costs of removal may be deducted from anticipated salvage even though the result is negative net salvage.[89]

Year of Sale Depreciation

The Internal Revenue Service takes the position that deduction for depreciation in the year of sale of a depreciable asset is limited to the amount by which the adjusted basis of the asset at the beginning of the year exceeds the amount realized from the sale.[90] But the courts have permitted year of sale depreciation even where assets are sold at a gain if the taxpayer can demonstrate that gain resulted from an increase in the value of the asset rather than unjustifiably high depreciation write-offs in preceding years.

Where the original estimates of a taxpayer as to useful life and salvage were judged by the IRS to be reasonable and accurate, the fact of sale above the adjusted basis by itself does not establish that there is no allowable depreciation in the year of sale.[91] A taxpayer may be able to demonstrate that gain was not the result of previous excessive depreciation, but rather the result of value enhancement that was greater than wear and tear.[92]

Leased Property

In the case of improvements on leased property, depreciation or amortization must be taken over the shorter of the following two periods of time: (1) the life of the asset or (2) the terms of the lease, including optional renewal periods. But depreciation may be taken over the term of the lease without renewal periods if: (1) the unexpired lease period (determined without regard to any unexercised option to renew) is 60 percent or more of the useful life of the improvement or (2) with respect to any cost of acquiring the lease, 75 percent or more of the cost is attributable to the unexpired lease period. But if the option to renew has been exercised or there is a reasonable certainty that it will be, the renewal period will be taken into account despite these tests.[93]

Where the lessee and lessor are related parties within the meaning of the following sentence, the lease is treated as including a period of not less than the useful life. "Related parties" for this purpose are:

(1) Members of an affiliated group.[94]
(2) Certain related parties.[95] (See chapter 18, Who, What, Where.)
The most common instances of this are:

(a) A corporation and a shareholder who owns 80 percent or more of the stock.

(b) Members of a family. This means transactions between an individual and his spouse, brothers and sisters, ancestors, or lineal descendants.

(c) Certain parties between whom there is a fiduciary relationship. (This will be detailed in chapter 18.)

Where the lease is for an indefinite period, depreciation must be taken over the life of the leasehold improvements.[96] Where the facts indicate that there is reasonable certainty that leases will be renewed, depreciation of improvements must be based upon useful life.[97]

Additional First Year Depreciation

For the first taxable year in which a deduction is allowable in the case of any tangible personal property, a taxpayer (other than a trust) may elect to take an *additional* allowance of 20 percent of the cost of this property up to a maximum in any one year of $10,000 ($20,000 in the case of a joint return).[98]

Depreciation Recapture

Where assets used in the taxpayer's trade or business are sold at a gain after they have been held for more than six months, this is treated as long-term capital gain. But under the *depreciation recapture* rules, some of this gain may be treated as ordinary income.

The depreciation recapture rules differ according to the nature of the asset:

(1) Gain on the sale of depreciable personal property is treated as ordinary income to the extent of depreciation taken after 1961.[99]

(2) Except in the case of residential real property (and certain contracts in effect when the law was changed in 1969), gains from the sale of real property after December 31, 1969, are subject to depreciation recapture to the extent of the excess of accelerated depreciation taken over the amount which straight-line depreciation would have produced after 1969.[100]

For recapture purposes, depreciable personal property includes livestock purchased, but not raised by the taxpayer. It also includes elevators and escalators, but not the building or structural components.

Depreciable real property includes intangible real property (such as a leasehold), buildings and their structural components, and other real property, except property used as an integral part of manufacturing, production, extraction, or furnishing facilities for utility, research, or storage.

Federal Tax Audit

The fact that depreciation rates, lives, or salvage values have been accepted by prior Internal Revenue agents does not mean that in the current taxable year the Internal Revenue Service is obliged to go along with previous treatment. If errors have been made in former years, they will not be perpetuated.[101]

After a tax examination, a taxpayer may make an agreement with the Internal Revenue Service as to the estimated useful life, depreciation method and rate, and treatment of salvage of any property which is subject to the depreciation allowance. This agreement is binding upon both parties, and whichever party wishes to modify the agreement subsequently has the burden of establishing any facts and circumstances which were not taken into account when the agreement was made.[102] This agreement is made on *Form 2271*.

Tax-Free Reorganizations

In most types of tax-free reorganization where the successor corporation is deemed to step into the tax shoes of the predecessor corporation, the successor is obliged to continue the depreciation methods used by the predecessor as an automatic carry-over. But for taxable years ending after July 24, 1969, the deduction under any of the accelerated depreciation methods is limited to that part of the basis of the assets in the successor's hands that does not exceed the basis in the predecessor's hands.[103]

Depreciation Required by Other Federal Agencies

The fact that a depreciation method was prescribed by another Federal agency for example, the Federal Power Commission does not mean that the method is acceptable to the Internal Revenue Service.[104]

Internal Revenue Service Rulings

In many areas of the tax law, it is possible to obtain a ruling from the Internal Revenue Service as to the tax consequences of a transaction. But it has been announced that no such ruling will be issued in the case of the useful lives, depreciation rates, and salvage values of assets.[105]

The Investment Credit

A seven percent credit (four percent in the case of public utilities) is available in the case of certain property—so-called Section 38 property—acquired by a taxpayer after August 15, 1971 or in the case of property which is constructed, reconstructed, or erected by the taxpayer where the construction, is completed after that date (regardless of when construction began). In the latter situation, however, the credit is available only with respect to that part of the basis of the property attributable to construction after the date cited. The credit also is available with respect to property whose construction by the taxpayer began after March 31, 1971 and property which was acquired after that date and before August 16, 1971 if the taxpayer can clearly establish that the acquisition was made pursuant to an order placed after March 31, 1971.[106]

Section 38 property includes only property as to which depreciation, or amortization in lieu of depreciation, is allowable and which is:

(1) Tangible personal property.

(2) Other tangible property (not including a building or its structural components), but only if this property:

(a) is used as an integral part of manufacturing, production, or extraction, or of furnishing transportation, communication, electrical energy, gas, water, or sewage disposal services, or

    (b) constitutes a research facility used in connection with any of the activities referred to in (a), or

    (c) constitutes a facility used in connection with any of the activities referred to in (a) for the storage of fungible commodities.

(3) Elevators and escalators under specified conditions.

Although buildings and their structural components do not qualify for the credit, storage facilities used by the taxpayer in connection with manufacturing and the like are eligible if the storage facility actually is used *principally as* a storage facility. The term "buildings" does not include a structure which houses property used as an integral part of a manufacturing activity if the use of the structure is so closely related to the use of the equipment it houses that the structure clearly can be expected to be replaced when the property it houses is replaced. Property which is used predominantly to furnish, or in connection with the furnishing of, lodging is not eligible for the credit except where the property is used by hotels or motels for transients. Livestock, with the exception of horses, is eligible for the credit.

New property fully qualifies for the investment credit, but used property does not qualify where the purchase price is in excess of $50,000 in the taxable year. The credit may be limited in the case of foreign-produced machinery and equipment at the discretion of the President of the United States.

Property with a useful life of seven or more years qualifies for the full seven percent credit. Property with a useful life of five to less than seven years qualifies for the credit to the extent of two-thirds of its cost. Property with a useful life of three years or more and less than five qualifies for a credit of one-third of its cost.[107]

The amount of the investment credit taken in any one year cannot exceed the first $25,000 of tax liability plus 50 percent of the tax liability in excess of $25,000. Carry-overs are provided for credits which cannot be used in the current year because of this limitation, there being a three-year carryback and a seven-year carry-forward. The 50 percent limitation for 1971 or a later year is to be absorbed first by carry-overs from pre-1971 years (under the investment credit provisions which existed prior to the Revenue Act of 1971) to that year and then, to the extent of any remaining limitations, by credits arising in that year. Carry-overs of unused credits from 1970 and earlier, to the extent they have not expired, are allowed a ten-year rather than the seven-year carry-forward. But in the case of carry-overs from 1971 and later, the 50 percent limitation for the year is first absorbed by carry-overs from the pre-1971 years, then by the credits generated in that year, and finally by carry-overs to that year from 1971 and later years.[108]

Noncorporate lessors are eligible for investment credit only where there are certain short-term leases or where the property was manufactured or produced by the lessor.

Taxpayers must employ the same useful life with respect to an asset in determining the useful life of the allowable investment credit as he uses in computing depreciation or amortization on the asset.

For purposes of accounting for the investment credit in financial reports, the taxpayer is not required to use any particular method of accounting. Certain alternative methods are set forth in reports to Federal agencies.[109]

NOTES

1. *United States v. Ludey*, 274 U.S. 295 (1927).
2. *Fribourg Navigation Company, Inc. v. Commissioner*, 335 F.2d 15 (2d Cir., 1964), *rev'd on another issue*, 383 U.S. 272 (1966).
3. *Detroit Edison Company v. Commissioner*, 319 U.S. 98 (1943).
4. *Commissioner v. Indiana Broadcasting Corporation*, 350 F.2d 580 (7th Cir., 1965).
5. *Occidental Loan Company v. United States*, 235 F. Supp. 519 (D.C., S.D. Cal., 1964).
6. I.R.C. Section 167(a).
7. *Macabe Company et al.*, 42 T.C. 1105 (1964).
8. *Indiana Broadcasting Corporation*, 42 T.C. 793 (1964), *rev'd on another issue*, 350 F.2d 580 (7th Cir., 1965).
9. *Tanforan Co., Inc. v. United States*, 313 F. Supp. 796 (D.C., N.D. Cal., 1970).
10. Regulations Section 1.167(a)-9.
11. *Del E. Webb Development Co.*, T.C. Memo. 1970-154 (filed June 15, 1970).
12. *Thomas W. Blake, Jr.*, 20 T.C. 721 (1953).
13. *Easter et al. v. Commissioner*, 338 F.2d 968 (4th Cir., 1964).
14. *Kem, Jr. et al. v. Commissioner*, 432 F.2d 961 (9th Cir., 1970).
15. I.R.C. Section 167(a)(1), (2).
16. *Johnson et al. v. United States*, D.C., W.D. Mo., 1970.
17. *Riss & Company, Inc. et al.*, T.C. Memo. 1964-190 (filed July 14, 1964).
18. Regulations Section 1.167(f)-1.
19. Regulations Section 1.167(a)-2.
20. *The Edinboro Company v. United States*, 224 F. Supp. 301 (D.C., W.D. Pa., 1963).
21. *The James Brothers Coal Company*, 41 T.C. 917 (1964).
22. *William C. Gregory*, T.C. Memo. 1954-12 (filed April 19, 1954).
23. Regulations Section 1.167(a)-3.
24. Regulations Section 1.167(a)-3.
25. Revenue Ruling 66-140, 1966-1 CB 45.
26. Revenue Ruling 68-232, 1968-1 CB 79.
27. *Commissioner v. Chicago National Baseball Club*, 74 F.2d 1010 (7th Cir., 1935).
28. Regulations Section 1.167(a)-10.
29. *Marigold Foods, Inc. v. United States*, D.C., Minn., 1965.
30. Revenue Ruling 69-77, 1969-1 CB 59.
31. *United States v. S & A Company*, 338 F.2d 629 (8th Cir., 1964).
32. Regulations Section 1.167(g)-1.
33. *Tanforan Co., Inc. v. United States*, 313 F. Supp. 796 (D.C., N.D. Cal., 1970).
34. *Ibid.*
35. *Bay Sound Transportation Company et al. v. United States*, 410 F.2d 505 (5th Cir., 1969).
36. Regulations Section 1.167(a)-1(b).
37. *Western Terminal Company v. United States*, D.C., E.D. Wash., 1970.
38. *Mary Z. Bryan Estate et al. v. Commissioner*, 364 F.2d 751 (4th Cir., 1966).
39. Revenue Procedure 62-21, 1962-2 CB 418.
40. Revenue Procedure 65-13, 1965-1 CB 759.
41. Regulations Section 1.167(a)-11(b)(4).
42. The Asset Depreciation Range System categories and ranges are published in Revenue Procedure 72-10, I.R.B. 1972-8, 13.
43. Regulations Section 1.167(a)-11(c).

44. Regulations Section 1.167(a)-11(d)(1).
45. Regulations Section 1.167(a)-11(d)(2)(iii).
46. Regulations Section 1.167(a)-11(b)(3)(i).
47. Regulations Section 1.167(a)-11(b)(3)(ii).
48. Regulations Section 1.167(a)-11(b)(4)(ii).
49. Regulations Section 1.167(a)-11(b)(2).
50. I.R.C. Section 381(a).
51. Regulations Section 1.167(a)-11(b)(5)(iii).
52. The detailed information which must be submitted with the election is listed in Regulations Section 1.167(a)-11(f)(2).
53. Revenue Ruling 68-192, 1968-1 CB 78.
54. *Potts, Davis & Co.*, T.C. Memo. 1968-257 (filed November 12, 1968).
55. *Hilaire P. Caussement*, T.C. Memo. 1966-179 (filed August 1, 1966), *aff'd*, 391 F.2d 227 (6th Cir., 1968).
56. *Nathaniel A. Denman et al.*, 48 T.C. 439 (1967).
57. *Adda, Inc.*, 9 T.C. 199 (1947), *rev'd on another issue*, 171 F.2d 367 (2d Cir., 1948).
58. *James D. Dunn et al.*, 42 T.C. 490 (1964).
59. *James Brothers Bakery, Inc. v. United States*, 411 F.2d 1282 (Ct. Cl., 1969).
60. Regulations Section 1.167(b)-1(a).
61. *Clarence Eaton et al.*, 10 T.C. 869 (1948).
62. *H. E. Harmon Coal Corporation v. Commissioner*, 200 F.2d 415 (4th Cir., 1952).
63. *Harmony Grove Mills*, 2 B.T.A. 1200 (1925).
64. *Otis Steel Company*, 6 B.T.A. 358 (1927); *The Avon Mills*, 7 B.T.A. 143 (1927).
65. *James Brothers Bakery, Inc. v. United States*, 411 F.2d 1282 (Ct. Cl., 1969).
66. Regulations Section 1.167(b)-2(c).
67. *Jones Brothers Bakery, Inc. v. United States*, 411 F.2d 1282 (Ct. Cl., 1969).
68. I.R.C. Section 167(b)(4).
69. Revenue Ruling 56-265, 1956-1 CB 156.
70. Revenue Ruling 67-286, 1967-2 CB 101.
71. Revenue Ruling 66-345, 1966-2 CB 67.
72. I.R.C. Section 167(j).
73. I.R.C. Section 312(m).
74. Regulations Section 1.167(c)-1.
75. I.R.C. Section 167(e).
76. *Virginian Hotel Corporation of Lynchburg v. Helvering*, 319 U.S. 523 (1953).
77. *Kittredge v. Commissioner*, 88 F.2d 532 (2d Cir., 1937).
78. *Dougherty v. Commissioner*, 159 F.2d 269 (4th Cir., 1946).
79. *Chester Witecki*, T.C. Memo. 1963-256 (filed September 19, 1963).
80. *Richmond Television Corporation v. United States*, 345 F.2d 901 (4th Cir., 1965).
81. Regulations Section 1.167(b)-2(a). (The special treatment of salvage under ADR was discussed earlier in this chapter.)
82. *R. E. Moorhead & Son, Inc.*, 40 T.C. 704 (1963).
83. *Catherine F. Dinkins et al.*, 45 T.C. 593 (1966).
84. *Engineers Limited Pipeline Co.*, 44 T.C. 226 (1965).
85. *Massey Motors, Inc. et al. v. United States*, 364 U.S. 92 (1960).
86. I.R.C. Section 167(f).
87. Regulations Section 1.167(a)-1(d).
88. *Brandtjen & Kluge, Inc.*, 34 T.C. 416 (1960).
89. *Portland General Electric Company v. United States*, 189 F. Supp. 290 (D.C., Ore., 1960), *aff'd*, 310 F.2d 877 (9th Cir., 1962).
90. Revenue Ruling 62-92, 1962-1 CB 29.
91. *Fribourg Navigation Company, Inc. v. Commissioner*, 383 U.S. 272 (1966).
92. *Macabe Company, Inc. et al.*, 42 T.C. 1105 (1964).
93. I.R.C. Section 178(a).

94. As defined in I.R.C. Section 1504.

95. As defined in I.R.C. Section 267.

96. *James L. Stinnett, Jr. et al.*, 54 T.C. 221 (1970).

97. *Radio City Trailer Park*, T.C. Memo. 1963-313 (filed November 26, 1963).

98. I.R.C. Section 179.

99. I.R.C. Section 1245.

100. I.R.C. Section 1250(a)(1), as amended by the Tax Reform Act of 1969.

101. *Engineers Limited Pipeline Company*, 44 T.C. 226 (1965).

102. Regulations Section 1.167(d)-1.

103. I.R.C. Section 381(c)(6).

104. *Gulf Power Company*, 10 T.C. 852 (1948).

105. Revenue Procedure 69-6, 1969-1 CB 396.

106. I.R.C. Sections 49 and 50.

107. I.R.C. Section 46(c)(2).

108. I.R.C. Section 46.

109. I.R.C. Sections 49 and 50.

CHAPTER 13

Bad Debts and Other Write-Offs

In general, reserves are not deductible for tax purposes except in the case of depreciation and bad debts, and, as to these, a deduction may be disallowed by the Internal Revenue Service because it is unreasonable. Deductions for reserves for contingencies or losses have been disallowed even though insurance was unavailable.[1] Likewise, a deduction for a reserve for estimated future costs has also been disallowed,[2] and additions to a renegotiation reserve were ruled not deductible even though the taxpayer had considerable experience with the renegotiation process and the additions to the reserve proved to be within two percent of the actual net amount of the renegotiation.[3]

The fact that a reserve for a contract refund was established according to generally accepted accounting principles does not, of itself, establish its propriety for Federal income tax purposes where the statutory scheme requires a different method.[4]

Sums set up as a warranty reserve by a dealer have been ruled not deductible; deductions would be allowed only when expenditures were incurred under the warranty.[5]

Bad Debts

Deductions may be taken for bad debts in either of two ways: (1) as a write-off in the year the debt becomes bad or (2) by making additions to a reserve for bad debts to bring the year-end balance to what experience shows to be the proper proportion of bad debts to measurable determinants such as sales or receivables. The two methods cannot be combined for tax purposes.[6]

For a debt to be deducted as bad, it must have been previously included in income. A taxpayer cannot reduce ordinary income he actually received by a sum which he never included as income.[7] A taxpayer cannot take a bad debt deduction for an advance which was never reflected in income, as in the case of an advance never regarded as collectible and thus never reflected in the income of an accrual-basis taxpayer.[8]

A bad debt must be an actual and existing debt. The obligation to repay cannot depend on a contingency that has not yet occurred.[9] So deductions cannot be taken where a demand is necessary and no demand has been made.[10]

To be deductible as a bad debt, the obligation must have been enforceable. So the deduction will be disallowed if it is based on an obligation which cannot be enforced because it is usurious.[11]

For a deduction to stand, the debt must not only have been bad at the close of the taxable year, but it must also not have been worthless when it was originally incurred.[12] The deduction will not be allowed in a taxable year if it appears that the debt was worthless before the start of that year.[13]

The Identifiable Event

A debt is deductible for tax purposes in the year in which an *identifiable event* establishing its worthlessness occurs.[14] Until there is such an event, the debt is not bad.[15] A mere opinion that a debt is worthless is not enough.[16] Worthlessness must be determined by objective standards.

If it can be shown that some identifiable event occured during the course of the year which effectively demonstrated the absence of potential value, this is sufficient.[17] Thus, an authoritative balance sheet showing that liabilities exceed assets so as to leave no equity for the corporate stock may be sufficient evidence of worthlessness.[18] Where there is no authoritative balance sheet available, worthlessness may be shown by an identifiable event in the corporate life of the debtor normally considered as effectively destroying the potential value of the debt (such as receivership, bankruptcy, liquidation, or cessation of business).[19] Also, the debtor corporation's filing along with its final Federal income tax return a notice of contemplated dissolution has been ruled sufficient.[20]

A taxpayer should strike a middle course between optimism and pessimism and determine debts to be worthless in the exercise of sound business judgment based upon as complete information as is reasonably obtainable.[21] Thus, even though a corporation's assets are less than its liabilities, if there is reasonable hope or expectation that its assets will exceed its liabilities sometime in the future, its stock has a potential value and is not worthless.[22]

The same identifiable event test that applies to bad debts applies to worthless securities. When the stock of a corporation becomes worthless, there is usually some identifiable event in the corporation's life which puts an end to any expectation that the corporate assets will exceed its liabilities.[23] The test is whether a prudent purchaser in an arm's length transaction would have regarded a stock investment as representing any equity at all.[24] Complete termination of a corporation's operations, where liabilities exceed assets and a receiver has been appointed, establishes worthlessness.[25] The immediate realities, realizations, and reasonable expectations must be considered.[26]

Sales by some of the security holders of their securities to afford a basis for claiming a loss deduction are not sufficient to show when the securities became worthless.[27] But once worthlessness at a particular time is established, the fact that at a subsequent time someone is willing to take a "flyer" at a nominal price is immaterial.[28]

As long as the taxpayer can show that an item is actually worthless, one judge ruled that he could write it off, when he chooses, provided he can show a good non-tax reason for his choice.[29]

Reserve for Bad Debts

By using the reserve method of handling bad debts, the taxpayer can take the deduction in anticipation of actual worthlessness.[30] A reserve is neither an asset nor a liability. It has no existence except upon the books and cannot be transferred to any other entity.[31]

In creating a reserve for bad debts, the taxpayer makes an estimate based upon his experience and knowledge. The amount he estimates lies within his discretion, but it must be reasonable; if unreasonable, it can be challenged by the Treasury.[32] Any additions to the reserve that are necessary are currently deductible. But if a reserve is adequate without any addition, no deduction will be allowed for an addition to the reserve in that taxable year.[33]

A taxpayer's past experience in collecting receivables is a reliable guide for measuring probable future losses.[34] The yardstick may be whatever amount is necessary to bring the year-end balance in the reserve account to what experience has shown to be the probable loss expressed in terms of such factors as sales, receivables, or the recommendations of a knowledgeable third party. The test, however, is whether the amount ultimately determined, regardless of the formula used, constitutes a reasonable addition to the taxpayer's reserve. What is a reasonable addition depends upon the facts and circumstances of the particular business and also on general business conditions.[35]

The Commissioner of Internal Revenue has discretion in determining the reasonableness of additions to a reserve for bad debts. He will be overruled by a court only when there is a clear showing of abuse of discretion. The Commissioner's determination may be upheld although the taxpayer's approach might be philosophically more accurate than his.[36]

Additions to a reserve for bad debts are not deductible if made merely on the basis of possibilities. This would be akin to a reserve for contingencies, which is not deductible. While additions to the reserve must be made in the light of existing conditions and cannot be based on trends which might develop in the future, subsequent loss experience may be considered as additional evidence tending to confirm the reasonableness of the taxpayer's judgment.[37]

Although a taxpayer may not retroactively adjust annual additions to the reserve because unanticipated future losses disclose them to have been inadequate, his subsequent loss experience may be considered as additional evidence tending to demonstrate whether the method used to compute annual additions was reasonable.[38]

Any balance in the reserve when the reserve is no longer necessary must be considered as taxable income at that time since that balance represents amounts which were previously deducted.[39] Where an individual transferred his business to a new corporation for all of that corporation's stock, a bad debt reserve which he had set up prior to incorporation was disallowed; he no longer was in business and so he did not need it.[40]

Partial Bad Debts

When satisfied that a debt is only in part recoverable, the Internal Revenue Service may allow a deduction for that part of the debt actually charged off on the books.[41] An actual charge-off on the books is required if the taxpayer takes a tax deduction for a partial bad debt.[42]

The write-off must be of specific debts.[43] One cannot take a specific percentage of total receivables or any other generalized figure. Anything showing an intent to eliminate an item from assets is sufficient to constitute a charge-off.[44]

Partial worthlessness must be evidenced by some event or change in the debtor's financial condition which change occurred after the debt was created and which adversely affected the debtor's ability to make repayment.[45]

Business and Nonbusiness Bad Debts

Business bad debts are deductible in full. *Nonbusiness* bad debts are deductible as short-term capital losses.[46] A business bad debt must be connected with the taxpayer's trade or business, but it can arise out of an isolated transaction.[47] If the creation of the debt was significantly motivated by the taxpayer's trade or business, it is immaterial that another, nonqualifying motivation was present as well.[48] The business motivation might be to commence, sustain, or sever a business relationship.[49]

An individual who advances funds to a corporation or guarantees its obligation is not entitled to a business bad debt deduction upon default unless he can establish that he was in the business of advancing funds to the corporation. An individual's devoting his time and energies to the affairs of a corporation is not, of itself, sufficient to show that he is in business. Although such activities may produce income or gain in the form of dividends or may enhance the value of an investment, this return is usually regarded as an investment return generated by the corporation's business as distinguished from the investor's business.[50] But a business bad debt deduction was permitted where the taxpayer invested in stocks and guaranteed loans of various corporations for a fee.[51]

If an employee makes a loan to his employer corporation in order to protect his job, any resulting loss is a business bad debt, especially where he is virtually unemployable because of age or personality factors.[52]

Guarantees

There is no real economic difference between the loss of an investment made in the form of a direct loan to a corporation or other party, and one made in the form of a guaranteed loan.[53] Thus, a reserve for bad debts is permissible even if the debts are owed to someone other than the taxpayer (such as under a guaranty).[54]

Change of Method of Accounting for Bad Debts

A taxpayer desiring to change his method of accounting for bad debts from the specific charge-off method to the reserve method may do so by filing an application on *Form 3115* with the District Director of Internal Revenue where the tax return is filed. The application must be filed within the first 180 days of the taxable year in which the change is to be effected. Unless a letter is received by the taxpayer from the District Director denying permission, it may be assumed that the change has been approved. Permission will be denied where the form is not filed within the required time. Revenue Procedure 64-51 shows the adjustments which must be made by reason of this change of method.[55]

Recovery of Bad Debts

Under the specific charge-off method, the recovery of a debt which was written off as bad does not involve any adjustment in the taxable year of the write-off. Instead, the recovered bad debt is income in the year it is received provided the original write-off produced a *tax benefit* at that time. Thus, where the original deduction reduced taxable income, a tax benefit was received, and the recovery of the debt was taxable income in the year of recovery. But if in the year of the charge-off the taxpayer had no taxable income and thus derived no benefit from the deduction, recovery of the debt would not create income.[56]

Where a taxpayer uses the reserve method, any recovered bad debt merely reduces the amount which would otherwise have to be added to bring the reserve balance up to the regular percentage of receivables or sales which measures proper additions to the reserve.

Abnormal Obsolescence

Under Section 167(a) of the Internal Revenue Code, a reasonable allowance for exhaustion, wear and tear, and obsolescence of property used in a trade or business is permitted in the form of a depreciation deduction.[57] Where abnormal obsolescence occurs, a special write-off is allowed. Where depreciable property is permanently withdrawn from use in a trade or business or in the production of income, the retirement is considered normal unless the taxpayer can show that the withdrawal resulted from a cause not contemplated when the depreciation rate was fixed. Thus, retirement of an asset is *normal retirement* where it occurs within the range of years used in fixing the depreciation rate and the asset has reached a condition at which, in the normal course of events, similar assets are usually retired in the business. However, the retirement may be considered abnormal if the asset is withdrawn earlier or under other circumstances as, for example, where the asset has been damaged by casualty or has lost its usefulness because of extraordinary obsolescence.

While a depreciation deduction is based on an allowance for the use of an asset, a write-off for *abnormal obsolescence* is based upon disuse.[58] Declining values in themselves will not support a claim for abnormal obsolescence.[59] Nor will overexpansion or similar management decisions support an abnormal obsolescence deduction.[60]

Obsolescence involves a loss of economic usefulness for any purpose.[61] It involves economic conditions which, in the picturesque language of one decision, "cause or contribute to the relentless march of physical property to the junk pile." [62]

The deduction cannot be based upon an expectation that future progress in the art will be so great that the assets will not be capable of profitable use, notwithstanding their workable condition. Thus, the deduction must be based on present conditions and the progress actually being made during the years when the deduction is claimed, which progress would have to lead to the conclusion that the assets are actually becoming obsolete. The state of becoming obsolete must be proven. What occurs after the taxable year is not sufficient to prove conditions existing during that year.[63] When property has become outmoded and the ordinary depreciation deduction is not enough to secure a return of original cost (less depreciation already taken) by the expiration of the useful life of the property, an obsolescence deduction may be available.[64] An obsolescence deduction may be denied in the absence of evidence that newer and better processes have been invented since the acquisition of the asset which render the asset obsolete.[65]

Affirmative action is needed to support an obsolescence deduction. So the deduction was denied where there was no evidence that the corporate officers had ever contemplated abandonment of equipment prior to the expiration of its normal life and where there was nothing to show that during the period in question, or since, there had been any change in the art of manufacturing the taxpayer's product or any development which rendered the taxpayer's equipment outmoded for the purposes for which it had been acquired.[66] Obsolescence deductions were disallowed to a ferry company that suffered losses because of competition where no effort was made to discontinue the service or to liquidate the company. Mere diminution in value of assets while they are still in use is not a proper basis for an obsolescence deduction.[67] To get the deduction, a taxpayer must show with reasonable certainty: (1) that the property is becoming obsolete; (2) when it will become obsolete, that is, when its normal useful life should expire; and (3) that the property will be obsolete before the end of that useful life.

Where a company president testified that if he were presently buying equipment, he would not buy the models used by his company because larger and more efficient equipment had made the former type of asset obsolete, but he admitted that equipment of the capabilities of his own still was being manufactured and used, the deduction was denied.[68]

In addition, giving up the use of property because of excess capacity after an acquisition does not support the deduction.[69]

Where a manufacturer lost its contract to manufacture shells for the government at war's end, the full value of specialized machinery for such production (less estimated salvage) was deductible as obsolescence upon the termination of the contract.[70] Additional buildings that had been constructed for a manufacturer under like circumstances could also be written off.[71]

Failure to acquire steel during a time of shortage did not make a tank manufacturer's production equipment obsolete even though the manufacturer was prevented from using machinery and equipment for the purpose originally intended. Although there was evidence that these facilities were not being used for their original purpose, there was no evidence that they had become obsolete by: (1) having lost economic usefulness for the purpose for which they had been acquired and (2) being useless for any other purpose.[72]

Where a hotel based its obsolescence claim primarily upon the advent of the motel or motor hotel, a court noted that the taxpayer had confused obsolescence with competition.[73] Obsolescence has not set in merely because equipment is useless for the reason that the owner has no business for which to use it.[74] Even if a building had been constructed for a specific commercial purpose, the deduction will not be allowed if the building is usable for other commercial purposes.[75] Equipment that is retained in place, ready for use if there is a demand for it, does not give rise to the deduction. More than nonuse or disuse is necessary.[76]

Facilities are not obsolete if they still are being used for their original purpose at the time the case is argued.[77] A corporation could not claim abnormal obsolescence in the case of a heavily reinforced, specialized building constructed to produce ceramic nuclear fuel elements for the Atomic Energy Commission, after the AEC cancelled the contract. The fact that the building was no longer being used did not mean that it could not be used for *some* other purpose, and admittedly, management was seeking to find another use for its building. Certain portions of it, in fact, still were being used.[78]

Changes in the character of a neighborhood can make a building economically valueless. An obsolescence deduction may be allowed where such conditions are known to exist at the end of the taxable year although the building is not abandoned until the following year.[79] But the deduction is not justified unless the taxpayer can show that the life of the asset or his use of it has been affected adversely by the neighborhood's deterioration or change.[80]

A retail furniture dealer was permitted, by reason of substantial changes in the art, to write off fixtures that were abandoned solely because of their unfitness for use in a modern store which was being established even though they were not discarded because of physical deterioration.[81]

Where a business was extinguished by law as being noxious, the owners could not demand partial compensation from the government in the form of an abatement of taxes otherwise due; the obsolescence deduction could not be used to provide partial compensation.[82] The obsolescence deduction was allowed for *tangible* assets after prohibitory legislation, but not for loss of good will as a result of such legislation.[83]

Obsolescence was not allowed on grain storage facilities which the taxpayer believed would be rendered useless because the government might terminate its present agricultural support policies. In the absence of reasonable foreseeability of a solution which would affect the taxpayer's business in a manner requiring abandonment of its grain storage facilities, agitation for such a solution to the farm surplus problem was held insufficient to support a claim for anticipated obsolescence.[84]

Deduction will be denied for a product or process that is "too far out." No deduction was allowed for obsolescence where improvements allegedly available to competitors had not as yet been put to use anywhere and, in fact, had not been perfected even to the extent that the consequences of research could be used by competitors.[85]

Loss on Abandonment

In the case of *abandonment,* the taxpayer recoups the unrecovered cost or other basis of an asset in that year without waiting for annual depreciation write-offs which, of course, would be nonexistent where real estate or property without an established useful life is involved.

Traditionally, the loss for physical abandonment has been based upon evidence establishing an intent to abandon the asset coupled with some overt external act or identifiable event to which the abandonment can be related.[86] The determination as to the year an asset loses its useful life or becomes worthless is a matter of sound business judgment, and that judgment is ordinarily given effect unless it appears from the facts that the decision as to the year of loss was unreasonable or unfair at the time the decision was made.[87]

For tax purposes, abandonment is defined as giving up property with the intention of never again reclaiming it. It requires not only a cessation of use, but also an *intent* to abandon. Disuse or nonuse is not sufficient to constitute an abandonment.[88]

An abandonment is deductible only in the taxable year in which it occurs.[89] It must be shown that the loss was actually sustained during the taxable year, that the loss became fixed by some identifiable event in such year, and that the owner intended to abandon the property.[90]

No abandonment loss was allowed in the case of a theatre merely because the owner decided to give no more performances. This was not tantamount to a permanent disposition.[91] Where it is not a remote possibility that the owner will alter its decision not to use a portion of the property for a particular purpose, no deduction is allowed.[92]

An abandonment requires an affirmative step by the taxpayer. One does not abandon title to an improvement to realty by his subjective decision to do so even though he may advise his attorney and his accountant that he intends to do so.[93]

Demolition

Demolition loss is not permitted where one acquires a building with the intention of tearing it down.[94] The cost of the property plus the demolition expenses are considered to be what was actually paid for the property. On the other hand, loss was allowed where there was no intent to demolish at the time of acquisition.[95]

If a change in circumstances makes a building unsuitable for the use for which it was purchased, the purchaser is entitled to a demolition loss in the year of demolition equal to the adjusted basis of the building less the net proceeds of salvage.[96] In one instance, a bank purchased land and a building with the intention of using the structure for bank purposes. The directors ultimately concluded that it was not feasible to perform the construction work necessary to adapt the old building to the conditions required by state law. Thus, five years later, the structure was torn down. A demolition loss was allowed in the year of razing; for this purpose, the original cost could be allocated between land and building.[97]

NOTES

1. *Ehlen et al. v. United States*, 163 Ct. Cl. 35 (Ct. Cl., 1963); *Spring Canyon Coal Company v. Commissioner*, 43 F.2d 78 (10th Cir., 1930); *L. A. Thompson Scenic Railway Company*, 2 B.T.A. 664 (1925).
2. *Simplified Tax Records, Inc.*, 41 T.C. 65 (1963).
3. *The Overlakes Corporation v. Commissioner*, 348 F.2d 462 (2d Cir., 1965).
4. *Portland Copper & Tank Works, Inc.*, 43 T.C. 182 (1964).
5. *Bell Electric Co. et al.*, 45 T.C. 158 (1965).
6. *Wengel, Inc. v. United States*, 306 F. Supp. 121 (D.C., E.D. Mich., 1969).
7. *Hendricks et al. v. Commissioner*, 406 F.2d 269 (5th Cir., 1969).
8. *Richard M. Drachman et al.*, 23 T.C. 558 (1954).
9. *Jeremiah J. O'Donnell et al.*, T.C. Memo. 1964-38 (filed February 19, 1964).
10. *Emzy T. Barker et al.*, T.C. Memo. 1963-314 (filed November 26, 1963).
11. *William K. Harriman et al.*, T.C. Memo. 1967-190 (filed October 4, 1967).
12. *I. D. Blumenthal et al.*, T.C. Memo. 1963-269 (filed September 30, 1963), *aff'd on another issue*, 334 F.2d 281 (4th Cir., 1964).
13. *Riss & Company, Inc. et al.*, T.C. Memo. 1964-190 (filed July 14, 1964).
14. *Industrial Rayon Corporation v. Commissioner*, 94 F.2d 383 (6th Cir., 1938).
15. *Iowa Southern Utilities Company v. United States*, 348 F.2d 492 (Ct. Cl., 1965).
16. *George M. Burger et al.*, T.C. Memo. 1964-92 (filed April 13, 1964).
17. *Herbert W. Dustin et al.*, 53 T.C. 491 (1969).
18. *Mahler v. Commissioner*, 119 F.2d 869 (2d Cir., 1941).
19. *Hans Christensen*, T.C. Memo. 1969-112 (filed May 29, 1969).
20. *Genecov v. United States*, 412 F.2d 556 (5th Cir., 1969).
21. *Minneapolis St. Paul & Sault Sainte Marie Railroad Company v. United States*, 164 Ct. Cl. 226 (1964).
22. *Bert Ruud et al.*, T.C. Memo. 1969-252 (filed November 26, 1969).
23. *Ibid.*
24. *Ainsley v. Commissioner*, 332 F.2d 555 (9th Cir., 1964).
25. *Charles W. Steadman et al.*, 50 T.C. 369 (1968).
26. *Powell White et al.*, T.C. Memo. 1970-132 (filed May 28, 1970).
27. *Keeney v. Commissioner*, 116 F.2d 401 (2d Cir., 1940).
28. *Gilbert H. Pearsall*, 10 B.T.A. 467 (1928).
29. *Charles W. Steadman et al.*, 50 T.C. 369 (1968).
30. *Foster Frosty Foods, Inc.*, 39 T.C. 772 (1963).
31. *Geyer, Cornell & Newell, Inc.*, 6 T.C. 96 (1946).
32. *Paramount Liquor Co. v. Commissioner*, 242 F.2d 249 (8th Cir., 1957).
33. *Nash et al. v. United States*, 398 U.S. 1 (1970); *Roanoke Vending Exchange, Inc.*, 40 T.C. 735 (1963).
34. *Home Ice Cream & Ice Co.*, 19 B.T.A. 762 (1930).
35. *Black Motor Company, Incorporated*, 41 B.T.A. 300 (1940).
36. *United States v. Haskel Engineering & Supply Co.*, 380 F.2d 786 (9th Cir., 1967).

37. *Massachusetts Business Development Corporation*, 52 T.C. 946 (1969).

38. *Rio Grande Building & Loan Association*, 36 T.C. 657 (1961).

39. *J. E. Hawes Corporation*, 44 T.C. 705 (1965).

40. *Max Schuster et al.*, 50 T.C. 98 (1968).

41. I.R.C. Section 166(a)(2).

42. *Ardele, Inc. et al.*, T.C. Memo. 1969-83 (filed April 23, 1969).

43. Regulations Section 1.166-3(a).

44. *Commissioner v. MacDonald Engineering Company*, 102 F.2d 942 (7th Cir., 1939).

45. *H. W. Findley*, 25 T.C. 311 (1955), aff'd, 236 F.2d 959 (5th Cir., 1956).

46. I.R.C. Section 166.

47. *Robert Cluett, 3d et al.*, 8 T.C. 1178 (1947).

48. *Weddle v. Commissioner*, 325 F.2d 849 (2d Cir., 1964).

49. *Axelrod v. Commissioner*, 320 F.2d 327 (6th Cir., 1963).

50. *Whipple et al. v. Commissioner*, 373 U.S. 193 (1963).

51. *Carpenter v. Erikson*, 255 F. Supp. 613 (D.C., Ore., 1966).

52. *Isador Jaffe et al.*, T.C. Memo. 1967-215 (filed October 30, 1967).

53. *Putnam et al. v. Commissioner*, 352 U.S. 82 (1956).

54. *Wilkins Pontiac v. Commissioner*, 298 F.2d 893 (9th Cir., 1962).

55. 1964-2 CB 1003.

56. I.R.C. Section 111.

57. I.R.C. Section 167(a).

58. *Renziehausen v. Commissioner*, 280 U.S. 387 (1930).

59. *State Line & Sullivan Railroad Co. v. Phillips*, 98 F.2d 651 (3d Cir., 1938).

60. *The Real Estate-Land Title & Trust Co. v. United States*, 309 U.S. 13 (1940).

61. *Mid-States Products*, 21 T.C. 696 (1954).

62. *The Real Estate-Land Title & Trust Co. v. United States*, 309 U.S. 13 (1940).

63. *Benjamin Booth & Co., Inc.*, 4 B.T.A. 248 (1926).

64. *Southeastern Building Corporation v. Commissioner*, 148 F.2d 879 (5th Cir., 1945).

65. *McKeever v. Eaton et al.*, 6 F. Supp. 697 (D.C., Conn., 1934).

66. *Mid-States Products*, 21 T.C. 696 (1954).

67. *Detroit & Windsor Ferry Company v. Woodworth*, 115 F.2d 795 (6th Cir., 1940).

68. *Kohinoor Coal Company*, T.C. Memo. 1956-79 (filed March 30, 1956).

69. *The Real Estate-Land Title & Trust Company v. United States*, 309 U.S. 13 (1940).

70. *United States v. Wagner Electric Mfg. Co.*, 61 F.2d 204 (8th Cir., 1932).

71. *United States Cartridge Company v. United States*, 284 U.S. 511 (1932).

72. *Ione Thompson et al.*, T.C. Memo. 1965-237 (filed August 20, 1965).

73. *Atlanta Biltmore Hotel Corporation et al. v. Commissioner*, 349 F.2d 677 (5th Cir., 1965).

74. *Roman S. Gontarek et al.*, T.C. Memo., Docket Nos. 28267 and 28275 (entered February 4, 1952).

75. *Olean Times-Herald Corporation*, 37 B.T.A. 922 (1938).

76. *Mid-States Products*, 21 T.C. 696 (1954).

77. *James D. Dunn et al.*, 42 T.C. 490 (1964).

78. *Coors Porcelain Company*, 52 T.C. 682 (1969), aff'd, 429 F.2d 1 (10th Cir., 1970).

79. *Cosmopolitan Corporation et al.*, T.C. Memo. 1959-112 (filed June 12, 1959).

80. *Northern Illinois College of Optometry*, T.C. Memo., Docket No. 108632 (entered August 23, 1943).

81. *Townsend-Ueberrhein Clothing Company v. Crooks*, 41 F.2d 66 (D.C., W.D. Mo., 1930).

82. *Burnet v. Niagara Falls Brewing Co.*, 282 U.S. 648 (1931).

83. *Moise v. Burnet*, 52 F.2d 1071 (9th Cir., 1931).

84. *James D. Dunn et al.*, 42 T.C. 490 (1964).

85. *Balaban & Katz Corporation v. Commissioner*, 30 F.2d 807 (7th Cir., 1929).

86. *Tanforan Co., Inc. v. United States*, 313 F. Supp. 796 (D.C., N.D. Cal., 1970).

87. *A. J. Industries, Inc. v. United States*, 388 F.2d 701 (Ct. Cl., 1967).

88. *Reid et al. v. United States*, D.C., E.D. Cal., 1969.

89. Revenue Ruling 54-481, 1954-2 CB 112.
90. *A. J. Industries, Inc. v. United States*, 388 F.2d 701 (Ct. Cl., 1967).
91. *Jones Beach Theatre Corporation*, T.C. Memo. 1966-100 (filed May 17, 1966).
92. *Citizens Bank of Weston v. Commissioner*, 252 F.2d 425 (4th Cir., 1958).
93. Concurring opinion, *Burke v. Commissioner*, 283 F.2d 487 (9th Cir., 1960).
94. *Dan L. Garrett, Jr. et al.*, T.C. Memo. 1966-170 (filed July 20, 1966).
95. *Jerome S. Murray et al.*, T.C. Memo. 1965-148 (filed May 27, 1965).
96. *William Heyman*, 6 T.C. 799 (1946).
97. *Panhandle State Bank*, 39 T.C. 813 (1963).

CHAPTER 14

Inventories

Income Tax Significance

Almost without exception, the Federal income tax laws are concerned with realized gains and losses. The provision authorizing the use of inventories in tax computation is an exception.[1] Whenever the production, purchase, or sale of merchandise of any kind is an income-producing factor, merchandise on hand (including finished goods, work in process, raw materials, and supplies) at the beginning and end of the year must be taken into account.[2] This puts every inventory-carrying taxpayer on the accrual basis with but insignificant exceptions.[3] A taxpayer does have the opportunity, rarely availed of, of showing that the cash method *does* properly reflect income in his particular case.[4] A company may have to be on the accrual basis even if it is in a service business where the sale of merchandise is an income-producing factor; for example, a funeral director who made package sales of funerals which included caskets.[5]

Inventory-Keeping Requirements

If inventories are not taken into account in the computation of taxable income or if the tax return interrogatory does not give proper information as to inventories, the return is characterized as "no return" and delinquency and negligence penalties may be assessed.[6] A negligence penalty also may be imposed if inventory records and supporting data are not preserved for the period during which the tax return is open for audit.[7]

Where a physical inventory is available, perpetual inventory records may not be used for Federal income tax purposes.[8] Book inventories should be adjusted to physical inventories at reasonable intervals.[9]

The precise manner in which inventory records are to be maintained is not specified. But they do not have to be an integral part of the books of account. Inventory data may be kept separately on loose sheets of paper.[10]

Inventory Requirements

The Treasury Regulations provide two tests to which each inventory must conform: (1) it must approach, as closely as possible, the best accounting practice in the trade or industry and (2) it must clearly reflect the income.[11]

Consistency should be given greater weight than any particular method of inventory valuation provided the method used conforms to the above requirements. An erroneous method does not become acceptable solely on the basis of consistent use for an extended period of time,[12] for where the method does not clearly reflect income, little weight is given to consistency.[13]

The Internal Revenue Service may change a taxpayer's inventory method even if prior tax returns had been examined without objection to the method used.[14]

What Is Included in Inventory?

The inventory used for Federal income tax purposes should include all finished or partly finished goods and, in the case of raw materials and supplies, only those which have been acquired for sale or which will physically become a part of the merchandise intended for sale. This includes containers (such as kegs, bottles, and cases) whether returnable or not, if title will pass to the purchaser of the product to be sold therein. Merchandise should be included in the inventory only if title is vested in the taxpayer. Accordingly, the seller should include in his inventory goods under contract for sale but not yet segregated and applied to the contract as well as goods out on consignment. But he should exclude from inventory goods sold (including containers), where title has passed to the purchaser.

A purchaser should include in inventory merchandise purchased, where title has passed to him, although such merchandise is in transit or for other reasons has not yet been reduced to physical possession. But he should not include goods ordered for future delivery, where transfer of title has not yet been effected.[15]

Direct costs are included in inventory; this means not only direct costs of labor and materials, but also those of overhead.[16] Overhead costs may not be considered expenses, even though that treatment had been used consistently over a long period of time.[17] A reasonable proration of management expenses should be included in inventory.[18]

Taxes, depreciation, and other items which are deductions from gross income are includable in overhead and allocable to inventory where these items are incident to and necessary for the production of the particular assets included in the closing inventory.[19]

Inventories of supplies are not usually used or required in computing income when the supplies have not been acquired for sale nor included physically as part of the merchandise intended for sale.[20]

The cost of returning defective merchandise to the producer was held not to be a deductible item. It was not an expenditure chargeable to inventory.[21]

A taxpayer engaged in the real estate business who holds real estate for sale to his customers is not permitted to include as inventory realty held for sale.[22]

A taxpayer can elect, in the first instance, to treat cash discounts on purchases either as a deduction from the cost of inventory purchased or as income. This election must be followed consistently. The election is limited to strictly cash discounts which approximate a fair rate of interest.[23]

Inventory Methods

The bases of valuation which are most commonly used by business concerns and which meet the statutory requirements[24] are (1) cost or (2) cost or market, whichever is lower.[25] But, as will be indicated later in this chapter, certain other methods also are available.

Cost or Market, Whichever Is Lower

The use of the lower of cost or market inventory is really a limited exception to the principle of annual accounting.[26] It is an instance where the tax law permits the deduction of an unrealized loss and is a recognized exception to the necessity of reflecting in income tax returns only closed transactions.[27]

Cost. "Cost" means:

(1) In the case of merchandise on hand at the beginning of the taxable year, the inventory price of such goods.

(2) In the case of merchandise purchased since the beginning of the taxable year, the invoice price less trade or other discounts, except strictly cash discounts approximating a fair interest rate, which, as mentioned previously, may or may not be deducted according to the taxpayer's original option. To this net invoice price should be added transportation or other necessary charges incurred in acquiring possession of the goods.

(3) In the case of merchandise produced by the taxpayer since the beginning of the taxable year: (a) the cost of raw materials and supplies entering into or consumed in connection with the product, (b) expenditures for direct labor; and (c) indirect expenses incident to and necessary for the production of the particular article, including a reasonable proportion of manufacturing expenses, but not including any cost of selling or return of capital, whether by way of interest or profit.

(4) In any industry in which the usual rules for computation of cost of production are inapplicable, costs may be approximated upon whatever basis is reasonable and in conformity with established trade practices in that particular industry.[28]

Specialized methods of inventory costing exist in the cases of:

(1) Dealers in securities.[29]

(2) Farmers and those who raise livestock.[30]

(3) Miners and manufacturers who, by a single process or a uniform series of processes, derive a product of two or more kinds, sizes, or grades, the unit cost of which is substantially alike.[31]

(4) Retail merchants who use what is known as the "retail method" in ascertaining approximate costs.[32]

Market. For normal goods in an inventory, the term "market" means the current bid price prevailing at the date of inventory for the particular merchandise in the volume in which that merchandise is usually purchased by the taxpayer. The term is applicable in the cases of:

(1) goods purchased and on hand; and

(2) basic elements of cost (materials, labor, and burden) in goods in the process of manufacture and in finished goods on hand. This does not refer to goods on hand or in the process of manufacture for delivery under firm contracts (that is, those contracts not legally subject to cancellation by either party) at a fixed priced entered into before the date of the inventory, under which contracts the taxpayer is protected against actual loss and where the goods must be inventoried at cost.

Where no open market exists or where quotations are nominal by reason of inactive market conditions, the taxpayer must use such evidence of a fair market value at the date or dates nearest the inventory as may be available (such as specific purchases or sales by the taxpayer or others in reasonable volume and in good faith or compensation paid for cancellation of contracts for purchase commitments). Where the taxpayer in the regular course of business has offered for sale such merchandise at prices lower than the current price, the inventory may be valued at the reduced prices less direct cost of disposition. The correctness of such prices will be determined by reference to the actual sales of the taxpayer for a reasonable period before and after the date of the inventory. Prices which vary materially from the actual prices so ascertained will not be accepted as reflecting the market.[33]

"Market" means the price which the taxpayer would have to pay for the merchandise on the inventory date, not the price at which he sells such merchandise or offers it for sale.[34] "Market" does not necessarily mean the prices prevailing in the market which is closest geographically to the taxpayer.[35] It may be determined by the taxpayer's actual offering of inventories for sale.[36] Or it may be determined by the taxpayer's own experience in this field if it has been substantial.[37] It may also be determined by actual quotations.[38]

Lower of Cost or Market. Where the inventory is valued upon the basis of cost or market, whichever is lower, the market value of each article on hand at the inventory date is compared with the cost of the article; the lower of the two is taken as the inventory value of the article.[39]

Where closing inventory includes goods that were on hand at the beginning of the year, the "cost" to be compared to "market" in determining the lower of cost or market should be the price at which the goods were included in the opening inventory.[40]

In order to show that the basis of its opening inventory is the lower of cost or market, a taxpayer has to present some evidence of both the cost and market values of its opening inventory.[41]

Last-In, First-Out Method

Under any method of inventory, "costing" the closing inventory is a necessary step in the calculation of taxable income. Alternative accounting methods for arriving at this cost are the first-in, first-out method (FIFO) and the last-in, first-out method (LIFO). FIFO assumes that the first article purchased was the first one sold so that articles left in the inventory at the end of the year were the last ones purchased. LIFO assumes the converse—that is, that the last articles purchased during the year were the first ones sold—so that articles left in the inventory at the end of the year were the first ones purchased. Obviously, neither FIFO nor LIFO corresponds with actual facts although the FIFO assumption seems more logical in the normal course of business operations. In a period of stable prices, the application of either theory renders the same result. But during an inflationary period, LIFO is distinctly advantageous to the taxpayer for, in effect, he is not required to include as profit increases in the value of inventory. This illustrates the real purpose of the method: to reflect accurately what is normally considered as profit during inflationary and deflationary periods in the economy.[42]

The assumption that underlies the LIFO is that businessmen are always able to purchase enough goods to maintain their inventories at a relatively stable level. The method permits the increases in price of articles purchased during an inflationary period to be allocated to cost, rather than to profits. But during a period of scarcity, it may not always be possible to replace inventories. As a result, the so-called "base-stock" inventory will be depleted, and the cost of goods sold will represent not current market prices, but the prices prevailing in previous years. And these are normally lower. This would tend to inflate profits unrealistically.

Where taxpayers can establish that a liquidation of inventory has occurred due to specified circumstances beyond their control and that in subsequent years they will replace the inventory, they may elect to adjust their net income for the year of liquidation by deducting from it the excess of the cost of goods replaced over the cost of the goods liquidated. Once the adjustment is made, taxes for the year of liquidation, the year of replacement, and all intervening and subsequent years must be redetermined accordingly.[43]

If one uses the LIFO method for inventory, he must also use this method on all reports or statements to shareholders, partners or other proprietors, and beneficiaries or for credit purposes.[44] Where a corporation uses the LIFO method for Federal income tax purposes, this method also must be used with respect to such inventories to the extent they are included in the consolidated financial statements of any other corporation.[45] That means that if one corporation in an affiliated group uses LIFO for filing consolidated Federal income tax returns, the use of the same method when consolidated financial statements are filed is mandatory. However, where a corporation used LIFO on tax returns and financial statements, it has been held that it may still compute officers' compensation under a formula which included five percent of compensation calculated under the FIFO method.[46]

The LIFO method may be used only if the taxpayer files a statement of his election on *Form 970* with his income tax return for the taxable year as of the close of which the method is first to be used. The necessary inventory analysis detail must accompany that form. Internal Revenue Service approval is required.[47] The election is irrevocable unless the Service authorizes or requires another method.[48]

Unacceptable Inventory Methods

The following inventory methods are not in accord with the Treasury Regulations:

(1) Deducting from the inventory a reserve for price changes or an estimated depreciation in the value thereof.

(2) Taking work in process, or other parts of the inventory, at a nominal price or at less than its proper value.

(3) Omitting portions of the stock on hand.

(4) Using a constant price or nominal value for so-called "normal quantity" of materials or goods in stock.

(5) Including stock in transit shipped either to or from the taxpayer, the title to which is not vested in the taxpayer.[49]

The "prime cost" method of valuing inventories reflects only direct labor and materials, but not manufacturing overhead. It is not an acceptable inventory method for tax purposes.[50]

There is no statutory authority for valuing finished goods on the basis of what it would cost (as disclosed by testimony) to replace them on the inventory date; that is, a "replacement market."[51]

Inventory Write-Downs

A simple fact about write-downs is: the greater the write-down of the inventory, the less the amount of income tax payable. Inventory write-downs fall into three principal categories:

(1) Write-down to market, or the lower of cost or market.

(2) Write-down in the case of damaged or other unsaleable goods.

(3) Inventory shortages.

Where the Internal Revenue Service disallows an inventory write-down, the taxpayer has the burden of showing that the Service acted arbitrarily.[52]

Write-down to Market, or to Lower of Cost or Market. An inventory write-down must be bottomed upon something specific. Thus, an estimated fixed percentage of write-down is not permitted.[53] The expert opinion of an accountant or other professional will probably be needed to back up the write-down.[54]

Where inventories are written down to a supposed market, but the merchandise is subsequently sold at the original figure, the question of the legitimacy of the write-downs arises. There may be no problem if it can be shown that prices fluctuate greatly in response to supply and demand.[55] But there is a burden of proof to be met.[56]

Inventory may not be written down to reflect a market drop by reason of the taxpayer's tarnished image despite his plea that no one would now do business with him unless he offered special prices.[57]

Damaged or Other Unsaleable Goods. Inventory which is unsaleable at normal prices or unusable in the normal way because of damage, imperfections, shop wear, changes of style, odd or broken lots, or like causes, including second-hand goods taken in exchange, should be valued at *bona fide* selling prices less direct cost of disposition. If the goods consist of raw materials or partly finished goods held for use or consumption, they are to be valued upon a reasonable basis, taking into consideration the usability and the condition of the goods. But in no such case may the value be less than scrap value. "*Bona fide* selling price" means the actual offering of goods during a period not more than 30 days after inventory date. The burden of proof is upon the taxpayer to show that the exceptional goods as are valued upon such selling basis come within the classifications indicated above. The taxpayer must maintain whatever records of the disposition of the goods as will enable verification of the inventory.[58] This procedure is available regardless of the method of valuation of normal inventory.

"Unsaleability" is not limited to damage, imperfections, shop wear, changes of style, odd or broken lots. Unsaleability was found where the only possible purchaser of the inventory terminated its contract.[59]

Inventory which became obsolete, worthless, and unsaleable by reason of the introduction of an entirely new and improved product during the taxable year may be included in closing inventory as zero.[60] But the obsolescence must be shown to have occurred during the taxable year.[61]

Discontinued items must be included in inventory at a figure no less than the salvage value that can be realized.[62]

Inventory may be revalued when large quantities of defective merchandise are discovered.[63] Loss of inventory by reason of leakage has been recognized.[64]

Inventory Shortage. Loss resulting from inventory shortage is deductible.[65]

Change in Inventory Method

A change in the method of valuing inventories is a change in the method of accounting. Thus, Internal Revenue Service approval is required.[66] Repricing of inventory may constitute a change in accounting method.[67]

A request to change an inventory method from cost to the lower of cost or market will be carefully scrutinized by the Service, and the request will be refused if it appears that the principal reason for it is to reduce Federal income taxes.[68]

Acquisition of Stock to Get Inventory

Ordinarily, the purchase and sale of corporate stock by a non-dealer in securities is a capital transaction. But where a taxpayer purchases shares of stock in a supplier corporation in order to ensure a steady supply of inventory for resale, the full cost of the stock may be deductible if the supplier fails.[69]

Where shares were purchased by a dealer in order to acquire rights to buy a commodity during a time of shortage, the sale of the shares as soon as the rights were exercised was held not to produce a capital loss, but it was ruled to be a part of the cost of the inventory.[70] In another case, the cost of debentures acquired to ensure a source of supply was held deductible when the debentures became worthless.[71]

Inventory Acquisition as "Ordinary and Necessary"

Prepayments for future inventory requirements by a cash-basis taxpayer will not be recognized as ordinary and necessary expenses where prepayment is not required by the seller and there is no other reason for it.[72] However, where, because of an acute inventory shortage, prepayment is necessary to assure the taxpayer a source of supply or at least a top priority position, the amounts prepaid may be deductible.[73]

The Accumulated Earnings Tax

A valid reason for retention of earnings is working capital requirements, taking into account the amount of inventories and rate of turnover.[74] However, the inventory must be needed in the business. To the extent that it is not, it cannot be accumulated with impunity and tax may be imposed.[75]

Inventory in 12-Month Liquidation

A corporation is not taxed where it is completely dissolved within 12 months of the adoption of a complete liquidation plan and its assets are sold either by the corporation or the shareholders. But this rule does not extend to inventory items unless they are sold to a single buyer in a single transaction.[76]

Reorganization Carry-overs

In the case of certain tax-free corporate reorganizations (such as a statutory merger or the complete liquidation by a parent of its subsidiary corporation), the inventories are taken over by the acquiring corporation on the same basis as they had been carried by the transferor corporation.[77]

Charitable Contributions

Contributions of inventories to *bona fide* charitable organizations are valued at cost, not fair market value.[78] (See chapter 16, What Can Be Done with Contributions.)

NOTES

1. *Wilson et al. v. Commissioner*, 76 F.2d 476 (10th Cir., 1935).
2. Regulations Section 1.446-1(a)(4)(i).
3. *Raymond F. Beels*, T.C. Memo., Docket No. 31476 (entered February 9, 1953).
4. *Glenn v. Kentucky Color & Chemical Co., Inc.*, 186 F.2d 975 (6th Cir., 1961).
5. *Wilkinson-Beane, Inc.*, T.C. Memo. 1969-70 (filed April 21, 1969), *aff'd*, 420 F.2d 352 (1st Cir., 1970). Revenue Ruling 69-537, 1969-2 CB 109.
6. *Carmichael Tile Company*, T.C. Memo., Docket No. 22858 (entered April 21, 1950), *aff'd on another issue*, 192 F.2d 209 (5th Cir., 1951).
7. *Bechelli v. Hofferbert*, 111 F. Supp. 631 (D.C., Md., 1953).
8. *Sprague Tire & Rubber Co.*, 11 B.T.A. 610 (1928).
9. *College Point Boat Corporation*, 1 B.T.A. 534 (1924).
10. *Commissioner v. Dwyer*, 203 F.2d 522 (2d Cir., 1953).
11. *John L. Ashe, Inc.*, T.C. Memo., Docket No. 26496 (entered February 29, 1942), *rem'd'd on another issue*, 214 F.2d 13 (5th Cir., 1954).
12. *Photo-Sonics, Inc.*, 42 T.C. 926 (1964), *aff'd*, 357 F.2d 656 (9th Cir., 1966).
13. *Otie M. Jones Estate*, T.C. Memo. 1961-5 (filed January 18, 1961)
14. *Caldwell v. Commissioner*, 202 F.2d 112 (2d Cir., 1953).
15. Regulations Section 1.471-1.
16. *Dearborn Gage Company*, 48 T.C. 190 (1967).
17. *Photo-Sonics, Inc. v. Commissioner*, 296 F.2d 732 (6th Cir., 1962).
18. Regulations Section 1.471-3(c).
19. *Frank G. Wikstrom & Sons, Inc.*, 20 T.C. 359 (1953).
20. *Smith Leasing Co., Inc.*, 43 T.C. 37 (1964).
21. *George C. Peterson Co.*, 1 B.T.A. 690 (1924).
22. Revenue Ruling 69-536, 1969-2 CB 109.
23. Revenue Ruling 69-619, 1969-2 CB 111.
24. I.R.C. Section 471.
25. Regulations Section 1.471-2(b).
26. *Space Controls, Inc. v. Commissioner*, 322 F.2d 144 (5th Cir., 1963).
27. *Sharp v. Commissioner*, 224 F.2d 920 (6th Cir., 1955).
28. Regulations Section 1.471-3.
29. *See* Regulations Section 1.471-5.
30. *See* Regulations Section 1.471-6.
31. *See* Regulations Section 1.471-7.
32. *See* Regulations Section 1.471-8.
33. Regulations Section 1.471-4.
34. *Elder Manufacturing Company v. United States*, 10 F. Supp. 125 (Ct. Cl., 1935).
35. *S. Weisbart and Company*, T.C. Memo. 1964-130 (filed May 8, 1954).

36. *Neustate Suit Co.*, 8 B.T.A. 903 (1927).

37. *T. B. Floyd*, 11 B.T.A. 903 (1928).

38. *A. P. Mitchell Auto Company*, 10 B.T.A. 1001 (1928).

39. Regulations Section 1.471-4(c).

40. Revenue Ruling 70-19, 1970-1 CB 123.

41. *National Fireworks, Inc. et al. v. Commissioner*, 243 F.2d 295 (1st Cir., 1957).

42. *R. H. Macy & Co., Inc. et al. v. United States*, 255 F.2d 884 (2d Cir., 1958).

43. *National Lead Company v. Commissioner*, 336 F.2d 134 (2d Cir., 1964).

44. I.R.C. Section 472(c).

45. Revenue Ruling 70-457, 1970-2 CB 109.

46. *Hammond Lead Products, Inc.*, T.C. Memo. 1969-14 (filed January 16, 1969).

47. Regulations Section 1.472-3.

48. Regulations Section 1.472-5.

49. Regulations Section 1.417-2(f).

50. *All-Steel Equipment, Inc.*, 54 T.C. 1749 (1970).

51. *Bedford Mills, Inc. v. United States*, 2 F. Supp. 769 (Ct. Cl., 1933).

52. *E. W. Bliss Company v. United States*, 351 F.2d 449 (6th Cir., 1965).

53. *John L. Ashe, Inc.*, T.C. Memo., Docket No. 26496 (entered February 29, 1952), *aff'd on this issue*, 214 F.2d 13 (5th Cir., 1954).

54. *E. W. Bliss Company et al. v. United States*, 351 F.2d 449 (6th Cir., 1965).

55. *Ernest, Holdeman & Collet, Inc.*, T.C. Memo. 1960-10 (filed January 29, 1960), *aff'd*, 290 F.2d 3 (7th Cir., 1961).

56. *Bennie Wolf et al.*, T.C. Memo., Docket Nos. 21249, 21253, and 13708 (entered October 25, 1950).

57. *Bernard H. Stauffer Estate*, 48 T.C. 277 (1967), *rev'd on another issue*, 403 F.2d 611 (9th Cir., 1968).

58. Regulations Section 1.471-2(c).

59. *Space Controls, Inc. v. Commissioner*, 322 F.2d 144 (5th Cir., 1963).

60. *Lucker v. United States*, 53 F.2d 418 (Ct. Cl., 1931); *Queen City Woodworks and Lumber Company v. Crooks*, 7 F. Supp. 684 (D.C., S.D. Mo., 1934).

61. *American Manganese Steel Co.*, 7 B.T.A. 659 (1927).

62. A.R.R. 921, I-1 CB 126.

63. *Celluloid Company*, 9 B.T.A. 989 (1927).

64. *Otto Huber Brewery Company*, 2 B.T.A. 1193 (1925).

65. *Lang Broom Co.*, 9 B.T.A. 39 (1927).

66. *F. S. Harmon Manufacturing Co.*, 34 T.C. 316 (1960).

67. *Fruehauf Trailer Co.*, 42 T.C. 83 (1964), *aff'd*, 356 F.2d 975 (6th Cir., 1966).

68. A.R.M. 38, 2 CB 54.

69. *Helen M. Livesley et al.*, T.C. Memo. 1960-24 (filed February 23, 1960).

70. *Western Wine & Liquor Co.*, 18 T.C. 1090 (1952).

71. *Tulane Hardware Co., Inc.*, 24 T.C. 1146 (1955).

72. *Tim W. Lillie et al.*, 45 T.C. 54 (1965).

73. *Cravens v. Commissioner*, 272 F.2d 895 (10th Cir., 1959).

74. *Smoot Sand & Gravel Corporation v. Commissioner*, 241 F.2d 197 (4th Cir., 1957).

75. *Sears Oil Co., Inc. v. Commissioner*, 359 F.2d 191 (2d Cir., 1966).

76. I.R.C. Section 337.

77. I.R.C. Section 381(c)(5).

78. I.R.C. Section 170(e).

CHAPTER 15

Casualties and Replacements

What Is a "Casualty"?

Deduction is allowed for any loss sustained during the taxable year if not compensated for by insurance or otherwise.[1] Many losses which are sustained by a business represent casualties. But for an occurrence to be recognized as a casualty for Federal income tax purposes, it must fall within the specialized intendment of the Internal Revenue Code.

Thus, for tax purposes, a casualty is an inevitable accident involving unforeseen circumstances, such as are not normally guarded against by human agency and in which man has no part.[2] An accident or casualty proceeds from an unknown cause or is an unusual effect of a known cause. Either may be said to occur by chance and unexpectedly.[3]

A casualty does not lose its deductible status because it resulted from negligence. An example is the loss arising from an ordinary highway mishap.[4] In holding that an earthslide caused by a builder's negligence was a casualty for tax purposes, even though this earthslide might have been foreseen or prevented by due care, the court likened it to a car accident. The owner of a damaged vehicle is not deprived of a casualty loss deduction merely because his negligence contributed to the mishap.[5]

In order to be embraced by the term "casualty," the occurrence need not be cataclysmic in character; the casualty does not have to be of great or near-tragic proportions to qualify.[6] Wherever force is applied to property and the owner-taxpayer is either unaware of that force because of its hidden nature or is powerless to act to prevent it because of sudden onset, and disability or damage results, the owner can be said to have suffered a loss which is, in that sense, similar to losses arising from a casualty.[7] The results of vandalism are regarded as a casualty loss.[8]

Suddenness Is Required

An otherwise deductible casualty loss, such as the collapse of a business structure, is not allowed for tax purposes unless the incidence of the event was *sudden.* Generally, the term "casualty" is interpreted by the courts as an event that is sudden, unexpected, and unusual. This has the practical advantage of confining losses to somewhat dramatic settings which are susceptible to identification and verification by the administrative authorities.[9] Thus, the concept of a casualty loss for tax purposes excludes the progressive deterioration of property through a steadily operating cause.[10] For a loss to qualify as a casualty, it must possess that suddenness which is common to fires, storms, and shipwrecks. The operating force giving rise to the loss must be shown to be the sudden, unexpected invasion by a hostile agency.[11]

Casualty loss for tax purposes was not found where damage to a wall had been developing over a long period of time.[12] Nor was there a deductible casualty loss when worms ate the piles on which a structure had rested, thereby causing a collapse, for this must have been taking place over a considerable period of time.[13] Injury to a structure which resulted from termite damage was not the result of an identifiable event of a sudden nature such as is necessary for a casualty deduction.[14] There was also no casualty loss where trees were damaged by a virus which was known to have been present prior to the start of the taxable year.[15] Casualty loss was not recognized in the case of destruction by carpet beetles where the element of suddenness was not proven; this situation differed from cases involving "fast termite" damage, which are extremely difficult to prove.[16] Loss of inventory in process by spoilage did not represent a casualty deduction where it could not be established that the spoilage was sudden rather than the result of a steadily operating cause. This was not a highly visible process, and consultation with an outside expert to establish just what had happened would have been an unacceptable risk at that stage of operations.[17]

Economic Loss Is Not Enough

A decrease in the monetary value of property is not enough to establish a deductible casualty loss for tax purposes. Thus, decline in the value of a taxpayer's property as the result of a landslide in the immediate vicinity was attributable to psychological, hypothetical, and temporary factors rather than a realized loss. Where there was a loss in the market place because of landslides, a court observed that this loss was in the heads of prospective buyers whose collective judgments established the market. It was likened to the situation of a notorious gangster buying a house next door to a taxpayer's home, a circumstance which would cause depreciation of the value of the latter's property. True, that might be a casualty, but it is not one for tax purposes.[18] Where a rain-induced washout seriously damaged properties next to a taxpayer's, he sought to deduct the loss on his tax return to the extent of the difference between the value of the property immediately before and that immediately after the casualty; additionally, an expert witness testified that considerable publicity had been given to the washout. As a result, there existed widespread fear about hillside properties, which had the potential for such damage. The effect was the discouraging of prospective purchasers and a substantial decline in the fair market value of this real estate. The deduction was disallowed insofar as it exceeded physical damage. Where the alleged loss results merely from a fluctuation in value and was not realized in a closed transaction (such as an actual sale) during the taxable year, the general rule for measuring casualty losses sustained on nonbusiness property is without application.[19]

Reductions in market value resulting from casualty-type occurrences are deductible where these reductions are the result of actual physical damage to the property. Only in such circumstances is the yardstick of market value used to measure the loss.[20] A deductible casualty loss must be more than a mere diminution in value demonstrable solely by some economic concept or theory. An appraiser's estimate of buyer resistance by itself has no real or tangible relation to the price at which a property may change hands in the market.[21]

No loss is allowed for temporary reduction in value of a taxpayer's property by reason of loss of the use of land during a period of rehabilitation. No deduction is permitted because of failure of profits or the loss of potential income.[22] It is vital to a deductible loss that something be parted with; that is, the taxpayer must have suffered a loss in the economic sense. Bookkeeping entries and paper losses are not sufficient.[23]

Prospect of Recovery

An otherwise eligible casualty loss is recognized to the extent that there is no reasonable prospect of recovery at the close of the taxable year.[24] The burden of proof is upon the taxpayer to show this.[25]

Although there is no litmus paper test of "reasonable prospect of recovery," the inquiry should be directed to the probability of recovery as opposed to the mere possibility. In one case, a court regarded a 40 to 50 percent or better chance of recovery as being "reasonable," while a lawsuit might well be justified by a ten percent chance.[26]

Where a loss is covered by insurance and there is a reasonable prospect of some recovery from the insurance company, deduction is permissible in the year of final determination of the insurance claim.[27] Until this claim is satisfied, rejected, or settled, the taxpayer cannot know the amount of the unreimbursed loss that he has sustained. Even if he has reasonable prospects of collecting some insurance, there is no deduction until he knows the amount he will collect or, more specifically, the amount of the loss he will not collect.[28]

A taxpayer claimed that a fire loss was deductible in the year after the casualty had taken place since at the end of the year of the fire there still was doubt as to the honesty of the claim. But deduction was disallowed for the subsequent year; investigations by the fire marshal and the insurance adjuster had revealed nothing suspicious which would have resulted in disqualification of the claim.[29]

If there is no dispute about recoverable amounts, fire and similar losses are deductible in the year of the casualty, although the amount of the loss is not ascertained until a subsequent year.[30] But in the case of theft, larceny, and embezzlement, loss deduction is taken in the year of discovery.[31]

Even if an insurance company rejects a taxpayer's claim for reimbursement, it does not follow that there is no reasonable prospect of recovery, which would make the loss deductible at that time. The taxpayer still has the burden of showing that there was no reasonable prospect of recovery at that time. An insurance company's rejection has to be taken with a grain of salt. It might be a routine formality in all claim matters, or it might be the first skirmish in an elaborate bargaining session. Even where the insurance carrier positively decided not to make payment, a court could decide otherwise if the insured brought suit and subsequently won.[32]

A taxpayer might have a prospect of recovery from a party other than an insurance company. A construction company which had erected the taxpayer's building guaranteed it for one year. Three years later, part of the roof collapsed. It was ascertained that the collapse was attributable to construction that did not meet the city building code requirements. Suit was not brought against the construction company, however, as search revealed that it had no assets to satisfy a judgment. Deduction was allowed in the year of the casualty since by year-end, there was no reasonable prospect of recovery by insurance or otherwise.[33]

Where a corporation, for whatever reason, fails to seek reimbursement from an insurance company or other party, a casualty loss will not be deductible, for there has not been a loss unreimbursed by insurance while the possibility of reimbursement still exists. Such was the case where a taxpayer sustained loss of heavy equipment by reason of an accident. Suit was not brought against the manufacturer of this equipment, for it might have meant that it would be impossible to buy equipment at advantageous terms in the future. Nor did the corporation wish to claim too much from its insurance company lest the rates be jacked up the following year. So the corporation sought no reimbursement for most of its loss, taking this loss instead as a tax return deduction. The court disagreed.[34]

Time of the Casualty Loss Deduction

A casualty loss might occur in any of three years: when the casualty occurred, when the claim was settled, or when the insurance company denied liability.[35] For cases where the loss is other than of the theft type, the first of these three alternatives prevails—subject to the possibility of reimbursement.[36] With an accrual-basis taxpayer, crystallization of the right to receive income, not prior expectation or subsequent receipt, determines the year in which the income must be declared for Federal income tax purposes.[37]

In the case of accrual of insurance proceeds, the amount thereof, even after the amount of the loss has been fully adjusted, is not accruable at all until the insurance company formally has waived co-insurance requirements which applied to the loss.[38] The insurance company settlement must be without strings before it can represent accruable income. Even a tender of partial payment to a property owner who has an unqualified right to file suit for just compensation as to the balance of his claim did not constitute an unconditional offer of payment upon which an accrual of income could be based.[39]

The "sale or exchange" of property by involuntary conversion (such as by fire) is not completed until the policy proceeds are received, an enforceable settlement of a determined amount is agreed upon, or a court judgment is obtained.[40]

Casualty Loss Limitation

Casualty losses on nonbusiness assets are limited to the amount by which they are in excess of $100.[41] In effect, this amounts to what insurance companies call a $100 deductible clause.

Involuntary Conversions

A taxpayer may have taxable gain as the result of a casualty loss. If the amount received as reimbursement from an insurance company or elsewhere exceeds the adjusted basis of the property, there is recognizable gain. But in the case of a statutory involuntary conversion, election may be made to include the gain in gross income only to the extent, if any, that the proceeds from the insurer or other party are not reinvested in property similar to or related in service or use to the lost property.[42]

The involuntary conversion replacement provision is a relief measure, which takes cognizance of the inequity of taxing a gain from the involuntary conversion of property, which conversion may have taken place at a time which was disadvantageous to the taxpayer.[43] The purpose is to relieve the owner of property of the immediate payment of tax when he does not liquidate his holding of his own will, but parts with it involuntarily by virtue of superior governmental power or loses it through flood or other circumstances over which he has no control.[44]

A *statutory involuntary conversion* means the destruction, theft, seizure, requisition, or condemnation of property or the sale or exchange of this property under imminence of requisition or condemnation. This includes destruction in whole or in part. There need not be a physical annihilation, for "destruction" also can mean rendering property useless for the purpose for which it was intended.[45]

If recognition of gain for tax purposes is to be avoided for property involuntarily converted after December 30, 1969, the property must be replaced within two years after the close of the first taxable year in which any part of the gain is realized.[46] This replacement time dates from the moment the award from the insurance company, governmental agency, or the like was available to the taxpayer; that is, from the time he *could* have gotten his money even if he did not actually claim it until later for any reason.[47]

The replacement property does not have to be *identical* to the property lost; but the service or use to which the property is put must be. There was a proper replacement when buildings used as an office for a used car lot and a repair shop were replaced with an office building. Both the original property and the replacement property were held solely for income purposes. The taxpayer did not occupy either, and as to all of the properties, his status was that of landlord.[48] But if property that had been rented is replaced with property that will be used by the taxpayer, this cannot be proper replacement. Replacement property must be used in the same manner as the original property.[49]

Tax-free replacement of property lost in an involuntary conversion may occur when a corporation owning similar property takes over more than 80 percent of the stock.[50] This is permissible even though the property was purchased by this corporation after its stock had been acquired.[51] Where two corporations with identical shareholders sustained involuntary conversions and the proceeds were used to acquire ownership of a third corporation which owned replacement assets, 50 percent of the stock of the acquired company went to each of the two corporations. This was not a tax-free replacement inasmuch as neither corporation had the requisite control.[52]

Where a partner replaces involuntarily converted property by buying the 50 percent of a partnership he did not own, this is a proper replacement of the lost property.[53]

No statutory involuntary conversion took place when a taxpayer decided for business reasons to sell rather than to repair a ship after settlement was made with the insurance company for damages which had been sustained.[54]

Casualty losses and gains with respect to (1) depreciable property and real estate used in a trade or business and (2) capital assets held for more than six months are consolidated. If the casualty losses exceed the casualty gains, the net loss is treated as an ordinary loss without regard to whether there are non-casualty gains under Section 1231 of the Code. (See chapter 6, Capital Assets, Capital Gains and Losses.) If, however, the casualty gains exceed the casualty losses, the net gain is treated as a Section 1231 gain and must be consolidated with other capital gains and losses.[55]

If a corporation is completely liquidated within 12 months of the adoption of a plan of complete liquidation, there is no taxable gain to the corporation upon the sale of assets during this period; however, the rule does not apply to inventories unless they are sold to a single purchaser in a single transaction.[56] Gain resulting from the collection of insurance proceeds is entitled to nonrecognition under this section, as where a corporation is liquidated after the destruction of its plant by fire.[57] The application of the rule is the same for both voluntary and involuntary conversions.[58]

Measure of a Casualty Loss

Where business property is destroyed by casualty, the tax deduction is the basis of this property less insurance or salvage recoveries. But where there is only a partial loss, the amount of the deduction is limited to either the decrease in market value of the property as a result of the casualty or the taxpayer's basis in the property, whichever is smaller.[59] The purpose of this rule is to prevent a taxpayer's obtaining a full deduction for every loss in market value his property suffers through a casualty. When he suffers a loss in market value greater than his cost or other basis of the property, that excess of value destroyed represents unrealized appreciation. He may not claim a deduction for that loss inasmuch as he never recognized or paid a tax on the gain.[60]

Another measure of the amount of the casualty loss is the cost of restoration or repair of the damage—but only if the following conditions are met:

(1) The repairs are necessary to restore the property to its condition immediately before the casualty.

(2) The amount spent for such repairs is not excessive.

(3) The value of the property as a result of the repairs does not exceed the value of the property immediately before the casualty. In other words, only the reasonable and necessary expenses of restoration and repair may be allowed, not improvements or additions to the original value of the property.[61]

In the case of an individual, casualty losses of property used for personal purposes are treated differently from losses of business property or property held for the production of income. The amount of the allowable deduction for nonbusiness property is the difference between the values of the property immediately before and immediately after the casualty—but not in excess of the cost or adjusted basis of the property—less any insurance or other compensation received or receivable.[62]

Casualty loss to a building which was fully depreciated was not deductible, but the cost of replacing the damage was ruled to be an ordinary and necessary expense.[63]

Unproven Basis

A taxpayer may not take a deduction for the destruction of property in which he had no cost or other basis.[64] Where there is a casualty loss, the tax basis of the assets is zero if the taxpayer cannot prove a higher figure.[65]

If property in a taxpayer's hands has the same tax basis it had in the hands of a transferor and that basis is unknown, the basis is whatever the Internal Revenue Service is disposed to allow (which could be nothing).[66]

In relatively few instances, taxpayers are fortunate enough to have casualty deductions (such as a fire loss) determined by a court in accordance with the so-called *Cohan* rule. In such cases, the court is willing to assume a certain cost basis where loss had occurred on property which presumably had *some* basis. (See chapter 17, The Burden of Proof.) Instances of the application of the *Cohan* rule to the establishment of casualty loss where basis was unproven may be seen in several decisions.[67] The rule has been applied on occasion to losses from theft[68] and from flood.[69] But the court will bear down heavily upon the taxpayer since the uncertainty is of his own making; that is, he should have had records to show what the basis really was.

Use and Occupancy Insurance

There are two basic forms of use and occupancy insurance; each has its own tax characteristics. *Non-valued* forms of such insurance usually define coverage in terms of reimbursement for estimated loss of net profits (to which may be added continuing expense) or in terms of net expense less expenses which continue during a shutdown. Reimbursement for lost profits resulting from the partial or total suspension of a business for stated reasons (such as a fire) is fully taxable.[70] Inasmuch as the net profits themselves would have been taxable as ordinary income, the insurance proceeds in lieu of these profits are similarly taxed.[71] Reimbursement by the insurer is regarded as mere replacement of taxable profits.[72] Such was the case where the insured taxpayer placed the entire proceeds of his insurance in buildings for business use. If income is taxable, the manner in which it is expressed does not relieve the owner thereof from tax.[73]

Valued forms of use and occupancy insurance generally provide for a fixed amount to be paid by the insurer for each day of business interruption for specified reasons, regardless of the profit factor. Receipt of income under such a policy is not taxable if such moneys are expended in the acquisition of similar property.[74] Proceeds from use and occupancy policies of this type are not treated differently from the proceeds of straight fire insurance policies.[75]

Reimbursed Living Expenses

Some property insurance policies provide that if the policyholder's residence is damaged or destroyed by fire or some other designated casualty, the insurance company will reimburse him for extra living expenses while his home is being repaired. Amounts received after January 1, 1969 under an insurance contract for reimbursement for living expenses for the insured and members of his household resulting from the loss of use or occupancy of their residence are not taxable. But this exclusion is limited to the excess of actual living expenses over the normal living expenses which would have been incurred during this period. Included are extraordinary expenses for transportation, food, utilities, and miscellaneous services. The casualty must involve the taxpayer's *principal* residence.[76]

Insurance Premium Deductability

Unlike certain types of life insurance premium, forms of business insurance premium are not specifically disallowed by the Internal Revenue Code. Deduction for most forms of business insurance premiums is permitted by the general language of the Code, which authorizes all the ordinary and necessary expenses paid or incurred during the taxable year in carrying on any trade or business.[77] But no business insurance premium may be included in business expense to the extent that it is used by a taxpayer in computing the cost of property included in inventory or in determining the gain or loss basis of plant, equipment, or other property.[78]

The cost of insurance for a building during construction operations is not deductible, being a capital expenditure.[79]

If a premium, as on an automobile insurance policy, is partially for business and partially for personal use, an allocation of the premium is required, and only that portion attributable to business use is deductible.[80]

Another type of allocation relates to advance premium payments, as where payments are made for a three-year period in order to obtain a lower rate. A prepaid asset, the cash value, has been created and is written off in the form of a deduction for the period covered by the payment.[81] This proration rule applies equally to taxpayers who are on the cash and on the accrual basis.[82]

Allocation of Insurance Proceeds

Where capital and noncapital assets are disposed of or converted for a lump sum (such as where an insurance policy is paid off), the gain or loss on each class of asset must be recognized separately if the basis therefor is established by the evidence.[83]

Usually, the fire or other casualty policies will be general in character; the policies do not provide that a specific amount of insurance is applicable to each separate class of property insured. Where the payment of the proceeds is in a lump sum, the only reasonable basis for assigning that sum to the different types of asset (such as capital and noncapital of various forms) is to apply the same percentage of loss to each class of property insured. That would be a proper basis for allocating the net proceeds of the insurance to each class of assets.[84]

Loss Prevention

The service provided by an insurance company frequently includes a risk minimization program. If steps taken by the insured to prevent loss are of a physical nature, deductibility involves the familiar choice between capital expenditure and deductible repair. (See chapter 7, Ordinary, Necessary, and Reasonable.) Expenditures to prevent future repair bills or even potential future damage customarily are not deductible as repairs. Thus, where a corporation raised the floors of its plant as a protection against floods on the basis of past experience and a governmental committee report, the cost was capital.[85] Protective devices for machinery are not regarded as repairs for tax purposes.[86]

Collection of Insurance Claims

The cost of hiring attorneys and adjusters to collect insurance claims arising in the ordinary course of a taxpayer's business is deductible where the reason for the expenditure involves neither title to a capital asset nor an additional expenditure which the taxpayer incurs to improve or increase the value of any of his capital assets.[87] However, expenses which are solely and directly related to the collection and maximization of capital assets (or those treated for tax purposes as though they were capital assets) are not deductible as ordinary and necessary expenses; they constitute capital expenditures.[88]

Self-Insurance

Sometimes a taxpayer will find that insurance is unobtainable, that the cost seems excessive, or that it is desirable for any other reason to be a self-insurer. The result is the same in each instance: A reserve set up for self-insurance equal to the estimated premiums which otherwise would be paid to an insurance company is nondeductible[89] even though no insurance is procurable and no other provision therefore seems possible.[90] Unless specifically authorized by the Internal Revenue Code (which self-insurance is not), reserves are not deductible for tax purposes, even in lieu of unobtainable insurance.[91]

Self-insurers do not provide the safeguards afforded by insurance companies and hence the tax treatment is not the same in the case of charges. A self-insurer customarily does not gauge the extent of the hazard for which he is providing; nor does any reserve computed upon an actuarial basis serve to offset a contingent casualty loss on a scientific basis.[92]

Accumulated Earnings Tax

Where insurance is too expensive or where it is unobtainable because of the hazards involved, earnings are retained for the reasonable needs of the business.[93] Risk of loss not fully covered by insurance is a justification for retention of earnings in an accumulated earnings tax matter.[94] If a corporation is a self-insurer, the possibility of substantial claims may justify the retention of earnings.[95]

But for this defense to prevail, there must be satisfactory evidence of the amount which may have to be committed to claims. The fact that a corporation is a self-insurer is not blanket permission to abandon dividend payments.[96] Nondeductible reserves for specific hazards or for general contingencies may be added by the Internal Revenue Service to earnings and profits for the purposes of the accumulated earnings tax.[97]

Personal Holding Company

A closely held corporation with nonoperating income may be subject to the penalty tax levied against personal holding companies. (See chapter 2, Corporations and Other Forms of Conducting Business.)

A corporation may sustain a casualty (such as a fire) that destroys the business. Loss is covered by insurance. While management deliberates over whether to reenter the original business, try something else, or liquidate, the insurance proceeds may be invested in income-producing securities. Income generated is personal holding company income and can trigger the personal holding company tax during this period of deliberation or uncertainty.[98]

Hedging

Being akin to insurance, losses and expenses of hedging are deductible as ordinary and necessary expenses of the business if the purpose of the operation is protection rather than speculation.[99]

Proof

In the case of a casualty loss, proof is necessary both to the insurance company and to the Internal Revenue agent. In one case, the court noted approvingly that in addition to the testimony of witnesses, evidence included photographs and a diagram of the property.[100] Elsewhere, the value of trees destroyed by hurricane was established to a considerable degree by pictures taken immediately after the storm.[101] (See chapter 17, The Burden of Proof.)

Disaster Losses

In sustaining a disaster loss in what the President of the United States subsequently designates a disaster area, a taxpayer may elect to take the deduction in the taxable year immediately preceding the taxable year in which the disaster occurred or, if he so desires, in the taxable year in which the casualty actually occurred.

NOTES

1. I.R.C. Section 165(a).
2. *Kipp et al. v. Bingler*, D.C., W.D. Pa., 1965.
3. *Chicago, St. Louis & New Orleans Rail Road Company v. Pullman Southern Car Co.*, 139 U.S. 79 (1891).
4. *Anderson v. Commissioner*, 81 F.2d 457 (10th Cir., 1936).
5. *Harry Heyn*, 46 T.C. 302 (1966).
6. *John P. White et al.*, 48 T.C. 430 (1967).
7. *William H. Carpenter et al.*, T.C. Memo. 1966-228 (filed October 18, 1966).
8. *Burrell E. Davis*, 34 T.C. 586 (1960).
9. *W. W. Bercaw*, T.C. Memo., Docket No. 7263 (entered January 21, 1947).
10. *Fay v. Helvering*, 120 F.2d 253 (2d Cir., 1941).
11. *Kipp et al. v. Bingler*, D.C., W.D. Pa., 1964.
12. *Richard C. Purdy et al.*, T.C. Memo. 1966-186 (filed August 9, 1966).
13. *Matheson v. Commissioner*, 54 F.2d 537 (2d Cir., 1931).

14. Revenue Ruling 63-232, 1963-2 CB 97.
15. *Appleman et al. v. United States*, 338 F.2d 729 (7th Cir., 1964).
16. *Meersman et al. v. United States*, 244 F. Supp. 278 (D.C., M.D. Tenn., 1965), *aff'd*, 370 F.2d 109 (6th Cir., 1967).
17. *Marko Durovic*, 54 T.C. 1364 (1970).
18. *Pulvers et al. v. Commissioner*, 407 F.2d 838 (9th Cir., 1969).
19. *Clarence A. Petersen et al.*, 30 T.C. 660 (1958).
20. *The Squirt Company*, 51 T.C. 543 (1969), *aff'd*, 423 F.2d 710 (9th Cir., 1970).
21. Revenue Ruling 66-242, 1966-2 CB 56.
22. *J. G. Boswell Company*, 34 T.C. 539 (1960).
23. *The Squirt Company*, 51 T.C. 543 (1969), *aff'd*, 423 F.2d 710 (9th Cir., 1970).
24. Regulations Section 1.165-1(d)(2)(i).
25. *Theodore A. Granger et al.*, T.C. Memo. 1970-155 (filed June 15, 1970).
26. *Parmelee Transportation Company v. United States*, 351 F.2d 619 (Ct. Cl., 1931).
27. *Allied Furriers Corporation*, 24 B.T.A. 457 (1931).
28. *Commissioner v. Harwick*, 184 F.2d 835 (5th Cir., 1950).
29. *Harry Brown*, 23 T.C. 156 (1954).
30. *Evans v. Commissioner*, 235 F.2d 586 (8th Cir., 1956).
31. I.R.C. Section 165(e).
32. *Theodore A. Granger et al.*, T.C. Memo. 1970-155 (filed June 15, 1970).
33. *The Wellston Company*, T.C. Memo. 1965 (filed March 18, 1965).
34. *Kentucky Utilities Company et al. v. Glenn*, 394 F.2d 631 (6th Cir., 1968).
35. *See Louis Gale et al.*, 41 T.C. 269 (1963).
36. Regulations Section 1.155-7(a).
37. *Maryland Shipbuilding and Drydock Company v. United States*, 409 F.2d 1363 (Ct. Cl., 1969).
38. *Georgia Carolina Chemical Company*, T.C. Memo., Docket No. 110326 (entered November 18, 1944).
39. *Luckenbach Steamship Co.*, 9 T.C. 662 (1947).
40. *United States v. Morton, Sr. et al.*, 387 F.2d 441 (8th Cir., 1968).
41. I.R.C. Section 165(c)(3).
42. I.R.C. Section 1033.
43. *Orders et al. v. United States*, D.C., W.D. S.C., 1964.
44. *Steuart Brothers v. Commissioner*, 261 F.2d 580 (4th Cir., 1958).
45. *Walter A. Henshaw*, 23 T.C. 176 (1954).
46. I.R.C. Section 1033.
47. *Town Hill Park Corporation*, T.C. Memo. 1970-261 (filed September 14, 1970).
48. *Ziegler v. United States*, 254 F. Supp. 202 (D.C., Colo., 1966).
49. Revenue Ruling 70-466, 1970-2 CB 165.
50. Regulations Section 1.1033(a)-2(c).
51. *John Richard Corp.*, 46 T.C. 41 (1966).
52. Revenue Ruling 57-454, 1957-2 CB 526.
53. Revenue Ruling 70-144, 1970-1 CB 170.
54. *C. G. Willis, Incorporated v. Commissioner*, 342 F.2d 996 (3d Cir., 1965).
55. I.R.C. Section 1231.
56. I.R.C. Section 337.
57. *United States v. Morton, Sr. et al.*, 387 F.2d 441 (8th Cir., 1968).
58. *The Covered Wagon, Inc. et al. v. Commissioner*, 369 F.2d 629 (8th Cir., 1966).
59. I.R.C. Section 165.
60. *Rosenthal et al. v. Commissioner*, 416 F.2d 491 (2d Cir., 1969).
61. *Kipp et al. v. Bingler*, D.C., W.D. Pa., 1964.
62. Regulations Section 1.165-7(b).
63. *Ralph S. Clark et al.*, T.C. Memo. 1966-22 (filed January 27, 1966).
64. *Rosenthal et al. v. Commissioner*, 416 F.2d 491 (2d Cir., 1969).

65. *Pasquale Colabella et al.*, T.C. Memo. 1958-136 (filed July 15, 1958).

66. *Ann Lader*, T.C. Memo. 1970-23 (filed February 3, 1970).

67. *E.g., Richard R. Hollington et al.*, T.C. Memo. 1956-132 (filed May 31, 1956); *Charles A. Harris et al.*, T.C. Memo., Docket No. 34256 (entered January 28, 1953); *Harold B. Adams*, T.C. Memo., Docket No. 35451 and 38238 (entered September 30, 1953).

68. *Thomas Miller*, 19 T.C. 1046 (1953).

69. *Clarence E. Stewart*, T.C. Memo., Docket Nos. 28637 and 31404-5, entered August 14, 1953.

70. *Mellinger et al. v. United States*, D.C., S.D. Texas, 1953, *rev'd on other issues*, 228 F.2d 688 (5th Cir., 1956).

71. *Massillon-Cleveland-Akron Sign Co.*, 15 T.C. 79 (1950).

72. *Oppenheim's, Inc. v. Kavanagh*, 90 F. Supp. 107 (D.C., E.D. Mich., 1950).

73. *Miller v. Hocking Glass Company*, 80 F.2d 436 (6th Cir., 1935).

74. *Piedmont-Mt. Airy Guano Co.*, 3 B.T.A. 1009 (1926).

75. *Flaxlinum Insulating Company*, 5 B.T.A. 676 (1926).

76. I.R.C. Section 124.

77. I.R.C. Section 162.

78. Regulations Section 1.162-1(a).

79. *Columbia Theatre Co.*, 3 B.T.A. 622 (1926).

80. *Marvin T. Blackwell et al.*, T.C. Memo. 1956-184 (filed August 9, 1956).

81. G.C.M. 23587, 1943 CB 118.

82. *Two-L Realty Co., Inc.*, T.C. Memo. 1955-297 (filed October 31, 1955).

83. *Watson et al. v. Commissioner*, 345 U.S. 544 (1953).

84. *The Lehman Company of America, Inc.*, 17 T.C. 422 (1951).

85. *Black Hardware Company v. Commissioner*, 39 F.2d 460 (5th Cir., 1930).

86. *International Building Company*, 21 B.T.A. 617 (1930).

87. *Ticket Office Equipment Co., Inc.*, 20 T.C. 272 (1953), *aff'd on another issue*, 213 F.2d 318 (2d Cir., 1954).

88. *United States v. Morton, Sr. et al.*, 387 F.2d 441 (8th Cir., 1968).

89. *Spring Canyon Coal Co. v. Commissioner*, 43 F.2d 78 (10th Cir., 1930).

90. *L. A. Thompson Scenic Railway Company*, 2 B.T.A. 664 (1925).

91. Revenue Ruling 69-512, 1969-2 CB 24.

92. *Electric Regulator Corporation*, 40 T.C. 757 (1963), *rev'd on another issue*, 336 F.2d 339 (2d Cir., 1964).

93. *Millane Nurseries & Tree Experts, Inc.*, T.C. Memo., Docket No. 110443 (entered December 15, 1942).

94. *Halby Chemical Company, Inc. et al. v. United States*, 180 Ct. Cl. 584 (Ct. Cl., 1967).

95. *California Motor Transport Co., Ltd. et al.*, T.C. Memo., Docket Nos. 108467-8 and 111612-3 (entered April 23, 1943).

96. *The Smoot Sand & Gravel Corporation*, T.C. Memo. 1956-82 (filed October 10, 1956), *rev'd and rem'd'd on other issues*, 241 F.2d 197 (4th Cir., 1957).

97. *Hemphill Schools, Inc. v. Commissioner*, 137 F.2d 961 (7th Cir., 1943).

98. *Eastern Railway and Lumber Company*, 12 T.C. 869 (1949).

99. *Ben Grote*, 41 B.T.A. 247 (1940).

100. *Ralph Walton et al.*, T.C. Memo. 1961-130 (filed May 12, 1961).

101. *Carl A. Hasslacher*, T.C. Memo., Docket No. 21662 (entered April 7, 1950).

102. I.R.C. Section 165(h).

CHAPTER 16

What Can Be Done with Contributions

Deductible Contributions

Corporate charitable contributions are generally limited to five percent of taxable income, computed without reference to charitable contributions, carrybacks, and the Western Hemisphere Trade Corporation deduction.[1]

A personal holding company is not subject to the maximum contributions deduction imposed upon other corporations; its limitation is that imposed upon individuals.[2]

An individual's deduction for charitable contributions is limited to 50 percent of his adjusted gross income for the taxable year. In the case of property which has appreciated in value, the taxpayer is entitled to this 50 percent ceiling only if he elects to take the unrealized appreciation in value into account for tax purposes. If he does not make this election, these contributions are limited to 30 percent of his adjusted gross income. Contributions to certain private nonoperating foundations and to certain other tax-exempt organizations, however, are limited to 20 percent of adjusted gross income.[3]

The percentage limitation on corporate charitable contributions can be bypassed if it is established that the payments constitute ordinary and necessary business expenses. Thus, a corporation's payments to a school board to improve educational standards were deductible without limitation as ordinary and necessary expenses where the purpose of the payments was to better the instructional service so that employees of the corporate donor would not leave to accept employment in areas with better schools.[4] A travel agency which made sizeable contributions to charitable organizations could deduct them as sales promotion expenses where the agency dealt primarily with charitable organizations and there was an expectation of increased business as a result of the contribution even though no conditions were imposed.[5]

Where a taxpayer was required by a local subdivision regulation to contribute a portion of its property for school and park purposes, this was ruled a business expenditure of a capital nature instead of a deductible contribution.[6] **203**

Elements of a Contribution

It is not sufficient that a contribution be actuated by charitable motives. The donee must fall within one of the classes specified in the Internal Revenue Code,[7] and there must be a gift.[8] For tax purposes, a gift is an irrevocable transfer without adequate or full consideration made by a donor competent to make a gift. The donor must manifest a clear and unmistakable intention to divest himself of title, dominion, and control over the property being transferred. The donee must be capable of accepting a gift; if not, he must be someone acting as a trustee or agent for the donee capable of accepting it.[9] The donee or his agent must *accept* the gift.[10] A *bona fide* gift also requires delivery of the subject matter of the gift or of the means of effecting dominion over it. Depending upon circumstances, delivery may be physical or symbolic.[11] (Examples of symbolic delivery are presenting a key to a car or a deed to a house.)

Charitable Motive Is Not Required

A purely charitable motive is not a prerequisite for a deductible charitable contribution. This was well described in one court's opinion: "Community good will, the desire to avoid community bad will, public pressures of other kinds, tax avoidance, prestige, conscience-salving, a vindictive desire to prevent relatives from inheriting family wealth—these are only some of the motives which may lie close to the heart, or so-called heart, of one who gives to a charity. If the policy of the income tax laws favoring charitable contributions is to be effectively carried out, there is good reason to avoid unnecessary intrusions of subjective judgments as to what prompts the financial support of the organized but non-governmental goods works of society."[12]

A corporation might find that it is "good business" to make conspicuous contributions to charity; this can enhance the corporate image and fulfill the aspirations of executives who would like to see worthy endeavors receive funds, but who personally are not in a position to help out in a substantial way.[13]

In most instances, corporate contributions are impelled by the prospect of favorable tax treatment. At times, the tax laws create a never-never land where a taxpayer can actually make money by giving away property to charity rather than by selling it.[14] That tax benefits result is not cause for the Internal Revenue Service to object.[15]

Qualified Charities

A *deductible charitable contribution* is one made to or for the use of:

(1) A state or a possession of the United States (or any political subdivision thereof), or the United States or the District of Columbia, but only if the contribution or gift is made exclusively for public purposes.

(2) A corporation, trust, or community chest, fund, or foundation

(a) created or organized in the manner described in (1);

(b) organized and operated exclusively for religious, charitable, scientific, literary, or educational purposes or for the prevention of cruelty to children or animals;

(c) no part of the net earnings of which inures to the benefit of any private shareholder or individual; and

(d) no substantial part of the activities of which consists of carrying on propaganda or otherwise attempting to influence legislation, and which does not participate or intervene in any political campaign on behalf of any candidate for public office.

(3) Under specified circumstances, a veterans' organization, a fraternal society operating under the lodge system, or a cemetery company exclusively for the benefit of its members may qualify.[16]

These classifications are necessarily broad.[17] The charitable deduction, within stipulated percentages, is only valid for contributions to organizations approved for this purpose by the Internal Revenue Service. The impressive, authentic-sounding name of an organization is no guarantee of deductibility. Every two years, the Treasury Department publishes a list of organizations, contributions to which are deductible for tax purposes. Supplements are issued regularly.[18]

An organization may be characterized as charitable for Federal income tax purposes even where its creator has provided that preference be given in its donations to his own relatives if the persons to whom the charity can give assistance are not limited by definition to his relatives.[19]

If a so-called charitable organization is removed from this official list by the Internal Revenue Service, contributions made to that organization by persons unaware of the change in status generally will be allowed if made on or before the date of publication of an announcement in the Internal Revenue Bulletin that contributions are no longer deductible.[20] Obviously, it is in the interest of a taxpayer to ascertain whether organizations to which he makes contributions are still on the eligible list.[21]

"Exclusively" for Charitable Purposes

In order to fall within the category covered by the Code, an organization must be devoted to purposes that are charitable, educational, or the like. The presence of a single non-charitable or other recognized purpose, if substantial in nature, will destroy the exemption, regardless of the number or importance of truly charitable purposes.[22] Where a charitable organization's efforts were devoted to legislative activity to the extent of five percent, this was deemed to be relatively insubstantial and the requirement that the organization be devoted exclusively to charity was not violated.[23]

The Internal Revenue Service argued fruitlessly in one case that an organization was not operated exclusively for charitable purposes because it was the practice of its founders to contribute appreciated-value properties to it, thereby obtaining personal tax advantages. But this motivation did not militate against the tax-exempt status of the organization or the deductibility of the contributions made to it.[24]

A trust organized and operated primarily for paying pensions to retired employees of a corporation is not organized exclusively for charitable purposes and therefore is not entitled to exemption. Contributions to such a trust are not considered charitable contributions.[25]

Absence of Consideration

Absence of consideration is a requirement for deductible contributions. Such a contribution does not include a payment made by a taxpayer in consideration of a service to be rendered to him by a charity.[26] Where a person or organization makes a payment to a charitable organization and receives something in return (such as a receipt of consideration in the form of tickets of admission or other privileges), a presumption exists to the effect that the payment is not a gift. The burden is on the taxpayer to overcome this presumption.[27]

Here are the Internal Revenue Service ground rules for tickets purchased for the "benefit" of charitable organizations:

(1) If the charity sells tickets for close to the established price for the concert, show, etc., no part of the "contribution" is deductible.

(2) If the charity charges an amount in excess of the established price of the ticket, only this excess is deductible by the payor as a contribution.

(3) If the buyer of a ticket sold by the charity at the established price has no intention of using the ticket and in fact does not use it, he gets no deduction. However, he would get the deduction if he refused to accept the ticket and merely made a contribution in the same amount to the charity.

(4) If a charity solicits contributions on a form where the "contributor" marks his check as being for a ticket to an event produced by the tax-exempt organization or as being a straight contribution, those checking the first option get no tax deduction.

(5) If friends of the charity pay the entire cost of staging an event for which tickets are sent to contributors to the charity, no part of the cost of the tickets is deductible.[28]

A contribution to an approved charitable organization is deductible to the extent permitted by the Internal Revenue Code even if the donor derives a commercial or other benefit from the transaction. In one instance, the officers of a real estate corporation contributed some acreage to a school board and claimed a charitable deduction. The Internal Revenue Service objected on the ground that the real purpose of the transfer was to attract persons with school-age children to the locality, where homes were available for sale by the donors' corporation. Property values clearly would be enhanced if a new school were built next to the donors' property. The court found that the deduction was proper, for regardless of the motivation, a transfer had been made without consideration to an approved donee.[29]

A corporation contributed land to a state highway department. This land ran through the corporation's property. The highway department improved and beautified the land given by the corporation and other parties at the same time. A contributions deduction was permitted since the authorizing section of the Code is not construed as applicable only in the event the donor receives no benefit, tangible or intangible, from a contribution. The motives of a taxpayer in making charitable contributions are not relevant if he complies with the statute in all other respects.[30]

But if the "contribution" to a governmental agency is nothing more than a payment in return for which benefits are anticipated, no contribution deduction is allowed. A taxpayer entered into an agreement to purchase real property, subject to its being rezoned to permit use for commercial purposes. To assure favorable rezoning, which otherwise was uncertain, the taxpayer deeded certain of the land to the city in which it was located as a gift. The rezoning was permitted and the purchase was formalized. But no charitable deduction was allowed inasmuch as the gift had been made, not for charitable or public purposes, but in expectation of the receipt of certain specific direct benefits within the power of the city to bestow, directly or indirectly.[31]

Voluntary payments by merchants and property owners to a municipality to provide public parking facilities in the general areas of their businesses and properties were held deductible as contributions where parking was not limited to the use of contributors or their customers and the amount of the contributions was not based upon the proximity or probable use of the facilities by the contributors, their tenants, or their customers.[32]

Actual Payment Is Required

A charitable deduction is not available in the case of a pledge; there must be actual payment.[33] Thus, a promissory note given to a charitable organization does not beget a deduction.[34]

Contributions are deductible in the year they are made, whether the payor is on the cash or the accrual basis. However, there is one exception: If an accrual-basis corporation's board of directors authorizes a contribution in one taxable year and the payment actually is made not later than the 15th day of the third month of the succeeding taxable year, the corporation may elect to treat the contribution as a deduction in the year of authorization. The election is made on that year's tax return.[35] This permits deduction in the year in which it will do the most good.

For tax purposes, one does not make a contribution by merely issuing instructions to someone that the formalities be carried out.[36] If a taxpayer unconditionally delivers or mails a properly endorsed stock certificate to a qualified organization or the organization's agent, the time of the contribution is the date of delivery (or mailing, provided the certificate is received in the ordinary course of the mails). If a taxpayer delivers his certificate to a bank or broker acting as his agent or to the issuing corporation or its agent for transfer into the name of the organization, the time of the contribution is the date the stock is transferred onto the books of the corporation, for this, in effect, is the date of delivery to the charitable organization.[37]

Form of Contributions

A charitable contribution is not restricted to cash or its equivalent. It may take the form of any kind of interest which has determinable value.[38]

A taxpayer's surrender to a charitable organization of its own debt obligation can constitute a contribution. But there must be a *bona fide*, pre-existent, enforceable debt before it can be considered the subject matter of a contribution.[39]

A restrictive easement in favor of the Federal government to enable it to preserve the scenic view afforded to certain public properties has been held to be deductible.[40]

If a prospective donor has nothing of value to contribute except his stock in a closely-held corporation, but he is disinclined to part with any of his shares in view of the fact that this would dilute his voting interest, a tax-free recapitalization could be effected from one-class voting stock into voting and nonvoting shares.[41] Then he could give away some or all of his nonvoting shares without disturbing his proportionate control of the corporation. This would also reduce his ultimate gross estate without diluting his voting stock interest.

Where stock is contributed to a charity, and shortly thereafter these shares are redeemed by the corporation that issued them, the reality of the contribution for tax purposes is not affected if the gift is not conditional on the charity's redeeming the shares and if the charity was not prevented from selling the shares elsewhere.[42]

A contributions deduction was allowed where stock was transferred in trust for charitable purposes. Although the donors were the officers and directors of the corporation the shares of which were transferred, the stock's value to the charity was not dependent upon the donors' whim; for if the corporation did not pay dividends, the accumulated earnings tax could have penalized not only the corporation, but also the directors.[42a]

A contributions deduction is allowed in the case of an irrevocable assignment of a life insurance policy to a charitable organization, the amount of the deduction being the interpolated terminal reserve of the policy at the time.[43]

No deduction is allowed for the contribution of services. But a taxpayer who gives his services gratuitously to a charitable organization may deduct his unreimbursed travel expenses (including meals and lodgings) incurred in connection with the affairs of the organization.[44] If an individual uses his car for the purpose of rendering gratuitous services to a charitable organization, a charitable deduction is allowed at a standard mileage rate of six cents per mile. This method is optional, and if the allowable non-reimbursed expenses for charitable purposes exceed this amount, the taxpayer may deduct his actual expenses.[45]

Gifts of the Use of Property

No charitable deduction is allowed for a donation of less than the donor's entire interest in property to, but not in trust for, a charitable organization in the case of gifts after July 31, 1969, unless the interest is a remainder interest in a personal residence, a farm or an undivided portion of the donor's entire interest in property, or the donation would have been includable if such interest had been transferred in trust. (A *remainder* is one's right to property after a period of time or a specified occurrence, such as the owner's death.) Therefore, no deduction is allowed where a contribution is made of the right to use property for a period of time.[46]

Contributions of Appreciated-Value Property

Prior to 1970, contributions in property which had increased in value since acquisition were deductible at fair market value at the time of gift, the donor having an additional saving of any income tax upon disposition of property at a figure higher than his cost or other basis. In certain instances, that is no longer possible. In the case of charitable contributions made after December 21, 1969, appreciation must be taken into account (that is, the amount of the charitable deduction is reduced) in these situations:

(1) where gifts are made to certain charitable private foundations;

(2) where gifts are made in the form of property which would give rise to *ordinary income* if sold (for example, inventory or works of art created by the donor); and

(3) where gifts are made in the form of tangible personal property (such as paintings, art objects, and books not produced by the donor) which would result in long-term capital gain if the property were sold.[47]

Thus, the appreciation element is deducted from the amount of the contribution allowed in the cases of short-term capital assets and inventory.

The amount of the charitable deduction is the fair market value reduced by $62\frac{1}{2}$ percent of the appreciation (50 percent in the case of individual donors) where gifts of long-term capital assets are made to private foundations other than operating foundations and private foundations which distribute an amount equivalent to the amount of the gift to public charitable foundations or private operating foundations within one year.

Bargain Sales to Charities

For contribution purposes, a "bargain sale" is one where a taxpayer sells property to a charitable organization for less than the property's fair market value; the sale is often made at the taxpayer's cost so that he can recover his investment and obtain a charitable deduction as well. The cost or other basis of the property must be allocated between the portion of the property "given" to the charity and the portion "sold" upon the basis of the fair market value of each portion.[48]

Here is an illustration of this treatment: If a taxpayer sold land with a fair market value of $20,000 to a charitable organization (not a private foundation) at his cost of $12,000, he would be required to allocate 60 percent of the cost ($7200) to the portion "sold" to the charity ($12,000; that is, 60 percent of $20,000 realization). He would allocate 40 percent of the cost ($4800) to the portion "given" to the charity ($8000; that is, 40 percent of $20,000 realization). Thus, he would be required to include $4800 as gain from the sale of a capital asset in his tax return and would be allowed a charitable deduction of $8000.

Conditional Contributions

No deduction is allowed for a contribution if the conditions accompanying it are so complex as to make valuation impossible.[49] Nor is deduction allowed where the mathematical possibility of a contingency is too complicated.[50]

A corporation contributed property to a tax-exempt organization on the condition that this property be used for religious or educational purposes. Some 18 years later, the donee decided not to use the property and reconveyed it to the donor. Inasmuch as the contribution had furnished the donor with a tax benefit (the deduction) in the first instance, the return of the property was income at the rate of tax prevailing in the year of recovery.[51]

Valuation of Property

The donor has the burden of establishing the fair market value of his contribution.[52] But on occasion, a court will allow *some* deduction for an unsubstantiated contribution if it can be established that a contribution had unquestionably been made.[53] This is in line with the so-called *Cohan* rule (See chapter 17, The Burden of Proof.)

Contributed securities are valued at the prices at which they actually were traded on an open public market on the date of the gift in the absence of exceptional circumstances which reduce their evidentiary worth.[54]

Cost does not establish the value of an article after it has been contributed to a charitable organization. The allowable deduction is the fair market value computed on the price an ultimate consumer would pay. What might be paid by a dealer buying for resale is not a proper consideration.[55]

The value of contributed property as set by an expert cannot ordinarily be used as the measure of the contributions deduction if the property is sold by the charitable organization immediately after the gift for a much lower figure.[56] Thus, the donor will lose out if the donee sells the property too soon for an inadequate price unless the donor can establish that the amount realized was below the fair market value of the property at the time of donation and that the charity did not take the proper steps to find the right market.[57]

Works of Art

Contributions of works of art have occasioned much litigation in the area of valuation. The Internal Revenue Service has laid down the following ground rules. The contribution should be buttressed by an appraisal to include:

(1) a complete description of the object, indicating the size, the subject matter, the medium, the name of the artist, the approximate date created, the interest transferred, and any other relevant information;

(2) the cost, date, and manner of acquisition;

(3) a history of the item including proof of authenticity;

(4) a photograph of a size and quality fully identifying the subject matter, preferably a print, 10 by 12 inches or larger; and

(5) a statement of the factors upon which an appraisal was based— such as sales of other works by the same artist around the valuation date, quoted prices in dealers' catalogs, the economic state of the art market at or around the time of valuation, a record of any exhibitions at which the particular art object had been displayed, and a statement as to the standing of the artist in his profession and in the particular school or time period.[58]

The Commissioner of Internal Revenue has a panel of art experts to advise him on valuations of contributed works of art. In any event, the Commissioner's finding as to the valuation will stand unless the donor can prove a higher figure.[59]

Limitations imposed by a donor upon the donee's right to dispose of paintings for a specified period (such as three years) will have a depressing effect upon the valuation.[60]

Proof of Contribution

In connection with claims for contributions deductions, a taxpayer must show on the appropriate schedule of his income tax return the names and addresses of the recipient organizations along with the amounts and approximate dates of the actual payment or delivery. If required by the Internal Revenue Service, the donee organization must supply a substantiating statement showing such data as the name of the donor and the amount of the contribution.[61] Some charitable organizations decline to report specific dollar amounts for non-cash contributions, but furnish only an identifying description of the property involved. A charitable organization cannot afford to be suspected of complicity with a donor in setting up an artificially high basis for a tax deduction. The organization's own tax-exempt status—and therefore its very survival—could be endangered by collusion.

Annuity from a Charitable Organization

The purchaser of an annuity from a commercial insurer may recover tax-free each year the cost of the annuity divided by the number of years in his life expectancy; that is, he excludes from income each year the cost divided by that number of years.[62] An individual may buy his annuity from a charitable organization, perhaps in response to an advertisement, paying more than the going rate for commercial annuities or transferring property valued at a greater amount. The "cost" he recovers tax-free over the remainder of his life is the fair market value of the annuity. The balance of his cost is deductible as a charitable contribution.[63]

Matching Contributions

Where a corporation's contributions to colleges match those of the company's employees, the corporation is entitled to a charitable contributions deduction, but the employee has not received the equivalent of income that would be taxed to him personally.[64] Ordinarily, an employee is taxed upon income which his employer pays on his behalf.

Appraisal Fees

Appraisal fees paid by a donor for determining the value of properties given to charity are deductible.[65]

Unused Contributions Carry-Over

Corporate contributions in excess of five percent of income may be carried over for five years.[66]

If an individual's charitable contributions are of the type which qualify for the 50 percent ceiling, any contributions which he makes in excess of 50 percent of adjusted gross income may be carried over into the next five years. However, no carry-over is permitted in the case of contributions geared to lesser percentages of adjusted gross income where the contributions exceed such percentages in any year.[67]

NOTES

1. I.R.C. Section 170(b)(2).
2. I.R.C. Section 556(b)(2).
3. I.R.C. Section 170(b)(1).
4. *United States v. The Jefferson Mills, Inc.*, 367 F.2d 392 (5th Cir., 1966).
5. *Sarah Marquis*, 49 T.C. 695 (1968).
6. *Jordan Perlmutter et al.*, 45 T.C. 311 (1965).
7. *Albion D. T. Libby*, B.T.A. Memo., Docket No. 107295 (entered May 6, 1942).
8. *Harold E. Wolfe et al.*, 54 T.C. 1707 (1970).

9. *Talge v. United States*, 229 F. Supp. 836 (D.C., W.D. Mo., 1964).
10. *Adolph Weil*, 31 B.T.A. 890 (1934), *aff'd*, 82 F.2d 561 (5th Cir., 1936).
11. *Adolph J. Urbanovsky*, T.C. Memo. 1965-276 (filed October 19, 1965).
12. *Crosby Valve & Gage Company v. Commissioner*, 380 F.2d 146 (1st Cir., 1967).
13. *The Why and How of Corporate Giving*, New York: National Industrial Conference Board, 1956.

14. *Sol Schildkraut Estate v. Commissioner*, 368 F.2d 40 (2d Cir., 1966).
15. *Curt Teich Foundation et al.*, 48 T.C. 963 (1967), *aff'd*, 407 F.2d 815 (7th Cir., 1969).
16. I.R.C. Section 170(c).
17. *Vaughn v. Chapman et al.*, 48 T.C. 358 (1967).
18. Publication No. 78.
19. *William Waller et al.*, 39 T.C. 665 (1965).
20. Revenue Procedure 68-17, 1968-1 CB 806.
21. I.R.S. News Release, July 10, 1970.
22. *Hammerstein v. Kelley*, 235 F. Supp. 60 (D.C., E.D. Mo., 1964), *aff'd*, 349 F.2d 928 (8th Cir., 1965).
23. *Seasongood v. Commissioner*, 227 F.2d 907 (6th Cir., 1955).
24. *William Waller et al.*, 39 T.C. 665 (1965).
25. *Watson et al. v. United States*, 355 F.2d 269 (2d Cir., 1965).
26. *Willis D. Wood Estate*, 39 T.C. 1 (1962).
27. Technical Information Release No. 747, June 30, 1965.
28. Revenue Ruling 67-246, 1967-2 CB 104.
29. *Ben I. Goldin et al.*, T.C. Memo. 1969-233 (filed November 3, 1969).
30. *The Citizens & Southern National Bank of South Carolina v. United States*, 243 F. Supp. 900 (D.C., W.D. S.C., 1965).
31. *Stubbs et al. v. United States*, 428 F.2d 885 (9th Cir., 1970).
32. Revenue Ruling 69-90, 1969-1 CB 63.
33. *Orr et al. v. United States*, 343 F.2d 553 (5th Cir., 1965).
34. Revenue Ruling 68-174, 1968-1 CB 81.
35. I.R.C. Section 179(a)(2).
36. *Jack Winston Londen et al.*, 45 T.C. 106 (1965).
37. I.R.S. Publication No. 561 (3-68).
38. Revenue Ruling 68-113, 1968-1 CB 80.
39. *Mervin R. Lippman et al.*, 52 T.C. 135 (1969).
40. Revenue Ruling 64-205, 1964-2 CB 62.
41. I.R.C. Section 368(a)(1)(E).
42. *Richard P. Makoff et al.*, T.C. Memo. 1967-113 (filed January 10, 1967).
42a. *United States v. Gates, Jr. et al.*, 376 F.2d 65 (10th Cir., 1967).
43. Revenue Ruling 69-79, 1969-1 CB 63.
44. Revenue Ruling 55-4, 1955-1 CB 291.
45. Revenue Procedure 70-26, 1970-2 CB 507.
46. I.R.C. Section 170(f)(3).
47. I.R.C. Section 170(e).
48. I.R.C. Section 1011(b).
49. *James L. Darling et al.*, 43 T.C. 520 (1965).
50. *Commissioner v. Louis Sternberger Estate*, 348 U.S. 187 (1955).
51. *Alice Phelan Sullivan Corporation v. United States*, 381 F.2d 399 (Ct. Cl., 1967).
52. *William Fox et al.*, T.C. Memo. 1968-154 (filed July 18, 1968).
53. *Charles A. Harris et al.*, T.C. Memo., Docket No. 34256 (entered January 28, 1953).
54. *Zanuck et al. v. Commissioner*, 149 F.2d 714 (9th Cir., 1948).
55. *Goldman et al. v. Commissioner*, 388 F.2d 476 (6th Cir., 1967).
56. *Philip Kaplan et al.*, 43 T.C. 663 (1965).
57. *Daniel S. McGuire et al.*, 44 T.C. 801 (1965).
58. Revenue Procedure 66-49, 1966-2 CB 1257.

59. *E.g., George Cukor*, T.C. Memo. 1968-17 (filed January 26, 1968); *Morris Schapiro et al.*, T.C. Memo. 1968-44 (filed March 15, 1968).

60. *Samuel S. Silverman et al.*, T.C. Memo. 1968-216 (filed September 26, 1968).

61. Regulations Section 1.170-1(a).

62. I.R.C. Section 72.

63. Revenue Ruling 70-15, 1970-1 CB 20.

64. Revenue Ruling 67-137, 1967-1 CB 63.

65. Revenue Ruling 67-461, 1967-2 CB 125.

66. I.R.C. Section 170(d)(2).

67. I.R.C. Section 170(d)(1).

CHAPTER 17

The Burden of Proof

Who Must Bear It

The taxpayer virtually always has the burden of proof.[1] Courts will extend to the finding of the Commissioner of Internal Revenue a presumption of correctness, unless the statute provides otherwise. The Commissioner's finding thus is *prima facie* correct, and the burden is on the taxpayer to overcome this presumption of its correctness.

A taxpayer's burden is a double one; it is not only to prove that the Commissioner's determination of the tax was wrong, but also to establish the essential facts from which a correct determination of his tax liability can be made.[2]

Who bears the burden is more than a question of tactics, for at times the evidence is in equipoise. The taxpayer has not met his burden of overcoming the presumption as to the Commissioner's correctness.[3] If there is some evidence that a taxpayer received income and no evidence that he did not, he is taxed. Such was the situation where the New York Racing Association sent a payment information return to an individual, showing his name and the daily double winnings that allegedly were paid to him. The Internal Revenue Service was sent a copy of this. Inasmuch as the individual could not meet the negative burden of proof requirement that he was not the winner-payee, he was subject to tax.[4]

What the Taxpayer Must Do

Taxpayers must prove statements made in connection with their tax returns. A court is not compelled to blindly accept their testimony.[5] It is not enough for a taxpayer to prove that his figures were reasonable; he must show that the Commissioner's action in changing these figures was unreasonable and an abuse of the Commissioner's permissible discretion.[6]

215

There Is No Presumption of Innocence

The time-honored presumption that a person is innocent until proven guilty does not extend to Federal income tax matters, except where fraud is alleged. (See the section on "Fraud" later in this chapter.)

Since the Commissioner's finding is presumptively correct, the taxpayer cannot sit back and wait for the Internal Revenue Service to prove *its* case. Once the Service has established its case, as by having the Commissioner make his finding, a taxpayer rests his at his peril.[7]

In certain areas, such as where there is administrative leeway in acceptance of an accounting method or the grant of an extension, the Commissioner has been given discretion in making his decision. In order to have an unfavorable action by the Commissioner overturned, the taxpayer must show that that official acted capriciously or arbitrarily.[8]

Difficulty of Meeting the Burden Does Not Excuse It

There is an ancient legal maxim, *lex non cogit ad impossibilia*—the law does not require the impossible. But meeting the burden of proof in a tax matter may require just that.

The fact that the circumstances may be such as to make it difficult or impossible, though that difficulty is not the fault of the taxpayer, to prove a material fact does not relieve the taxpayer of this burden.[9]

For example, when the taxpayer must establish the probable useful life of a business asset, it is not enough that a court recognizes the difficulty facing the taxpayer who must assign some realistic, meaningful evaluation to that life.[10] The taxpayer still has that responsibility.[11]

Sometimes, the statute has deliberately made the problem of proof difficult so as to prevent abuses, as in the establishment of just how much of one's personal residence was used for business purposes.[12]

The *Cohan* Rule

Since 1930, courts have been following the *Cohan* rule, which was named after the great entertainer George M. Cohan, whose tax troubles resulted in the rule. If a taxpayer unquestionably has business expenses of a certain type but lacks proof to substantiate them, a court may "approximate" the amount of allowable deduction, bearing down, if the court chooses, upon the taxpayer whose inexactitude is of his own making.[13]

The *Cohan* rule is a judicial attempt at dispensing practical justice in the best way possible.[14] Its use by a court depends upon a showing that expenses of the type claimed unquestionably had been borne, proof of the amount being the only element in question.[15]

The application of the *Cohan* rule is exemplified by a court's determination of the portion of automobile expenses that were deductible after it had been established that the car definitely was being used for business purposes part of the time.[16] So, where a court believed that a taxpayer had made charitable contributions, but there was no substantiation of the amount, the *Cohan* rule authorized a court-created substitute.[17] The amount of allowable theft loss, in the absence of verification of amounts, may also be determined under this rule.[18]

Where the Internal Revenue Service claimed that parties under common control were dealing at less than arm's length, and hence all of the profits had to be reallocated to one of the parties (see chapter 5, Arm's Length Transactions), the court agreed that such a situation existed, but noted that *not all* of the profits were subject to reallocation. Here, one of the corporations from which a reallocation was sought by the Service unquestionably had earned some of its income. The amount which was subject to reallocation was found by the court under its application of the *Cohan* rule to be 70 percent.[19]

Where an individual maintained an office in his own home but could not prove the portion of the home's total maintenance and other relevant expenses apportionable to the office as business expenses, the court arrived at a figure by using the *Cohan* rule.[20]

In the absence of proper substantiation, a taxpayer may be able to get *some* deduction under the *Cohan* rule. But he may be subjected to a negligence penalty for not having kept better records.[21]

Travel and Entertainment

The *Cohan* rule was specifically made inapplicable to travel and entertainment expenses by the requirement of specific substantiation for such expenses. Thus, all such expenses must be substantiated thoroughly before they can be allowed to offset gross income.[22]

No deduction is allowed as an ordinary and necessary expense, or as an expense for the production of income, for traveling expenses, entertainment, or gifts unless the taxpayer substantiates by adequate records or sufficient evidence corroborating his own statement: (1) the amount of such expenses or other items; (2) the time and place of the travel, entertainment, amusement, recreation, or use of the facility, or the date and description of the gift; (3) the business purpose of the expense or other item, and (4) the business relationship to the taxpayer of the persons being entertained, using the facility, or receiving the gift.[23]

In order to substantiate the requirements enumerated in the preceding paragraph, a taxpayer must keep adequate records or other evidence sufficient to corroborate his own statements. Adequate records means detailed records, such as account books, diaries, or statements of expenses in support of each element of the expenditure.[24] The expenses must be proximately related to the taxpayer's trade or business.[25] For example, it must be demonstrated that Christmas presents to customers are necessary for business purposes in order that deduction for them can be justified.[26]

Dates and amounts of payments and names of payees do not constitute proof. The expenditures must be explained and identified with the business benefit sought to be gained.[27] Nor does a canceled check, which might satisfy a corporation's own auditor, meet the requirements of the Internal Revenue Service, since it does not follow that a canceled check had been used for payment of a business expense.[28] Sometimes a taxpayer is called upon to show the business benefit contemplated by the expenditure or the business actually developed as a result of it.[29]

Detailed substantiation is not required in the case of expenditures not in excess of $25, and diary notations of the party entertained, etc., will be sufficient.[30]

Where a businessman takes his wife with him on a trip which unquestionably is related to his trade or business, no deduction is allowed for her expenses in the absence of proof of her specific business purpose on the trip.[31]

Corporate Payments to an Officer's Widow

An increasingly common practice is for a corporation to make certain payments to the widow of an officer who dies in harness. In one case, in holding that such payments were not taxable income to her, but were a gift, the court listed five factors to be considered: (1) the payments had been made to the wife of the deceased employee and not to the employee's estate, (2) there was no obligation on the part of the corporation to pay any additional compensation to the deceased employee, (3) the corporation derived no benefit from the payment, (4) the widow performed no services for the corporation, and (5) the services of the husband had been compensated fully.[32] In a similar case, another court used the same criteria and added these additional ones: (6) the company had no established plan or policy for making payments to widows of deceased officers and employees, (7) the payment was not made in accordance with the husband's salary, (8) the amount was not included in the company's bonus schedule, (9) the payment was debited on the corporate books to "voluntary death benefit" and credited to "expenses payable," and (10) the payment resulted from detached and disinterested generosity.[33]

Thus, as many of the above criteria as possible should be established in order that the payment be treated as a tax-free gift to the widow.

Turning to the other side of the coin, it is necessary to show that the corporation derived a business benefit from the payment in order to get a tax deduction. That can cause a conflict with (3) above. Thus, corporate payments to an officer's widow were not regarded as deductible business expenses in the absence of proof that the payment was for the benefit of employee morale. The payments were not referred to in the company's annual report, nor were they made known to the public, the key personnel, or the customers.[34] Establishment of a corporation's right to the deduction requires proof of the business benefit contemplated—such as publicizing the payment to the widow (without its being a firm commitment) to highlight the fact that this is a good company for which to work.

Reasonableness of Compensation

In order for a corporation to be entitled to a deduction for the full compensation paid to officers or other highly compensated persons, it must establish three things: that the payment is (1) in fact made as compensation; (2) compensation for personal services actually rendered; and (3) is a reasonable amount.[35] (How this can be done is considered in chapter 8, Compensation.)

Actions of the board of directors of a corporation in voting salaries for any given period are presumed reasonable and proper.[36] Obviously, the minutes should set the stage for a reasonable compensation deduction. Minutes also should indicate that changes in executive compensation were related to the services performed rather than to corporate profits, especially where the officers are stockholders.[37] Bonuses to employees who also were stockholders were accepted by a court as compensation rather than dividends where the payments demonstrably were based upon individual performances.[38]

One of the factors used to determine the reasonableness of an officer's compensation is the time he devotes to the business. A court may well ask if he has other time-consuming interests and activities.[39] Of course, time spent at a corporation's business in itself is not enough to justify a high salary. Background, knowledge, experience, results, and other factors are important as well.[40]

Reasonableness of compensation may be established by the testimony of a qualified management consultant.[41] Evidence that a competitor had been trying to lure away the persons whose salaries are being questioned by the Serivce, is persuasive.[42]

Casualty Loss

Substantiation of a casualty loss must include proof that the asset in question was worth its purported value. The fact that there had been a loss by casualty was recognized after storm damage to a taxpayer's building. But inasmuch as the property had not been in very good condition at the time of the damage (one wall was "out of line"), only a portion of the loss was regarded as deductible.[43]

A taxpayer claimed a casualty loss after its insurance company denied liability. Deduction was denied, the court pointing out that the burden was on the taxpayer to show that its prospect for recovery was no longer reasonable at the end of the taxable year, which burden had not been met.[44]

If a casualty loss is claimed, it must be established that the loss actually was the result of a casualty.[45] Ordinarily, termite damage is not regarded as a casualty loss, for the element of "suddenness" is lacking. But deduction is allowed where it can be demonstrated that the termite invasion took place within a short period of time.[46]

Depreciation

A depreciation deduction requires the establishment of various forms of proof, although the Asset Depreciation Range System alleviates this problem considerably. (See chapter 12, Depreciation.) Estimated useful life, intended length of use if that is shorter than physical life, and probable resale or salvage value must be substantiated in most situations.[47] No depreciation is allowed where a taxpayer fails to adduce any evidence to prove that assets had a useful life capable of reasonable calculation.[48]

Depreciation may be taken at a faster rate than previously even where the straight-line method is used if it can be proven that during the taxable year(s) the assets are being subjected to faster wear and tear. In the case of road building equipment, this was demonstrated where the owner used the equipment an excessive number of hours, where the equipment was subjected to unusual weather conditions, where the equipment was near a coastal line where flooding occurred, and where the operators were not fully trained.[49] But mere demonstration of extra-long use of equipment does not prove the extent, if any, to which accelerated straight-line depreciation is appropriate.[50]

Depreciation has been permitted for a period shorter than physical life where it was established that the assets were useful only in connection with a contract which might not be renewed.[51]

The taxpayer will not be entitled to a depreciation deduction for an asset in the year in which it is sold at a profit unless he is prepared to show that any profit on sale was by reason of market enhancement in value, not by reason of excessive depreciation taken in prior years.[52]

Bad Debts

A bad debt must be deducted in the year in which it becomes worthless.[53] The unsupported opinion of the taxpayer by itself will not be accepted as proof of worthlessness.[54] The taxpayer has the burden of proving the year of worthlessness.[55] This may be shown by an identifiable event which either makes the debt worthless or from which the worthlessness can be ascertained.[56] (See chapter 13, Bad Debts and Other Write-Offs.)

If a state statute of limitations on debts ran before the taxable year, a creditor has the burden of showing why he believed the debt still was collectible.[57]

For a taxpayer to be entitled to a business bad debt deduction, he must show that the indebtedness was necessary for, and proximately related to, his trade or business.[58]

Inventories

In order for a taxpayer to prevail where the Internal Revenue Service seeks to change an inventory method, it must show that the method of valuing inventories most clearly reflects its income and that the method conforms as nearly as may be to the best accounting practice in the trade or business.[59]

The use of the lower of cost or market valuation method for inventories is not established by reference to an election to this effect upon a prior tax return.

An election may not have been available when that prior return had been filed; for example, the taxpayer at that time might have been bound by an earlier election.[60]

In order to have a write-down for unsaleable goods, a taxpayer has the burden of showing that inventories cannot be sold at normal prices.[61]

Abnormal Obsolescence

Proof is required in various areas in order to justify a write-off for abnormal obsolescence. A taxpayer must prove that the alleged brooding omnipresence of obsolescence was impending during the taxable year;[62] a taxpayer must establish with reasonable certainty that his assets will have little or no value at the end of their projected useful life, by reason of changing conditions or models;[63] and a taxpayer must demonstrate that the asset in question was permanently withdrawn, or earmarked for permanent withdrawal, during the taxable year.[64]

One corporation justified its obsolescence deduction for equipment which was being replaced by another type with testimony from its largest customer to the effect that the products turned out by the replacement machinery were better and cheaper than those produced by the old equipment.[65]

Repairs

A deductible repair is one which merely restores the *status quo ante* of property. In order that an expense be fully deductible as a repair and not depreciated as a capital improvement, a taxpayer must show that the items for which it made payment did not add to the value of the property or prolong its life, but merely kept the property in operating condition during its probable useful life.[66]

Transaction Entered into for Profit

To get a deduction as a business expense, the taxpayer must proffer evidence that a transaction was profit-oriented.[67]

Tax-Exempt Organizations

An individual may lose his charitable contributions deduction for failure of proof. Such was the case when a taxpayer refused to name the parties to whom he made his contributions on the ground that his religious beliefs forbade this disclosure and that his right of free speech under the First Amendment was being violated. The court disagreed.[68]

An allegedly tax-exempt organization must meet several forms of proof: (1) that it was organized exclusively for charitable purposes; (2) that it was operated exclusively for charitable purposes; (3) that no part of its net earnings inured to the benefit of any private shareholder or individual; and (4) that no substantial part of its activities consisted of carrying on propaganda or otherwise attempting to influence legislation.[69]

A tax-exempt foundation will lose its exempt status if income is allowed to accumulate unreasonably.[70] That is what happened where a foundation failed to establish that its programs, as budgeted, would begin to use expected annual income, let alone that accumulated before the questioned period. There was no showing of any attempt to relate the programs to anticipated income.[71] Elsewhere, a court noted disapprovingly that nothing in the record indicated any particular use to which a foundation's accumulated income or the then current income would be put.[72]

Failure to File Return

The burden is upon a taxpayer to prove reasonable cause for failure to file a tax return on time.[73] If a taxpayer would avoid a negligence penalty for failure to comply with the Federal income tax requirements, he must show that he had requested and relied upon the advice of a competent advisor to whom a full disclosure of the facts had been made.[74] Where an accountant had been fed inadequate information, it could not be shown that his recommendations had been based upon knowledge of the facts, and hence, there was no reasonable cause for the resultant penalty.[75]

Status of the Expert Witness

The rules of evidence ordinarily do not permit the opinion of a witness to be received in evidence. An exception to this rule exists in the case of expert witnesses. A person who, by education, study, and experience, has become an expert in any field and who is called as a witness may give his opinion as to any matter in which he is versed and which is material to the case.[76]

A taxpayer generally will prevail if the testimony of his expert witness is not controverted by the Internal Revenue Service's.[77] If a taxpayer has a qualified expert witness and the Service also has such a witness, the opinion of the latter will usually be preferred by the court, other things being equal, inasmuch as the Service's expert is presumptively completely disinterested as to the outcome of this particular litigation.[78] But in the final analysis, a court is not bound by the conclusory statements of any witness, even an "expert." [79] The testimony of an expert witness is no better than the convincing nature of the reasons offered in support of his testimony.[80]

Credibility of Witness

With reference to expert and other witnesses, there are certain qualities to be stressed. One court pointed out that in weighing testimony it would consider: (1) the recognized tests of the witnesses' testimony while on the stand; (2) any interest the witnesses might have in the outcome of the case; (3) any bias or prejudice for or against either party; (4) their opportunity to observe; (5) any reason to remember or forget; (6) the inherent improbability of their testimony; (7) the consistency or lack of consistency of the testimony; and (8) its corroboration or lack of corroboration with other credible evidence. Exhibits also could be significant.[81]

Taxpayer Credibility

Of no less importance in the substantiation of a tax case than an expert witness' plausibility is the taxpayer's. A charitable contribution was allowed although there was no documentary evidence to support it where the court found the donor's testimony to be candid and forthright, whether or not his testimony was contrary to his self-interest.[82]

A taxpayer's credibility can be fatally undermined if, in a different and perhaps minor area, he admits on cross-examination something which he had denied upon direct examination.[83]

Photography and the Burden of Proof

If, as the old Chinese proverb declares, "a picture is worth ten thousand words," the process of proof may be greatly simplified by a telling photograph. This can furnish the proof of what something looked like before, during, or after a taxable event. Unlike a legal brief, a photograph may not be developed years after the fact by a person who actually has no personal knowledge of what really took place. The taxpayer must realize at once what he wants to say in his photograph. There will be no opportunity for afterthought or editing.

Thus, a photograph can show what a building looked like before and after reconstruction; a series of photographs can show the original delapidated condition, the condition after various phases of the work were done, and the final result.[84] In the case of a casualty loss, pictures can show the property immediately before and immediately after the event.[85] Photographs can add plausibility to the statements of witnesses.[86]

Nature of Payment Received

Where a vendor sells his going business for a bulk price, he has the burden of establishing the proper division among the several types of assets of the lump consideration which was received.[87]

For example, two suits were brought, (1) for breach of contract with injury to good will and (2) for unfair competition and injury to income, and both actions were settled for one lump sum. Inasmuch as the Internal Revenue Service found the payment was taxable, the taxpayer had the burden of showing what portion should be allocated to each suit, for only income attributable to (1) was nontaxable. Failing to fix this amount, the taxpayer was bound by the Service's allocation.[88]

A corporation received $125,000 from its insurer as a compromise settlement under a policy affording "direct damage" and "use and occupancy" coverage. The Internal Revenue Service reallocation of $25,000 to the first category (compensatory) and $100,000 to the second category (fully taxable) was sustained for failure of proof of a more reasonable allocation.[89]

On a compromise settlement, a taxpayer has the burden of proving what portion of the payment, if any, is entitled to capital gains treatment.[90]

Where a compromise payment is made to the Internal Revenue Service in lieu of tax, penalty, and interest, the taxpayer has the burden of showing how much is for interest if he seeks an interest expense deduction. Customarily, this cannot be done; for there is no breakdown on a compromise settlement which is in lieu of all amounts assessed.[91]

Receipts by an Accrual-Basis Taxpayer

If an accrual-basis taxpayer would avoid the reporting of income upon a sale, he must show that receipt is contingent on an unresolved and allegedly intervening right. Postponement of payment without such accompanying doubts is not enough to omit the reporting of the income.[92]

Where the Internal Revenue Service treats advance payment receipts by an accrual-basis corporation as income, the corporation has the burden of showing what portion of these payments is excludable as a return of capital (costs).[93]

A taxpayer using a hybrid method of accounting has the burden of showing that such a method is permitted by law.[94]

Fraud

The burden of proof is upon the Internal Revenue Service when fraud is alleged.[95] For tax purposes, "fraud" means intentional wrongdoing on the part of a taxpayer, which wrongdoing is motivated by a specific purpose to evade a tax known or believed to be owing.[96]

To sustain a conviction of fraud, the Internal Revenue Service must prove three things:

(1) an attempt to evade and to defeat the tax laws;
(2) willfulness; and
(3) that an additional tax is due and owing.[97]

Fraud is never presumed. The Service must establish it affirmatively by clear and convincing evidence.[98] But willfulness may be inferred from the facts. For example, such inference may be drawn where a taxpayer keeps a double set of books, makes false entries or alterations, conceals assets or covers up sources of income, handles his affairs to avoid making the usual records in transactions of a particular nature, and engages in any conduct, the likely effect of which would be to mislead or to conceal.[99] Willfulness may also be indicated by a reckless disregard for obvious or known risks.[100] Consistent under-reporting of income has been deemed to constitute fraud if accompanied by other circumstances which are "badges of fraud."[101] These "badges of fraud" include:

(1) Deductions taken carelessly.[102]

(2) Records which purposely were kept incomplete.[103]

(3) Failure to notify one's own accountant of certain transactions.[104]

(4) Insisting upon cash receipts even when the payor wished to give a check.[105]

One of the factors which lead courts to conclude that understatements of income are the result of fraud rather than negligence is the taxpayer's high degree of intelligence.[106] But fraud was not found where a taxpayer was merely, as a lower court had pointed out in the same suit, "stubborn or stupid, careless, negligent, or grossly negligent."[107]

One taxpayer was found guilty of fraud because of his excellent financial background. He was a securities dealer, well versed in affairs of the financial world; thus, the omissions from his income seemed to have been deliberate under the circumstances.[108] Fraud was also found in the case of an individual who, despite her lack of formal education, was highly knowledgeable about her business affairs.[109] An allegation of fraud was accepted as well in the case of one individual who, in addition to operating his regular business, took in several thousand dollars a year for preparing tex returns for other people.[110]

Payment of tax subsequent to acts of willful evasion is no defense to prosecution for fraud.[111]

Reconstruction of Taxpayer's Income

If a taxpayer does not supply adequate proof to justify the figures on his income tax return, the Internal Revenue Service may reconstruct that income. A classic case for using the net worth method is where the Service is deprived of any taxpayer documentation.[112] If a taxpayer's net worth has increased over a period of time and the increase is not due to nontaxable receipts or nontaxable appreciation of assets, the conclusion is inescapable (at least to the Service) that taxable income has been received.[113] If a taxpayer is unable or refuses to produce any records or substantiation for his tax return verification, approximation in the calculation of his taxable income is permitted on the basis of apparent and unaccounted for enhancement of net worth.[114]

Where the net worth method is used, the Internal Revenue Service, with its vast inquisitorial powers, must follow up leads furnished by the taxpayer as to the existence of nontaxable receipts.[115] The taxpayer will prevail if he can prove the nonexistence of all possible sources of taxable income.[116] Likewise, the taxpayer will win if he can show that the increase in net worth was attributable to nontaxable receipts such as gifts.[117]

In the absence of explanation or proof to the contrary, unidentified deposits in a checking account will be considered income.[118] Where the Internal Revenue Service resorts to the bank deposit method, the Service must establish that a taxpayer's allowable deductions do not exceed an amount which, when deducted from gross income, leaves a substantial amount of unreported net income.[119]

Other Instances Where the Service Has the Burden of Proof

In addition to matters of fraud, the Internal Revenue Service also has the burden of proof in these areas:

(1) *Transferee liability.* Under certain circumstances, the transferee of assets may be responsible for unpaid Federal taxes of the transferor up to the amount of the assets so received. The Service has the burden of showing that the transferee is liable for unpaid taxes of the transferor.[120] This burden consists of showing the *liability* of the transferee for the unpaid taxes of the transferor, but the Service's determination that there are unpaid taxes and the amount thereof is presumed to be correct.[121] To meet this burden, the Service must show that the transfer of assets was without adequate consideration, that the transferor was insolvent at the time of the transfer or was made insolvent by it, and either that the Service had exhausted his remedies against the transferor or that to proceed against him would be a useless gesture.[122] The Service also has the burden of establishing the value of the assets received by the transferee.[123] In considering whether the transferor was insolvent at the time of the transfer, the Service must take into account his liability for Federal income tax, even if unknown or contingent.[124] A transferee cannot divest himself of liabilities for taxes by a contract providing for the payment of these taxes by another if the Service is not a party to this contract.[125]

(2) *Understatement of gross income.* The ordinary three-year period for the running of the statute of limitations on assessment of income tax (see chapter 23, Dealing with the Internal Revenue Service) is extended to six years in the case of understatement of gross income in excess of 25 percent.[126] The Service must prove: (a) that the taxpayer omitted from gross income an amount in excess of 25 percent of the gross income stated in the tax return and (b) that the omitted income was properly includable.[127]

(3) *"Self-dealing" by foundation.* In any proceeding involving the issue of whether a charitable foundation manager had "knowingly" participated in an act of self-dealing, participated in an investment which jeopardized the carrying out of exempt purposes, or agreed to make a taxable expenditure which would cause the foundation to lose its exempt status, the Service must shoulder the burden of proof.[128]

(4) *Mailing of deficiency notice to taxpayer.* The Internal Revenue Service must prove that it sent a deficiency notice to the taxpayer's last known address on time.[129]

(5) *Where arbitrariness is shown.* If the Service's determination of tax liability is shown by the taxpayer to be arbitrary or capricious, the presumption in favor of the correctness of the determination disappears, and the Service then must prove the correctness of the determination.[130]

(6) *Public policy.* If the Service would disallow a deduction on the grounds of public policy, the Service must show that there is such a clearly defined policy which is being enforced.[131]

Timely Filing of Tax Returns and Other Forms and Documents

If any tax return document must be filed within a prescribed time and it is received by the Internal Revenue Service after the permissible date, the date postmarked on the cover in which the document is mailed will be deemed to be the date of delivery.[132] Where no postmark appears upon the envelope, the taxpayer has not met its burden of proof by filing an affidavit that the communication was placed in a mailbox before the due date.[133] But the actual date of mailing may be established by the taxpayer by any form of evidence.[134]

Where a private postage meter is used and the document is not delivered within the required time, timely delivery requires proof of: (1) the document's actually being deposited in the mail on or before the last date prescribed for filing; (2) the delay in delivery's being attributable to delay in the transmission of the mail; and (3) the cause of that delay.[135]

Health

If an individual claims that he should not be compelled to appear at a tax investigation because an appearance would endanger his health, he has the burden of proving this. Where his physician's testimony and that of the Internal Revenue Service's physician conflict and appear to be of equal validity, the taxpayer has not proven his case.[136]

The Problem of Negative Proof

Up to now, this chapter has been concerned primarily with *affirmative proof;* that is, proof that something happened or coincided with something else. A much more difficult type of proof is *negative proof;* that is, proof that something did not happen. But in a variety of situations, this is the type of proof which a taxpayer must establish. The first step toward solution is to recognize the problem so that the negative proof may be established at the least impossible time—namely, at the time something did not happen.

Losses. A stockholder in a corporation advanced funds to the company. He could not deduct this amount as a business bad debt upon the subsequent failure of the company, for there was no proof that the loans had not been made as an investment or to protect an investment.[137]

A taxpayer claiming a loss must show that it was not compensated for by insurance or otherwise.[138] Or he must show that he did not have a reasonable expectation of recovery from insurance or otherwise at the close of the taxable year. The standard applied is what a "reasonable man" would have determined the prospects of recovery to have been at that time. One court believed that a lawsuit might well be justified by a ten percent chance of recovery.[139] That there was not a reasonable chance of recovery by lawsuit must be shown.

Where a taxpayer did not even make a claim against the manufacturer of equipment which had broken down and the claim against the insurer was not for the full amount of the loss sustained, loss was denied on the tax return.[140]

This rule as to non-reimbursed losses applies equally to non-reimbursed expenses. An individual must show that he could not have obtained reimbursement from his employer-corporation for entertainment or other expenses allegedly incurred for business reasons. An individual could not deduct expenses paid for corporate entertaining where he could not show that the company would have refused to assume the bill.[141]

Income. Where a corporation created an account payable to its president on the books, the latter had the burden of showing that he never received the money. To rebut a constructive receipt argument, he also had to show that the corporation could not have paid him the sum because of pending insolvency.[142]

A debit to accounts payable and a credit to earned surplus was made to eliminate a long-standing excess of the accounts payable control account over the accounts payable detailed schedules. This could be treated by the Internal Revenue Service as taxable, the restoration to income of previously deducted items. The taxpayer could not meet its burden of proving the deduction never had been taken.[143]

If a person is found to have cash that he cannot explain (for example, money found in a decedent's safe deposit box after his death), the taxpayer has the burden of proving that these funds were not unreported taxable income.[144]

Sales. If a taxpayer argues that the actual sales price of an item should be disregarded as fair market value, he has the burden of showing that the sales price was not the true value at the time.[145]

A taxpayer claiming a loss on the sale of stock may be confronted with the burden of establishing that there was no understanding that he would repurchase the shares.[146]

In order to avoid the wash sale disallowance of loss when shares are sold and repurchased, a taxpayer may be called upon to prove that he had entered into no contract or option to reacquire the stock within 30 days.[147]

Worthless stock. To get a deduction, it is not enough for a taxpayer to show that stock was worthless at the close of the taxable year; it is equally important to show that the stock was not worthless at the beginning of that year.[148]

Qualified employee benefit plans. Where an individual claims long-term capital gains treatment for the permissible portion of sums received from an employee trust within one of his taxable years upon separation from service, he must show that he did not retain any vestige of employment.[149]

If a qualified pension or deferred profit-sharing plan is abandoned for any reason other than business necessity within a few years after this plan has taken effect, to prevent disqualification of contributions which had been made into the plan, the employer must establish that it had not intended discontinuance of the plan at the time it was qualified.[150]

Travel and entertainment. In the case of an expenditure for travel or entertainment, an individual must prove that the expense was not personal.[151] He must establish that the expenditure was not so remotely related to his business as to fall within the area of nondeductible personal expense.[152]

Where an individual argued that he had used his automobile to go to work only for the purpose of transporting his tools to his place of work, he had to show that he would not have used his car to drive to and from work if he had not had to transport his equipment.[153]

In order to deduct away-from-home expenses, a taxpayer must show that the place where he works is not his home for tax purposes.[154]

Accumulated earnings tax. If a corporation's earnings accumulate beyond the reasonable needs of the business, the corporation must establish by the preponderance of the evidence that avoidance of shareholder taxes was not one of the purposes for the accumulation.[155]

A court may properly place upon a corporation a burden to prove not only the negative (that is, that it did not accumulate its earnings and profits to avoid shareholder taxes), but also the affirmative (that is, that it accumulated its earnings and profits for some specific reason other than avoidance of shareholder taxes—for example, to meet definite reasonable business needs).[156]

NOTES

1. *Burnet v. Houston*, 283 U.S. 223 (1931).
2. *Warwick et al. v. United States*, 236 F. Supp. 761 (D.C., E.D. Va., 1964).
3. *Sydney J. Carter Estate*, T.C. Memo. 1970-305 (filed November 2, 1970).
4. *Rocco Joseph Rosato*, T.C. Memo. 1967-226 (filed November 9, 1967).
5. *Rand v. Helvering*, 77 F.2d 450 (8th Cir., 1935).
6. *Ehlen et al. v. United States*, 163 Ct. Cl. 35 (Ct. Cl., 1963).
7. *Percifield v. United States*, 241 F.2d 225 (9th Cir., 1957).
8. *E. W. Bliss Company v. United States*, 203 F. Supp. 175 (D.C., N.D. Ohio, 1953).
9. *Bishop v. Commissioner*, 342 F.2d 757 (6th Cir., 1965).
10. *Potts, Davis & Company v. Commissioner*, 431 F.2d 1222 (9th Cir., 1970).
11. *Allen Hoffman et al.*, 54 T.C. 1607 (1970).
12. *International Artists, Ltd. et al.*, 55 T.C. 94 (1970).
13. *Cohan v. Commissioner*, 39 F.2d 540 (2d Cir., 1930).
14. *Custer Robinson*, T.C. Memo., Docket No. 28184 (entered June 19, 1951).
15. *Eugene J. Rogers et al.*, T.C. Memo. 1959-192 (filed October 20, 1959).
16. *Thomas C. St. John et al.*, T.C. Memo. 1970-238 (filed August 24, 1970).
17. *Julian Peck et al.*, T.C. Memo. 1965-128, (filed May 12, 1965).
18. *Norman A. Pharr*, T.C. Memo. 1971-28 (filed February 8, 1971).
19. *Pauline W. Ach et al.*, 42 T.C. 114 (1964), aff'd, 358 F.2d 342 (6th Cir., 1966).
20. *Joseph Sheban et al.*, T.C. Memo. 1970-163 (filed June 22, 1970).

21. *Abe Brenner et al.*, T.C. Memo. 1967-239 (filed November 28, 1967).

22. *Albert N. Dibs et al.*, T.C. Memo. 1970-204 (filed July 21, 1970).

23. I.R.C. Section 274(d). (Detailed requirements under this statute are contained in Regulations Section 1.274-2.)

24. *William Andress, Jr.*, 51 T.C. 863 (1969), *aff'd*, 423 F.2d 679 (5th Cir., 1970).

25. *William F. Sanford*, 50 T.C. 823 (1968), *aff'd*, 412 F.2d 201 (2d Cir., 1969).

26. *James J. Glenn et al.*, T.C. Memo. 1970-184 (filed June 30, 1970).

27. *Martin Bromley et al.*, T.C. Memo. 1964-316 (filed December 9, 1964).

28. *William H. Johnson et al.*, T.C. Memo. 1966-164 (filed July 12, 1966).

29. *Otho B. Ross, Jr. et al.*, T.C. Memo. 1970-110 (filed May 11, 1970).

30. *William F. Sanford*, 50 T.C. 823 (1968), *aff'd*, 412 F.2d 201 (2d Cir., 1969).

31. *Weatherford et al. v. United States*, 418 F.2d 895 (9th Cir., 1969).

32. *Florence S. Luntz*, 29 T.C. 647 (1958).

33. *Greely v. United States*, 247 F. Supp. 37 (D.C., Mont., 1965).

34. *Allen Industries, Inc. v. Commissioner*, 414 F.2d 983 (6th Cir., 1969).

35. *Hyneman Gin, Inc. v. United States*, D.C., E.D. Ark., 1964.

36. *Coca-Cola Bottling Company of Mitchell, South Dakota v. United States* (D.C., S.D., 1958).

37. *Riss & Company, Inc. et al.*, T.C. Memo. 1964-190 (filed July 14, 1964).

38. *Penn Perry Roofing, Inc.*, T.C. Memo. 1965-31 (filed March 9, 1965).

39. *Hyneman Gin, Inc. v. United States*, D.C., E.D. Ark., 1964.

40. *Bromley Plating Company*, T.C. Memo. 1958-217 (filed December 31, 1958).

41. *W. Braun Co., Inc.*, T.C. Memo. 1967-66 (filed April 5, 1967).

42. *James J. Glenn et al.*, T.C. Memo. 1970-184 (filed June 30, 1970).

43. *Richard E. Stein*, T.C. Memo. 1955-57 (filed March 11, 1955).

44. *Louis Gale et al.*, 41 T.C. 269 (1963).

45. *E.g.*, *Clyde v. Jackson et al.*, T.C. Memo. 1965-56 (filed March 18, 1965); *Robert W. Raddatz*, T.C. Memo. 1966-119 (filed June 3, 1966); *James I. Goski et al.*, T.C. Memo. 1965-155 (filed June 7, 1965).

46. *Denton et al. v. Bingler*, D.C., W.D. Pa., 1963.

47. *S & A Company v. United States*, 218 F. Supp. 677 (D.C., Minn., 1963), *aff'd*, 338 F.2d 629 (8th Cir., 1964).

48. *Westinghouse Broadcasting Co. v. Commissioner*, 309 F.2d 279 (3d Cir., 1962).

49. *United States v. Livengood et al.*, D.C., E.D. Pa., 1969.

50. *The Challenger, Inc.*, T.C. Memo. 1964-338 (filed December 31, 1964).

51. *Gordon Lubricating Company*, T.C. Memo. 1965-132 (filed May 18, 1965).

52. *Macabe Company et al.*, 42 T.C. 1105 (1964).

53. *Watkins v. Glenn*, 88 F. Supp. 70 (D.C., W.D. Ky., 1950).

54. *Herbert W. Dustin et al.*, 53 T.C. 491 (1969).

55. *Raffold Process Corp. v. Commissioner*, 153 F.2d 168 (1st Cir., 1946).

56. *Helvering v. Smith*, 132 F.2d 965 (4th Cir., 1942).

57. *Duffin v. Lucas*, 55 F.2d 786 (6th Cir., 1932).

58. *D. G. Bradley*, 26 T.C. 970 (1956).

59. *Photo-Sonics, Inc.*, 42 T.C. 926 (1964), *aff'd*, 357 F.2d 656 (9th Cir., 1966).

60. *Rogers, Brown & Crocker Bros., Inc.*, 32 B.T.A. 307 (1935).

61. *Dunn Manufacturing Company*, 14 B.T.A. 225 (1928).

62. *Stevens Realty Co.*, T.C. Memo. 1967-113 (filed May 19, 1967).

63. *Colin M. Peters et al.*, T.C. Memo. 1969-52 (filed March 17, 1969).

64. *Coors Porcelain Company*, 52 T.C. 682 (1969), *aff'd*, 429 F.2d 1 (10th Cir., 1970).

65. *The Bolta Company*, T.C. Memo., Docket No. 5638 (entered November 28, 1945).

66. *Gibbs et al. v. Tomlinson*, D.C., M.D. Fla., 1964.

67. *Everett R. Taylor et al.*, T.C. Memo. 1969-186 (filed September 16, 1969).

68. *Oscar Hearde et al.*, T.C. Memo. 1968-78 (filed April 30, 1968), *aff'd*, 421 F.2d 846 (9th Cir., 1970).

69. *Hammerstein, Jr. v. Kelley*, 235 F. Supp. 60 (D.C., E.D. Mo., 1964), *aff'd*, 349 F.2d 928 (8th Cir., 1965).

70. I.R.C. Section 504(a).

71. *The Danforth Foundation v. United States*, 222 F. Supp. 761 (D.C., E.D. Mo., 1963), *aff'd*, 347 F.2d 673 (8th Cir., 1965).

72. *Stevens Bros. Foundation, Inc.*, 39 T.C. 93 (1962), *aff'd on this ground*, 324 F.2d 633 (8th Cir., 1963).

73. *Heman et al. v. Commissioner*, 283 F.2d 227 (8th Cir., 1960).

74. *New York State Association of Real Estate Boards Group Insurance Fund*, 54 T.C. 1325 (1970).

75. *Leonhart et al. v. Commissioner*, 414 F.2d 749 (4th Cir., 1969).

76. *Reid et al. v. United States*, D.C., E.D. Cal., 1969.

77. *Smith Leasing Co., Inc.*, 43 T.C. 37 (1964).

78. *Gulf Television Corporation*, 52 T.C. 1038 (1969).

79. *South Texas Rice Warehouse Co. v. Commissioner*, 366 F.2d 890 (5th Cir., 1966).

80. *Potts, Davis & Company v. Commissioner*, 431 F.2d 1222 (9th Cir., 1970).

81. *Locke Manufacturing Companies v. United States*, 237 F. Supp. 80 (D.C., Conn., 1964).

82. *Henry W. Berry et al.*, T.C. Memo. 1969-162 (filed August 12, 1969).

83. *Cross et al. v. United States*, 250 F. Supp. 609 (D.C., S.D. N.Y., 1966).

84. *Philip W. Conrad et al.*, T.C. Memo. 1965-149 (filed May 27, 1965).

85. *Carl A. Hasslacher*, T.C. Memo., Docket No. 21662 (entered April 7, 1950).

86. *Ralph Walton et al.*, T.C. Memo. 1961-130 (filed May 12, 1961); *C. E. R. Howard et al.*, T.C. Memo. 1969-277 (filed December 18, 1969).

87. *Green v. Allen*, 67 F. Supp. 1004 (D.C., M.D. Ga., 1946).

88. *Armstrong Knitting Mills*, 19 B.T.A. 318 (1930).

89. *Marcalus Manufacturing Co., Inc. et al.*, 30 T.C. 1345 (1958), *aff'd*, 268 F.2d 739 (3d Cir., 1959).

90. *Commissioner et al. v. Murdoch et al.*, 318 F.2d 414 (3d Cir., 1963).

91. *Marion W. Brink*, 39 T.C. 802 (1962).

92. *Georgia Schoolbook Depository, Inc.*, 1 T.C. 463 (1943).

93. *Hagen Advertising Displays, Inc. v. Commissioner*, 407 F.2d 1105 (6th Cir., 1969).

94. *Leo Sheep Company v. Schuster*, 234 F. Supp. 761 (D.C., Wyo., 1964).

95. I.R.C. Section 7454(a).

96. *Powell v. Granquist*, 252 F.2d 56 (9th Cir., 1958).

97. *United States v. Fronek et al.*, 231 F. Supp. 8 (D.C., W.D. Pa., 1964).

98. *Anson Beaver et al.*, 55 T.C. 85 (1970).

99. *Spies v. United States*, 317 U.S. 492 (1943).

100. *Monday et al. v. United States et al.*, 421 F.2d 1210 (7th Cir., 1970).

101. *United States v. Florida et al.*, 252 F. Supp. 806 (D.C., E.D. Ark., 1965).

102. *G. Douglas Strachan*, 48 T.C. 335 (1967).

103. *Victor Mecca et al.*, T.C. Memo. 1968-258 (filed November 12, 1968).

104. *United States v. Procario*, 356 F.2d 614 (2d Cir., 1966).

105. *Ibid.*

106. *Albert R. McGovern et al.*, 42 T.C. 1148 (1964), *aff'd*, 6th Cir., 1966; *Isaac T. Mitchell et al.*, T.C. Memo. 1968-137 (filed June 27, 1968).

107. *United States v. Stone*, 431 F.2d 1286 (5th Cir., 1970).

108. *Carl Trotte*, T.C. Memo. 1966-129 (filed June 16, 1966).

109. *Louis B. Libby et al.*, T.C. Memo. 1969-68 (filed September 8, 1969).

110. *Richard W. Chominski et al.*, T.C. Memo. 1971-1 (filed January 5, 1971).

111. *United States v. Campbell*, 351 F.2d 336 (2d Cir., 1965).

112. *United States v. Stone*, 431 F.2d 1286 (5th Cir., 1970).

113. *Davis v. Commissioner*, 239 F.2d 187 (7th Cir., 1956).

114. *Harris v. Commissioner*, 174 F.2d 70 (4th Cir., 1949).

115. *United States v. Procario*, 356 F.2d 614 (2d Cir., 1966).

116. *Commissioner v. Thomas*, 261 F.2d 643 (1st Cir., 1958).

117. *Doris Loisell Mullin*, T.C. Memo., Docket No. 22884 (entered May 23, 1950).

118. *Goe v. Commissioner*, 198 F.2d 851 (3d Cir., 1952).

119. *Lloyd J. Lowe*, T.C. Memo. 1955-150 (filed June 14, 1955).

120. I.R.C. Section 6902(a).

121. *Francis L. Hine*, 54 T.C. 1552 (1970).

122. *Krebs v. Commissioner*, 351 F.2d 1 (2d Cir., 1965).

123. *R. E. Burdick*, 24 B.T.A. 1297 (1931).

124. *J. Warren Leach*, 21 T.C. 70 (1953).

125. *John H. Humbert*, 24 B.T.A. 828 (1931).

126. I.R.C. Section 6501(e).

127. *Barth A. Easton et al.*, T.C. Memo., Docket Nos. 11094-7 (entered February 5, 1943).

128. I.R.C. Section 7454(b).

129. *Raymond S. August*, 54 T.C. 1535 (1970).

130. *Robert H. Welch et al.*, T.C. Memo. 1960-163 (filed August 10, 1960).

131. *Aetna-Standard Engineering Company*, 15 T.C. 284 (1950).

132. I.R.C. Section 7502(a).

133. *Luther A. Madison*, 28 T.C. 1301 (1957).

134. *Skolski v. Commissioner*, 351 F.2d 485 (3d Cir., 1965).

135. Regulations Section 301.7502-1(b).

136. *United States v. Miriani*, 310 F. Supp. 217 (D.C., E.D. Mich., 1967).

137. *Charles J. Ginsberg Estate*, T.C. Memo. 1958-95 (filed May 26, 1958), *aff'd*, 271 F.2d 511 (5th Cir., 1959).

138. *Kelly v. Patterson*, 331 F.2d 753 (5th Cir., 1964).

139. *Parmalee Transportation Company v. United States*, 351 F.2d 619 (Ct. Cl., 1965).

140. *Kentucky Utilities Company et al. v. Glenn et al.*, 394 F.2d 631 (6th Cir., 1968).

141. *William H. Johnson et al.*, T.C. Memo. 1966-164 (filed July 12, 1966).

142. *James Klein Bowen*, 27 B.T.A. 824 (1933).

143. *Lime Cola Company*, 22 T.C. 493 (1954).

144. *Frank Scotto Estate*, T.C. Memo., Docket Nos. 19744-5 (entered October 31, 1950).

145. *Rogers et al. v. Helvering*, 107 F.2d 394 (2d Cir., 1939).

146. *Rand v. Helvering*, 77 F.2d 450 (8th Cir., 1935).

147. *A. W. Mellon*, 36 B.T.A. 977 (1937).

148. *Squier v. Commissioner*, 68 F.2d 25 (2d Cir., 1933).

149. *Barrus et al. v. United States*, D.C., E.D. N.C., 1969.

150. Revenue Ruling 69-25, 1969-1 CB 113.

151. *Fred A. De Cain*, T.C. Memo., Docket No. 27327 (entered June 18, 1951).

152. *Henry B. Kelsey et al.*, T.C. Memo. 1968-62 (filed April 15, 1968), *aff'd*, 2d Cir., 1969.

153. *Tyne, Jr. v. Commissioner*, 409 F.2d 485 (7th Cir., 1969).

154. *I. Jay Green et al.*, 35 T.C. 764 (1961), *aff'd*, 321 F.2d 504 (6th Cir., 1962).

155. *United States v. The Donruss Company*, 393 U.S. 297 (1969).

156. *Young Motor Company, Inc. v. Commissioner*, 339 F.2d 481 (1st Cir., 1965).

CHAPTER 18

Who, What, Where

How Relationships Affect Taxes

The Federal income tax consequences of a transaction may depend upon the relationship of the parties, the subject matter of the transaction, and where it takes place. In this chapter, we look at each element separately, starting with a consideration of the relationships between the parties. One phase of this subject has been considered in chapter 5, Arm's Length Transactions.

The Internal Revenue Service subjects transactions within a "family" group, individual or corporate, to special scrutiny in order to determine if they are actually and economically what they appear to be on their face.

Intra-family transactions between individuals or related business corporations or other entities offer a potential for establishing losses or deductions.[1] One way in which the Internal Revenue Service attempts to cope with these potential transactions is through the statutory provision for mandatory disallowance of losses where the parties stand in certain relationships.

Losses Where Parties Are Related

The statute providing for mandatory disallowance of losses in transactions between certain related parties was enacted to prevent tax avoidance through such transactions.[2] Losses are disallowed regardless of subjective intent or good faith.[3]

No deduction is allowed for tax purposes in the case of losses from sales or exchanges of property, directly or indirectly, between or with specified persons. Included are losses suffered in transactions between:

(1) A person and his spouse, brothers and sisters, ancestors, and lineal descendants.

(2) An individual and a corporation, more than 50 percent of the value of the stock of which is owned by or for this individual.

(3) Two corporations more than 50 percent of the value of the stock of

both of which is owned by or for the same individual if either corporation in its taxable year preceding the sale or exchange was a personal holding company or a foreign personal holding company.

(4) A grantor and a fiduciary of any trust.

(5) A fiduciary of a trust and a fiduciary of another trust, if the same person is a grantor of both trusts.

(6) A fiduciary of a trust and a beneficiary of that trust.

(7) A fiduciary of a trust and a beneficiary of another trust, if the same person is a grantor of both trusts.

(8) A fiduciary of a trust and a corporation, more than 50 percent of the value of the outstanding stock of which is owned by or for a person who is a grantor of the trust.

(9) A person and a tax-exempt organization which is controlled, directly or indirectly, by that person or, if this person is an individual, by members of his family.[4]

In determining whether loss should be disallowed because of the relationship of the parties, for this purpose, the Internal Revenue Service may consider that a person owns shares which are owned by designated related parties. "Constructive ownership" or "constructive attribution" rules provide:

(1) Stock owned by or for a corporation, partnership, estate, or trust is considered as being owned proportionately by or for its shareholders, partners, or beneficiaries.

(2) An individual is deemed to own the stock owned by his spouse, brothers and sisters, ancestors, and lineal descendants.

(3) An individual owning stock (otherwise than by the application of (2) immediately above) is considered to own the stock owned by or for his partner.

(4) Stock constructively owned by a person by reason of the application of (1), (2), and (3) will be treated as actually owned by that person. But stock owned by an individual by reason of the application of (2) and (3) will not be treated as owned by him for the purpose of *again* applying either (2) or (3) in order to make another person the constructive owner of this stock.[5] In other words, presumption will not be built on presumption.

The automatic loss disallowance provision obviously cannot be applied by the Service to transactions between related parties not spelled out in the statute. Members of a family for this purpose include *only* the parties named in the statute. Collateral relatives—uncles and aunts, for example—cannot be included.[6] However, adoptive relatives are treated in the same manner as blood relatives.[7]

This rule applies to involuntary sales as well as to voluntary ones. So, where the Internal Revenue Service seized an individual's stock for back taxes and the successful bidder at public auction was his wife, his loss was not recognized for tax purposes.[8] This provision applies to sales in the ordinary course of a trade or business as well as to capital transactions.[9]

No loss is allowed on redemptions of stock by a corporation which is owned to a greater extent than 50 percent by the person whose shares are being redeemed.[10] But losses are recognized in the case of corporate liquidations and partial liquidations.[11]

The statute speaks only of losses. It does not provide that gains from such sales are not to be recognized.[12] This can be a trap. If a taxpayer sells property to a related party on two different occasions within one taxable year, one transaction resulting in a gain and the other in a loss, the transactions cannot be added to obtain a net result. They must be reported in full; the loss is not deductible.[13]

Transactions between relatives who are not on the ineligible list may still breed suspicion and invite sharp scrutiny by the Service.[14]

Loss of Capital Gains Treatment

Capital gains treatment is not allowed on sales of depreciable property used in the trade or business in transactions between: (1) a husband and wife or (2) an individual and a corporation more than 80 percent of the stock of which is owned by that individual, his spouse, minor children, and minor grandchildren.[15] Property used in a trade or business in this context refers to the so-called "Section 1231 assets." (See chapter 6, Capital Assets, Capital Gains and Losses.)

Without this rule, a taxpayer who owned property which had been depreciated to a low basis could sell it to his spouse or a controlled corporation, pay only capital gains rates on the gain, while his transferee could then re-depreciate the property, using the sale price as a new basis and deducting depreciation from ordinary income. But such a scheme is rendered profitless by the gains being taxed at ordinary rather than capital rates.[16]

In applying the 80 percent rule, the Service does not consider beneficial ownership of stock. So, shares held by an irrevocable trust for the benefit of minor children are not to be counted.[17]

The Internal Revenue Service has ruled that if a sale takes place between two corporations where more than 80 percent of the stock of each is owned by the same individual, the sale will not be entitled to capital gains treatment because it is, in effect, a sale between the individual and the transferee corporation.[18] This could be quite a trap, for the statute does not hint at the possibility of ordinary income resulting from such a sale. Nor is it apparent which income would be treated as ordinary: that of the individual or that of the corporation (the seller) whose identity would thus be fused into his.

Partnership Disallowance

A loss deduction is denied in the case of a sale of property between a partnership and an individual who owns, directly or indirectly, more than 50 percent of the capital interest or profits interest in the partnership.[19] Capital gains treatment is denied for gains realized from the sale of depreciable property in a transaction between a partnership and an individual with a greater than 80 percent interest in the capital or profits of the partnership.[20]

For both of these purposes, ownership rules are applied (discussed earlier in this chapter), which rules include the provision attributing to the beneficial owners stock held in trust for them.[21]

Title May Be Ignored

The Internal Revenue Service may attempt to set aside the legal title to property in order to impose tax upon an entity other than the purported taxpayer.[22] Courts likewise may look beyond the naked legal title to ascertain true ownership.[23]

A sale by one person cannot be transformed for tax purposes into a sale by another by using the latter as a conduit through which to pass title.[24] Where a closely-held corporation, manipulated by its shareholders, distributes property with the knowledge that it will be sold immediately as a device to avoid corporate taxes, but the corporation plays an active role in the subsequent disposal, a sale for tax purposes may be imputed to the corporation.[25]

But there is an important exception to the above rule. If a corporation adopts a plan of complete liquidation and all assets are distributed within the 12-month period following the date of adoption of the plan, no gain or loss is recognized to the corporation on the sale or exchange of its assets during that period, except as to assets retained to meet claims. Inventory is not subject to this liberal treatment unless sold to a one purchaser in a single transaction.[26]

The Entity Concept

Ordinarily, if an enterprise elects to do business as two or more separate entities, the separate existence of each one for tax purposes cannot be denied. The entity of a corporation is separate from that of the person who owns 100 percent of its stock. This doctrine of corporate entity serves a useful purpose in business life. Whether that purpose is to gain an advantage under the laws of the state of incorporation to limit liability, to comply with the demands of creditors, or to serve the creator's personal or undisclosed convenience, so long as that purpose is the equivalent of business activity or results in the carrying on of business by the corporation, the corporation remains a separate taxable entity.[27]

A corporation's purchase of replacement property to take the place of assets condemned while in an individual's hands does not qualify as a tax-free involuntary conversion replacement. The corporation is not the same entity as the party (the individual) whose property had been lost.[28]

Separate existence is justified where there is a business purpose—as distinguished from a mere tax scheme; for example, to provide insulation against creditor suits.[29] On the other hand, a corporate entity may be disregarded by the Internal Revenue Service where the corporation serves no legitimate business purpose.[30] Thus, an individual was taxed upon income of a corporation formed to handle certain of his subsidiary rights from performing personal services where the corporation had no assets or employees and performed no services.[31]

Ordinarily, the creation of additional entities means that the creator cannot ignore their existence even when the tax results are unfortunate. If a party proliferates his fiscal self, he must take all the consequences, not merely those which are agreeable.[32] However, special circumstances may permit an exception. So where a corporation was formed solely to liquidate real estate and had no right, power, or discretion with respect to the disposition of income, it was held that the corporation was a mere conduit and was not taxable. The corporation had been formed for one purpose, to hold property, and it had no control over income.[33]

Assignments of Income

Federal income tax is imposed upon the person who earns income, even though by contract the payment is made to another party. The tax cannot be escaped by anticipatory arrangements and contracts, however skillfully devised.[34] Here, the court has made use of a horticultural allusion which commonly crops up when efforts are made to tax income to someone other than its earner or the owner of property which had produced the income. The Internal Revenue Service is not bound to an arrangement "by which the fruits are attributed to a different tree from that on which they grew." Similarly, where a father gave his son unmatured bonds still held by the father, the income was taxed to the donor, for "the fruit is not to be attributed to a different tree from that on which it grew." [35]

One who retains property from which income is produced is obligated to account for it even though he has assigned it, thereby divesting himself of all control, and even though the income actually is received by the assignee and not by him.[36]

Carry-Overs

Customarily, a net operating loss or an unused capital loss may be utilized only by the party who had sustained it. But in the case of certain types of tax-free reorganization, the successor corporation is permitted to make use of the predecessor's carry-overs, the theory being that in a tax-free reorganization, the successor steps into the "tax shoes" of the predecessor.[37]

Subject Matter, What Is Being Bought and Sold, Price

What is being bought and sold can determine the tax consequences for both buyer and seller.

While the descriptive words used by the parties in an agreement cannot be completely ignored by the Internal Revenue Service or the courts, inquiry must be addressed to the substance and not to the form of the agreement to determine its essential character for tax purposes.[38] So in determining sales price, the recitations of the contract or other instrument involved are not conclusive. It is always competent to show by parol or other extrinsic evidence what the real consideration was.[39]

Allocation of Sales Price

Where a going business is sold as such via a sale of assets and good will, as distinguished from a sale of shares of stock, the parties will usually make an allocation of part of the sales price to different items sold.[40] Ordinarily, if the sale is at arm's length, no reallocation by the Internal Revenue Service of the allocations made by the parties is in order.[41] Countervailing tax considerations as between buyer and seller will tend to limit tax avoidance schemes unless one of the parties is disadvantaged because of a factor such as ignorance.[42] But for the allocation of the parties to be sustained, it must be negotiated bilaterally. Where the buyer informed the seller that unless the buyer's allocation were agreed to there would be no deal, the Internal Revenue Service was not bound by the terms and could make its own allocation in accordance with the relative values of the assets.[43]

Neither the Internal Revenue Code nor the Treasury Regulations provide any additional assistance in determining the cost of the separate items in a lump-sum purchase of an integral business. However, it has been established that when a taxpayer buys a mixed aggregate of assets for a bulk price, an allocation of the purchase price will be made to the separate items upon the proportionate value of each item to the value of the whole. As a further refinement of this method, it has also been established that the purchaser should eliminate from the allocation whatever cash, or its equivalent, he acquires. A sufficient part of the purchase price is apportioned to these assets so that their bases are their face or book values. The balance of the purchase price is allocated to the remaining assets.[44] Separate computations must be made of the gain or loss with respect to each asset sold for which there is a separately identifiable basis for making this computation possible.[45]

Where an agreement provides for the total consideration, but not the breakdown, the Internal Revenue Service will make its own allocation as between capital and noncapital assets, good will, and the like.[46] If a taxpayer objects to that allocation, the taxpayer assumes the burden of proof, which is apt to be difficult.[47] There is nothing which prevents the Service from allocating the sales price in one manner on the seller's tax return and in a different manner on the buyer's. Quite different is the situation where the bill of sale noted the allocation of the total consideration because both buyer and seller felt such an itemization was desirable.[48]

Allocation of Payments Involving Principal, Interest, and Taxes

Where a compromise settlement is made on a claim which includes both principal and interest, it is important to specify how much is for interest and how much is for principal. Lacking agreement, the payment is treated by both debtor and creditor as applicable first to the interest due and then to the principal.[49]

If a Federal income tax assessment is made for one or more years and there are no specific instructions as to the application of a partial payment made by the taxpayer, the payment will be applied by the Internal Revenue Service first to tax, then to penalty, and then to interest, starting with the earliest year involved and continuing until the payment is absorbed.[50] A taxpayer's instructions to the Service merely to apply payments to the tax assessment do not serve to modify this sequence.[51]

Allocation of Casualty Loss

The separate identification and different tax treatment of each asset is required for tax purposes when there is a single payment for a casualty loss. Property normally considered as a single unit often must be subjected to allocation between different types of assets.[52]

Claim Settlements

As far as a payor is concerned, the origin and character of the claim with respect to which a settlement is made, rather than its potential consequences on the business operation of a taxpayer, is the controlling test of whether a settlement payment constitutes a deductible expense or a nondeductible capital outlay.[53]

As far as the payee is concerned, proceeds from the settlement of litigation or other claims are taxable in the same manner as those for which they are a substitute.[54] Although a contract is generally regarded as a capital asset, payments for cancellation of a contract are taxable according to what the payment actually represents. The important consideration is the nature of the contract rights surrendered rather than the method of computing the payments for the cancellation.[55]

Good Will

Regardless of whether the parties include good will with the assets bought and sold, good will may in fact exist. This allows the Internal Revenue Service to reallocate a portion of the consideration to good will, the result being that the basis of other assets is reduced accordingly. When sold, these reduced-basis assets obviously produce greater gain or less loss. Good will is an unfortunate asset for a taxpayer to acquire or to have attributed to him, inasmuch as it cannot be written off in the form of depreciation or obsolescence.[56]

The essence of good will is the expectancy of continued patronage.[57] It is tangible only as an incident of its connection with a going concern or business having a locality or name and it is not susceptible of being disposed of independently.[58]

Ordinarily, a fair allocation made by the parties will not be disturbed. But where the valuations are not in accord with the realities of the transaction, a court may determine whether the business possessed good will of any fair market value and thus make a proper allocation.[59]

Good will may be found even though the books of the seller do not show it. For example, in one case, the court noted that the asset purchase agreement required the seller (the taxpayer) to deliver to the buyer a list of customers and prospective customers along with their credit status.[60]

Where both tangible and intangible assets are acquired, the value of good will is frequently determined by the residual method; that is, the value of the tangible assets is subtracted from the total price.[61]

Covenant Not to Compete

Frequently, a buyer wishes to have the protection of a covenant that the seller will not compete with him. To the extent that the payments by the buyer were for such a covenant, they constitute ordinary income to the seller and an amortizable expense to the buyer. But if the covenant is not separately bargained for and is merely incidental to the transfer of the overall business, the seller is generally entitled to capital gains treatment for the entire proceeds of the sale, but the buyer gets no deduction.[62]

Where the contract for the sale of a business contains a separately stated and valued covenant not to compete, it is valid for tax purposes in the absence of strong proof that it is a sham.[63]

Sale and Lease-Back

In a *sale and lease-back transaction,* the owner of property sells it to another party (sometimes called, for the purpose of convenience, the "investor") and then immediately leases it back. The reasons for this may be non-tax:

(1) The seller can improve his balance sheet position by liquidating a fixed asset.

(2) The seller may get additional funds despite contractual or other restrictions against borrowing.

(3) The seller may be able to obtain funds equivalent to the fair market value of his property, which he ordinarily could not do in the case of a loan.

Here are the tax aspects of a sale and lease-back:

(1) Property which has appreciated in value may be sold without present recognition of gain if the sale is for cost or adjusted basis. The "bargain" which the investor has received is reciprocated by future rental payments in reduced amounts. If the interest factor is ignored, what the seller receives for his property and what he is to pay in rent tend to be equal.

(2) Property may be sold below adjusted basis to establish a loss for tax purposes. Here again, the investor would equate his bargain with future lower rentals.

(3) If the seller has a loss which might otherwise be wasted, the gain on a sale at a price in excess of fair market value may be offset by the loss, and the buyer may equate the higher price with future above-market rentals.

(4) By selling nondepreciable property such as land and leasing it back, one gets deductible rent, whereas his land produced no depreciation deduction for tax purposes.

The fact that the sale and lease-back transaction was devised to provide the seller with a tax advantage will not disqualify it. The seller would be entitled to deduct rent if he had sold the property in an arm's length transaction to a buyer having adverse interests and then had leased it back at a fair rental.[64] The presence or absence of a business purpose in lessor-lessee transactions between unrelated parties is not in and of itself determinative. Thus, the fact that there may be a business purpose for a transaction does not necessarily mean that the transaction has economic substance for tax purposes. Conversely, the lack of a business purpose does not necessarily mean that there is no economic substance.[65] The important ingredient is *reality*. Did the seller derive an advantage other than the saving of taxes? When the "other party" to a sale and lease-back transaction is a related party, the tax advantages otherwise available may be denied, even though the terms are the same as those an outside party would have offered.[66]

A sale and lease-back was not recognized for tax purposes where an individual sold property to himself as trustee for a trust he created for his children.[67] The element of transactions between two parties with adverse interests was lacking.

Where a sale and lease-back transaction is disqualified for valid reasons, the Internal Revenue Service may disallow rent deductions in excess of fair rental values.[68]

A sale and lease-back may be of intangibles, such as a mailing list.[69]

Where there is a sale and lease-back, the depreciation recapture rules incident to a disposition apply.[70]

Gift and Lease-Back

A gift in trust and lease-back involves the transfer of property to donees and its simultaneous lease-back by the donor. The motivation for such a transaction is immaterial if the donee retains no control over the trust and the trustee is independent of the donor.[71] To preclude sham, subterfuge, and abuse in trust-lease transactions, the fiduciary obligation of a trustee requires that he act strictly in accordance with the terms of the trust instrument and without direct or indirect control of the person who created the trust.[72] The donor-lessee was not permitted to deduct rent where he was a co-trustee with his attorney and his accountant and these two worthies had never ascertained the proper rental value that should have been used, but merely had accepted the donor's figures.[73] A similar arrangement was accepted where the donor acted as trustee for the beneficiaries, his minor children. But here, the terms were fair; and thus, the gift was recognized as taking the property out of the donor's ultimate gross estate for Federal estate tax purposes.[74]

Percentage Lease

Rent may be paid for business premises upon a percentage basis rather than in a flat sum. This has the advantage of providing a self-adjusting rent according to the lessee's business. When business is poor, the tenant is not saddled with a high rent; when business is good, he can afford to make a generous payment, which is tax-deductible.

However, in the case of parties under common control or related parties, rent paid under the percentage method in a good year may produce a figure which is much higher than a flat rental would have been, and that portion of the rent deemed excessive may be disallowed.[75]

Percentage leases based on the tenant's sales or income generally are used only in prime retail areas where the particular value of the property is derived from its location. They are rarely used for industrial property. This factor was taken into account where a portion of the rent paid under a percentage lease was disallowed in the case of industrial property rented to a related corporation. That court deemed it unlikely that such a transaction would have been entered into by unrelated parties.[76]

Where there is an escalator clause based upon income, the fact that the landlord may provide competent assistance on how to increase income does not affect the tax consequences.[77]

Special Assessments

Property taxes are deductible whether they are on business or personal property. A *special assessment* is a tax which is limited to the property to be benefitted by the work being financed by the assessment (such as streets, sidewalks, and like improvements). The special assessment is imposed because of and is measured by some benefit going directly to the property involved. Special assessments generally are not deductible.[78] Instead, they are added to the cost or other basis of the property. However, special assessments may be deductible to the extent that the tax is properly allocable to maintenance and interest charges, but this is very difficult for a taxpayer to establish, especially in the case of new property.[79]

Tax-Free Reorganization

The general rule is that when property is sold or exchanged, there is gain or loss to the extent of the difference between realization and adjusted basis. But in the case of a tax-free reorganization, the replacement is deemed to have taken the place of the original property and there is no gain or loss at the time of the exchange.[80]

Tax-Free Exchange

Property held for productive use in a trade or business or for investment may be exchanged for property of like kind without recognition of gain or loss; that is, property of the same character, though it need not be identical in grade or quality.[81] But there is no tax-free exchange where property is sold for cash, even though the cash is used by the seller to acquire other property.[82] However, where a wholly-owned subsidiary purchased equipment from a manufacturer for cash while at the same time the parent-taxpayer sold its old equipment to the manufacturer, this was regarded as being in effect a tax-free exchange, and no gain or loss was recognized on the sale of the old equipment.[83]

Where property held for productive use or investment is exchanged without any thought of the tax consequences, but merely to save brokerage commissions, this still qualifies as a tax-free exchange and loss is not recognized for tax purposes.[84]

Right to Future Income

Assignment of the rights to future income for a lump-sum consideration is ordinary income where the time at which payment will be completed can reasonably be estimated.[85] Even if the present form of future income is a capital asset, the sale of that asset will not ordinarily result in capital gain. The ground rule is that a right to receive ordinary income produced by a capital asset is not transmuted into a capital asset by the sale or assignment of the capital asset together with the right to receive the ordinary income.[86]

Where a taxpayer sells a life (or term of years) interest in property or an income interest in a trust (which was acquired by gift, bequest, inheritance, or transfer in trust), the entire amount received is taxable.[87]

Inducement to Locate

Property or money given to a corporation as an inducement to locate in a particular community by the community or by a chamber of commerce is not taxable income, but is a contribution to capital.[88] The cost basis of such property is zero in the hands of the recipient. If money is provided instead of that property, any property purchased with this money in less than 12 months will have its basis reduced by the amount of money received.[89]

Is It a Sale?

Even if a transaction is cast in the form of a sale, it will not be treated as one for tax purposes if it is not really a sale.[90] Substance, not form, governs.[91]

Sometimes, the question is whether a transaction was a sale (where gain or loss would be recognized) or an exchange (where there would be no gain or loss if a tax-free exchange had taken place). The very essence of an exchange is the transfer of property between owners, while the mark of a sale is the receipt of cash for the property.[92]

Where a lease gives the lessee the option to purchase the property, in which event prior rent payments will be applied against the purchase price, the question often arises as to whether this is in reality a sale or lease. If it is a sale, the periodic payments by the payor are not deductible, but are part of the cost of the property. Theoretically, the distinction between an ordinary lease and a conditional sale is well settled: a lease contemplates only the use of property for a limited time and its return to the lessor at the end of that time; whereas a conditional sale contemplates the ultimate ownership of property by the buyer together with its use in the meantime. In reality, however, certain transfers of property may exhibit characteristics of both sale and lease.[93]

In the absence of compelling factors of contrary implication, an intent warranting treatment of a transaction for tax purposes as a purchase and sale rather than as a lease or rental may in general be said to exist if one or more of the following factors are present:

(1) Portions of the periodic payments are specifically made applicable to an equity to be acquired by the lessee.

(2) The lessee will acquire title upon the payment of a stated amount of "rentals" which he is required to make under the contract.

(3) The total amount which the lessee is required to pay for a relatively short period of use constitutes an inordinately large proportion of the total sum to be paid to secure the transfer of the title.

(4) The agreed upon "rental" payments materially exceed the current fair rental value. This may be indicative of the fact that the payments include an element other than compensation for the use of property.

(5) The property may be acquired under a purchase option at a price which is nominal in relation to the value of the property at the time when the option may be exercised, as determined at the time of entering into the original agreement, or at a price which is relatively small when compared with the total payments which are to be made.

(6) Some portion of the periodic payments is specifically designated as interest or is otherwise readily recognizable as the equivalent of interest.[94]

Where Does the Transaction Take Place?

The question of *where* a transaction takes place for tax matters is customarily of more concern for state than for Federal purposes. For Federal purposes, the matter is important in determining the percentage of income derived within and without the United States in the cases of Western Hemisphere Trade Corporations and taxpayers doing business within a possession of the United States. The question also may be significant in the case of income allegedly earned by individuals outside of the United States.

In determining whether income is from sources within the United States, the Internal Revenue Service will consider a sale of personal property to have been consummated where the seller's rights, title, and interest in the property are transferred to the buyer. Where bare legal title is retained by the seller, the sale is deemed to have occurred at the time and place of passage to the buyer of beneficial ownership and the risk of loss. But these rules are not applied where the sales transaction is arranged in a particular manner for the primary purpose of tax avoidance. In such a situation, regard will also be given to negotiations, the execution of the agreement, the location of the property, and the place of payment; and the sale will be treated as having been consummated at the place at which the substance of the sale occurred.[95]

Determination of the place of sale by using the locality where title passed has its advantages. This method provides for certainty and ease of application in international trade.[96] Despite its shortcomings, this test serves a purpose because it provides a measure of certainty upon which corporations may plan their contracts and, indeed, their business operations with an eye to the tax benefits attendant upon qualifying for such preferential treatment as that accorded to Western Hemisphere Trade Corporations.[97]

But one cannot avoid Federal income tax by merely manipulating the language of legal documents, such as to cause title to pass outside of the United States.[98]

In the case of transactions which take place entirely within the United States, state law determines where title changes for the purpose of contractual liability and specific performance.[99] Thus, state law creates legal interests; but the Federal statutes still determine when and how they will be taxed.[100]

NOTES

1. *Jeanette W. Fitz Gibbon*, 19 T.C. 78 (1952).
2. *Dillard Paper Company*, 42 T.C. 588 (1964), *aff'd*, 341 F.2d 897 (4th Cir., 1965).
3. *Federal Cement Tile Company v. Commissioner*, 338 F.2d 691 (7th Cir., 1964).
4. I.R.C. Section 267; *see also Coyle, Jr. et al. v. United States*, 415 F.2d 488 (4th Cir., 1968).
5. I.R.C. Section 267(c).
6. *Graves Brothers Company*, 17 T.C. 1499 (1952).
7. *Wanvig, Jr. et al. v. United States*, 423 F.2d 769 (7th Cir., 1970).
8. *Merritt, Sr. et al. v. Commissioner*, 400 F.2d 417 (5th Cir., 1968).
9. *Melvin W. McGrew et al.*, T.C. Memo. 1965-256 (filed September 22, 1956).
10. Revenue Ruling 57-387, 1957-2 CB 225.

11. *McCarthy et al. v. Conley, Jr.*, 341 F.2d 948 (2d Cir., 1965).

12. *Edwin H. Johnson Estate*, 42 T.C. 441 (1964).

13. *United States Holding Co.*, 44 T.C. 323 (1965).

14. *Greer, Sr. et al. v. United States*, 269 F. Supp. 801 (D.C., E.D. Tenn., 1967), *aff'd*, 408 F.2d 631 (6th Cir., 1969).

15. I.R.C. Section 1239.

16. *United States v. Parker et al.*, 376 F.2d 402 (5th Cir., 1967).

17. *Mitchell et al. v. Commissioner*, 300 F.2d 533 (4th Cir., 1962).

18. Revenue Ruling 69-109, 1969-1 CB 255.

19. I.R.C. Section 707(b)(1).

20. I.R.C. Section 707(b)(2).

21. I.R.C. Section 707(b)(3).

22. *United States v. Schroeder et al.*, D.C., S.D. Iowa, 1965, *aff'd*, 348 F.2d 223 (8th Cir., 1965).

23. *Austin National Bank v. Scofield*, 84 F. Supp. 483 (D.C., W.D. Texas, 1948).

24. *Commissioner v. Court Holding Company*, 324 U.S. 331 (1945).

25. *Henry A. Rosenberg Estate*, 36 T.C. 716 (1961).

26. I.R.C. Section 337.

27. *Moline Properties, Inc. v. Commissioner*, 319 U.S. 436 (1943).

28. *Feinberg et al. v. Commissioner*, 377 F.2d 21 (8th Cir., 1967).

29. *Alcorn Wholesale Co. et al.*, 16 T.C. 75 (1951).

30. *United States v. Martin et al.*, 337 F.2d 171 (8th Cir., 1964).

31. *Patterson v. Commissioner*, 2d Cir., 1968.

32. *Palmer et al. v. Commissioner*, 354 F.2d 974 (1st Cir., 1965).

33. *Silver Bluff Estates, Inc.*, T.C. Memo., Docket No. 12303 (entered June 24, 1947).

34. *Lucas v. Earl*, 281 U.S. 111 (1930).

35. *Helvering v. Hort*, 311 U.S. 112 (1940).

36. *Galt v. Commissioner*, 216 F.2d 41 (7th Cir., 1954).

37. I.R.C. Section 381.

38. *Green v. United States*, D.C., M.D. Fla., 1965, *rev'd on another issue*, 377 F.2d 550 (5th Cir., 1967).

39. *Philadelphia Steel & Iron Corporation*, T.C. Memo. 1964-93 (filed April 13, 1964).

40. *Williams v. McGowan*, 152 F.2d 570 (2d Cir., 1945).

41. *Thomas J. McCoy*, 15 T.C. 828 (1950).

42. *Schulz v. Commissioner*, 294 F.2d 52 (9th Cir., 1961).

43. *F. & D. Rentals, Inc.*, 44 T.C. 335 (1965), *aff'd*, 365 F.2d 34 (7th Cir., 1966).

44. *Victor Meat Co., Inc.*, 52 T.C. 929 (1969).

45. Revenue Ruling 70-465, 1970-2 CB 162.

46. *Winn-Dixie Montgomery, Inc. v. United States*, 307 F. Supp. 1304 (D.C., N.D. Ala., 1970)

47. *Commissioner v. Chatsworth Stations, Inc.*, 282 F.2d 132 (2d Cir., 1960).

48. *Coastal Oil Company*, 50 T.C. 528 (1968).

49. *Theodore A. Granger et al.*, T.C. Memo. 1970-155 (filed June 15, 1970).

50. Revenue Ruling 58-239, 1958-1 CB 94.

51. *Moloney et al. v. United States*, D.C., N.D. Ohio, 1970.

52. *Carloate Industries, Inc., v. United States*, 230 F. Supp. 282 (D.C., S.D. Texas, 1964).

53. *Anchor Coupling Company, Inc. v. United States*, 427 F.2d 429 (7th Cir., 1970).

54. *Raytheon Production Co. v. Commissioner*, 144 F.2d 110 (1st Cir., 1944).

55. *Commercial Solvents Corporation v. United States*, 427 F.2d 749 (Ct. Cl., 1970).

56. *Dodge Brothers, Inc. v. United States*, 118 F.2d 95 (4th Cir., 1941).

57. *Bee v. Commissioner*, 307 F.2d 339 (9th Cir., 1962).

58. *Metropolitan Bank v. St. Louis Dispatch Co.*, 149 U.S. 436 (1893).

59. *Philadelphia Steel & Iron Corporation*, T.C. Memo. 1964-93 (filed April 13, 1964).

60. *Fulton Container Co., Inc. v. United States*, 355 F.2d 319 (9th Cir., 1966).

61. *Plantation Patterns, Inc. et al.*, T.C. Memo. 1970-182 (filed June 30, 1970).

62. *General Insurance Agency, Inc. et al. v. Commissioner et al.*, 401 F.2d 324 (4th Cir., 1968).

63. *Barran v. Commissioner*, 334 F.2d 58 (5th Cir., 1964).

64. *Riverpoint Lace Works, Inc.*, T.C. Memo. 1954-39 (filed May 13, 1954).

65. *Irvine K. Furman et al.*, 45 T.C. 360 (1966), *aff'd*, 381 F.2d 22 (5th Cir., 1967).

66. *Shaffer Terminals, Inc. v. Commissioner*, 194 F.2d 539 (9th Cir., 1952).

67. *Van Zandt et al. v. Commissioner*, 341 F.2d 440 (5th Cir., 1965).

68. *Southeastern Canteen Co. et al. v. Commissioner*, 410 F.2d 615 (6th Cir., 1969).

69. *In the Matter of David W. Margulies*, 271 F. Supp. 50 (D.C., N.J., 1967).

70. Regulations Section 1.1245-1(a)(3).

71. *Alden B. Oakes et al.*, 44 T.C. 524 (1965).

72. *Failor et al. v. United States*, D.C., W.D. Wash., 1966.

73. *Audano et al. v. United States*, 428 F.2d 251 (5th Cir., 1970).

74. *McMillian et al. v. United States*, D.C., W.D. Texas, 1969.

75. *Ray's Clothes, Inc.*, 22 T.C. 1332 (1954).

76. *Tube Processing Corporation v. United States*, D.C., S.D. Ind., 1964.

77. *See Dahlem Foundation, Inc.*, 54 T.C. 1566 (1970).

78. Regulations Section 1.164-4(a).

79. *Brecklein et al. v. Bookwalter*, 313 F. Supp. 550 (D.C., W.D. Mo., 1970).

80. I.R.C. Section 368; see Robert S. Holzman, *Tax-Free Reorganizations after the Tax Reform Act of 1969*, Lynbrook, N.Y.: Farnsworth Publishing Company, 1970.

81. I.R.C. Section 1031.

82. *Halpern et al. v. United States*, 286 F. Supp. 255 (D.C., N.D. Ga., 1968).

83. *Redwing Carriers, Inc. et al. v. Tomlinson*, 399 F.2d 652 (5th Cir., 1968).

84. *W. D. Haden Company v. Commissioner*, 165 F.2d 588 (5th Cir., 1948).

85. *Commissioner v. P. G. Lake, Inc. et al.*, 356 U.S. 260 (1958).

86. *Tunnell v. United States*, 259 F.2d 916 (3d Cir., 1958).

87. I.R.C. Section 1001(e)(2).

88. *Federated Department Stores, Inc. v. Commissioner*, 426 F.2d 417 (6th Cir., 1970).

89. I.R.C. Section 362.

90. Under I.R.C. Section 351.

91. *Stanley, Inc. v. Schuster*, 295 F. Supp. 812 (D.C., S.D. Ohio, 1969), *aff'd*, 421 F.2d 1360 (6th Cir., 1970).

92. *Carlton et al. v. United States*, 385 F.2d 238 (5th Cir., 1967).

93. *Adam Holzworth Estate et al.*, T.C. Memo. 1965-304 (filed November 22, 1965).

94. Revenue Ruling 55-540, 1955-2 CB 39.

95. Regulations Section 1.861-7.

96. *United States v. Balanovski*, 236 F.2d 298 (2d Cir., 1956).

97. *Commissioner v. Pfaudler Inter-American Corporation*, 330 F.2d 471 (2d Cir., 1964).

98. *Philipp Brothers Inter-Continent Corporation v. United States*, D.C., S.D. N.Y., 1966.

99. *See e.g., Joseph v. Krull Wholesale Drug Co.*, 245 F.2d 231 (3d Cir., 1957).

100. *Burnet v. Harmel*, 287 U.S. 103 (1932).

CHAPTER 19

When

Significance

The Federal income tax system is based on an annual accounting. Whether there has been taxable income is determined annually from the result of the operations of that year.[1] Thus, the year in which a transaction is reported can make a decided difference for Federal income tax purposes.

Cash or Accrual Method

Basically, there are two methods for reporting income and expenditures: the cash method and the accrual method.

Under the cash method, income ordinarily is reported when payment is received, and deductions are taken into account when payment is made. But actual receipt is not required. A cash-basis taxpayer is taxable when income is available to him, even though he does not take the income at that time.[2] In the case of deductions, giving a note is not payment.[3]

An accrual-basis taxpayer must report income when he acquires a fixed right to receive a reasonably ascertainable amount.[4] Under the accrual method, it is the *right to receipt* not the actual receipt, which determines the inclusion of an amount in gross income. When the right to receive an amount becomes fixed, the right accrues.[5]

The right to receive income or the liability to make payment must be definite. Thus, when the cases refer to "a fixed right to receive" an amount as the touchstone of accruability, they comprehend a "right" that is enforceable with no strings attached, not a "right" one obtains only by relinquishing some other related and valuable right.[6]

Where there is a contingency which may preclude ultimate payment, the right need not be accrued when it arises. For example, a taxpayer need not accrue a debt if later experience, available at the time the question is adjudged, confirms a belief reasonably held at the time the debt was due to the effect that

248

it never would be paid. In order to avoid the accruability of a sale, a taxpayer must make a definite showing that an unresolved question makes receipt contingent. Postponement of payments without such accompanying doubts is not enough to suspend the reporting of income.[7] Where the right to keep payments is conditional, the payments do not result in income to an accrual-basis taxpayer until the condition is fulfilled.[8] However, the mere fact that fees were subject to some adjustment was ruled insufficient to permit their deferment.[9]

The fact that an accrual method of reporting income does not always give a precise method of matching income and expenses does not mean that it does not clearly reflect the income of a taxpayer; the vital point is consistency.[10]

Under the accrual method, an expense is deductible for the taxable year in which *all the events* have occurred which determine the fact of liability and the amount thereof with reasonable accuracy.[11] The phrase "all the events" is the essential factor in accruals. Thus, in order to reflect the income of a given year, all the events must occur in that year, which events fix the amount and the fact of the taxpayer's liability for items of indebtedness deducted though not paid; and this cannot be the case where the liability is contingent and is contested by the taxpayer.[12]

Books can be kept on an accounting basis different from that used in the Federal income tax returns so long as the adjusting figures are placed on the books at year-end.[13] For example, a corporation permitted to be on the cash basis because it has no inventories may reflect income on the accrual basis for managerial evaluation purposes, but it still reports for tax purposes on the cash basis.

Hybrid Methods

In certain instances or in certain years, the cash basis may have advantages; in others, the accrual method may be more advantageous. Except in a stipulated situation, as where the taxpayer must use the accrual method because he has inventories, the taxpayer chooses his own method, which must be followed in subsequent years unless permission to make a change is obtained. The Internal Revenue Service does not permit a taxpayer to use a hybrid method by which the taxpayer selects certain advantages of both the cash and the accrual methods.[14]

But in certain instances, a hybrid method is *required*. Thus, Federal Social Security taxes are deductible on the cash basis regardless of a taxpayer's accounting method. Social Security taxes attributable to accrued bonuses and vacation pay of an accrual-basis taxpayer are deductible only for the taxable year in which these bonuses and vacation amounts actually are paid.[15] There are other instances of identical treatment for cash and for accrual basis taxpayers. The cost of insurance covering a period of more than one year must be prorated. Contributions are deductible only when actually paid, except in the case of accrual-basis corporations which elect to deduct a contribution in the year of accrual where payment is actually made within the first 75 days of the following taxable year.[16] Both methods are similar in that they require the capitalization of acquisition costs in the case of capital assets, property used in the trade or business, and inventory.[17]

Constructive Receipt

A cash-basis taxpayer must report income not actually received if it is deemed to have been *constructively received*. The doctrine of constructive receipt treats as taxable any income which unqualifiedly is subject to the demand of a cash-basis taxpayer, whether or not such income actually has been received in cash or its equivalent.[18]

However, income not unqualifiedly subject to demand will not be deemed constructively received. So, where a fighter had earned a purse which, under his contract, could not be paid to him except in installments over a period of years, he was taxed upon this income only at such times as he actually received it.[19]

Advance Payments

Unrestricted advance payments have long been held to be income to an accrual-basis taxpayer in a service industry (such as a dance studio or an automobile club), for the taxpayer never has to return the payments and may never have to perform any further services if none are demanded.[20] But unrestricted advance payments for merchandise are now regarded as income, even if the payments cover items which are included in the recipient taxpayer's closing inventory.[21]

An accrual basis corporation tailored fur coats for customers, who were obliged to make advance payments. The advance payments were carried on the books as liabilities, income being deferred until the garments were ready for delivery. It was held that the deposits were taxable income upon receipt, for there were no restrictions upon the use of this money and no deposits had ever been returned.[22] Advance payments were taxed as income even where a corporation returned deposits to dissatisfied customers, for there was no obligation to do so and the returns were merely regarded as a matter of good business practice.[23] An accrual-basis funeral service was taxed upon amounts received from individuals under a "Pre-Need Funeral Plan Agreement," even though these amounts were received in trust for the ultimate payment of funeral services. The economic benefit received by the company (use of the money) made the receipts taxable, regardless of any power the payors might have had to enforce the trust terms under state law.[24]

However, a sum of money which was deposited with a lessor by a lessee under a ten-year lease as security for payment of rent and other covenants and which ultimately was to be applied as rent for the last year of the lease was not taxable to the lessor as advance rent in the year it was received.[25]

Claim of Right

A taxpayer must include as income any moneys which both he and the payor believed were correct at the time of payment, even though he is subsequently obliged to return some or all of the funds. Under the *claim of right* doctrine, if a taxpayer receives earnings without restriction as to the use of the money and both parties believe that the payment is due and proper, it is taxable income in the year of receipt. The principle applies even though in a later year the taxpayer may be required to refund all or part of the money; it applies whether returns are on the cash or the accrual basis. Any amount repaid is deductible in the year of repayment (on the cash basis) or in the year in which the liability to repay becomes fixed (on the accrual basis).[26]

The claim of right doctrine depends not upon the legitimacy of the claim, but upon a taxpayer's treatment of the funds as his own. Consequently, the fact that the claim was erroneous does not prevent the operation of the doctrine where the taxpayer actually had the benefit of the money at the time of receipt.[27]

Contested Liabilities

An accrual-basis taxpayer does not deduct a liability until it is admitted. By contesting a liability, he can control the time of the deduction; it is the year in which he ceases to contest the liability and concedes it.

But a contest must be in good faith.[28] A contest requires some objective act, such as lodging a formal protest against the claimed liability, starting suit, and the like.[29] If a state law requires that payment of taxes under protest is a condition to contesting a liability, mere discussion with the state authorities does not constitute a contest which would delay deductibility until the issue is conceded.[30]

Sales

There are no hard and fast rules of thumb that can be used in determining for tax purposes when a sale is consummated, and no single factor is controlling. The transaction must be viewed as a whole and in the light of realism and practicality. Passage of title is perhaps the most conclusive circumstance. Transfer of possession is also significant. Another factor often considered is whether there has been such substantial performance of conditions precedent as to impose upon the purchaser an unconditional duty to pay.[31]

A cash-basis taxpayer reports sales income in the year of receipt, whether that receipt be actual or constructive.[32] An accrual-basis taxpayer reports income when there is an unconditional liability on the part of the buyer for the purchase price.[33] An accrual-basis taxpayer must include credit sales in income in the year when the sale occurs.[34]

However, a sale is not necessarily completed by the passing of cash or the creation of a liability, for the right of action to rescind the transaction upon proof of fraudulent representation still may be open.[35]

Where a contract is executory, the payments received thereon are not income until the sale is completed.[36] However, where the only obligation remaining on a contract is contingent, deferral of income is not justified.[37] The income tax laws operate on an annual basis, and there is no assurance that there will be complete correlation between items of income and deductions pertinent thereto.[38]

In the case of securities, the sale takes place when the broker executes it, not when the taxpayer receives the money.[39] The settlement date, when title actually passes, may be set by the rules of the particular stock exchange where the transaction takes place.[40] Under the "wash sales" provision, no loss deduction can be claimed on the sale or other disposition of stock or securities if the taxpayer acquires substantially identical stock or securities 30 days before or after this disposition.[41] The rule does not apply to dealers in securities.

For tax purposes, a short sale is not consummated or closed until delivery of the shares to cover the short sale. The time of purchase of shares which could cover the short sale is not decisive, for delivery could always be made with shares other than the ones supposedly purchased for the purpose. Thus, until actual delivery of shares earmarked as coverage of the short sale, such a sale is not consummated.[42]

A seller's retention of title under a conditional sales contract until all deferred payments have been received does not prevent the sale from being a closed transaction for tax purposes. Such retention of title is merely for security purposes, and the security thus provided for the seller is comparable to what he would have acquired if he had first transferred the title to the purchaser and had then reacquired the same simultaneously for security purposes through a mortgage from the purchaser.[43]

One does not establish a loss for tax purposes by selling for a nominal sum a property which had become worthless in an earlier year.[44]

The death of a taxpayer does not constitute a sale or other disposition of his property; gain or loss does not result when property passes from the decedent to his executor or administrator.[45]

Installment Method

The installment method of reporting sales offers relief from the necessity of paying income tax on the profit from a sale where the entire proceeds of the sale are not realized until a later period or periods.[46]

A person who regularly sells or otherwise disposes of personal property on the installment plan may use the installment method for tax purposes. The method also may be used to report gain on a casual sale of real estate or personal property (other than inventory) where the price is in excess of $1000. But the method is available for casual sales only if the payments received by the seller in the year of sale (ignoring purchase obligations of the buyer) do not exceed 30 percent of the sales price.[47]

However, certain types of debt instruments may be treated as payments received in the year of sale. Thus, bonds or debentures designed to be readily tradeable in an established securities market may be so treated if steps necessary to create such a market for the securities had been taken at the time of issuance (or later, if taken pursuant to an agreement or understanding which existed at the time of issuance), or if the bonds or debentures had been a part of an issue which normally would have been traded through brokers dealing in corporate or government securities.[48]

Taxpayers using the installment method may return as income from installment sales in any taxable year that proportion of the installment payments actually received in that year which the gross profit realized or to be realized when the property is sold bears to the total contract price. In the case of dealers in personal property, "gross profit" means sales less cost of goods sold. In the case of sales of real estate or casual sales of personal property, gross profit means the selling price less the adjusted basis.[49]

Carrying charges of dealers in personal property are not included in the total contract price.[50] Sales under a revolving credit plan are, in general, treated as sales on the installment method.[51]

The installment method applies only to gains. Losses cannot be spread in this manner.[52]

Where a sale involves components not subject to installment reporting, such as inventory, an allocation of the components is necessary to determine whether the 30 percent rule is satisfied.[53]

A controlling stockholder may use the installment method for the sale of his property to his controlled corporation.[54] Sales of corporate stock may be made on the installment method.[55]

A taxpayer selling on the installment basis may use the reserve method of accounting for bad debts.[56]

A taxpayer's employment of the installment basis for tax purposes is optional.[57] (See chapter 22, Elections and Their Consequences.)

Gain or loss results from the disposition of installment obligations to the extent of the difference between realization and basis. But there is no gain upon the disposition of installment obligations at death.[58]

Deferred Payment Sales

A gain or loss from a deferred payment sale which does not meet the requirements for installment method reporting must be reflected in gross income in the year of sale, even though the sale is covered by obligations of the buyer which are payable to the seller over a period of years. The gain or loss recognized at the time of sale is the difference between the sale price (including the purchaser's obligations at their fair market value), reduced by the cost of making the sale, and the adjusted basis of the property.[59]

Imputed Interest on Deferred Payments

Where property is sold and some of the payments are due more than one year from the date of sale and no interest is provided for or the interest is below the rate prescribed by the Treasury regulations (currently four percent), a part of each payment due after the first six months from the date of sale is treated as interest.[60] This prevents a seller from avoiding ordinary income tax liability by merely labeling receipts as selling price rather than interest.[61]

The amount to be treated as interest is determined by multiplying each payment made by the buyer by a fraction, the numerator of which is the total unstated interest under the contract and the denominator of which is the total of all payments under the contract, which payments are subject to this rule.[62] Interest is imputed where the rate under the agreement is less than four percent per annum simple interest;[63] it is imputed at a rate of five percent.

This rule applies only where the contract price for an item sold on the deferred payment plan exceeds $3000. But the Internal Revenue Service is authorized to disregard any breaking down of the contract price to amounts less than $3000 by casting a transaction as though several sales were involved.[64]

Long-Term Contracts

Long-term contracts for present purposes are building, installation, or construction contracts covering a period in excess of one year from the date of execution of the contract to the date on which the contract is finally completed and performance is accepted.[65]

Income from such long-term contracts may be reported by a taxpayer under either of two methods:

(1) *Percentage of completion method.* Under this method, the percentage of the gross contract price which corresponds to the percentage of the entire contract which has been completed during the taxable year is included in the gross income of that year. Deduction is then permitted for all expenditures made during the taxable year in connection with the contract; the material and supplies on hand at the beginning and end of the taxable year are taken into account. The percentage of completion may be established by certificates of architects or engineers.[66]

(2) *Completed contract method.* Under this method, gross income is reported for the taxable year in which the contract is finally completed and accepted. All expenses which are properly allocable to the contract are deducted from gross income for that year; any material and supplies charged to the contract but remaining on hand at the time of completion are taken into account.[67] The completed contract method is a modification of the accrual method of accounting. It differs from the accrual method in that items of accrued income and accrued expense, though recorded in primary accounts, are carried into profit and loss not at the end of an annual accounting period, but only when the contract is completed and accepted.[68] Whether or not there has been a "substantial completion" of a

particular contract is not subject to a definite rule or formula.[69] A contract is finally completed within the meaning of the requirement if the contractor has performed substantially all of the important particulars of the contract.[70]

Assignment of Right to Future Income

An assignment of a right to future income is taxed not as a sale of a right, but as a substitute for the income which otherwise would be obtained. Thus, a sale of a right to future income is taxed as ordinary income if it is essentially a substitute for what otherwise would be received at a future time as ordinary income.[71]

Loss Disallowance on Belated Payments to Related Parties

Under certain circumstances, payments of even *bona fide* liabilities to specified related parties will not beget tax deductions. Unpaid expenses and interest are not deductible in the case of payments (even at arm's length) between designated classes of related parties—even though the payor is on the accrual basis—if the payee is on the cash basis, and payment is not made within 75 days after the close of the taxable year. Transactions between a taxpayer and the following members of his family are within the rule: spouse, ancestors, brothers and sisters, and lineal descendants. The following relationships are also within the rule: that between an individual and a corporation more than 50 percent of the value of the stock of which is owned (directly or indirectly) by that individual; two corporations more than 50 percent of the value of the stock of which is owned by the same individual if either one is a personal holding company; a grantor and a fiduciary of any trust. Various other fiduciary-beneficiary relationships also fall within the rule. Likewise covered is a transaction between a person and an organization which is tax-exempt, if that organization is directly or indirectly controlled by that person or, if that person is an individual, by members of his family.[72]

The purpose of this rule is to eliminate a taxpayer's avoiding tax by accruing unpaid expenses and interest payable to a closely related taxpayer who, because he is on a cash basis, reports no income. Because of the relationship between the taxpayers, payment might never be required or might be postponed until the related taxpayer has offsetting losses.[73]

A payment disallowed under this rule is not deductible in any year.[74] Voluntary inclusion of unpaid corporate accruals by a cash-basis stockholder will not save the lost corporate deduction.[75] Nor is a deduction saved by the fact that the corporation was dissolved prior to the 75-day limit for payments.[76]

Time of Loss

In general, losses are recognized only when they have been realized. However, an exception is made in certain circumstances in the case of losses which are so reasonably certain in fact and ascertainable in amount as to justify their deduction before they are absolutely realized.[77]

In the case of stock losses, the burden of proof rests upon the taxpayer to show by some fixed and identifiable event that the stock has become worthless in the year for which the deduction is claimed.[78] This event is not fixed by selling a stock which has become worthless in an earlier year for a nominal sum.[79] When it is reasonably certain that stockholders will receive a further liquidating dividend, a loss is not allowable until there is a distribution of such a dividend in property or money. Until this is done, the stock has a value of its own, and the mere fact that, because the corporation is in process of liquidation, its value has declined to a figure which is less than cost does not entitle the stockholder to elect the year in which he will take his loss.[80]

A casualty loss is deductible in the year in which the insurance company or other party responsible for reimbursement has admitted liability; this may well be after the year in which the casualty actually took place.[81] Deduction is allowed in the year of the loss where there is no reasonable prospect of recovery in a future year.[82]

Where property is lost by casualty in what the President of the United States subsequently proclaims to be a disaster area, the taxpayer can elect to claim the deduction in the taxable year immediately preceding the taxable year in which the disaster occurred.[83]

Deductions for Benefits of More Than One Year's Duration

Expenditures which provide a benefit lasting more than one year are not deductible, but must be capitalized over the life of the expected benefit. (See chapter 6, Capital Assets, Capital Gains and Losses.)

Expenses incidental to securing a mortgage loan are not deductible as business expenses in the year in which the loan is made, but must be prorated over the life of the bond.[84]

Inventory

A taxpayer may write down his inventory to reflect obsolete and worthless items. But a tax deduction is permitted only where there is evidence that corporate officials considered the inventory to be obsolete and worthless during the taxable year.[85] No deduction is allowed for shopworn and obsolete inventory which has been in that condition for many years.[86]

Depreciation

The depreciation deduction is dependent upon the estimated number of years of useful life of an asset to a particular taxpayer. The essential concept of the deduction is prediction or estimation.[87] Estimates are made at the time of the acquisition of the property.[88]

Depreciation or amortization is dependent upon whether the length of an asset's life can be estimated with reasonable accuracy.[89]

Employee Benefit Plan Contributions

An employer corporation may deduct contributions to a qualified employee benefit plan only where the contributions are made not later than the time prescribed by law for the filing of the Federal income tax return for the taxable year to which the contribution applies (including extensions).[90] Payments to the plan must be made in cash or its equivalent by the time the return is due, extensions being taken into consideration.[91]

Fiscal Year

Taxable income is computed, and a tax return is filed for a period known as the *taxable year*.[92] It is often desirable to use a period other than the calendar year. A fiscal year is a year ending on the last day of any month other than December. The use of such a year other than the calendar year may be productive of tax advantages.

If a corporation's first taxable year closes at the end of the calendar year, early expenses may not have allowed income to produce a profit. If the taxable year is extended through the mechanism of a fiscal year, the losses may then be offset by income instead of being wasted. Conversely, if a corporation is formed to effectuate a transaction which is immediately profitable and the taxable year ends very shortly thereafter, it may mean that this profit is taxed without being offset by expenses that will subsequently be incurred.

Where management does not anticipate a very liberal dividend policy, the resultant accumulated earnings tax hazard could be mitigated by proper selection of a fiscal year. The accumulated earnings tax is imposed, if at all, upon the basis of the year-end balance sheet and other factors as of the time covered by the income tax return. If this corporation selects the fiscal year which ends at the time of year when liquidity is poorest and accounts payable are most overpowering, the force of this tax is softened.

There are highly persuasive non-tax reasons for the use of a fiscal year. Most businesses have a natural operating cycle, and a fiscal year which reflects the operation of that cycle is far more meaningful than an arbitrary calendar year. A fiscal year might be selected to conform to that time of the year when operations would be least affected by the closing of the books, which, at a less propitious time, could involve shutting down a plant to take inventory.

A change of accounting period, as from a calendar to a fiscal year, customarily requires an application to the Internal Revenue Service on *Form 1128*. This form makes inquiries as to the reason (which should be non-tax) for the change. In one case, it was noted that there were valid business reasons for changing the accounting period of a cotton ginner. At the close of the season, several months were required for repair of the equipment, which ran day and night during the ginning season. It was logical to conform the accounting period to the usage of the equipment.[93]

Permission for change of accounting period is not required where:

(1) A corporation has not changed its accounting period at any time within the past ten years.

(2) The short period required to effect the change is not one in which the corporation showed a net operating loss.

(3) The taxable income for the short period, when annualized, is at least 80 percent of the taxable income for the preceding taxable year.

(4) The corporation retains any special status it had in the preceding period. Thus, a personal holding company, Western Hemisphere Trade Corporation, etc., must keep such a characterization.[94]

Under certain circumstances, the Internal Revenue Service will approve a change in accounting period even though in the short taxable year resulting from the change the taxpayer would show a net operating loss.[95]

If a tax return is for a period shorter than 12 months because of a change of accounting period, the income of this "short period" must be annualized. This is done by projecting the income for the period ending with the newly selected year-end date to a full year. Thus, if a calendar year is changed to a fiscal year ending April 30, there will be a short period from January 1 to April 30 for the first period of the change. Annualization is effected by multiplying the income for that short period by a fraction, the numerator of which is the number of days in the full year and the denominator of which is the number of days in the short taxable year. Tax is computed on this projected income. The tax is then "de-annualized" by the application of a fraction, the numerator of which is the number of days in the short period and the denominator of which is the number of days in the full year.[96] No annualization is required where a taxable year covers fewer than 12 months solely because it is the taxpayer's first or last year.

Where a corporation becomes a member of an affiliated group and participates in a consolidated tax return, it is not required to annualize its income.[97] Nor is annualization required for purposes of the accumulated earnings tax.[98]

Dividends

The date of payment, not the date of the declaration of the dividend, is the date of the distribution.[99]

A distribution made by a corporation to its shareholders must be included in the gross income of the distributees when the cash or other property is unqualifiedly made subject to their demands.[100]

Timeliness of Tax Return

The question of timely filing of Federal income tax returns and related documents is treated in chapter 23, Dealing with the Internal Revenue Service.

Final Tax Return

The final Federal income tax return of a corporation must be filed by the 15th day of the third month following dissolution.[101]

Carry-Overs

The purpose of the carry-over provisions is to make available a method for "evening out" the peaks and troughs of the profit curve of a business which has fluctuating gains and losses.[102] The sequence of time application of carry-overs is set by the Internal Revenue Code, with no election available to the taxpayer.

In the case of a net operating loss, there is a three-year carryback, starting with the earliest of these years.[103] Unused losses are then carried forward for as long as five years, starting with the earliest year.[104]

In the case of a capital loss, carrybacks are available only to corporations, and the loss must have been in a taxable year beginning after December 31, 1969. Carry-forwards are five years for corporations and an unlimited time for individuals.[105] A decedent's unused capital loss dies with him.[106]

Accumulated Earnings Tax

The term "reasonable needs of the business" for the purposes of reasonable retention of earnings must be interpreted in the light of what is known at the close of the taxable year.[107] Thus subsequent events cannot be taken into account as justification for earnings which had been retained at year-end. However, the Internal Revenue Service may consider subsequent events in determining whether the taxpayer actually intended to consummate or actually has consummated the plans for which the earnings and profits were accumulated. In this connection, projected expansion or investment plans should be reviewed in the light of that fact during each year and as they exist at the close of the taxable year.[108]

The controlling intention of a corporation is that which is manifested at the time of the accumulation, not a subsequently declared intention which is merely the product of afterthought.[109]

A persuasive argument in support of retention is based upon the cash requirements of an operating cycle. (See chapter 11, Dividends and the Tax on Accumulated Earnings.) This is based upon projected fiscal requirements for one operating cycle.[110]

Controlled Foreign Corporation

260

When

If a foreign corporation meets the test for qualification of a controlled foreign corporation for an uninterrupted period of 30 days or more, every United States shareholder who owns ten percent or more of the stock on the last day of that year must include in his gross income his *pro rata* share of the corporation's income, whether distributed or not.[111]

Holding Period of Capital Assets

Time plays a major role in the tax treatment of disposition of capital assets inasmuch as such assets held for one day more than six months are generally characterized as long-term and thus accorded different tax treatment.[112] The holding period for capital gains treatment for animals held for draft, breeding, or sporting is two years and for other livestock, one year. The taxpayer has the burden of proof of establishing how long property has been held.[113]

In the case of securities, the holding period may be affected by the rules of the securities exchange on which the securities are listed.[114]

The Tax Benefit Rule

The tax benefit rule determines the Federal income tax treatment of the recovery of items previously claimed as deductions on a tax return for a prior period. As a general rule, each taxable period is treated as separate and independent, and items of income and deductions for one year cannot be set off and adjusted in computing the tax for another year. Yet there are situations where the proper treatment of one year cannot be resolved without reference to events in a prior year. For example, if an amount deducted from gross income in one year is recovered in a later year, the tax return of the earlier year is not amended; in fact, it may have been closed by the statute of limitations. Instead, subject to the tax benefit rule, the amount of the recovery is taxed when the recovery takes place.[115]

Under the tax benefit rule, recovery of an item previously shown as a deduction on a tax return constitutes income in the year of recovery, provided the taxpayer had previously had the tax benefit of this deduction. When a prior deduction which had created a tax benefit is recovered, the tax imposed upon the recovery is at the rate that prevailed in the year of recovery, not at the rate that prevailed when the tax benefit was determined.[116] If the deduction had been claimed in a year when there was insufficient income to absorb the loss so that no tax benefit resulted, the recovery is not taxed.

This rule is applied most frequently in the case of recoveries of amounts deducted as bad debts, worthless securities, or taxes.

Time of Book Entries

When made substantially contemporaneously with events and long before any tax controversy arises, book entries are entitled to great evidentiary weight.[117]

A schedule showing the financial considerations which allegedly actuated the directors in adopting a certain course of action obviously could not have established what the real motivation for a transaction had been when the schedules had not been prepared until the time of trial of the tax issues and the preparation of the schedule had been at the suggestion of the attorney who was handling the litigation.[118]

A transaction which is effected to legitimize a transaction after an Internal Revenue agent had asked about it is customarily regarded as being too late.[119]

NOTES

1. *Heiner v. Mellon*, 304 U.S. 271 (1938).
2. *Helvering v. Horst*, 311 U.S. 112 (1940).
3. *Eckert v. Burnet*, 283 U.S. 140 (1931).
4. *Stephens Marine, Inc. v. Commissioner*, 430 F.2d 679 (9th Cir., 1970).
5. *Spring City Foundry Company v. Commissioner*, 292 U.S. 182 (1934).
6. *Maryland Shipbuilding and Drydock Company v. United States*, 409 F.2d 1363 (Ct. Cl., 1969).
7. *Georgia Schoolbook Depository, Inc.*, 1 T.C. 463 (1943).
8. *Consolidated-Hammer Dry Plate & Film Company*, T.C. Memo. 1962-97 (filed April 25, 1962).
9. *E. Morris Cox et al.*, 43 T.C. 448 (1965).
10. *Koebig & Koebig, Inc.*, T.C. Memo. 1964-32 (filed February 12, 1964).
11. Regulations Section 1.461-1(a)(2).
12. *Dixie Pine Company v. Commissioner*, 320 U.S. 516 (1944).
13. Revenue Ruling 68-35, 1968-1 CB 190.
14. *Little v. Commissioner*, 294 F.2d 661 (9th Cir., 1961).
15. Revenue Ruling 69-587, 1969-2 CB 108.
16. I.R.C. Section 170(a)(2).
17. *United States v. Catto, Jr. et al.*, 384 U.S. 102 (1966).
18. *Ross v. Commissioner*, 169 F.2d 483 (1st Cir., 1948).
19. *Ray S. Robinson et al.*, 44 T.C. 20 (1965).
20. *Schlude v. Commissioner*, 372 U.S. 128 (1963); *Automobile Club of Michigan v. Commissioner*, 353 U.S. 180 (1957).
21. *Hagen Advertising Displays, Inc. v. Commissioner*, 407 F.2d 1105 (6th Cir., 1969).
22. *S. Garber, Inc.*, 51 T.C. 733 (1969).
23. *Modernaire Interiors, Inc.*, T.C. Memo. 1968-252 (filed October 30, 1968).
24. *Angelus Funeral Home v. Commissioner*, 407 F.2d 210 (9th Cir., 1969).
25. *Clinton Hotel Realty Corporation v. Commissioner*, 128 F.2d 968 (5th Cir., 1942).
26. *Whitaker v. Commissioner*, 259 F.2d 379 (5th Cir., 1958).
27. *Bramlette Building Corporation, Inc. v. Commissioner*, 427 F.2d 661 (5th Cir., 1970).
28. *Southwest Exploration Company et al. v. Riddell*, 232 F. Supp. 13 (D.C., S.D. Cal., 1964).
29. *Dravo Corporation v. United States*, 384 F.2d 542 (Ct. Cl., 1965).
30. *Woodmont Terrace, Inc. v. United States*, 261 F. Supp. 789 (D.C., M.D. Tenn., 1966).
31. *Commissioner v. Segall et al.*, 114 F.2d 706 (6th Cir., 1940).
32. I.R.C. Section 451(a).
33. *Lucas v. North Texas Lumber Company*, 281 U.S. 11 (1930).

34. *Spring City Company v. Commissioner*, 292 U.S. 182 (1934).

35. *James N. Collins Estate*, 46 B.T.A. 765 (1942).

36. *Watkins v. United States*, 287 F.2d 932 (1st Cir., 1961).

37. *Schlude v. Commissioner*, 372 U.S. 128 (1963).

38. *The Marquardt Corporation*, 39 T.C. 42 (1962).

39. *Huntington National Bank v. Commissioner*, 90 F.2d 876 (6th Cir., 1937).

40. I.T. 3705, 1945 CB 174.

41. I.R.C. Section 1091.

42. *Hendricks et al. v. Commissioner*, 423 F.2d 485 (4th Cir., 1970).

43. *Floyd R. Clodfelter et al.*, 48 T.C. 694 (1967), *aff'd*, 426 F.2d 1391 (9th Cir., 1970).

44. *Genecov et al. v. United States*, 412 F.2d 556 (5th Cir., 1969).

45. O.D. 731, 3 CB 210.

46. *Ackerman v. United States*, 318 F.2d 402 (10th Cir., 1963).

47. I.R.C. Section 453(a).

48. I.R.C. Section 453(b)(3).

49. Regulations Section 1.453-1(b).

50. I.R.C. Section 453(e).

51. Regulations Section 1.453-2(d).

52. *Martin v. Commissioner*, 61 F.2d 942 (2d Cir., 1932).

53. Revenue Ruling 68-13, 1968-1 CB 195.

54. *Warren Brown*, 27 T.C. 27 (1956).

55. *50 East 75th Street Corporation v. Commissioner*, 78 F.2d 158 (2d Cir., 1935).

56. Revenue Ruling 70-139, 1970-1 CB 39.

57. Regulations Section 1.453-1(c).

58. I.R.C. Section 453(d)(3).

59. Regulations Section 1.453-6.

60. I.R.C. Section 483.

61. *Robinson et al. v. Commissioner*, 439 F.2d 767 (8th Cir., 1970).

62. Regulations Section 1.483-1(a)(1).

63. Regulations Section 1.483-1(d).

64. Regulations Section 1.483-2(b).

65. Regulations Section 1.451-3.

66. Regulations Section 1.451-3(b)(1).

67. Regulations Section 1.451-3(b)(2).

68. *C. H. Leavell & Company*, 53 T.C. 426 (1969).

69. *King, Jr. et al. v. United States*, 220 F. Supp. 350 (D.C., E.D. Texas, 1963).

70. *Ehret-Day Company*, 2 T.C. 25 (1943).

71. *Commissioner et al. v. P. G. Lake, Inc. et al.*, 356 U.S. 260 (1958).

72. I.R.C. Section 267(a)(2).

73. *Young Door Company*, 40 T.C. 890 (1963).

74. *L. R. McKee et al.*, 18 T.C. 512 (1952).

75. *Century Transit Company v. United States*, 124 F. Supp. 148 (D.C., N.J., 1951), *rev'd on another ground sub nomine Fiorentino v. United States*, 266 F.2d 619 (3d Cir., 1955).

76. *Susan J. Carter*, 9 T.C. 346 (1947), *aff'd on another issue*, 170 F.2d 911 (2d Cir., 1948).

77. *Lucas v. American Code Company*, 280 U.S. 445 (1930).

78. *875 Park Avenue Company v. Commissioner*, 217 F.2d 699 (2d Cir., 1954).

79. *Keeney v. Commissioner*, 116 F.2d 401 (2d Cir., 1940).

80. *Dresser v. United States*, 55 F.2d 499 (Ct. Cl., 1932).

81. *Commissioner v. Harwick*, 184 F.2d 835 (5th Cir., 1950).

82. *Paul H. Schweitzer et al.*, T.C. Memo. 1965-308 (filed November 30, 1965).

83. I.R.C. Section 165(h).

84. Revenue Ruling 70-360, 1970-2 CB 103.

85. *Dunn Manufacturing Co.*, 14 B.T.A. 225 (1928).

86. *Hug & Sarachek Art Co.*, 14 B.T.A. 990 (1929).

87. *Macabe Company et al.*, 42 T.C. 1105 (1964).
88. *S & A Company v. United States*, 218 F. Supp. 677 (D.C., Minn., 1963), *aff'd,* 338 F.2d 629 (8th Cir., 1964).
89. *Times-World Publishing Corporation v. United States*, 250 F. Supp. 43 (D.C., W.D. Va., 1966).
90. I.R.C. Section 404(a)(6).
91. *F. & D. Rentals, Inc.*, 44 T.C. 335 (1965).
92. I.R.C. Section 441.
93. *Wilson et al. v. United States*, 267 F. Supp. 89 (D.C., E.D. Mo., 1967).
94. Regulations Section 1.442-1(c).
95. Revenue Procedure 66-6, 1966-1 CB 615.
96. I.R.C. Section 443(b).
97. Revenue Ruling 67-189, 1967-1 CB 255.
98. I.R.C. Section 536.
99. *Mason v. Routzahn*, 275 U.S. 775 (1927).
100. Regulations Section 1.301-1(b).
101. Revenue Ruling 215, 1953-2 CB 149.
102. *Huyler's, Inc.*, 38 T.C. 773 (1962).
103. I.R.C. Section 172(b)(1)(A)(i).
104. I.R.C. Section 172(b)(1)(B).
105. I.R.C. Section 1212.
106. Revenue Ruling 54-207, 1954-1 CB 147.
107. I.R.C. Section 537.
108. *Havens & Martin v. United States*, D.C., E.D. Va., 1965.
109. *The Smoot Sand & Gravel Corporation v. Commissioner*, 241 F.2d 197 (4th Cir., 1957).
110. *Bardahl Manufacturing Corporation*, T.C. Memo. 1965-200 (filed July 23, 1965).
111. I.R.C. Section 951.
112. I.R.C. Section 1223(3).
113. *Taylor v. Commissioner*, 76 F.2d 904 (2d Cir., 1935).
114. For an extended consideration of the holding period, *see* Robert S. Holzman, *Federal Taxation Of Capital Assets*, Lynbrook, N.Y.: Farnsworth Publishing Company, 1969, chapter 4.
115. *Mayfair Minerals, Inc.*, 56 T.C. 82 (1971), *aff'd*, 456 F.2d 622 (5th Cir., 1972).
116. *Alice Phelan Sullivan Corporation v. United States*, 381 F.2d 399 (Ct. Cl., 1967).
117. *Stout et al. v. Commissioner*, 273 F.2d 345 (4th Cir., 1959).
118. *Apollo Industries, Inc.*, 44 T.C. 1 (1965), *rev'd on another issue*, 358 F.2d 867 (1st Cir., 1966).
119. *Tabery et al. v. Commissioner*, 354 F.2d 422 (9th Cir., 1965).

CHAPTER 20

Intention and Purpose

The instances are many in which purpose or state of mind determines the incidence of an income tax.[1] *Why* was a transaction entered into? The primary intent or motive of a taxpayer always has been the ultimate test for determining whether losses are deductible because incurred in a trade or business or in a transaction entered upon for profit, or, on the other hand, are nondeductible because they are personal expenses.[2] Similarly, in determining whether an expenditure is capital or is chargeable against operating income, one must bear in mind the purpose for which the expenditure was made.[3] Purpose is an important criterion in distinguishing between capital outlays and ordinary and necessary expenses.[4]

This chapter will deal with these and other areas where intention and purpose are crucial in determining taxability. Areas will also be considered where motivation is irrelevant, where purpose is not enough, and where a business purpose will not suffice to gain for a transaction the tax treatment the taxpayer desires because of certain specific statutory requirements that there be a *principal* purpose which is not related to tax advantages.

The Internal Revenue Code does not specifically state that the purpose of a transaction must be something other than the avoidance of taxes if it is to be recognized for tax purposes. Thus, there may be a twilight zone of resolving two conflicting propositions: the precept that the courts cannot impose restrictive conditions not authorized by the law, and the rule that the courts cannot give tax benefits to a transaction that is without business or commercial purpose and motivated only by a desire to avoid taxes.[5]

The Internal Revenue Service may disregard the tax consequences of corporate transactions which do not relate to the corporation's business. And escaping taxation is not regarded as a business activity.[6] Arrangements entered into solely to suit the personal convenience of stockholders do not relate to the business or the business purposes of a corporation.[7]

Sound Business Purpose

The fact that a sound business purpose was specified by a taxpayer does not necessarily mean that this is what actually motivated the transaction.[8] Nor does the presence of a business purpose automatically mean that the transaction had enough economic reality to be recognized for tax purposes.[9] A taxpayer must be unusually persuasive in its arguments when it attempts to demonstrate that Congress intended to give favorable tax treatment to the kind of transaction which never would occur without the motive of tax avoidance.[10]

A taxpayer has a perfect right to take advantage of all the leverage that the tax laws give him, and he is not to be deprived of that right simply because his situation gives him more leverage than the Internal Revenue Service thinks he ought to have. Nor is a taxpayer forbidden to kill two birds with one stone if he can do so under the tax laws.[11] But the transaction must be real. The substance of a transaction will always prevail over the mere form for tax purposes. However, the parties may structure a transaction in the light of their awareness of its tax consequences, provided the substantive nature of the transaction has economic reality.[12]

Establishment of Intent

Generally, the taxpayer has the burden of proving the true intent and purpose of a transaction. Intent may be proved by the words and conduct of the actor and also by the presumption that the actor intends the legal consequences of his act.[13] The court need not take the actor at his word;[14] his actions speak louder than his words.[15] The normal and natural consequences which flow from the acts of interested parties frequently will reveal their intent and purpose more clearly than their declarations with respect thereto.[16]

Rarely is there only one purpose or motive, or even one dominant purpose or motive, for corporate decisions. Numerous factors contribute to the course of action ultimately decided upon.[17] Any given intention or purpose is likely to yield to circumstances. Thus the "intention" which is contemplated for tax purposes is an intention or purpose to be followed under circumstances which are foreseen as more probable than not.[18]

Survival as a Business Motive

Efforts of a corporation to continue its existence clearly are related to its business purpose. No purpose is more germane to business than its profitable perpetuation.[19]

The promotion of harmony in the conduct of a venture may be a proper business purpose. This rule applies where the shares of a minority shareholder are purchased by a corporation after his complaints about the conduct of affairs make forward steps impossible.[20] A separation of a corporation into two separate companies may be justified by the existence of serious differences of opinion among the principal stockholders.[21]

Complying with the law assuredly is a valid business purpose.[22]

Inasmuch as customers are essential for the survival of a business enterprise, the expressed preference of a major customer was sufficient business justification for a transaction.[23]

"Held . . . Primarily for Sale to Customers"

By definition, a capital asset does not include property held by the taxpayer primarily for sale to customers in the ordinary course of its trade or business.[24] This phrase has been construed to cover property held with a purpose to sell that is "substantial" or "essential," even if not "principal" or "chief." [25]

In determining why property is held, a court may look at such factors as: (1) the intent of the taxpayer with respect to the asset; (2) the purpose for its acquisition; (3) the purpose of its disposition; (4) the period it was held; (5) the number, frequency, and substantiality of sales; and (6) the extent of development, improvement, and sales activity.[26] The vocation of the taxpayer at the time of the sales or prior thereto also may be significant.[27] But the most important criterion of all is the purpose for which the property is held at the time of sale.[28]

Even where property had been acquired for sale to customers in the ordinary course of business, it may be treated as a capital asset if it can be shown that the property was being held for investment at the time of sale.[29] On the other hand, a manufacturer which leased equipment to customers of its regular products was required by the United States Department of Justice to divest itself of the equipment being leased. Although the sale was under compulsion, the equipment was being held for sale at the time of disposition, and the resultant gain was ordinary income.[30]

Property may be held for a dual purpose. If one of the purposes is to sell to customers in the ordinary course of the business, a sale will fail to qualify for capital gain treatment.[31] This may be the case where an asset is acquired for sale or rental; the outcome depends upon customer demands.

"Transaction Entered into for Profit"

Deductions are allowed for losses resulting from any transaction entered into for profit.[32] Essentially, the test is whether the intention of the taxpayer was to carry on a business for profit.[33]

Profit has been defined as the advantages or gains resulting from the investment of capital or the acquisition of money beyond the amount expended.[34] Where an individual entered upon a transaction to help a relative and not primarily with a view to earning a profit, a loss deduction was not allowed.[35] The deduction was also denied where the purpose of acquiring property was to give financial assistance to a corporation rather than to make a profit.[36] In another case, the deduction was denied to an artist who admitted that his motive for painting was to give mankind a better vision of beauty and to establish for himself a reputation as a great artist rather than to make a profit from the deal.[37]

The deduction of "hobby losses" has been made more difficult by the Tax Reform Act of 1969. Individuals and Subchapter S corporations (see chapter 2, Corporations and Other Forms of Conducting Business) cannot deduct losses arising from an activity not engaged in for profit if deductions with respect to the activity are not allowable as trade or business expenses or as expenses incurred for the production of income. Where an activity is not engaged in for profit, a deduction is allowed for expenses which may be deducted without regard to whether they are incurred in a trade or business or for the production of income; for example, interest, or state and local property taxes. A deduction is also allowed for items which would be deductible if the activity were engaged in for profit, but only to the extent that these items do not exceed the amount of gross income derived from the activity reduced by the deductions which are allowable in any event. A taxpayer is presumed to be engaged in an activity for profit in a taxable year if in two or more years of the period of five consecutive taxable years ending with the current taxable year, the activity was carried on at a profit; that is, if the gross income from the activity exceeds the deductions attributable to the activity which would be allowed if it were engaged in for profit. If the major part of the activity consists of breeding, training, showing, or racing horses, the five-year figure becomes seven.[38]

An amendment to the Revenue Act of 1971 allows a taxpayer to elect to suspend the application of the presumption until there are five consecutive taxable years (or seven in the case of horses) in existence from the time he first engages in the activity and then to apply the presumption to any years in the five- or seven-year period. For this purpose, a taxpayer is not treated as having engaged in any activity covered by this provision for any taxable year beginning before 1970.[39]

Interest

In the case of a deduction for interest, the Code says nothing about the motive or purpose for incurring the indebtedness and paying the interest.[40] But the statutory allowance presupposes that the indebtedness be neither a sham nor incurred in a sham transaction.[41] This question is one of fact based upon intent, and the taxpayer has the burden of establishing his right to the interest deduction.[42] Whether a transfer of money creates a *bona fide* debt depends upon the existence of an intent by both parties, substantially contemporaneous with the transfer, to establish an enforceable obligation of repayment.[43]

In the case of stockholders' "loans" to their corporation, the intention of the parties is important in determining the nature of such advances.[44]

The intent that advances create indebtedness can change. Interest ceases to be a real cost if, with the passage of time, it becomes apparent that the parties have no intention of continuing the debtor-creditor relationship.[45]

Where the indebtedness was genuine, the fact that the parties deliberately had chosen a technique which provided a tax advantage was deemed to be irrelevant. The mere fact that a more favorable tax treatment may result from the way in which a corporation's management conducted its affairs does not entitle the Internal Revenue Service to revise or to rewrite the corporate books and to show to be capital what was intended at all times to be a loan or indebtedness.[46]

Ordinarily, no deduction is allowed for interest paid or incurred to purchase or to carry tax-exempt bonds. (See chapter 3, Is It Stock or Are They Bonds?) But where business reasons not related to obtaining tax-free interest dominate the incurring of an indebtedness, a taxpayer may deduct interest on such indebtedness.[47]

Dividends

An intention to distribute corporate earnings is not a requirement for a finding that a taxable dividend has been paid. Taxability exists if there was a *constructive* dividend by reason of a shareholder's having received an economic benefit which was essentially equivalent to the payment of a taxable dividend.[48] The motive or expressed intent of the corporation is not determinative, and constructive dividends have been found despite the expressed intent of the corporation to the contrary. The courts, as arbiters of the true nature of corporate payments, have consistently used as a standard the measure of receipt of economic benefits as the proper occasion of taxation.[49]

In resolving the question of whether corporate payments to shareholders are dividends or loans, courts look to the intention of the parties.[50] Ordinarily, a legitimate corporate business purpose for the payment to a stockholder is enough to bar the transaction's being characterized as equivalent to a dividend.[51] But the existence of a single *bona fide* business purpose will not conclusively establish that the transaction does not result in a taxable dividend.[52]

Redemptions are even more suspect as being dividends. Where a corporation redeems some of its own stock which is held by a shareholder at a time when the corporation has earnings and profits, the evidence of a business motive is not relevant to the question of whether the transaction is essentially equivalent to a dividend; it *is* a dividend.[53]

Depreciation

Where the taxpayer does not have a predetermined plan for disposing of an asset before its useful life expires, the period during which the asset might reasonably be expected to be employed in the business is its physical or economic life.[54] Or the period of the asset's use could be considered a guideline life where the Asset Depreciation Range System is used.

In general, the Internal Revenue Service will disallow a depreciation deduction in the taxable year in which the assets are sold at a gain on the theory that if proper depreciation had been taken in earlier years, there would have been no gain. (See chapter 12, Depreciation.) But where excessive depreciation had not been taken with the intent of subsequently disposing of the property before the end of its useful life, the courts will not apply this rule. Again, the intent of the taxpayer is of prime importance.[55]

The depreciation recapture rules apply upon the disposition of certain depreciable property upon which accelerated depreciation had been taken, regardless of why the disposition took place. Various exceptions to this rule are spelled out in the statute in the case of gifts, transfers at death, and specified tax-free transactions.[56]

Repairs

The tax treatment of a repair, as opposed to an improvement, may depend upon the taxpayer's purpose. The "purpose of expenditure" test governs the deductibility: Was it to reestablish the *status quo ante* of an asset, or was it to add to the life, utility, or performance of the asset? [57]

The taxpayer's motive or purpose is also crucial in determining the treatment of expenditures where many "repairs" are taken care of at approximately the same time. If a general plan of renovation was contemplated, the expenditures must be capitalized.[58]

Loss on Abandonment

Deduction for loss on abandonment requires an intent to abandon the assets in question during the taxable year. The intent to abandon, which is a state of mind, must be coupled with cessation of activity with respect to the project.[59]

"Mere mental attitude" is not enough to establish an abandonment.[60] Nor is an intent which is, in the language of one decision, "ill-defined or floating." [61]

Demolition

If land and buildings are acquired with the intent of razing the structure, no demolition loss deduction is allowed and the entire cost of acquiring the combined property is allocated to the land. If an intent to raze the building existed, the fact that the actual demolition was to take place at some future time is immaterial.[62]

Where land and building were purchased with the intention of using the structure, but subsequently it was found unfeasible to perform the construction work necessary to convert the building to the use for which it was originally intended, a demolition loss was allowed when the structure was razed five years after acquisition.[63]

Advertising

Whether the cost of an advertisement is deductible is a matter of motivation. An inquiry must be made: For what purpose was the expenditure made? If the answer is lobbying purposes, for example, the expense is not a tax deduction.[64]

Travel

A deduction is allowed for the costs of business travel. The dominant purpose of the trip is the critical inquiry, and the presence of some pleasurable features will not negate the finding of an overall business purpose.[65]

When an employee's travel expenses are paid for him by another, such as by his employer, he does not realize taxable income if he is serving a legitimate business purpose of the party paying the expenses.[66] Thus, a corporate executive was not obliged to include in income employer-paid expenses of his wife who accompanied him on his business trips. It was established to the court's satisfaction that her presence had a *bona fide* purpose with respect to his business amounting to more than the rendition of some merely incidental service.[67]

Sale or Lease?

Frequently there is a purported lease with an option to purchase, and the question is whether payments made by the alleged lessee are deductible rent or merely nondeductible payments to purchase property upon a deferred basis. If the parties enter into a transaction which, in actuality, has all the elements of a contract of sale, it will be considered a contract of sale no matter what they call it or how they treat it on their books.[68]

Even if there is a contract which purportedly establishes the nature of the transaction, courts will scan the language to ascertain the real intent of the parties.[69]

Acquisition of Stock to Get Assets

An investor's gain or loss on the sale of stock or securities is usually a capital gain or loss. The rule is otherwise where a securities dealer is involved. If the intent was to serve a business need and not to make an investment, ordinary gain or loss results.

One who purchased stock in a manufacturing company in order to assure himself of a steady supply for his business and then sold the stock at a loss suffered an ordinary loss.[70] Similarly, a wholesale liquor company was allowed to take an ordinary loss on the sale of stock in a whiskey manufacturing company which it had acquired solely for the purpose of obtaining merchandise which otherwise was unobtainable.[71] A manufacturer was permitted to deduct as a business expense the loss upon disposition of stock in a retail organization which had been acquired to assure continued patronage.[72] A salesman who bought stock in the business of a customer which incorporated could deduct his cost as a business expense when the stock was ultimately rendered worthless. The purchase had been for the purpose of assuring the salesman the exclusive orders of the customer, and the business purpose for which the shares were held continued until the very day they became worthless.[73]

A corporation was permitted to deduct as an ordinary and necessary business expense the cost of the stock of a company that was the purchaser's selling agency, where it appeared that the purchaser's reputation would have been injured had not this agency been eliminated from the economic scene via liquidation. The only way to achieve this result was to purchase the stock, which was not desirable as an investment.[74]

Loss on the sale of stock of a corporation which had been purchased for the purpose of obtaining scarce inventory was capital, however, when the stock was retained after inventory again became plentiful. The retention of the shares indicated that the stock now was being held for investment purposes and not for a business purpose.[75]

Morality of Business Purpose

From the tax point of view, an acceptable and sound business purpose may involve a situation whose moral justification is lacking. For tax purposes, that is irrelevant so long as the one deluded or defrauded is not the Commissioner of Internal Revenue. For example, the transfer of property or the incorporation of an enterprise may be to remove assets from the reach of attachment by judgment creditors.[76]

A transaction was recognized for tax purposes where the objective was minimization of vulnerability to personal damage suits.[77]

Gifts

In determining whether a payment has the tax status of a gift, the Internal Revenue Service will give most critical consideration to the transferor's intention.[78] As long as there is an intention to make a gift and such a gift is actually made, the fact that it was tax-inspired is not fatal.[79]

In ascertaining whether payments by a corporation were compensation or nontaxable gifts to the recipients, one court spelled out various criteria to be considered, the first of which was the motive or intent of the corporation in making the payments.[80] This question frequently arises where gratuitous payments are made to the widow of an officer or other employee who died during employment. In one such case, the court pointed out that the widow was taxable upon payment for services (her late husband's), for there was no evidence that the employer had made any inquiry into her financial circumstances. This failure to consider her financial posture was described as a very relevant factor in indicating that the motive of the employer was not to make a gift to her.[81]

Deductibility of a corporation's payment to the widow of a deceased employee also depends upon the payor's intent. A corporation was permitted to deduct voluntary payments made to the widow of a deceased officer where the court was satisfied that such payments served a business purpose in maintaining the morale and incentive of its executive and managerial staff.[82] Where the dominant, if not the sole, reason for the payment was to provide for the financial needs of the widow, no business purpose existed and the corporation's deduction was lost.[83]

Where Intent or Purpose Is Irrelevant

In certain areas, taxability is not affected by the existence or nonexistence of a sound business purpose. Instances of this are taxability as constructive dividends of corporate distributions where there was no intent to distribute earnings;[84] sales to establish a tax gain or loss;[85] personal holding company status where the motivation for creation of the corporation may have been the operation of a business and not tax avoidance;[86] loss on transfer of securities to a related party at fair market value;[87] reallocation of income or expenses in a transaction between parties under common control, which transaction is at less than arm's length;[88] redemption of part of a major shareholder's stock at a time when the corporation has earnings and profits;[89] corporate spin-offs or split-ups where the five-year requirement of active conduct of the business has not been met;[90] deductibility of charitable contributions;[91] and where multiple trusts are created and the progressive income tax structure of a single trust is thus mitigated, a business purpose test for plural entities is not necessary.[92]

Principal Purpose

Except in instances where a business purpose is irrelevant, the existence of a business purpose customarily serves to ensure the validity of a transaction, regardless of the mathematical weighing of business and nonbusiness purposes which may coexist in the same transaction. But in a few clearly defined areas, the taxpayer must show that the *principal purpose* of the transaction was business as opposed to tax avoidance.

In the case of acquisition of control of a corporation where the principal purpose is evasion or avoidance of Federal income tax by securing the benefit of a deduction, credit, or other allowance, the Internal Revenue Service may disallow the deduction.[93] A common example occurs where control of a corporation which has a net operating loss carry-over is acquired. If the principal purpose of the acquisition was tax avoidance, it is immaterial that there also were valid business reasons for the transaction.[94]

Ordinarily, any redemption of shares by a corporation at a time when it has earnings and profits will be treated as a dividend. One of the exceptions to this rule is complete termination of a shareholder's interest in the corporation. But this exception does not apply where a shareholder reacquires stock other than by bequest within the next ten years, unless he can establish that the transaction did not have as one of its principal purposes the avoidance of Federal income tax.[95]

A foreign corporation cannot be a party to a tax-free reorganization unless it is established that the transaction has not been entered into pursuant to a plan having as one of its principal purposes the avoidance of Federal income taxes.[96] The principal purpose for use of a foreign subsidiary by a United States corporation was found to be non-tax where that subsidiary desired to employ lower-priced foreign labor on contracts outside of the country and there would have been "difficulties" had a United States company made such arrangements.[97]

If a shareholder disposes of stock received as a nontaxable stock dividend at a time when the corporation had earnings and profits, the portion of his gain which is equivalent to his share of these earnings and profits will have ordinary income status unless he proves that his principal purpose was not tax avoidance.[98]

Sometimes, the doctrine of *principal purpose* is applied even where the Internal Revenue Code does not specifically so provide. Where several purposes exist as to the motivation for undertaking an expenditure, the primary one may be decisive in determining its deductibility.[99] Thus, where an individual seeks to deduct the cost of attending law school, the test is what his primary purpose was—for example, serving the requirements of his present employment, seeking to qualify himself for a better position, or personal gratification.[100] Thus, the deduction was allowed where an employee's primary purpose was to retain his position.[101]

Tax Awareness as Intent

If a person is demonstrably aware that Federal income taxes can be saved by casting a transaction in a certain form, does this imply that his purpose in selecting that form was tax avoidance rather than commercial? In holding that a corporation with losses could not be included in a consolidated Federal income tax return filed by its purchaser, the court noted that the chief stockholder of the purchasing corporation had made his offer only after consultation with his tax advisor.[102] In supporting positions adverse to those of the taxpayer, some courts have, for example, observed that a certain resolution was passed because "the accountant requested that the board of directors adopt a resolution," [103] or that a corporation's accountant suggested and drafted a gift resolution.[104] One court ruled in favor of the taxpayer since a transaction had been conceived by the taxpayer's regular attorney, not by its tax advisor.[105]

Where earnings have accumulated beyond the reasonable needs of the business, it is still permissible for the taxpayer to show that even though knowledge of the tax savings to the shareholders was in the directors' minds when the dividend policy was decided upon, such knowledge did not contribute to the decision to accumulate earnings.[106]

Establishment of the Business Purpose

A sound business purpose must not only have existed in the taxable year, but the taxpayer must show that he knew about it and was actuated by it.[107] Thus, evidence to support a sound business purpose was not persuasive where the decision to carry out the transaction and the terms for it had been agreed to before the purpose came into being.[108]

The motive or purpose of a taxpayer at the time a transaction took place must be considered. Subsequent knowledge retrospectively applied is not sufficient.[109]

Request for Ruling

A taxpayer request to the Internal Revenue Service for a ruling must contain certain specified information, including a full and precise statement of the business reasons for the transaction in question.[110]

NOTES

1. *Helvering v. National Grocery Company*, 304 U.S. 282 (1938).
2. *Nadalin et al. v. United States*, 304 F.2d 431 (Ct. Cl., 1966).
3. *Illinois Merchants Trust Co.*, 4 B.T.A. 103 (1926).
4. *Kennecott Copper Corporation v. United States*, 374 F.2d 275 (Ct. Cl., 1965).
5. *Evans et al. v. Dudley et al.*, 188 F. Supp. 9 (D.C., W.D. Pa., 1960), *aff'd*, 295 F.2d 713 (3d Cir., 1961).
6. *National Carbide Corporation et al. v. Commissioner*, 336 U.S. 422 (1949).
7. *The Humko Co.*, T.C. Memo., Docket Nos. 112235 and 75 (entered December 11, 1943).
8. *Commissioner v. Wilson et al.*, 353 F.2d 194 (9th Cir., 1965).
9. *Irvine K. Furman et al.*, 45 T.C. 360 (1966), *aff'd*, 381 F.2d 22 (5th Cir., 1967).
10. *A.B.C.D. Lands, Inc.*, 41 T.C. 840 (1964).
11. *Stephens, Inc. v. United States*, 321 F. Supp. 1159 (D.C., E.D. Ark., 1970).
12. *Murphy Logging Co. et al. v. United States*, 378 F.2d 222 (9th Cir., 1967); *Zilkla & Sons, Inc. et al.*, 52 T.C. 607 (1969).
13. *The Reuben H. Donnelley Corporation v. United States*, 257 F. Supp. 747 (D.C., S.D. N.Y., 1966).
14. *House Beautiful Homes, Inc. et al. v. Commissioner*, 405 F.2d 61 (10th Cir., 1968).
15. *Markham et al. v. United States*, 245 F. Supp. 505 (D.C., S.D. N.Y., 1965).
16. *Von's Investment Co., Ltd.*, 39 B.T.A. 114 (1939), *aff'd*, 111 F.2d 440 (9th Cir., 1940).
17. *United States v. The Donruss Company*, 390 U.S. 1023 (1969).
18. *Meyer et al. v. United States*, 247 F. Supp. 939 (D.C., Mass., 1965), *aff'd*, 362 F.2d 264 (1st Cir., 1966).

19. *John G. Stoll Estate et al.*, 38 T.C. 223 (1962).
20. *Fred F. Fischer*, T.C. Memo., Docket No. 8737 (entered May 8, 1947).
21. Revenue Ruling 56-117, 1956-1 CB 180.
22. *Mary Archer W. Morris Trust*, 42 T.C. 779 (1964), *aff'd*, 367 F.2d 794 (4th Cir., 1966).
23. *Buffalo Meter Company*, 10 T.C. 83 (1948).
24. I.R.C. Section 1221(1).
25. *S.E.C. Corporation v. United States*, 140 F. Supp. 717 (D.C., S.D. N.Y., 1956), *aff'd*, 241 F.2d 416 (2d Cir., 1957).
26. *Sylvester A. Lowery*, T.C. Memo. 1964-30 (filed February 10, 1964), *aff'd*, 335 F.2d 680 (3d Cir., 1964).
27. *Kaltreider v. Commissioner*, 255 F.2d 833 (3d Cir., 1958).
28. *Eline Realty Company*, 35 T.C. 1 (1960).
29. *Ralph W. Simmers and Son, Inc.*, T.C. Memo. 1968-150 (filed July 16, 1968).
30. *American Can Co. et al. v. Commissioner et al.*, 317 F.2d 604 (2d Cir., 1963).
31. *S.E.C. Corporation v. United States*, 241 F.2d 416 (2d Cir., 1957).
32. I.R.C. Section 165(c)(2).
33. *Joseph V. Curran et al.*, T.C. Memo. 1970-160 (filed June 18, 1970).
34. *Goldsborough v. Burnet*, 46 F.2d 432 (2d Cir., 1931).
35. *Howell et al. v. Commissioner*, 332 F.2d 428 (3d Cir., 1964).
36. *Nat Tully Semel*, T.C. Memo. 1965-232 (filed August 27, 1965).
37. *Porter v. Commissioner*, 437 F.2d 39 (2d Cir., 1970).
38. I.R.C. Section 183.
39. I.R.C. Section 183(e).
40. *Joseph H. Bridges*, 39 T.C. 1064 (1963), *aff'd*, 325 F.2d 180 (4th Cir., 1964).
41. *Knetsch v. United States*, 364 U.S. 361 (1960).
42. *Gounares Bros. & Co., Inc. v. United States*, 185 F. Supp. 794 (D.C., S.D. Ala., 1960), *rev'd and rem'd'd on another issue*, 292 F.2d 79 (5th Cir., 1961).
43. *Delta Plastics Corporation*, 54 T.C. 1287 (1970).
44. *Ortmayer et al. v. Commissioner*, 265 F.2d 848 (7th Cir., 1959).
45. *Cuyuna Realty Company v. United States*, 382 F.2d 298 (Ct. Cl., 1967).
46. *The 1661 Corporation v. Tomlinson*, 247 F. Supp. 936 (D.C., M.D. Fla., 1965), *aff'd*, 377 F.2d 291 (5th Cir., 1967).
47. *Wisconsin Cheeseman, Inc. v. United States*, 388 F.2d 420 (7th Cir., 1968).
48. *Sammons v. United States*, 433 F.2d 728 (5th Cir., 1970).
49. *Sachs v. Commissioner*, 277 F.2d 879 (8th Cir., 1960).
50. *Gurtman et al. v. United States*, 237 F. Supp. 533 (D.C., N.J., 1965).
51. *Keefe v. Cote*, 213 F.2d 651 (1st Cir., 1954).
52. *Heman et al. v. Commissioner*, 283 F.2d 227 (8th Cir., 1960).
53. *United States v. Davis et al.*, 397 U.S. 301 (1970).
54. *S & A Company v. United States*, 218 F. Supp. 677 (D.C., Minn., 1963), *aff'd*, 338 F.2d 629 (8th Cir., 1964).
55. *Desilu Productions, Inc.*, T.C. Memo. 1965-307 (filed November 20, 1965).
56. *See* I.R.C. Section 1250(d).
57. *Oberman Manufacturing Company*, 47 T.C. 471 (1967).
58. *Herman Barron et al.*, T.C. Memo. 1963-315 (filed November 29, 1963).
59. *Custer Robinson*, T.C. Memo., Docket No. 28184 (entered June 19, 1951).
60. *Wilton Bentley*, T.C. Memo., Docket No. 32170 (entered December 11, 1952).
61. *Orrin W. Fox et al.*, 50 T.C. 813 (1968).
62. *Hughes v. United States*, 241 F. Supp. 677 (D.C., S.D. Ohio, 1965).
63. *Panhandle State Bank*, 39 T.C. 813 (1963).
64. Regulations Section 1.162-15(c).
65. *United States v. Gotcher et al.*, 401 F.2d 118 (5th Cir., 1968).
66. *Allen J. McDonnell*, T.C. Memo. 1968-18 (filed January 29, 1968).
67. *United States v. Disney et al.*, 413 F.2d 783 (9th Cir., 1969).

68. *Osterreich v. Commissioner*, 226 F.2d 798 (9th Cir., 1955).

69. *Albritton et al. v. Commissioner*, 248 F.2d 49 (5th Cir., 1957).

70. *Arlington Bowling Corporation*, T.C. Memo. 1959-201 (filed October 26, 1959).

71. *Hogg et al. v. Allen*, 105 F. Supp. 12 (D.C., M.D. Ga., 1952), *aff'd sub nomine Edwards v. Hogg*, 214 F.2d 640 (5th Cir., 1954).

72. *Weather-Seal, Inc.*, T.C. Memo. 1963-102 (filed April 8, 1963).

73. *Hagan et al. v. United States*, 221 F. Supp. 248 (D.C., W.D. Ark., 1963).

74. *Helvering v. Community Bond and Mortgage Corporation*, 74 F.2d 727 (2d Cir., 1935).

75. *Missiquoi Corporation*, 37 T.C. 791 (1962).

76. *Raymond M. Cassidy*, T.C. Memo., Docket No. 24110 (entered June 15, 1951).

77. *Alcorn Wholesale Co. et al.*, 16 T.C. 75 (1951).

78. *McCarthy et al. v. United States*, 232 F. Supp. 605 (D.C., Mass., 1964).

79. *Commissioner v. Newman*, 159 F.2d 848 (2d Cir., 1947).

80. *Collins, Jr. et al. v. Tomlinson*, D.C., M.D. Fla., 1963.

81. *Sydney J. Carter Estate*, T.C. Memo. 1970-305 (filed November 2, 1970).

82. *Weyenberg Shoe Manufacturing Company*, T.C. Memo. 1964-322 (filed December 17, 1964).

83. *Loewy Drug Company of Baltimore City v. United States*, 356 F.2d 928 (4th Cir., 1966).

84. *Sammons v. United States*, 433 F.2d 728 (5th Cir., 1970).

85. *Sun Properties, Inc. v. United States*, 220 F.2d 171 (5th Cir., 1955).

86. *American Package Corporation v. Commissioner*, 125 F.2d 413 (4th Cir., 1942).

87. *Dillard Paper Company*, 42 T.C. 588 (1964), *aff'd*, 341 F.2d 897 (4th Cir., 1965).

88. *Philipp Brothers Chemicals, Inc.* (Md.), 52 T.C. 240 (1969), *aff'd*, 435 F.2d 53 (2d Cir., 1970).

89. *United States v. Davis et al.*, 397 U.S. 301 (1970).

90. *Lloyd Boettger et al.*, 51 T.C. 324 (1968).

91. *Orr et al. v. United States*, 343 F.2d 553 (5th Cir., 1965).

92. *Estelle Morris Trusts et al.*, 51 T.C. 20 (1968), *aff'd*, 367 F.2d 794 (4th Cir., 1970).

93. I.R.C. Section 269(a).

94. *Meridan Corporation v. United States*, 253 F. Supp. 636 (D.C., S.D. N.Y., 1966).

95. I.R.C. Section 302(c)(2)(B).

96. I.R.C. Section 367(a).

97. *Nat Harrison Associates, Inc. et al.*, 42 T.C. 601 (1964).

98. I.R.C. Section 306(b)(4).

99. *Sandt v. Commissioner*, 303 F.2d 111 (3d Cir., 1962).

100. *Ronald F. Weiszmann et al.*, 52 T.C. 1106 (1969).

101. *Williams et al. v. United States*, 238 F. Supp. 351 (D.C., S.D. N.Y., 1965).

102. *R. P. Collins & Company v. United States*, 303 F.2d 142 (1st Cir., 1962).

103. *Sarfert Hosiery Mills, Inc.*, T.C. Memo., Docket No. 9512 (entered November 13, 1947).

104. *Evans v. Commissioner*, 330 F.2d 518 (6th Cir., 1964).

105. *The Esrenco Truck Company*, T.C. Memo. 1963-72 (filed March 13, 1963).

106. *United States v. The Donruss Company*, 390 U.S. 1023 (1969).

107. *The Smoot Sand & Gravel Corporation v. Commissioner*, 241 F.2d 197 (4th Cir., 1957).

108. *General Guaranty Mortgage Co., Inc. v. Tomlinson*, 335 F.2d 518 (5th Cir., 1964).

109. *Arthur Cronin Estate et al. v. Commissioner*, 164 F.2d 561 (6th Cir., 1947).

110. Regulations Section 601.201(e)(2).

CHAPTER 21

What Happens When
a Major Stockholder Dies

The Alternatives

When an important shareholder in a closely-held corporation dies, his executor or estate has these principal alternatives:

(1) *Keep the stock.* But cash may have to be raised for the Federal estate tax and for the immediate needs of beneficiaries.

(2) *Sell the stock.* But bringing in outside interests may create an impossible operational situation. Sales of stock to certain related parties could bring about a loss which is not recognized for tax purposes. (See chapter 18, Who, What, Where.) The consolidation of shares in the hands of the existing shareholders or their families could create a personal holding company. (See chapter 2, Corporations and Other Forms of Conducting Business.)

(3) *Liquidate the corporation in order to raise funds.* But most corporations are worth more alive than dead. And liquidation could create an unfortunate situation for the estate, the remaining stockholders, the employees, and possibly the creditors.

The injection of a new owner of a decedent's interest in a corporation would certainly complicate matters in the case of most closely-held organizations.[1] Many closely-held corporations are worth substantially more to those who are able and anxious to manage them than to passive investors who look only to prospective dividends for a return upon their investments. This sort of situation can lead to demands for dividends without appropriate regard for the needs of the corporation.[2]

Realization upon Decedent's Shares

Liquidation of a corporation may seem to be a necessary step where the directors are pressured by the estate of a deceased principal stockholder to make cash available.[3] Yet greater value could be realized from the sale of most businesses as going concerns than from liquidation.[4]

If the decedent's family retains his stock, the corporation's continued existence could be jeopardized by the interference of inexperienced co-owners.[5] Or the executor may believe that one or more corporate officers have been doing a poor job; this could lead to unworkable animosity or even litigation.[6]

A sale of the decedent's shares might be the best solution for the estate, the surviving shareholders, the employees, and the corporation itself. But it can be difficult to arrive at a price. Closely held corporate stock cannot be valued with the standard yardsticks. Financial data are important only to the extent that they furnish a basis for an informed judgment of future performance.[7] An unlisted closely held stock usually is less attractive than a similar stock listed on an exchange to which the investing public has ready access. While in some very rare circumstances an unlisted stock of truly exceptional quality may not suffer from lack of marketability, usually marketability is important in determining fair market value.[8]

Another deterrent to investors is uncertainty as to what the enterprise really is worth. Because the company is closely held, records have probably been kept informally. There may never have been an audit by a truly independent certified public accountant.

It is difficult enough to set a value upon the stock of a closely held corporation. The problem is infinitely more difficult when the decedent's shares represented a minority interest in the corporation. Unlisted stock representing a minority interest in a family-controlled or close corporation has limited marketability.[9] The fact that the stock represents a minority interest in a corporation dominated by a single family or other group serves to depress its value.[10]

Not without reason, a potential buyer of a minority interest in a closely held corporation might fear that the majority shareholders would "gang up" against him and that his ideas and experience would be ignored. In one case, the sale of a 20 percent stock interest in a closely held corporation at public auction produced no bids except from the seller's wife. In addition, the sale to her at a loss was not recognized for tax purposes, as she was a related party and thus the transaction was in a category of those where losses automatically are disallowed.[11]

Buy-Out Agreements

The multiple problems of putting the decedent's estate or family in funds, obtaining a viable valuation for stock, financing payment of the Federal estate tax, and assuring the continued existence of a corporation may be solved by the single mechanism of a *buy-out agreement* which is properly funded.

Many businessmen now anticipate such problems and provide for them through agreements and implementing devices which are designed to be fair to the estate, the enterprise, and the surviving co-venturers.[12]

A buy-out agreement may take either of two forms: under a *buy-and-sell agreement*, the surviving stockholders agree to buy a decedent's shares; under a *stock retirement agreement,* the corporation and one or more shareholders arrange that the corporation will buy up a decedent's shares. Even where there is a buy-and-sell agreement, it may be assigned to the corporation by the participating shareholders, and the corporation will actually redeem its stock from the shareholder who dies.[13]

Even apart from tax considerations, stock redemption arrangements between a closely-held corporation and its stockholders present advantages to both company and stockholders. Continuity of stock control, management, and the concomitant security afforded company personnel and creditors benefit the corporation and are valid business purposes. The assurance of a sale of stock at an agreed upon price where otherwise the stock might be unmarketable also gives comfort to the stockholders.[14] Thus, the sound business purpose that is required in the case of most transactions to assure tax recognition is present. No purpose is more germane to business than its profitable perpetuation, which is the objective of a buy-out agreement.[15] Conceivably, a corporation and its shareholders would also be benefitted by a change of management.

Funding a Buy-Out Agreement

A buy-out agreement may be funded by any method agreed upon or on a strictly *ad hoc* basis. Shareholders may dip into their own fortunes to finance the acquisition of the shares; the funds, however, might not be there when needed. A corporation may utilize its retained earnings for the purpose or it may borrow the necessary money. But corporate accumulations of earnings for this purpose might be characterized as retention beyond the reasonable needs of the business. (See chapter 11, Dividends and the Tax on Accumulated Earnings and the discussion in this chapter under the heading "Redemption of Stock to Pay Death Taxes.") Utilization of surplus for the purpose of redeeming a shareholder's stock might be assailed as a fraud against creditors.

In most circumstances, the best mechanism for funding the buy-out agreement with assurance that the money will be there when needed and without fear of priority claims of other parties is life insurance. Where two or more stockholders enter upon a buy-and-sell agreement, each shareholder may take out insurance on the life of the other shareholder; the proceeds payable upon the death of a shareholder would be used to pay for his stock. Or each shareholder could take out insurance on his own life, the policies being assigned to all the shareholders collectively or to a trustee. Under a stock redemption agreement, the corporation would take out the insurance on the lives of each of the participants.

Where there is a buy-and-sell agreement for the purchase of the shares of a stockholder who dies, there may be a supplementary agreement which not only recites how the purchase is to be financed but also requires that the insurance proceeds be used for that purpose.[16]

Where a corporation purchases life insurance on the lives of its stockholders, the proceeds of which are to be used in payment for the stock of any shareholder, the premiums on the insurance are not treated as income to any stockholder—even though he has the right to designate a beneficiary—if his beneficiary's right to receive the proceeds is conditioned upon the transfer of his stock to the corporation. The payment of the premiums by the corporation is merely an independent act by the corporation by which it converts one asset (cash) into another asset (an insurance policy), and such action has no relationship whatsoever to the receipt of income by the stockholders.[17]

If corporation-financed life insurance proceeds are used to redeem the shares of a deceased stockholder, each of the surviving shareholders will automatically have a greater equity in the corporation because the total number of shares outstanding has been reduced. But these benefits operate only to increase the value of the shareholder's stock; they do not give rise to taxable income within the meaning of the Sixteenth Amendment until the corporation makes a distribution to the shareholder or until his stock is sold. There is no authority supporting the proposition that redemption of one shareholder's stock at fair market value constitutes a dividend to the remaining stockholders.[18]

Despite the many advantages to a corporation in having a stock retirement plan funded by life insurance, the insurance premiums the corporation pays are not deductible by it since they are paid for the acquisition of a capital asset—that is, stock.[19]

If a corporation's growing prosperity has increased the value of its stock so that the amount of insurance provided is no longer sufficient, additional insurance or other funding could be provided to supplement the insurance, or a tax-free recapitalization could bring down the value of the voting stock to a level where it is compatible to the insurance protection available. A corporation with one class of voting stock could be recapitalized into voting and nonvoting common stock. The value of the voting stock, which by itself would be significant in a buy-out agreement under most circumstances, could be reduced to as low a figure as desired. Such a procedure also could supply a shareholder with greater flexibility; for example, he could make gifts or charitable contributions in the form of nonvoting stock without diluting his ownership of voting stock.

If a corporation possesses all of the incidents of ownership of insurance on the life of the sole stockholder, the insurance proceeds are included in his gross estate when he dies.[20]

The Buy-Out Price

One of the great advantages of the buy-out technique is that a value of the stock is set for Federal estate tax purposes. The valuation of stock in a closely-held corporation is one of the most difficult and frequently litigated of all tax questions; only rarely has an arm's length sale that would set a fair market value taken place. In the absence of evidence provided by *bona fide* stock sales in the recent past, the Internal Revenue Service may make a finding as to valuation which is quite different from that which the shareholders believe is proper. The burden of proving a more acceptable value is then upon the estate or other interested party. Usually, this burden is difficult to meet in the absence of an arm's length sale.

The buy-out agreement comes to grips with this problem. An actual sale of stock takes place between the estate and the surviving shareholders or the corporation. It is an arm's length sale because at the time the agreement is made no one knows whether he is going to be a buyer (survivor) or seller (decedent). Each stockholder may survive the others; but if he does not, then he wants to be certain that his estate will promptly receive full value for his stock. If he outlives the others, he wants to be certain of ready cash with which to buy the stock owned by the decedent.[21] He also wants the highest price for his stock if his estate is eventually the seller and he wants to pay the lowest price if he is eventually the buyer. Thus, the price ultimately paid is deemed to be a fair one. This is true despite differences in the age and health of the parties.[22]

The stock should be valued in the buy-out agreement according to some self-adjusting formula that will assure validity at some unknown future date or dates. If the price is set inflexibly in the agreement at its value when the agreement is signed, that price may be unrealistic 20 years later when a party dies, and the Internal Revenue Service will disregard the price as a basis for valuation for estate tax purposes. A buy-sell agreement that is binding upon all the parties is not necessarily binding upon the Commissioner of Internal Revenue in fixing valuation for estate tax purposes.[23]

Any standard, objective valuation method may be provided in the buy-out agreement. Thus, the stock may be valued according to net worth at the time of death, according to net worth at the nearest financial statement date, or according to the *pro rata* net value of the assets, the purchase price to be increased or decreased if, in the unanimous opinion of the parties to the arrangement, substantial profit or loss was likely to result from pending contracts or arrangements.[24] Good will should not be overlooked [25] and the valuation formula may call for the book value of the stock plus a good will value to be determined by arbitration.[26] The purchase price may be agreed upon annually by the shareholders or it may be based on billings to certain customers during a specified period, less direct wages.[27] The formula price may be the value ultimately used for Federal estate tax purposes.[28] Actually, this is approaching the problem from the wrong end, for one of the greatest advantages of the formula method is that it establishes a valuation which may be used on the estate tax returns. And it could be several years before the estate and the Internal Revenue Service agree upon the proper figure to be used for this purpose or a court makes its judgment.

Other standard formulæ could be based upon average earnings, to be capitalized at a stipulated rate, for a specified number of years. There also could be a post-death appraisal of the underlying assets or a valuation to be determined by an independent agency or by arbitration.

The existence at death of a valid enforceable option, the exercise of which would compel the executor to sell the decedent's shares at a stipulated price, fixes their value for Federal estate tax purposes.[29] But this rule applies only where the restriction was imposed in settlement of a business problem by persons dealing at arm's length.[30] The specified price is not controlling for estate tax purposes unless the restrictive provision: (1) prevents transfer of the shares during the holder's life at a figure higher than the specified price and (2) grants an option to purchase or requires a transfer at that price on the shareholder's death.[31]

Where there is a buy-out agreement, it may be advisable for the parties to agree in writing that they will not pledge, mortgage, or otherwise encumber the stock.[32] Certain predictable practical difficulties may be avoided if these restrictions are stamped upon the face of the stock certificates.

Other Controls to Keep Stock from Getting into "Outside" Hands

A contract between a corporation and its employees or one among designated employees may provide that shares must be sold back to the corporation (or sold to the other shareholders) on termination of employment at a stipulated price or formula and that, meanwhile, the shares may not be mortgaged, hypothecated, transferred, or subjected to any circumstance which would bring them beyond the control of the other parties to the agreement.[33]

A buy-and-sell agreement may provide that the parties can dispose of stock only by *inter vivos* gifts to family members or by sale to the other parties.[34] Or the shareholders might be required to offer to sell to the corporation or the other stockholders before offering to sell to outsiders.[35]

In order to make restrictions upon the transfer of stock effective, one should give notice of the restrictions to prospective purchasers of the stock. This is sometimes required by state law.

Another device to prevent corporate stock from getting into the hands of outside parties is for the shareholders to adopt a policy, at a time when they are still compatible, of having all the voting stock placed in a voting trust to be voted by trustees designated for the purpose.[36]

Anticipating the Implementation of a Buy-Out Agreement

Even if the shareholders of a corporation have a buy-and-sell agreement which is to take effect at the death of the first party to die, this arrangement may not prove financially feasible as circumstances change. One shareholder may feel that for some reason, perhaps because he is younger, he will become the buyer. But under the corporation's indicated growth pattern, he may believe that the value of the stock at the time of the death of the other shareholder or shareholders will be so high that he could not finance acquisition of the stock. So the worried stockholder may demand that the other parties presently sell their shares to him or buy him out.[37]

Are Buy-Out Agreements "in Contemplation of Death"?

For Federal estate tax purposes, any transaction within three years of a decedent's death is presumed to be in contemplation of death unless the executor can establish to the contrary.[38] This means that property covered by a transfer or other transaction will be included in the decedent's estate. If a buy-and-sell agreement between the shareholders of a family-owned corporation is entered into at a time when the health of one of the parties is failing, this may create an inference that the agreement actually was testamentary in character and, thus, a device for the avoidance of Federal estate taxes.[39] But this presumption may be refuted by showing that the purpose for the agreement was not related to thoughts of imminent death, but rather to keeping control of a business for present operational purposes. Under such circumstances and in the absence of an actual transfer of property by the decedent in his lifetime, this would not be characterized as a transaction in contemplation of death.[40]

Dividend Implications of Redemption

Ordinarily, if a corporation with accumulated earnings and profits redeems a stockholder's shares, there is a strong implication that the transaction was essentially equivalent to the payment of a dividend. But there is no dividend implied if a shareholder's interest is completely terminated by the redemption.[41] For this purpose, an individual is deemed to own shares actually owned by certain members of his family. These "constructive ownership" rules do not apply if each of five tests is met: (1) the person whose shares are redeemed retains no interest in the corporation except as a creditor; (2) no shares are reacquired within ten years except by bequest; (3) notice of any reacquisition is given to the Internal Revenue Service; (4) none of the redeemed shares was acquired from a related party within the past ten years; and (5) any shares that were transferred to related parties within ten years are redeemed at the same time. (Related parties for the purpose of these requirements are one's spouse, children, grandchildren, and ancestors.)

Stock owned by a beneficiary is deemed to be owned by the executor for this purpose.[42] Thus, if one wishes a complete redemption of stock to be without dividend implications, it is necessary that he redeem not only the decedent's stock, but also that of any beneficiaries of his stock. A person is not a beneficiary for this purpose if he has received all that he is entitled to, if he no longer has a claim against the estate, and if he is not likely to have to repay anything to the estate.[43]

If an individual is contractually responsible to purchase the stock of another individual and the former arranges for the corporation itself to buy up its own shares, this represents a constructive dividend to the individual primarily responsible for buying the stock. The corporation provided him with an economic benefit by relieving him of his personal obligation to buy the stock.[44] But there was no constructive dividend to a shareholder where his obligation regarding the stock was to "purchase or cause to be purchased." [45]

Redemption of Stock to Pay Death Taxes

A decedent's shares may be purchased by the issuing corporation under a buy-out agreement or otherwise without dividend implications if the transaction qualifies as a redemption of stock to pay death taxes.[46] Dividend implications are inapplicable to the extent that the proceeds of the redemption are used to pay Federal and state death taxes and administrative expenses of the estate. For this purpose, the shares need not actually be "redeemed" in the sense of being retired by the corporation; they may be held as treasury stock or reissued to other parties.[47]

This preferential treatment applies only if the value of the company's stock included in the decedent's gross estate comprises more than 35 percent of the value of the gross estate or 50 percent of the value of the taxable estate. If stock in two or more corporations is held to the extent of more than 75 percent of the value of each, the corporations may be aggregated for the purpose of applying these percentages.

A certain amount of pre-death planning is necessary. The corporation must have enough funds to buy the stock without interfering with regular operational requirements. Life insurance may be provided for this purpose.

Customarily, courts tend to look askance at a corporation's claimed need to redeem its own shares in the event of a chief stockholder's death, particularly where there is no evidence that there were dissenting or competing shareholder factions which threatened corporate health. Thus, the accumulated earnings tax may be applied in the case of earnings retained to redeem shares of a decedent.[48] But in the case of a redemption of stock to pay death taxes, which redemption meets the tests just described, earnings which have been accumulated by the corporation may be deemed part of the permissibly retained funds for the reasonable needs of the business.[49]

Taxability of Insurance Proceeds

The proceeds of a life insurance policy matured by death are not taxable income.[50] However, proceeds in excess of the cost of the policy are taxable where the policy had been acquired from a third party for consideration.[51]

Where Life Insurance Is Unobtainable

If one or more of the parties subject to a buy-out agreement is uninsurable because of health or age factors, the arrangement could be funded by any other procedure (such as a sinking fund). But this involves grave elements of risk until funding is complete.

Frequently, the life of a supposedly uninsurable person can be insured by means of life insurance issued on a high-risk premium basis. This can be very expensive. But a buy-out agreement which is not funded by life insurance can be even more costly in the long run.

Alternatively, insurance that was taken out on the life of a stockholder when he was still insurable can be transferred to the corporation in which he is a shareholder or officer without triggering the rule that provides that proceeds of insurance which have been transferred are tax-free only to the extent of the consideration paid.[52]

Insurance Used to Support the Market

Life insurance proceeds or other buy-out agreement pay-outs are useful for a shareholder who wishes to buy up the shares of a deceased stockholder in a closely held corporation. They are also useful where a major shareholder in a publicly held corporation dies. Upon his death, the shares could be sold off in the market place to the detriment of a company which has loans secured by its own stock or which is contemplating the issuance of additional shares in the future. The pay-out could be used to support stock values until the first shock of the officer's death has worn off.

Payments by a Corporation to Its Shareholders

Life insurance proceeds received by a corporation as beneficiary do not retain their nontaxable character when distributed to shareholders, but are taxable as dividends to the extent of earnings and profits available for the payment of dividends.[53]

Nonvoting Stock

While a buy-out agreement usually concerns voting stock, it may be desirable to eliminate the decedent's family from any future interest in the corporation, or the family or estate may require additional funds for other forms of their property. Thus, a buy-sell agreement may also cover a corporation's preferred stock.[54]

Disability Insurance

One rarely finds a buy-out agreement which does not cover the *death* of a shareholder, particularly where the arrangement is funded by insurance. But it may be just as important to deal with a shareholder who becomes totally disabled. From the point of view of the stockholder and his family, demands for cash may be very compelling. Thus, a buy-out agreement may include a provision for total disability and be funded in part by disability insurance.

Capital Status

A stockholder's right under a buy-out agreement is a capital asset.[55] Litigation expenses to determine rights under a buy-out agreement are not deductible as ordinary and necessary expenses or as expenses in connection with the maintenance, conservation, or management of property. Such expenses are capital in nature, being related to stock transactions.[56]

NOTES

1. *See Obermer v. United States,* 238 F. Supp. 29 (D.C., Hawaii, 1964).
2. *Mountain State Steel Foundries, Inc. et al. v. Commissioner et al.,* 284 F.2d 737 (4th Cir., 1960).
3. *See Macabe Company et al.,* 42 T.C. 1105 (1964).
4. *See Halby Chemical Corporation, Inc. et al. v. United States,* 180 Ct. Cl. 584 (Ct. Cl., 1967).
5. *See Salvatori et al. v. United States,* D.C., S.D. Cal., 1966.
6. *See Richard Rubin et al.,* 51 T.C. 251 (1968), *rev'd and rem'd'd on another issue,* 429 F.2d 650 (2d Cir., 1970).
7. *J. Luther Snyder Estate v. United States,* 285 F.2d 857 (4th Cir., 1961).
8. *Sidney L. Katz Estate,* T.C. Memo. 1968-171 (filed July 5, 1968).
9. *Betty Hansen et al.,* T.C. Memo., Docket Nos. 29419-21 (entered July 20, 1952).
10. *Sidney L. Katz Estate,* T.C. Memo. 1968-171 (filed July 5, 1968).
11. *Merritt, Sr. et al. v. Commissioner,* 400 F.2d 417 (5th Cir., 1968).
12. *Mountain State Steel Foundries, Inc. et al. v. Commissioner et al.,* 284 F.2d 737 (4th Cir., 1960).
13. Revenue Ruling 69-608, 1969-2 CB 42.
14. *Sanders et al. v. Fox,* 253 F.2d 855 (10th Cir., 1958).
15. *John G. Stoll Estate et al.,* 38 T.C. 223 (1962); *Orville B. Littick Estate et al.,* 31 T.C. 181 (1958).
16. *First National Bank of Birmingham v. United States,* 358 F.2d 625 (5th Cir., 1966).
17. Revenue Ruling 59-184, 1959-1 CB 65.
18. Revenue Ruling 59-286, 1959-2 CB 103.
19. Revenue Ruling 70-117, 1970-1 CB 30.
20. Regulations Section 20.2042-1(c)(2).
21. *First National Bank of Birmingham v. United States,* 358 F.2d 625 (5th Cir., 1966).
22. *Orville B. Littick Estate,* 31 T.C. 181 (1958).
23. *George Marshall Trammell Estate,* 18 T.C. 662 (1952).
24. *First National Bank of Birmingham v. United States,* 358 F.2d 625 (5th Cir., 1966).
25. Revenue Ruling 157, 1953-2 CB 255.
26. *Brown v. Commissioner,* 95 F.2d 184 (6th Cir., 1938).
27. *See Lewis & Taylor, Inc.,* T.C. Memo. 1969-82 (filed April 22, 1969).
28. *See Davis et al. v. United States,* 277 F. Supp. 602 (D.C., W.D. Pa., 1967).
29. *Lomb v. Sugden,* 82 F.2d 166 (2d Cir., 1936).
30. *Commissioner v. Bensel,* 100 F.2d 639 (3d Cir., 1938).
31. *Baltimore National Bank et al. v. United States,* 136 F. Supp. 642 (D.C., Md., 1955).
32. *See First National Bank of Birmingham v. United States,* 358 F.2d 625 (5th Cir., 1966).
33. *Sullivan et al. v. United States,* 363 F.2d 824 (8th Cir., 1966).
34. *See Lake v. United States,* D.C., E.D. Texas, 1968, *aff'd,* 406 F.2d 941 (5th Cir., 1969).
35. *Henry C. Goss et al.,* T.C. Memo. 1963-242 (filed September 10, 1963).
36. *See Howard P. Blount et al.,* 51 T.C. 1023 (1969), *aff'd,* 425 F.2d 921 (2d Cir., 1969).

37. *See Farmers and Merchants Investment Co.,* T.C. Memo. 1970-161 (filed June 22, 1970).
38. I.R.C. Section 2035.
39. *Slocum v. United States,* 256 F. Supp. 753 (D.C., S.D. N.Y., 1966).
40. *Lionel Weil Estate,* 22 T.C. 1267 (1954).
41. I.R.C. Section 302(b)(3).
42. I.R.C. Section 318(a)(2)(A).
43. Revenue Ruling 60-18, 1960-1 CB 145.
44. *Sullivan et al. v. United States,* 363 F.2d 724 (8th Cir., 1966).
45. *S. K. Ames, Inc.,* 46 B.T.A. 1020 (1942).
46. I.R.C. Section 303.
47. *United States v. Lake,* 406 F.2d 941 (5th Cir., 1969).
48. *See Faber Cement Block Co., Inc.,* 50 T.C. 317 (1968).
49. I.R.C. Section 537(a)(2).
50. I.R.C. Section 101(a)(1).
51. *See United States v. Supplee-Biddle Hardware Co.,* 265 U.S. 189 (1924).
52. I.R.C. Section 101(a)(1)(B).
53. Revenue Ruling 71-79, I.R.B. 1971-7, 14.
54. *See Arthur D. McDonald et al.,* 52 T.C. 82 (1969).
55. *Turzillo v. Commissioner,* 346 F.2d 884 (6th Cir., 1965).
56. *Ransburg v. United States,* 440 F.2d 1140 (10th Cir., 1971).

CHAPTER 22

Elections and Their Consequences

What Is an Election?

Frequently, a taxpayer has the right to elect one of several different courses of action. Once he has clearly exercised his choice by some act or failure to act, the election is binding on him. This may be true despite an oversight, error of judgment, miscalculation, or unawareness of tax consequences.[1]

This chapter will discuss the circumstances under which a taxpayer is bound by the choices he makes and those under which he may not be bound on the theory that he has made an irrevocable election.

Where the statute or the implementing regulations specify the manner in which an election is to be made, there is no election unless it appears that those requirements are met.[2] Where a specific form is prescribed for making an election, an election in any other manner is not acceptable.[3] But in the absence of any specific mode set up in the Internal Revenue Code or the Treasury Regulations, the term "election" means that a taxpayer must make a choice and manifest that choice in some overt manner—that is, any reasonable manner.[4]

Consequences of Election

Once a taxpayer elects to use a particular method of reporting income or deductions, he may not be able to use another method simply because he subsequently realizes that he has not chosen the method most advantageous to him.[5] Even though the taxpayer was put to a hard choice, he is bound by his election.[6]

Time for Making the Election

The time when an election is to be made may depend on statute or regulation.

An election may not be effective if made prematurely or if the right to make an election is lost because it was not exercised within the required time. An election made even one day late may fail.[7] An election can be too late if delivered personally one day after the critical date even if a timely mailing made one day earlier would have arrived later.[8] An election was ruled tardy when forms were deposited in a post office in the early evening of the last day for filing and the postmark was 3.A.M. of the following day.[9] Where an election requires an affirmative act by the taxpayer (such as the filing of a return or other form), he has the burden of showing that the filing was in fact made on time.[10]

If an election has to be made on a timely tax return, a tardy return will mean that no effective election has been made even though the taxpayer did not then realize that his election was not timely.[11]

Amended Returns

Where an election is to be made by a taxpayer upon his first tax return or upon the first tax return after the occurrence of a specified event, the election may be made or changed upon a timely amendment of the return.[12] An election which may be exercised validly only upon a timely tax return may be filed upon an amended return filed within the period provided by the tax law for filing the original return.[13]

A timely tax return election to use the last-in, first-out inventory method (LIFO) can be revoked before the final date for making the election.[14] An election as to an accounting period on a taxpayer's first return can be revised prior to the running of the statute of limitations on that return.[15]

An election to use the installment method of reporting gain may be made upon an amended return which is filed prior to the final date for filing an income tax return.[16] So where an Internal Revenue Service audit revealed a casual and unreported sale of real estate, the taxpayer could make an election to report this sale on the installment method since the statute of limitations applicable to the tax return had not yet run and the transaction qualified for installment reporting.[17]

An amended return must be filed within the required time. It is ineffective if filed too late even though the late filing resulted from ill-advised opposition or representations on the part of the Internal Revenue Service.[18]

The right to make an election may be lost even though the failure to make a timely election results from reliance upon an Internal Revenue Agent; the government is not bound by an erroneous interpretation of the law made by its subordinate agent.[19]

Extension of Time
for Making an Election

The Commissioner of Internal Revenue may, upon a showing of good cause, grant a reasonable extension of the time fixed by Treasury Regulations for the making of an election provided three conditions are met:

(1) The time for making the election is not expressly prescribed by law.

(2) Request for the extension is filed with the Commissioner before the time fixed by the regulations for making the election expires or within such time thereafter as the Commissioners may consider reasonable under the circumstances.

(3) It is shown to the satisfaction of the Commissioner that the granting of the extension will not jeopardize the interests of the government.[20]

Where the authority to grant an extension lies within the Commissioner's discretion, the court will not interfere even though the Commissioner might have taken a more lenient view on the facts presented.[21]

Selection of Business Form

While one is entitled to choose the form in which he does business, even if his choice is based solely on Federal income tax considerations, the Internal Revenue Service may ignore the form if it lacks business or economic substance.[22] So, if a corporation is to be recognized for Federal income tax purposes, it must do some "business" within the ordinary meaning of the word.[23]

Where a taxpayer elects to do business in corporate form, it must accept disadvantages that go with that form. Thus, even if a corporation is wholly owned by one individual and its records might tend to incriminate him, any claim to personal privilege under the Fifth Amendment becomes unavailable as a corporation does not have the right to remain silent.[24]

If a tax-exempt corporation foregoes its exempt status and becomes a regular taxpaying corporation, it is nonetheless the same corporation. Thus, an election which was binding upon the corporation when it enjoyed tax-exempt status is still binding on it when it yields its tax-exempt status, and no new election is possible without the consent of the Internal Revenue Service.[25]

Subchapter S Corporation

Under appropriate circumstances and under carefully circumscribed conditions, an election may be made under Subchapter S of the Code for corporate earnings to be taxed only at the shareholder level. (See chapter 2, Corporations and Other Forms of Conducting Business.) The election must be made by all of the shareholders. Even after a Subchapter S election is made, the corporation is still the same entity, and, therefore, an accounting or other election made prior to the attainment of Subchapter S status still is binding.[26]

Stock of a Subchapter S corporation issued to an individual in a community property state was deemed to be owned to the extent of 50 percent by each spouse. Thus, each spouse should have filed an election to make

Subchapter S status available; and where only the husband, the sole stockholder of record, had made an election, election had not been made, by all of the stockholders, as the law requires.[27]

Where an individual purported to transfer 50 percent of the stock of a wholly-owned corporation to his children and then elected to have the corporation as a Subchapter S corporation, all of the corporation's income was taxed to him. The stock transfer lacked reality since he still exercised complete control and management of the corporation for all practical purposes.[28]

The election to be taxed as a Subchapter S corporation, as already has been indicated, must be made by all of the shareholders. This does not mean only shareholders of record. The shareholders of record are not always accountable for tax purposes for the income of the corporation. Many shareholders of record hold only legal title,—for example, as in a fiduciary capacity as agent, or merely as security for payment of a debt. The election also must be made by persons who own the shares beneficially.[29]

Accounting Method

In general, a taxpayer may choose his own accounting method. But if inventories are used, the accrual basis must be used unless otherwise authorized by the Internal Revenue Service.[30]

A taxpayer must obtain the Service's permission to make a substantive change in the accounting method used. But a change from single- to double-entry accounting does not require permission where, for example, income is reported on the accrual basis both before and after the change.[31]

A taxpayer must submit an application for change in accounting method to the Service on *Form 3115* within 180 days after the beginning of the taxable year in which he desires to make the change. A taxpayer may be deemed to have obtained consent for the change merely by filing the application on the proper form and on time. An example would be a properly filed application for a change from the cash method to the accrual method.[32]

A request for a change in accounting method which is made after the 180-day period, but within nine months after the beginning of the taxable year for which the change is requested may nevertheless be considered timely upon a showing of good cause by the taxpayer.[33]

If there is to be a change from the specific charge-off method of accounting for bad debts to the reserve method, an application therefore must similarly be timely made on *Form 3115*. This will be deemed accepted by the Internal Revenue Service unless the taxpayer is advised to the contrary.[34]

Where a cash-basis taxpayer prepays interest in substantial amounts and this results in a material distortion of income for the taxable year, the interest prepayment will be reallocated so that the amount deducted for interest in the taxable year will not result in a material distortion of income.[35]

Accrual of Real Property Taxes

An accrual-basis taxpayer may elect to accrue real property taxes ratably over the period covered by the tax payment. The election may be made without the consent of the Internal Revenue Service for the first taxable year in which the taxpayer incurs this type of tax. The election must be made not later than the filing date of the return, excluding extension periods. The election applies to all real property taxes of the trade, business, or nonbusiness activity for which the election is made. An election to accrue real property taxes ratably is binding upon the taxpayer unless the Service agrees to a change.[36] A change from the ratable method of accruing property taxes to the lump-sum method is a change of accounting and, as such, requires prior approval.

Where consent to accrue real property taxes ratably is necessary, a taxpayer must file a written request for permission within 90 days after the beginning of the taxable year to which the election is first applicable.[37]

Consolidated Returns

An election to file consolidated Federal income tax returns by corporations eligible for such treatment must be exercised at the time the common parent corporation of the companies involved makes its return. For this purpose, the return is considered to have been made on the due date of such return (including any extensions which have been granted), regardless of the fact that the actual date of filing was previous to that. Under no circumstances can the privilege be exercised at any time thereafter.[38]

Wholly-owned Canadian and Mexican subsidiaries which had been formed to comply with local law as to title and operation of the property may be included in a consolidated return, despite the fact that only domestic (United States) corporations ordinarily may be covered in a consolidated return. The inclusion of the Canadian or Mexican subsidiaries in a consolidated return is a binding election as long as consolidated returns are filed.[39]

A consolidated return could not be filed by parent and subsidiary corporations where consents had not been filed by the subsidiaries and all fiscal years were not the same.[40]

The initial filing of a return on a consolidated basis is optional. But once the return is filed, consolidated returns must be filed in all future years unless one of the following circumstances exists: (1) the common parent ceases to be such; (2) permission is obtained from the Service to revert to separate return status; (3) there is an amendment of the Code or Regulations which makes the filing of consolidated returns less advantageous to affiliated groups as a class.[41]

Time for Reporting Income

For a detailed discussion of the elective procedures available for the reporting of income on a deferred basis, such as installment sales, long-term contracts, and deferred payments, see chapter 19.

Inventory

Any method of valuing inventory items is permitted if it clearly and accurately reflects income.[42] A change in inventory method is a change in accounting method and, thus, subject to the same rules as to permission to make a change. Thus, a corporation was not permitted to use the last-in, first-out method although the three proprietorships which had been merged to form the corporation had obtained permission to do so. This was the case because the corporation had not filed an election on its own behalf.[43]

Depreciation

In general, the initial choice of depreciation method is the taxpayer's. It may be adopted without permission, and no formal election is required.[44] But accelerated depreciation methods (such as double-declining balance and sum-of-the-years-digits) may be used only in the case of tangible property having a useful life of three years or more, which was acquired new by the taxpayer.[45]

Any change in the method of computing depreciation requires the consent of the Internal Revenue Service, except that a change from a declining-balance to straight-line method is permitted without consent.[46]

As pointed out in chapter 12, the Asset Depreciation Range System (ADR) came into being in 1971. The use of ADR is optional and an annual election is provided for. In general, an election for a taxable year will apply to all additions of eligible property during the taxable year of election, but not to additions of eligible property in any other taxable year. The election, which is made with the return for the taxable year, may not be revoked or modified for any property included in the election. An election to compute the allowance for depreciation under ADR is an election as to a method of accounting, but the Service's consent to the election will be deemed granted.[47]

A taxpayer may elect not to take salvage into consideration in the case of tangible personal property where salvage does not amount to more than ten percent of the adjusted basis of the property.[48]

A 20 percent additional first year depreciation is allowed on tangible personal property costing not in excess of $10,000 ($20,000 in the case of a married couple filing a joint return). Election for this treatment, which is irrevocable, must be made by the filing date of the return, including extensions.[49] But this additional first year depreciation is not allowed in the absence of proof that an election had been made.[50]

Organizational Expenditures

A corporation may elect to take current deductions for organizational expenses. Such expenses must be: (1) incidental to the creation of the corporation; (2) chargeable to the capital account of the corporation; and (3) of such a character that, if expended incident to the creation of a corporation having a limited life, they would be amortizable over that life.[51] The current deduction is allowed even though the items are reflected on the books as capital expenditures.[52]

Capitalization of Carrying Charges

A taxpayer may elect to capitalize rather than to expense certain taxes and carrying charges. In the case of unimproved and unproductive real property, these include annual taxes, mortgage interest, and other carrying charges. In the case of improved real property, these expenses include interest, payroll taxes, taxes imposed upon the purchase or use of materials, and other necessary expenses in connection with development and construction. In the case of personal property, they include payroll taxes in connection with the transportation and installation of fixed assets to a plant, interest on a loan to purchase such property, and taxes relating to the purchase, use, or consumption of such property. Also included may be other taxes and carrying charges which the Internal Revenue Service feels are chargeable to capital accounts under sound accounting principles.[53]

Election is made by means of a statement attached to the income tax return,[54] but may not be made on a refund claim.[55]

Tax-Free Reorganizations

The consequences of a tax-free reorganization are automatic if a transaction falls within the language and intendment of the statute.[56] But sometimes a taxpayer desires that such consequences should not apply; for example, a loss upon liquidation of an 80 percent controlled subsidiary would not be recognized in a tax-free reorganization. Or there might be carry-overs of accounting treatment in a tax-free reorganization which the taxpayer does not desire.

In order to avoid the tax consequences of a tax-free reorganization, a taxpayer may elect to structure the transaction in such a way that it does not qualify as a tax-free reorganization. But a failure to abide by a requirement imposed by the Treasury Regulations (as distinguished from a requirement of the code) may be waived by the Internal Revenue Service.[57]

Reduction or Cancellation of Indebtedness

Gross income includes income resulting from the reduction, cancellation, or discharge of indebtedness.[58] But a taxpayer may elect to have a reduction in the basis of its assets in lieu of reporting a cancellation or a reduction of indebtedness as income.

Ordinarily, the reduction is applicable to property liable or subject to the indebtedness. If the taxpayer desires to have the property basis adjusted in any other manner, the Commissioner's approval is required. Details as to this are provided on *Form 982*, which is used to make the election for reduction in basis of assets.

Involuntary Conversion

A taxpayer who has sustained an involuntary conversion can avoid the recognition of gain only by making an affirmative election as to the utilization of the proceeds.[59] Specifically, the taxpayer must elect not to have gain recognized and must apply the proceeds to the acquisition of qualified replacement property within the prescribed time. The taxpayer makes the election by not including the proceeds in income on the tax return except to the extent that they were not utilized in making the replacement.[60]

Research and Development Expense

Research and development expenses are charged to the capital account unless the taxpayer elects to have them expensed in the year they are incurred.[61] A company's treatment of these expenses on the tax return need not be the same as that reflected on its books and financial statements.[62]

Ordinarily, "pre-business" expenses are not deductible. (See chapter 7, Ordinary, Necessary, and Reasonable.) But research and development expenses may be deducted even before a taxpayer is actually engaged in the particular business to which these expenses relate. The aim of this provision is to encourage research and experimentation.[63] Expenditures for research and experiments to develop new products or processes that are not related to the current product lines or manufacturing processes of the taxpayer's trade or business may, at the taxpayer's election, be deducted if incurred in connection with his trade or business.[64]

Even though a formal statement that research and development expenses will be treated as deferred expenditures was not filed by the taxpayer, the election was deemed to be effective where these expenses were actually deferred on the tax return for that year. The election was also deemed effective for subsequent years.[65]

Payment in Restricted Property

In the case of property received by a person as compensation for services where the property is subject to a restriction, the ordinary rule is that the property is taxed at the time of receipt unless it is subject to a substantial risk of forfeiture. But an election may be made within 30 days of the transfer to pick up the value of the property (without regard to restrictions, except those which by their own terms never will lapse) in the year of transfer. This election may not be revoked without the consent of the Internal Revenue Service. If the taxpayer makes the election and subsequently forfeits his right to the property, he will not recover the tax he paid, nor will he receive any deduction for the amount forfeited.[66]

Election is indicated if the property is likely to increase in value, so that it will be picked up as ordinary income at as low a figure as possible. A later increase in the value of the property, if it is a capital asset, may be picked up as capital gain.

Government Subsidized Low- and Moderate-Income Housing Rental

If a qualified government subsidized low- or moderate-income rental housing project has been sold or disposed of in an approved disposition after October 9, 1969, and the proceeds have been invested in another qualified housing project within one year after the close of the first taxable year in which any part of the gain is realized, the taxpayer may elect to have the gain recognized only to the extent the proceeds are not reinvested in the new project.[67]

Repayment of Money Received under a Claim of Right

Ordinarily, if an individual receives income in one year and believes that it is his, any subsequent repayment he makes of this income does not result in a reopening of the accounts of the year in which he paid tax on the income. Thus, the repayment will reduce his tax (if at all) in the year of repayment when he may be in a lower tax bracket or when he may not be able to justify the deduction. But if he had received the payment subject to a legal obligation to repay it under stipulated circumstances and if the repayment is in excess of $3000, he may elect to make the adjustment as of the year of receipt *or* as of the year of repayment.[68] In one case, the president of a corporation was a party to an agreement whereby if an officer's salary were disallowed in part as a corporate deduction, the officer would repay the company that amount. After $5000 of the president's compensation for 1960 was disallowed as unreasonable in 1964, he repaid the company that amount. He deducted the payment in 1964, and the court held that the election was available to him as his obligation to repay existed legally before the corporation made the salary payments to him.[69]

Automobile Mileage

Where an individual uses an automobile for business purposes, in lieu of keeping detailed records of the actual cost of operations, he may elect to take a tax deduction at a standard mileage rate of: (1) 12¢ per mile for the first 15,000 miles each year for business purposes and (2) 9¢ per mile for distances in excess of 15,000 miles. This optional allowance takes the place of all operating and fixed costs of the car allocable to business purposes; it includes gasoline (including all taxes on it), oil, repairs, license tags, insurance, and depreciation. But parking fees and tolls attributable to use for business purposes may be deducted as separate items if documented. Gasoline taxes allocable to nonbusiness purposes are allowed in addition to this deduction, as are interest and state and local taxes.[70]

An individual who elects to use the standard mileage rate is not permitted to substitute for the specified mileage allowances a figure which allegedly represents national averages. The taxpayer's election requires that he use the Treasury's published figures.[71]

Life Insurance Proceeds

A widow who elects to leave life insurance proceeds payable by reason of the death of her husband, with the insurer and to receive only interest payments thereon must include such payments in gross income. But she is not precluded from obtaining the benefit of any exclusions allowed to widows electing to receive insurance proceeds over a period of years if she elects at a later date to receive future payments under another mode of settlement which would have qualified for such exclusions had such an election been made in the first instance.[72]

Dividends

No election is available either to the corporate payor or to the shareholder as to the character of a distribution when the corporation has earnings and profits. Unless the contrary can be established, any such distribution *is*, by definition, a dividend.[73]

If a shareholder has the right to receive a dividend in the distributing corporation's stock or in cash, this is a taxable dividend, regardless of the form he elects.[74]

For taxable years beginning after December 31, 1969, a corporation may elect to take a deduction for dividends paid on or before the 15th day of the third month following the close of its taxable year, provided the dividend deduction does not exceed 20 percent of the dividends paid by the corporation during the year.[75]

Carry-Overs

In the case of certain types of corporate reorganization, the statute provides for many carry-overs, including a net operating loss carry-over. Among the forms of reorganization are a statutory merger or consolidation, a complete liquidation of a subsidiary corporation by its parent where there is a continuance of the basis of the subsidiary's assets in the parent's hands, and the acquisition by one corporation of substantially all of the properties of another corporation solely in exchange for stock.

In such a reorganization, the predecessor's tax attributes as enumerated in the Code must be carried over by the successor—for example, accounting methods, inventory election, method of computing depreciation, etc. This is not subject to election; it is mandatory.[76]

Where the method of accounting employed by the predecessor on the date of the reorganization is continued, it is not necessary for the successor corporation to renew any election previously made with respect to that method of accounting. The successor corporation is bound by any election previously made—as though the taxfree reorganization had not taken place.[77]

Choice of Tribunal

Under certain circumstances, it may appear that a taxpayer engaged in litigation with the Internal Revenue Service is likely to fare better if decision is left to a jury rather than to a judge. (See chapter 23, Dealing with the Internal Revenue Service.) The taxpayer may be able to make an election as to who will hear the matter.

Charitable Contributions

Ordinarily, contributions are deductible in the year paid, whether the taxpayer is on the cash or the accrual method. But an accrual-basis corporation which authorizes a contribution in one taxable year and actually makes payment in the first 75 days of the succeeding taxable year has a choice of the taxable year in which to take this deduction.[78] The corporation must make this election at the time the return for the taxable year is filed by reporting the contribution on the return. There must be attached to the return when filed a written declaration that the resolution authorizing the contribution was adopted by the board of directors during the taxable year, and the declaration must be verified by a statement signed by an officer authorized to sign the tax return that it is made under the penalties of perjury. There also must be attached to the tax return a copy of the directors' resolution authorizing the contribution.[79]

Disaster Area

Ordinarily, a casualty loss, as by storm, is deductible in the year of the casualty.[80] But if the casualty is sustained in what the President of the United States subsequently proclaims a disaster area, the taxpayer has a choice as to the year of deduction: in the taxable year it took place or the year preceding the close of the taxable year.[81] Thus, in the case of a calendar year taxpayer, if the loss takes place on May 15, 1973, it may be claimed on either the 1972 or the 1973 return at the taxpayer's election.

NOTES

1. *Bay Sound Transportation Co. et al. v. United States*, D.C., S.D. Texas, 1967, *aff'd, rev'd and rem'd'd on other issues*, 410 F.2d 505 (5th Cir., 1969).
2. *Anthony Granata et al.*, T.C. Memo. 1963-309 (filed November 21, 1963).
3. *M. H. McDonnell et al.*, T.C. Memo. 1965-125 (filed May 11, 1965).
4. *Arthur William Peterson et al.*, T.C. Memo. 1970-181 (filed June 29, 1970).
5. *Mamula v. Commissioner*, 346 F.2d 1016 (9th Cir., 1965).
6. *George Stamos Estate et al.*, 55 T.C. 468 (1970); *Ewing v. Rountree*, 228 F. Supp. 137 (D.C., M.D. Tenn., 1964).
7. *Frentz et al. v. Commissioner*, 375 F.2d 662 (6th Cir., 1967).
8. *Simons v. United States*, 208 F. Supp. 744 (D.C., Conn., 1962).
9. *Joseph W. Feldman*, 47 T.C. 329 (1966).
10. *In re The Round Table, Inc.*, D.C., S.D. N.Y., 1965.
11. *Gimbel Brothers, Inc. et al. v. United States*, 404 F.2d 939 (Ct. Cl., 1968).
12. *Haggar Company v. Helvering*, 308 U.S. 389 (1940).
13. *Robert B. Dupree Estate v. United States*, 391 F.2d 753 (5th Cir., 1967).
14. *National Lead Co. v. Commissioner*, 336 F.2d 134 (2d Cir., 1964).
15. *Wilson et al. v. United States*, 267 F. Supp. 89 (D.C., E.D. No., 1967).
16. *John P. Reaver*, 42 T.C. 72 (1964).
17. *Robert L. Griffin et al.*, T.C. Memo. 1965-91 (filed April 9, 1965).
18. *R. H. Macy & Co., Inc. et al. v. United States*, 255 F.2d 884 (2d Cir., 1958).
19. *Bookwalter v. Mayer et al.*, 345 F.2d 476 (8th Cir., 1965).
20. Regulations Section 1.9100-1(a).
21. *Lambert et al. v. Commissioner*, 338 F.2d 4 (2d Cir., 1964).
22. *Haberman Farms, Inc. et al. v. United States*, 182 F. Supp. 829 (D.C., Neb., 1960).
23. *Morrow v. Deal*, 197 F.2d 821 (5th Cir., 1952); *National Investors Corporation v. Hoey*, 144 F.2d 466 (2d Cir., 1944).
24. *Caro et al. v. Bingler et al.*, D.C., W.D. Pa., 1965.
25. *Forrest City Production Credit Association v. United States*, 426 F.2d 819 (8th Cir., 1970).
26. *Leonhart et al. v. Commissioner*, 414 F.2d 749 (4th Cir., 1969).
27. *Homer W. Forrester*, 49 T.C. 499 (1968).
28. *Henry D. Duarte et al.*, 44 T.C. 193 (1965).
29. *Harold C. Kean et al.*, 51 T.C. 337 (1968).
30. Regulations Section 1.446-1(c)(2).
31. *Abe B. Adler et al.*, T.C. Memo. 1968-100 (filed May 28, 1968).
32. Revenue Procedure 67-10, 1967-1 CB 585.
33. Revenue Procedure 70-27, 1970-2 CB 509.
34. Revenue Procedure 64-51, 1964-2 CB 1003.
35. Revenue Ruling 68-643, 1968-2 CB 76.

36. Regulations Section 1.461-1(c).
37. *Woodward Iron Company v. United States*, 396 F.2d 552 (5th Cir., 1968).
38. Regulations Section 1.1502-10(a).
39. Regulations Section 1.1502-2.
40. *General Manufacturing Corp.*, 44 T.C. 513 (1965).
41. Regulations Section 1.1502-11(a).
42. Regulations Section 1.471-2(c).
43. *Textile Apron Co., Inc.*, 21 T.C. 147 (1953).
44. Regulations Section 1.167(c)-1(c).
45. Regulations Section 1.167(c)-1(a).
46. Regulations Section 1.167(e)-1(a).
47. Regulations Section 1.167(a)-11(f).
48. I.R.C. Section 167(f)(1).
49. I.R.C. Section 179.
50. *Samuel Horowitz et al.*, T.C. Memo. 1968-74 (filed April 23, 1968).
51. I.R.C. Section 248.
52. Revenue Ruling 67-15, 1967-1 CB 71.
53. Regulations Section 1.266-1(b).
54. Regulations Section 1.266-1(c).
55. *Parkland Place Company v. United States*, 354 F.2d 916 (5th Cir., 1966).
56. *Braunstein et al. v. Commissioner*, 374 U.S. 65 (1963).
57. *Hamilton et al. v. United States*, 324 F.2d 960 (Ct. Cl., 1963).
58. I.R.C. Section 61(a)(12).
59. I.R.C. Section 1033(a).
60. *See Adolph K. Feinberg et al.*, 45 T.C. 635 (1966).
61. I.R.C. Section 174.
62. Revenue Ruling 57-78, 1958-1 CB 148.
63. *Best Universal Lock Co., Inc. et al.*, 45 T.C. 1 (1965).
64. Revenue Ruling 71-162, I.R.B. 1971-13, 12.
65. Revenue Ruling 71-136, I.R.B. 1971-11, 13.
66. I.R.C. Section 83(b).
67. I.R.C. Section 1039.
68. I.R.C. Section 1311(a).
69. *Vincent E. Oswald*, 49 T.C. 645 (1968).
70. Revenue Procedure 70-25, 1970-2 CB 506.
71. *Ralph E. Schumaker et al.*, T.C. Memo. 1970-281 (filed October 5, 1970).
72. Revenue Ruling 65-284, 1965-1 CB 613.
73. I.R.C. Section 316(a).
74. I.R.C. Section 305.
75. I.R.C. Section 563(b).
76. I.R.C. Section 381.
77. Regulations Section 1.381(c)(4)-1(b)(4).
78. I.R.C. Section 170(a)(2).
79. Regulations Section 1.170-3(b).
80. I.R.C. Section 165(a).
81. I.R.C. Section 165(h).

CHAPTER 23

Dealing with the Internal Revenue Service

What Is Expected of Taxpayers

A taxpayer is required to meet the obligations the Federal income tax laws impose upon him. He is deemed to be aware of those laws. He must honestly and fully furnish correct information regarding his income and pay the taxes which he owes to the government. He is subject to criminal liability where he is guilty of filing a false return or of fraudulently evading income taxes.[1]

The rendering of a proper return by a taxpayer is of vital importance.[2] The return must be properly filled out and properly filed and the amount of income tax due must be paid within the required time. Timely mailing of a tax return is something which a taxpayer must be prepared to prove. A return which is mailed to the Internal Revenue Service cannot be regarded as filed on time if it is received belatedly and there is no postmark on the envelope[3] or where it is postmarked the morning after the last day for filing.[4] Where a private postage meter is used and the tax return or other document is not received on time, the printed date will not establish timely mailing. The taxpayer still has to prove that the item was mailed on time and that any delay was by reason of tardy transmission of the mail without any fault on his part.[5]

If a tax return is not filed on time, both penalties and interest may be imposed. An election which must be made upon a timely filed return is lost where the return is tardy. (See chapter 22, Elections and Their Consequences.)

Where a tax return cannot be filed on time, a request for an extension should be made before the due date to the Internal Revenue Service. A taxpayer will not be excused for failure to file on time or failure to apply for an extension even in the case of harsh circumstances.[6]

A corporation may obtain an automatic extension for the filing of a return by filing *Form 7004* and making payment not later than the regular due date of the first installment of the tax.[7] If a corporation expects a net operating loss carryback, an extension for the time of paying taxes otherwise due is made by an application on *Form 1138.*

Signatures

If a person's signature appears upon a tax return, it is presumed to be a correct signature. A closing agreement with the Internal Revenue Service was held to be binding upon a taxpayer because his signature was on it.[8]

The only signatures which may properly be used on a corporate income tax return are those of the president, vice-president, treasurer, assistant-treasurer, chief accounting officer, or any other officer duly authorized so to act.[9] The authorization of a secretary, an assistant secretary, or other person should appear in the corporate minutes. There may be some factual question in a particular corporation as to who the "chief accounting officer" actually is. Conceivably, it could be the chief accountant, controller, vice-president of finance, or any one of a variety of other persons. The signature of a bookkeeper in his capacity as a notary was ruled not to be equivalent to signature by an officer.[10]

An unsigned tax return is not regarded as a tax return at all.[11] Thus, even though the form which was filed reflected the taxpayer's income and deductions, the statute of limitation never began to run (it begins with the timely filing of a tax return). An unsigned document, which otherwise would be a tax return, is a nullity.[12] A typed "signature" is not enough.[13] A so-called return signed by someone other than the proper party is not a tax return.[14] A statement by a taxpayer that he confirmed and adopted a previously filed unsigned return as a true return is not enough.[15]

The fact that the Internal Revenue Service accepted and held an unsigned or improperly signed return for several years did not mean the requirement of a valid signature was waived.[16]

Statute of Limitations

The purpose of the statute of limitations is to put to rest controversies with respect to old transactions, the evidence in relation to which may be stale or unavailable.[17] It would be unrealistic to have an income tax system under which there never would be a day of final settlement and one which required both the taxpayer and the government to stand ready forever to produce vouchers, prove events, establish values, and recall details of everything which is contestable from a tax point of view. Thus, a statute of limitations is an almost indispensable element of fairness as well as a valuable aid in the practical administration of an income tax policy.[18]

Income taxes must be assessed within three years after the date on which the return must be filed. Even if the return was filed before the due date, the three-year period starts running on the due date. After this three-year period, the return is closed as to both the taxpayer and the Internal Revenue Service. Here are the general exceptions:

(1) If a taxpayer understimates gross income by 25 percent or more, the three-year figure becomes six.

(2) Where the assessment period has been extended by agreement of the parties, the agreement date supersedes the statutory date.

(3) If there is a false or fraudulent return, there is no statute of limitations.[19]

The Internal Revenue Service is not required to prove the grounds for its belief that a 25 percent understatement of gross income triggering the six-year statute has taken place in order for it to examine the only records which will provide the ultimate proof.[20]

The Service is entitled to make an inspection to determine the existence or nonexistence of any deficiency or fault which would allow the tolling of, or substitution for, the normal three-year statute of limitations.[21]

Where the Service proceeds on the basis of its belief that the taxpayer is guilty of fraud, the former has the burden of proof as to the fraud.[22]

A claim for a refund by reason of bad debts or worthless securities may be made within seven years after the due date of the tax return.[23]

The amount of income or loss for a closed year may be scrutinized where necessary for the purpose of ascertaining carrybacks or carry-forwards to years still open under the statute of limitations.[24]

Retention of Records

The Internal Revenue Service may require the production of records necessary to show income tax liability.[25] The government publication *Guide to Record Retention Requirements* spells out the requirements of income tax laws under the heading "Department of the Treasury." Failure of a taxpayer to keep books and records of his income-producing activities gives the Internal Revenue Service the right to use the best evidence available to determine taxable income.[26]

There are special guidelines for record requirements to be followed where accounting records are maintained with automatic data processing systems.[27]

Examination by Revenue Agent

For the purpose of determining the tax liability of any party, the Internal Revenue Service is authorized to examine any books and records which may be relevant or material to the inquiry.[28] The Service may summon not only the person liable for the tax, but any other person deemed to be "proper"; such person may be compelled to produce relevant books and records. A third party (such as a bank) may not complain that turning over material for the purpose of the audit gives the government, free of charge, information which may have cost that third party a considerable amount of time and money to accumulate.[29]

Those affected by an attempt by the Internal Revenue Service to obtain records from banks, brokers, accountants, etc., may intervene by asserting their rights, constitutional or otherwise, or other claims.[30] But a taxpayer may not intervene to prevent the Service from seeing another person's records on the ground that the examination might tend to incriminate the former.[31]

A subpoena for the production of records cannot be regarded as an invitation to a game of hare and hounds in which the witness must testify only if cornered at the end of the chase.[32] Rather, the subpoena must specify precisely which records are to be produced in order not to violate the Fourth Amendment's prohibition against unreasonable searches and seizures.[33] But records such as corporate minutes may be demanded by the Internal Revenue Service even if the precise objective of the examination is vague.[34] It does a taxpayer no good to characterize a Revenue agent's efforts to see the books as a "fishing expedition," for the statute[35] has specifically licensed the Secretary of the Treasury or his delegate, the Commissioner of Internal Revenue, to fish.[36]

Examination of a taxpayer usually occurs at his place of business, where his books and other supporting documents are maintained. But a taxpayer's wishes as to the place of examination will be given due consideration as, for example, where he prefers the office of his accountant, attorney, or other person.[37]

A taxpayer's failure to cooperate with the Service in uncovering unreported income may amount to fraud.[38]

Privileged Communications

While the Internal Revenue Service cannot inquire into material protected as a privileged communication between attorney and client, not everything claimed to be protected as a privileged communication actually is.[39] The protection does not apply unless all of the following are satisfied: (1) the party claiming the protection was, or sought to become, a client; (2) the person to whom the communication was addressed was a member of the bar or his subordinate; acted as a lawyer or his subordinate in connection with the communication; (3) the communication related to a fact of which the attorney was informed by his client, not in the presence of strangers, for the purpose of securing an opinion as to the law, legal services, or assistance in some legal proceeding, and not for the purpose of committing a crime or tort; and (4) the privilege has been claimed and not waived by the client.[40]

The mere fact that a person is an attorney does not mean that everything he does for and with a client is privileged. Thus, the Service can compel a lawyer to produce information if he merely performed ministerial or clerical services.[41]

Communications between a client and an accountant are not privileged.[42] Thus, where a taxpayer's affairs were handled by a person who was both an attorney and a certified public accountant, the Service could not subpoena records which he handled as an attorney; but the privilege did not protect the papers and schedules he prepared for the taxpayer that were primarily of an accounting nature.[43]

The Service is also not bound by a state law which makes a physician's records about his patients inviolate.[44]

Confidential Nature of Tax Returns

No officer or employee of the United States may make known the amount or source of any income, loss, etc., shown on a tax return in a manner not specified by law.[45] But this does not protect a taxpayer from the demands of state authorities for the filing of copies of the Federal income tax return along with the required state returns.[46] In addition, the Internal Revenue Service can advise a law enforcement agency (such as the Department of Justice) of possible violations of law as indicated by a tax return. The details of that violation may be made available to the enforcement agency.[47]

The President of the United States is authorized to order that certain Federal income tax returns be open to inspection.[48] For example, the House Committee on Un-American Activities has been allowed to examine tax returns in connection with its inquiries.[49]

Second Examination by Internal Revenue Service

A taxpayer is sometimes requested to disclose books and records after an examination has already been made. A taxpayer can avoid unnecessary harrassment by an Internal Revenue agent by insisting that the appropriate District Director of Internal Revenue approve this request on *Form L-153* or by letter. The purpose of this provision is to curb the investigatory powers of low-echelon agents by requiring them to clear any repetitive examination with a superior.[50] A second examination may be ordered by the District Director where, for example, the Service has received a complaint about alleged irregularities on the part of the agent who had conducted the original examination.[51]

If a taxpayer does not formally object to a request for a second examination by a Revenue agent without the order of the District Director, the right not to have an unauthorized second examination is deemed to have been waived.[52] Information obtained by means of a second examination could not be suppressed by a taxpayer in court when he had voluntarily furnished a second Revenue agent with the records.[53]

A second examination did not violate the rights of taxpayers where this examination was of the books of a corporation whose taxpayers were shareholders. The "only one inspection" prohibition applies only to a taxpayer's books, not to the books of a third party.[54] Where a bank was required by the Service to produce its records relating to the account of a person undergoing a tax examination, this person could not object that this was a second examination of his records or books without notice. His returns for the period had already been examined once by the Service, but the statute refers only to the inspection of a *taxpayer's* records or books without notice; hence, examination of the bank's records was not barred.[55] Where a taxpayer refused the Service's request to make a second examination, additional adjustments then made by a Revenue agent without recourse to the books were not barred as contrary to the prohibition against a second examination.[56]

An office audit of a tax return is not an examination of a taxpayer's books and records; hence, an actual examination of the records is not a second examination.[57] There was no second examination when a Revenue agent wished to return to audits he had left incomplete at an earlier date; the original examination was in fact a continuing one.[58] A second examination is not involved when all of the necessary records requested by the Service were not made available by the taxpayer the first time around.[59] A second examination is not deemed to have taken place when a taxpayer has filed an application for a tentative loss carryback adjustment. Once a taxable year is reopened for one purpose without objection, it is validly reopened for all purposes.[60]

Double Jeopardy

A Federal income tax indictment was not subject to dismissal on the ground of double jeopardy simply because the accused had already been indicted by the state of New York for filing a parallel state return using the same income data. The state and Federal offenses are distinct.[61]

Assessment of Tax

A Revenue agent examines tax returns to ascertain whether the proper tax liability has been disclosed. After the agent has completed his examination, he discusses his findings with the taxpayer. If the latter agrees with the proposed changes, he will be expected to sign a form, which will stop the running of interest.[62]

In the absence of an agreement, the taxpayer may request an informal conference in the office of the District Director of Internal Revenue. If the request is not made within ten days, a so-called "30-day letter" will be issued along with a copy of the assessment. A request may be made for a hearing in the Appellate Division of the District within 30 days. If no request is made, the formal demand of deficiency, the so-called "90-day letter," is issued. A taxpayer may file a petition with the United States Tax Court for a redetermination of the proposed deficiency within 90 days from the mailing date; if he fails to do so, the tax will become due and payable. The 90-day period includes nonbusiness days and holidays, except that those days will not be counted as the last day of the period.[63] During that 90-day period, the Service is barred from action by way of assessment or levy. The taxpayer may obtain further unconditional respite from assessment or collection if he sends a timely petition to the Tax Court, inasmuch as the Service cannot act during the pendency of the Tax Court litigation.[64]

Litigation

Litigation is necessary if the taxpayer and the Service cannot agree upon how a tax matter is to be settled. Most tax litigation begins in the United States Tax Court. Nothing has to be paid until that court has rendered a decision unfavorable to the taxpayer. Such a decision will become final because of affirmation by a higher court or because no appeal is taken. But if tax has already been paid, the taxpayer may file a suit for a refund. This suit would be filed in a United States District Court or in the Court of Claims.

A taxpayer may deliberately choose to bypass the Tax Court in the belief that he will receive a more sympathetic hearing from a jury rather than from one or more judges. Thus where managerial judgment is involved—as, for example, in a case involving accumulated earnings or the reasonableness of executive compensation—the taxpayer may prefer to rely on the thinking of other businessmen.[65]

A jury trial is available in the district court, if requested by either party in an action against the United States for a refund of taxes paid.[66] But a taxpayer is not entitled to a jury trial where the claim asserted is a lien against his property.[67]

The burden of proof in an accumulated earnings tax matter, where there is a timely filing of a statement of grounds for retention of earnings, is on the Service only in proceedings before the Tax Court.[68] (See chapter 11, Dividends and the Tax on Accumulated Earnings.) The tactical advantage of having the burden of proof on the Service must be weighed against the conspicuous success scored by taxpayers when these actions are disposed of by juries.

Offers in Compromise

The Service may reach a compromise in any civil or criminal case arising under the Internal Revenue laws before the matter is referred to the Department of Justice.[69] An offer in compromise of taxes, interest, or penalty may be based upon an inability to pay the tax or doubt as to liability.

Where a compromise agreement is reached, the taxpayer usually is required to agree that, in the event of default in payment of principal or interest, he will not contest the amount due and that the Service has the option of immediately suing for the entire balance of the compromise or disregarding it and collecting, by distraint or suit, the balance of the liability after applying all amounts previously paid. Where the Service accepts amounts smaller than provided for by the compromise agreement, the government does not thereby waive the right to collect the balance at a later date.[70]

Amounts tendered in partial payment of deficiencies mutually agreed upon as to the amount of liability, but unassessed at the time of tender, for one or more years will be applied by the Service to tax, penalty, and interest, in that order, due for the earliest year where there are no instructions from the taxpayer as to the application of the payment.[71]

Tax Liens

If any person liable to pay any tax neglects or refuses to pay it after demand, the amount (including any interest, penalty, or other additions) will be a lien in favor of the United States upon all property and rights to property belonging to that person.[72]

The Federal Tax Lien Act of 1966 provides a direct method by which the Internal Revenue Service can obtain free from an insurance company the cash loan value of a delinquent taxpayer's unmatured life insurance and endowment contracts. The insurance company is not required to pay over the cash loan value until 90 days after the service of a notice of levy. If the tax liability is not satisfied within this period, the amount to be levied on is the cash loan value of the contract with certain adjustments.[73] A lien may also be imposed against a taxpayer's intangible property (such as a liquor license).[74]

Seizure of Property

The United States has the authority to seize the property of any person to satisfy unpaid Federal taxes. If this authority is in conflict with state law, constitutional or statutory, the latter must yield.[75] Federal seizure power extends to property set aside by a state court for support and to property subject to state-created exemptions (such as the property of a state highway or tunnel authority).[76]

Jeopardy Assessment

Whenever the Internal Revenue Service believes that delay will jeopardize the assessment or collection of a tax deficiency, the Service is authorized to make an assessment immediately and to send a notice and demand for tax.[77] To do this, the Service need only to offer evidence: (1) of the assessment's having been made; (2) of demand for payment; and (3) that the taxes are still due.[78] A *jeopardy assessment* has been characterized as a "pay first-litigate later scheme." [79]

A jeopardy assessment will not stand if the Service has no evidence that money was earned in, or was the income of a citizen or resident of, the United States.[80]

The Service could not issue a jeopardy assessment against an individual entirely upon the basis of information received from the Secret Service that that individual was in possession of currency obtained from a source he would not identify. The Internal Revenue Service must make its own findings and issue its own declaration that it is necessary to institute such an action.[81]

A taxpayer has these safeguards against jeopardy assessments:

(1) The Service must send him a deficiency notice within 60 days, thus allowing him to litigate in the Tax Court.

(2) The jeopardy taxpayer can stay all collection pending the Tax Court's decision if he is able to post adequate bond.

(3) Property seized pursuant to the assessment may not, in general, be sold during the pendency of litigation in the Tax Court.

(4) The Service may abate the jeopardy assessment if it finds that the jeopardy does not exist.[82]

No penalty is asserted in the case of a jeopardy assessment except where the taxpayer performs or attempts to perform an act tending to prejudice or to render ineffectual any proceedings to collect the tax by his quick departure from the United States.[83]

Prevention of Departure

A writ of *ne exeat republica* ("he may not leave the country") may be issued by Federal District Courts of the United States in tax cases. This is appropriate only when the Service can show that the taxpayer's departure from the country would substantially prejudice the government in the collection of its taxes, penalties, and interest, assuming such claims are just. For example, there must be substantial evidence that the taxpayer had been transferring assets, or the proceeds from assets, from the United States to another country.[84]

Transferee Liability

Under certain circumstances, a person's unpaid taxes may be collected from a party who had received property from him in an amount not greater than the value of the property received. Transferee liability applies to corporations in the same way it does to individuals.

Transferee liability generally requires proof by the Service: (1) that the assets were transferred by a taxpayer to a transferee without adequate consideration; (2) that the taxpayer was insolvent or was rendered insolvent by the transfer; (3) that the assets had value and what that value was on the date of the transfer; and (4) that the Service has made every reasonable effort to collect the sums due from the transferor.[85] In order to discharge its burden, the Service must also establish that it would have been pointless to proceed further against the taxpayer-transferor.[86] The burden of establishing that, in fact, there was no tax liability on the part of the insolvent transferor is on the transferee.[87]

Transferee liability may be assessed up to one year after the expiration of the statute of limitation against the transferor even if a prompt assessment had been requested and obtained by the transferor as a result of a corporate liquidation.[88]

Penalties

In the case of failure to file a tax return without willful neglect, there is a penalty of five percent with another five percent for each additional month or fraction thereof during which the failure to file continues, not to exceed 25 percent in the aggregate.[89]

One who fails to pay taxes because of negligence is subject to a five percent penalty. If the failure is by reason of fraud, the penalty is 50 percent.[90] Conviction for willful violation of the tax laws may result in a fine of not more than $10,000, or imprisonment for not more than five years, or both.[91] Any person who willfully attempts in any manner to evade or to defeat the tax will, upon conviction, incur similar fines and penalties.[92]

Persons other than the taxpayer may be convicted under this provision.[93] So the taxpayer's accountant may also be convicted.[94] The statute extends to persons who conspire with a taxpayer by keeping fraudulent books or hiding assets.[95]

Any person required to pay a tax, keep records, or supply any information and who willfully fails to do so, will, upon conviction, be fined not more than $10,000, or imprisoned for not more than one year.[96] Any person who willfully makes and subscribes any return, statement, or other document which contains or is verified by a written declaration that it is made under the penalties of perjury and which he does not believe to be true as to every material aspect will, upon conviction, be fined not more than $5000, or imprisoned for not more than three years, or both.[97]

Any person who, being duly summoned to appear to testify or to produce books, accounts, records, memoranda, or other papers, neglects to comply with the terms of the summons, will be subject to a fine of not more than $1000 upon conviction, or imprisonment for not more than one year, or both.[98]

An attempt to interfere with the administration of Internal Revenue laws is punishable, upon conviction, by a fine of not more than $5000, or imprisonment for not more than three years, or both. If the offense is committed only by threats of force, the maximum penalties are $3000 and/or one year.[99]

In addition to six percent interest on tax delinquencies per year, which is deductible, there is a nondeductible penalty of one-half of one percent per month (up to a maximum of 25 percent) for failure to pay income tax (other than estimated tax) when due and for failure to pay a deficiency within ten days after the date of notice and demand. In the case of failure to pay income tax when due, the penalty is imposed upon the amount shown on the tax return as due, less amounts which have been withheld, estimated tax payments, partial payments, and other applicable credits. The penalty is not imposed if it is shown that the failure to pay the tax or deficiency is due to a reasonable cause and not to willful neglect.[100]

Damage Suits Against Revenue Officials

A taxpayer has no means of redress against the government where he is injured by the carelessness or other action of a Revenue agent. In addition a damage suit may not be brought against a District Director or other revenue official unless the taxpayer can show that the act complained of was not done in the line of regular duty.[101] There are means of punishing public officers who have been truant in their duties; but that is quite apart from exposing officers who have been honestly mistaken to a lawsuit by anyone who has suffered from their errors.[102] But bias of an Internal Revenue agent is a cause for reversal of a lower court finding for the Internal Revenue Service.[103]

Suits to Restrain Collection of Taxes

The Internal Revenue Service has the authority to assess and collect taxes alleged to be due without judicial intervention. The Service can also determine if the legal right to disputed sums will be relegated to actions for refunds. In this manner, the Service can be assured of the prompt collection of revenues.[104]

A taxpayer is not entitled to injunctive relief on the ground that payment of an asserted tax would result in insolvency.[105] But an injunction against seizure of a taxpayer's property may be allowed where the taxpayer testified that he was not subject to the tax, that he did not have the funds to pay it, and that any effort by the Service to collect the tax would work a complete cessation of his business, ruin him financially, and inflict such irreparable and profound losses that he would have no adequate remedy at law.[106]

Where the Service issued a jeopardy assessment for three times the total admitted assets of a taxpayer, the court enjoined the collection of any amount the taxpayer would have to retain to defend the case.[107]

Motion for the Production of Records

A taxpayer is entitled to know the basis of an assessment. Thus, where the Service asserted a deficiency "on the basis of information on file in this office," the taxpayer could demand production of the basis of the imposition.[108] But where an accumulated earnings tax was imposed, the corporation was not entitled to see any of the Service's workpapers; for if the company showed that there was justification for the retention of its earnings, the Service's workpapers would be of no significance.[109]

Where the Service valued the shares of a closely-held corporation for tax purposes, the taxpayer was able to obtain a court order requiring the Service to produce for inspection and copying the materials, reports, and information upon which the valuation was based.[110]

Refund Claims

A taxpayer may file a refund claim within three years from the time the return was filed or two years from the time the tax was paid, whichever is later.[111]

A refund claim may not be filed after two years from the date of mailing of a disallowance of a claim.[112] A second claim based upon the same grounds as a rejected first claim cannot operate to extend the statutory period of an otherwise stale claim.[113]

rejected first claim cannot operate to extend the statutory period of an otherwise stale claim.[113]

Even after a taxpayer had given his consent to a deficiency or overassessment of tax on *Form 870,* he can still file a refund claim if the statutory period for closing that year has not yet run.[114] Similarly, the Service may assess further liability even after *Form 870* has been signed.[115] The only document which really will close a taxable year is a *closing agreement,* which is signed both by the taxpayer and by the Commissioner of Internal Revenue. Generally, the Commissioner will sign the agreement only when it appears that it would be advantageous to have the case permanently closed or when the taxpayer argues with sufficient persuasiveness that it would be in the interest of all parties to get the matter settled permanently, for example, when a creditor wishes to know the true tax liability of its debtor or a liquidating corporation wishes to know its tax liability before all assets are distributed. A closing agreement may be on *Form 866,* "Agreement as to Final Determination of Tax Liability"; or it may be on *Form 906,* "Closing Agreement as to Final Determination Covering Specific Matters."

A closing agreement is final and conclusive except upon a showing of fraud or misrepresentation of a material fact.[116]

Rulings

Treasury rulings, which constitute interpretations of revenue statutes by the Service or other agencies charged with enforcing them, are not lightly overturned by a court. They will be sustained unless they are inconsistent with statutory law or are unreasonable.[117] However, Treasury regulations cannot change the meaning or effect of the tax law.[118] Regulations may be applied retroactively if by their express terms they are made retroactive and they manifest no new approach.[119]

Each year the Service publishes hundreds of "Revenue Rulings," which set out the tax consequences of particular situations presented to the Service for disposition. Revenue Rulings are applied retroactively unless there is a specific statement to the contrary. But where a ruling revokes or modifies a previously published ruling, the new ruling will usually not be applied retroactively to the extent that it has unfavorable consequences to taxpayers.[120]

Sometimes, a taxpayer or his counsel may obtain from the Service a ruling on the taxpayer's special problem. This "special ruling" may not be utilized by any party except the one to whom it is addressed.[121]

The Internal Revenue Service has announced that it will no longer issue special rulings in various designated areas, including: whether compensation is reasonable; whether an acquisition was made to evade or avoid tax; whether a sale of property received by a shareholder as a distribution in kind will be taxable to him or to the corporation; whether a family partnership is valid; whether a transaction is in contemplation of death; and the results of transactions which lack a *bona fide* business purpose or have as their principal purpose the reduction of Federal taxes.

In all, there are 17 areas where these rulings will not be issued. In ten other areas, rulings "will not ordinarily be issued." They include: whether advances to undercapitalized corporations constitute loans; the useful lives of assets, depreciation rates, and salvage values; and situations where the ruling requested is primarily one of fact (such as the market value of property) or those where the ruling involves the tax effect of any transaction to be consummated at some indefinite time in the future.[122]

The Tax Informant

To promote the enforcement of the tax law, private persons are encouraged to give information to the Internal Revenue Service. The law promises informants anonymity.[123]

Persons who know something about a taxpayer's financial affairs may have reason to believe that his tax returns do not tell the whole story. Informants may submit information relating to violations of tax laws to the office of the Director of the Intelligence Division, Internal Revenue Service, Washington, D.C. 20025, or to the office of a District Director, preferably to a representative of the Intelligence Division there.[124] Most complaints are of the "squeal letter" variety and entitle the authors to no reward. But before an informant reveals his information, he may make a claim for compensation for his services on *Form 211.*[125] A written agreement is essential to any reward; an oral promise by a Revenue agent to an individual that he would be rewarded to the extent of ten percent of the taxes collected from leads furnished was not enforceable against the Service.[126]

The Secretary of the Treasury is authorized to pay whatever amount is necessary for information used for detecting, bringing to trial and obtaining verdicts against persons guilty of violating the tax laws or conniving at the same.[127] The Service will make agreements with individuals, other than governmental employees, to pay them up to ten percent of taxes recovered as the result of leads they furnish. This covers tax deficiencies, penalties, and fines.[128]

No unauthorized person is advised by the Internal Revenue Service of the identity of the informant.[129] Were it otherwise, few people would come forward to disclose to the Service their knowledge of evaded taxes. What is usually referred to as the informant's privilege is in reality the government's privilege to withhold from disclosure the identity of persons who furnish information of violations of the tax law to officers charged with enforcement of that law.[130]

The informants may be clerical help or disenchanted or displaced executives. Where a taxpayer is aided by others in falsifying corporate records, those coconspirators may be granted immunity by the government for testimony and cooperation in the proceedings against the taxpayer.[131] The informant may be the taxpayer's own spouse although one spouse cannot be *compelled* to testify against the other. However, when notified of her rights, a wife may *volunteer* information.[132]

NOTES

1. *United States v. Caiello*, 420 F.2d 471 (2d Cir., 1970).
2. *Ned Wayburn*, 32 B.T.A. 813 (1935).
3. *Jacob I. Rappoport*, 55 T.C. 709 (1971).
4. *Joseph W. Feldman*, 47 T.C. 329 (1966).
5. Regulations Section 301.7502-1(c)iii)(*b*). *See Fishman et al. v. Commissioner*, 420 F.2d 491 (2d Cir., 1970).
6. *Boyce v. United States*, 405 F.2d 526 (Ct. Cl., 1968).
7. Regulations Section 1.6081-3(c).
8. *Lincoln v. United States*, 356 F.2d 145 (Ct. Cl., 1966).
9. I.R.C. Section 6062.
10. *Western Supply & Furnace Company et al.*, T.C. Memo. 1959-57 (filed March 30, 1959), *aff'd*, 295 F.2d 341 (7th Cir., 1961).
11. *Reaves v. Commissioner*, 295 F.2d 336 (5th Cir., 1961).
12. *Charles L. Kotovic*, T.C. Memo. 1959-177 (filed September 21, 1959).
13. *Jacob A. Doll et al.*, T.C. Memo. 1965-191 (filed July 14, 1965).
14. *Uhl Estate Company v. Commissioner*, 116 F.2d 403 (9th Cir., 1940).
15. *Roy Dixon et al.*, 28 T.C. 338 (1957).
16. *Lucas v. Pilliod Lumber Co.*, 281 U.S. 245 (1930).
17. *Irving Bartel et al.*, 54 T.C. 25 (1970).
18. *Rothensies v. Electric Battery Company*, 329 U.S. 296 (1946).
19. I.R.C. Section 6501.
20. *United States v. United Distillers Products Corporation*, 156 F.2d 872 (2d Cir., 1946).
21. *United States et al. v. Giordano*, 301 F. Supp. 884 (D.C., E.D. Mo., 1969), *aff'd*, 419 F.2d 564 (8th Cir., 1969).
22. *Kreps v. Commissioner*, 351 F.2d 1 (2d Cir., 1965).
23. I.R.C. Section 6511(d)(1).
24. *Pacific Transport Company et al.*, T.C. Memo. 1970-41 (filed February 17, 1970).
25. I.R.C. Section 6001.
26. *Fuller v. Commissioner*, 313 F.2d 73 (6th Cir., 1963).
27. Revenue Procedure 64-12, 1964-1 CB (Part 1) 672.
28. I.R.C. Section 7602.
29. *In re Samuel W. Kearney*, 235 F. Supp. 618 (D.C., S.D. N.Y., 1964).
30. *Reisman v. Caplin*, 375 U.S. 440 (1964).
31. *United States v. Benford*, D.C., N.D. Ind., 1968.
32. *United States v. Bryan*, 339 U.S. 323 (1950).
33. *United States et al. v. Dauphin Deposit Trust Company et al.*, 385 F.2d 129 (3d Cir., 1967).
34. *United States et al. v. Acker*, 325 F. Supp. 857 (D.C., S.D. N.Y., 1971).
35. I.R.C. Section 7602.
36. *United States et al. v. Giordano*, 419 F.2d 564 (8th Cir., 1969).
37. Technical Information Release No. 985 (August 14, 1968).
38. *Escobar v. United States*, 388 F.2d 661 (5th Cir., 1967).
39. *Colton v. United States*, 306 F.2d 633 (2d Cir., 1962).
40. *United States v. United Shoe Machinery Corporation*, 89 F. Supp. 357 (D.C., Mass., 1950).
41. *United States v. Bartone*, 400 F.2d 459 (6th Cir., 1968).
42. *Lustman v. Commissioner*, 322 F.2d 253 (3d Cir., 1963).
43. *United States et al. v. Higgins*, 266 F. Supp. 596 (D.C., S.D. W.V., 1966).
44. *United States et al. v. Kansas City Lutheran Home and Hospital Association et al.*, 297 F. Supp. 239 (D.C., W.D. Mo., 1969).
45. I.R.C. Section 7213(a)(1).
46. Revenue Ruling 70-454, 1970-2 CB 296.
47. *United States v. Tucker et al.*, D.C., Conn., 1970.
48. I.R.C. Section 6103(a).

49. Executive Order No. 11217, 30 F.R. 5819.
50. *United States et al. v. Powell et al.*, 379 U.S. 48 (1964).
51. *See Fort Howard Paper Company*, 49 T.C. 275 (1967).
52. *United States v. Florida et al.*, 252 F. Supp. 806 (D.C., E.D. Ark., 1965).
53. *Field Enterprises, Inc. v. United States*, 348 F.2d 485 (Ct. Cl. 1965).
54. *Geurink et al. v. United States*, D.C., N.D. Ill., 1965, *aff'd*, 354 F.2d 629 (7th Cir., 1965).
55. *Brunwasser v. Pittsburgh National Bank*, 351 F.2d 951 (3d Cir., 1966).
56. *United States Holding Co.*, 44 T.C. 323 (1965).
57. *Geurink et al. v. United States*, 354 F.2d 629 (7th Cir., 1965).
58. *United States et al. v. Crespo et al.*, 281 F. Supp. 928 (D.C., Md., 1968).
59. *Giordano v. United States*, 419 F.2d 564 (8th Cir., 1969).
60. *Rife, Jr. et al. v. Commissioner*, 356 F.2d 883 (5th Cir., 1966).
61. *United States v. Page*, D.C., E.D. N.Y., 1965.
62. *United States v. Frank*, 245 F.2d 284 (3d Cir., 1957); I.R.C. Section 6213(d).
63. *Julie K. McGuire*, 52 T.C. 468 (1969).
64. I.R.C. Section 6213(a).
65. *See* Robert S. Holzman, "Should You Use a Jury?" *TAXES—The Tax Magazine*, May 1958, Volume XXXVI, No. 5, p. 301.
66. 28 U.S.C. 2402 (1969).
67. *Damsky v. Zavatt*, 289 F.2d 46 (2d Cir., 1961).
68. I.R.C. Section 534.
69. I.R.C. Section 7122.
70. *United States v. Saladoff*, 372 F.2d 352 (3d Cir., 1965).
71. Revenue Ruling 58-239, 1958-1 CB 94.
72. I.R.C. Section 3670.
73. I.R.C. Section 6332(b).
74. *Paramount Finance Company v. United States*, 379 F.2d 543 (6th Cir., 1967).
75. *United States v. Greenville*, 118 F.2d 963 (4th Cir., 1941).
76. *Davis v. Birdsong*, 275 F.2d 113 (5th Cir., 1960).
77. I.R.C. Section 6861.
78. *United States v. Mauro*, 243 F. Supp. 413 (D.C., S.D. N.Y., 1965).
79. *Schreck v. United States et al.*, 301 F. Supp. 1265 (D.C., Md., 1969).
80. *Rinieri v. Scanlon*, 254 F. Supp. 469 (D.C., S.D. N.Y., 1966).
81. *United States v. Bonaguro*, 294 F. Supp. 750 (D.C., E.D. N.Y., 1969).
82. *See Schreck v. United States et al.*, 301 F. Supp. 1265 (D.C., Md., 1969).
83. Revenue Ruling 68-96, 1968-1 CB 566.
84. *United States v. Robbins et al.*, 235 F. Supp. 353 (D.C., E.D. Ark., 1964).
85. *Samuel Napsky et al.*, T.C. Memo. 1966-284 (filed October 27, 1965), *aff'd*, 371 F.2d 189 (7th Cir., 1967).
86. *Kreps v. Commissioner*, 351 F.2d 1 (2d Cir., 1965).
87. I.R.C. Section 6902(a).
88. Revenue Ruling 64-305, 1964-2 CB 503.
89. I.R.C. Section 6651.
90. I.R.C. Section 6653.
91. I.R.C. Section 7202.
92. I.R.C. Section 7201.
93. *United States v. Donovan*, 250 F. Supp. 463 (D.C., W.D. Texas, 1966).
94. *Leathers v. United States*, 250 F.2d 159 (9th Cir., 1957).
95. *Tinkoff v. United States*, 86 F.2d 868 (7th Cir., 1936).
96. I.R.C. Section 7203.
97. I.R.C. Section 7206.
98. I.R.C. Section 7210.
99. I.R.C. Section 7212.
100. I.R.C. Section 6651(a).

101. *See National Dairy Products Corporation v. O'Connell* (D.C., R.I., 1950).

102. *Gregoire v. Biddle*, 177 F.2d 579 (2d Cir., 1950).

103. *Lenske v. United States*, 383 F.2d 20 (9th Cir., 1966).

104. *Enochs v. Williams Packing & Navigation Co., Inc.*, 370 U.S. 1 (1962).

105. *Bynum v. O'Donnell, Jr.*, 243 F. Supp. 63 (D.C., N.D. Ala., 1965).

106. *Ralston v. Wood*, D.C., Arizona, 1954.

107. *Homan Manufacturing Co., Inc. v. Sauber et al.*, D.C., N.D. Ill., 1955.

108. *Frazier v. Phinney*, 24 F.R.D. 406 (D.C., S.D. Texas, 1959).

109. *Unistruct Corporation v. United States*, 37 F.R.D. 478 (D.C., E.D. Mich., 1965).

110. *United States v. Gates, Jr. et al.*, D.C., Colo., 1964, *aff'd*, 376 F.2d 65 (10th Cir., 1967).

111. I.R.C. Section 6511(a).

112. I.R.C. Section 6532(a)(1).

113. *Golden Gate Motor Inn, Inc. v. United States*, D.C., E.D. N.Y., 1971.

114. *Uinta Livestock Corporation v. United States*, 355 F.2d 761 (10th Cir., 1966).

115. *United States v. Prince*, 348 F.2d 746 (2d Cir., 1965).

116. I.R.C. Section 7121.

117. *Commissioner v. South Texas Co.*, 333 U.S. 496 (1948).

118. *Saks v. Higgins*, 29 F. Supp. 996 (D.C., S.D. N.Y., 1939).

119. *United States v. California Portland Cement Company*, 413 F.2d 161 (9th Cir., 1969).

120. Revenue Procedure 68-37, 1968-2 CB 926.

121. *Bookwalter v. Brecklein et al.*, 357 F.2d 78 (8th Cir., 1966).

122. Revenue Procedure 69-6, 1969-1 CB 396.

123. *The Timken Roller Bearing Company v. United States*, 38 F.R.D. 57 (D.C., N.D. Ohio, 1964).

124. Regulations Section 301.7623-1(d).

125. Revenue Ruling 140, 1953-2 CB 470.

126. *Chase v. United States*, 59 F. Supp. 211 (Ct. Cl., 1945).

127. I.R.C. Section 7623.

128. T.D. 5183, 1942-2 CB 344.

129. Regulations Section 301.7623-1(e).

130. *Roviaro v. United States*, 353 U.S. 53 (1957).

131. *See United States v. Goldberg et al.*, 330 F.2d 30 (3d Cir., 1904).

132. *United States v. Winfree*, 170 F. Supp. 659 (D.C., E.D. Pa., 1959).

CHAPTER 24

Unnecessary and Unwitting Disclosure

Who Talks?

Disclosures by executives and other employees may compromise a corporation's income tax returns. However, low-echelon employees rarely know enough to cause difficulties. It is the key executives who are apt to be the worst offenders.

Sometimes an executive will say more than was necessary in a speech, a letter, an annual report, or elsewhere. On other occasions, knowledgeable or just suspicious stockholders, by pointed questions at annual shareholders' meetings, can wring reluctant admissions from officers which may be of great interest to the Internal Revenue Service. For example, at the annual meeting of a major listed corporation, a shareholder compelled the company president to admit that the corporation paid the wages of a six-man crew who served on a yacht belonging to the board chairman.[1] At another meeting, it was brought out that the corporation had made loans to company executives.[2] The latter might, among other things, be indicative of retention of earnings beyond the reasonable needs of the business. (See chapter 11, Dividends and the Tax on Accumulated Earnings.)

Accumulated Earnings Tax

Where a corporation sought to justify retained earnings by arguing the need for future expansion, the president's testimony, "We wouldn't build a doghouse without an architect," rendered the explanation dubious where no architect had been consulted.[3]

Another company's retention of earnings for improvements was fatally undermined when the president, in response to a question as to when expenditures would be made, replied, "at a propitious time." To the court, that could mean never.[4]

One officer testified that he never intended that his corporation would pay dividends.[5] Another officer, when asked what amount of corporate accumulations would be reasonable in his judgment, naively replied, "The sky was the limit, to me." [6] A taxman's arguments as to the business reasons for retention are not apt to be very persuasive when the officer who really makes the decisions has something else to say.

Where it was argued on behalf of a corporation that earnings had been retained for diversification or expansion, but the minutes at the year-end meeting stated that the directors were seriously considering liquidation of the company, diversification or expansion scarcely seemed likely reasons for retention and an accumulated earnings tax was imposed.[7]

For tax purposes, the effectiveness of minutes will be weakened, if not destroyed, by a statement that a specific resolution was passed, not for listed business reasons, but because "the accountant had requested that the board of directors adopt a resolution." [8]

Where the representatives of a corporation sought to justify retention of earnings for purposes of diversification, the corporate minutes, through the frequent use of the present tense in describing the corporation's alleged plans, left room for the inference that such plans did not exist during the years in question.[9]

Reasonableness of Compensation

A corporation is not helped in a reasonable compensation dispute with the Internal Revenue Service when an officer testifies that he "worked almost 25 hours a day performing . . . services. . . ." [10] No one can take such testimony seriously even though the fact may be that the officer did work long hours. His entire testimony is apt to be discredited.

Nor is it helpful to the corporation, in a case challenging a president's salary as unreasonable, to have the president testify that his filial relationship to the corporation's sole stockholder could have been instrumental in his appointment.[11]

Likewise, the president's admission at a stockholders' meeting that his corporation paid generous executive salaries might later prove prejudicial to the corporation on the issue of the reasonableness of salaries.[12]

Payments to Wives of Deceased Officers

If a corporation makes payments to the widow of an executive or other employee who dies in harness, tax treatment may depend upon the motivation for such payments. Payments to a widow from an account labeled "Widows' Severance Pay Account" may be taxed as compensation rather than gifts by reason of the account's label.[13] If a corporate payment to an officer's widow is intended as a gift, it should certainly not be recorded on the books as "Compensation of Officers." However, that the payment really was a gift still may be proven by external evidence.[14] But that is doing it the hard way. Management can make it impossible for a widow to characterize payments as tax-free gifts by its own unwitting testimony. Such was the case where a director testified that one of the reasons for such payments was to compensate the widows for unpaid services rendered by the wives in support of and in furtherance of the corporation's business.[15] The word "services" virtually assures taxability as compensation. To assist the widow's tax posture, the record (if justified by the facts) should establish that the payments were made because of such factors as the payee's financial needs and the corporation's desire to help her. A widow was taxed upon payments where a director testified that the board had not been informed and did not consider her financial needs and that generosity toward her was not a factor in enacting the resolution of payment.[16]

Payments of this nature are deductible by a corporation which makes the payment for business reasons, such as to help company morale by showing that it is a fine place to work. Deduction was not allowed, however, where a director testified that he had voted for payments to the widow "to keep her off my back." [17] That was a personal motivation, not a business one.

Corporate Charter and Bylaw Provisions

A corporation's articles of incorporation may spell out taxability of income. A sporting club argued that it was not liable for the Federal tax on dues as the charter granted no power to levy such dues; for this reason such dues were not legally enforceable and not taxable. But the certificate of incorporation *did* authorize the club "to do and perform all acts in any wise appertaining to the specific objects hereinbefore set forth." This was deemed to be sufficiently broad to cover the levy of dues; and the club was taxed.[18]

Membership fees were not deductible when the bylaws of an association receiving the payments disclosed that the association had an illegal purpose: to effect a combination proscribed by law in restraint of trade in pinball machines.[19]

A medical society alleged that it was a tax-exempt organization. Its charter, however, showed that the society had been formed not only to promote the art and science of medicine, but also the unity, harmony, and welfare of the medical profession. In holding that this was not an organization devoted exclusively to charitable, non-profit purposes, the court cited the charter provisions and declared that the society would not be satisfying its stated purposes if it did not seek to promote the welfare of the profession *and* the welfare of its individual members.[20]

Transaction Entered into for Profit

The desire to be helpful may be more noble than the desire to make money; but the expenses incurred thereby are not business-related and hence cannot be deducted.

Where an individual sought to deduct his expenses as a painter, but he testified that he painted to give beauty to the world, his expenses were disallowed as being unrelated to a transaction entered upon for profit.[21]

Reality of Debt

The sole stockholder of a corporation argued that advances to him from the corporation were not dividends but loans, for he had always regarded the withdrawals as loans and recognized an obligation to repay them to the corporation. But on a number of loan applications which he had personally addressed to lending institutions during the years when the withdrawals were in effect, his applications did not disclose his recognition of any liability to his own corporation. On the lines provided in these statements for the disclosure of his liabilities, he entered the word "none." Without an admitted intention to repay the moneys, his withdrawals were taxed as dividends.[22]

Interest on so-called bonds was disallowed as a deduction where a letter from the issuing corporation to a commercial lending institution stated that these securities "are regarded by us like preferred stock and not as an obligation." [23] If management regarded the issue as a stock, why should not the Internal Revenue Service take the same attitude? [24]

In one case, a taxpayer made sales to a wholly-owned corporation, according to his own testimony, to help build up volume and thus get a lower unit price from his supplier. The sales were not for the purpose of making a profit, and hence, a business bad debt did not result.[25]

If a corporation gratuitously forgoes the indebtedness of a subsidiary company on the stated ground that the subsidiary at all times since its organization had been hopelessly insolvent and there was no possibility that it would ever be able to pay any part of the accrued interest, the subsidiary is likely to lose its accrued interest deduction for any years not yet closed by the statute of limitations. If repayment had never been contemplated, there would not have been a *bona fide* indebtedness.[26]

Write-Offs

A corporation claimed a property abandonment loss on its income tax return. But insurance coverage against fire and other hazards was continued on this property. Moreover, the corporation continued to carry the assets on its books and to record depreciation thereon. These acts spoke conclusively against the alleged abandonment, and loss was denied.[27]

Similar was the situation where an obsolescence deduction was claimed by a taxpayer which, up to the time of the trial, was still using the alleged obsolescent facilities for their original purpose.[28]

In one instance, a difference of opinion among corporate officers as to when machinery became obsolete was fatal to a tax deduction, for this prevented establishment of the time when the equipment really could be considered to be outmoded. The court noted that a wide divergence existed in the opinions of various plant executives relative to the use of a substitution.[29] These differences of opinion should have been worked out before the tax returns were filed.

After the Atomic Energy Commission had canceled a contract with a corporation which had had a specialized building constructed for the implementation of the contract, the corporation sought to write off the unrecovered cost of the structure as abnormal obsolescence. The write-off was denied, however, after this exchange between a corporate officer and an Internal Revenue Service interrogator:

"Q: Do you know whether or not there is any contemplated use for that building in the future?

"A: I'm sure we will attempt to use it, but I don't know what it will be. No."

Deduction was denied because this indicated that the taxpayer had no definite intention of withdrawing the building from use in its trade or business, during the taxable year.[30]

Demolition loss was not allowed where the taxpayer's own architect, who had inspected a building allegedly sought as an additional terminal facility when land was acquired, described the structure at that time as "a very, very old sheep barn . . . in a terrible shape." [31] Under such circumstances, it did not appear that the taxpayer had purchased the building with the intention of using it, and the entire cost of land and building must have been to acquire the land.

Entertainment

A businessman sought to deduct the cost of entertaining business associates at his club. Deduction for business meals is permitted where the surroundings in which they are furnished "are of a type generally considered to be conducive to a business discussion." [32] But in the case of one chit which was marked "2 Las Vegas," the expense was disallowed for tax purposes. The court felt that this notation indicated that the atmosphere at the club on that night was not of the type generally considered conducive to business discussion. The inference of "Las Vegas" was that this was not a quiet business setting.[33]

Where an insurance company invited agents and their wives to a convention in a resort city, the amounts expended by the company on behalf of the wives was taxable income to the husbands. In making arrangements for the convention, a vice-president of the insurance company flatly stated in a letter to the hotel that "business was secondary," the main objective of the expenditure being "to give our people a good time." [34] There was no reason why both business and pleasure could not have been involved, but here, the corporate payor had stated the dominant motivation in writing.

Valuation

Where a deduction of $42,500 was claimed for a contribution of antique jewelry made to a university, but two years before the donor had only insured it for

$15,000 and there was no showing that the property had since become more valuable, deduction for contribution purposes was limited to the $15,000 insurance valuation.[35]

A certain individual contributed many paintings to charitable organizations and took deductions on the basis of values supplied by an appraiser, but the donor had made gifts of paintings and had used much lower values, for gift tax purposes. The court ruled that he had failed in the establishment of his income tax deduction.[36]

In his will, a decedent had directed his executors to hold a specified stock, despite fluctuations in market quotations, as long as they deemed appropriate because he believed the stock had a higher potential value than ordinary market quotations would indicate. Although the executors were ultimately successful in having the court accept the mean between bid and ask quotations at the time of death as the basis for valuation, the Internal Revenue Service, in seeking a higher valuation, laid much stress upon the language of the will which stated that this stock was worth more than the market quotations.[37] A court could not be faulted for concluding that the decedent, by reason of his intimate knowledge of the corporation's potentialities which still were unsuspected by the investing public, was better aware of the much higher valuation which was indicated than outsiders had been.

Fraud

When asked by a Revenue Agent why tax returns never were filed, one taxpayer replied, "Next year I'll do it, but next year never comes." It was held that he was guilty of fraud for willfully failing to file income tax returns, for this glib statement was an admission of intent not to pay taxes known to be due.[38]

In this connection, a taxpayer should not allow himself the luxury of speaking too frankly, however personally gratifying that may be. When a special agent of the Internal Revenue Service asked an individual who had not filed tax returns whether he knew about the law which covers a taxpayer's not filing with intent to evade tax, the individual exclaimed, "Well, I will tell you. It is a God damn fraud, and what I did, I did deliberately." [39]

Statements Made by Other Parties

A taxpayer may be hurt not only by statements he makes, but also by statements made by other persons who are deemed to know what he had in mind.

In one instance, various business reasons, all unrelated to saving Federal income taxes, were advanced for the splitting of one corporation into three companies. But the Service refused to recognize certain resulting tax advantages on the ground that there was no real business reason for the transaction. The corporation's attorney's statement, "whether [the tax saving] was [the chief stockholder's] principal purpose, I don't know, but as far as I was concerned, yes [it was]" lost the case for the corporation. The attorney was in a position to know from personal discussions what the actual motivation had been.[40]

A Revenue agent found in a taxpayer's files a letter from an attorney to his corporate client, which stated in part: "Certainly in this instance there is ample reason for retaining funds in the business, and, actually, from a purely business viewpoint, you should retain in the company all the present capital." But fairly substantial dividends should be paid, advised the lawyer, "because, as we have experienced before, sound business judgment is not a part of the stock-in-trade of the examining agent." That virtually compelled the Revenue agent to take action, which he did in the form of an accumulated earnings tax deficiency, to show that *his* "business judgment" was better than that of the attorney who had written the insulting letter. In the court's opinion, the agent had made such a showing.[41]

Another type of letter, if found by a Revenue agent, also tends to cause tax trouble; it is one that provides an analysis of the effect of a corporation's dividend policy upon personal taxes of shareholders. A Revenue agent discovered in the files of a corporation's accountants a copy of a letter from the accountants to the major stockholder of a corporate client which stressed the competing disadvantages of increasing the individual's own surtaxes as against subjecting the corporation to accumulated earnings tax upon undistributed earnings. The court was greatly disturbed by this letter, which suggested that corporate objectives were not the sole factor considered in setting the dividend rate. Eventually, the court decided in the corporation's favor, pointing out that there was no evidence that the directors had ever received the letter or even that it had been mailed.[42] But it was a narrow escape.

Subject to a few statutory exceptions, ordinary income rather than capital gain is found in the case of a corporation which is liquidated ("collapsed") within three years of its formation if the company had been formed with a view to liquidation while its gains or profits were still unrealized.[43] It was argued by the shareholders of one liquidated corporation that at the time they had formed the corporation, they had no intention of liquidating it. But after the conference of interested parties when the corporation was formed, the chief stockholder's tax attorney drafted a memorandum which he sent to his law partner. This stated in part: "All of the foregoing is to be done by it in contemplating [*sic*] of keeping consistent record with a view to a subsequent plan of liquidation, and the liquidation of the corporation to be along the lines which we discussed with Van on his recent trip to Newark." The court decided that any doubt that the shareholders had contemplated distributions in liquidation at the time of formation of the corporation was dispelled by the attorney's letter to his partner since the former had been present and presumably was aware of what had been discussed by and with the shareholders.[44]

The remarks of an agent might show willful intent to evade taxes which can result in a penalty for the principal. Thus, where a corporation had failed to turn over taxes withheld from the government and the responsible corporate officer sought to delegate this responsibility to a certified public accountant, testimony by the accountant that, "[f]or the past two years, the butcher was paid because he was outside the door with his hand out, whereas the government did not press its claim,"[45] showed a deliberate failure to pay taxes. (See chapter 1, Management's Tax Responsibilities.)

Knowledgeable outside parties may be compelled by the Internal Revenue Service to divulge what they know about the actual commission of a tax-related felony over which Federal courts of the United States are given exclusive jurisdiction.[46]

The testimony or other statements of a taxpayer's employees or associates may be used against a taxpayer. (See the section titled "Tax Informants" in chapter 23, Dealing with the Internal Revenue Service.) Where a taxpayer was aided by others in falsifying the corporate records, these coconspirators may testify against him in exchange for a promise by the government that in return for their cooperation, they will be granted immunity from prosecution.[47]

Employer Book Treatment

Alleged scholarship payments to employees of a major corporation on "educational leave of absence" were regarded by a United States Court of Appeals as taxable compensation where the employer showed the amounts on the books as "indirect labor." [48] However, the Supreme Court ultimately decided that, despite the employer's characterization of the payments, external evidence established that they were nontaxable scholarship payments.[49] The employees were extremely fortunate here, since it is ordinarily extremely difficult to upset the presumption created by entries in an employer's books.

The Peril of Dubious Statements

Officers who are not familiar with all of the facts should not be permitted by management to testify, lest the record be hopelessly damaged by their words. An executive testified on behalf of an officer who sought to exclude certain payments as sick pay under an established plan that "[i]t's always been the policy of our board or the Association to continue the pay of employees when they are ill." But he could name only one instance when this had actually been done.[50] A bad debt was not regarded as a business bad debt for tax purposes when the party who had made the loans testified that he really did not know why he had made them.[51] In testifying about a claim for accelerated straight-line depreciation, one witness stated that he had never been able to determine what life a piece of machinery had.[52] The value of such observations is not affirmative; it is not neutral. It is negative.

Non-Statements by Taxpayers

Not saying what should have been said also can have unfavorable tax consequences. As stated in chapter 13, Bad Debts and Other Write-Offs, no demolition loss is allowed where land and building have been acquired with the intention of tearing down the structure. After a corporation had purchased land

and building, a newspaper article reported: "N. W. Ayer & Son has purchased property in Philadelphia on which they intend to erect an office building for their own use. The property . . . adjoins their present location . . . . The buildings now standing on it will be removed." Demolition loss was denied for tax purposes although management argued at trial that there definitely had been no intention of tearing down the existing structure when the land was purchased.[53] At the time of publication of the newspaper article, no executive had gone on record to state that that was not the corporation's intention at all. Silence in tax matters is not always a virtue.

NOTES

1. *Twenty-fifth Annual Report of Stockholder Activities at Corporations During 1964,* New York: Lewis D. and John J. Gilbert, 1965, page 82.
2. *Thirty-first Annual Report of Stockholder Activities at Corporations During 1970,* New York: Lewis D. and John J. Gilbert, 1971, page 122.
3. *Battelstein Investment Company v. United States,* 302 F. Supp. 320 (D.C., S.D. Texas, 1969), *aff'd,* 442 F.2d 87 (5th Cir., 1971).
4. *Southland Industries, Inc.,* T.C. Memo., Docket No. 3387 (entered October 31, 1946).
5. *Albert L. Allen Company, Inc.,* T.C. Memo., Docket No. 112025 (entered November 25, 1944).
6. *Trico Products Corporation v. McGowan,* 67 F. Supp. 31 (D.C., W.D. N.Y., 1946), *aff'd,* 169 F.2d 43 (2d Cir., 1948).
7. *In re W. T. Ray et al.,* D.C., M.D. Tenn., 1967, *aff'd,* 420 F. 2d 1322 (6th Cir., 1969).
8. *Sarfert Hosiery Mills, Inc.,* T.C. Memo., Docket No. 9512 (entered November 13, 1947).
9. *Henry Van Hummel, Inc.,* T.C. Memo. 1964-290 (filed November 5, 1964), *aff'd,* 364 F.2d 746 (10th Cir., 1966).
10. *Isaac Engle Realty Company et al.,* T.C. Memo. 1963-273 (filed October 2, 1963).
11. *Transport Manufacturing & Equipment Company et al. v. Commissioner,* 434 F.2d 373 (8th Cir., 1970).
12. *Thirty-first Annual Report of Stockholder Activities at Corporation Meetings During 1970,* New York: Lewis D. and John J. Gilbert, 1971, page 108.
13. *Elliman v. United States,* (D.C., E.D. Mich., 1967).
14. *See United States v. Frankel,* 302 F. 2d 666 (8th Cir., 1962).
15. *Carper v. Wall,* 292 F. Supp. 340 (D.C., W.D. N.C., 1968).
16. *Fritzel v. United States,* 339 F.2d 995 (7th Cir., 1964).
17. *Loewy Drug Company of Baltimore City v. United States,* 232 F. Supp. 143 (D.C., Md., 1964), *aff'd,* 356 F.2d 928 (4th Cir., 1966).
18. *Century Country Club v. United States,* 116 F. Supp. 727 (Ct. Cl., 1953).
19. *Domenico E. Fazzio et al.,* T.C. Memo., Docket Nos. 111857 and 112564 (entered September 17, 1943).
20. *Krohn et al. v. United States,* 246 F. Supp. 341 (D.C., Colo., 1965).
21. *Porter v. Commissioner,* 437 F.2d 39 (2d Cir., 1970).
22. *Gurtman et al. v. United States,* 237 F. Supp. 533 (D.C., N.J., 1965), *aff'd,* 353 F.2d 212 (3d Cir., 1966).
23. *Covey Investment Company v. United States,* 377 F.2d 403 (10th Cir., 1967).
24. *The Rappold Company,* T.C. Memo., Docket No. 23393 (entered November 18, 1950).
25. *Ernest E. Dison et al.,* T.C. Memo. 1965-150 (filed June 1, 1965).
26. *Cuyuna Realty Company v. United States,* 382 F.2d 298 (Ct. Cl., 1967).
27. *United California Bank,* 41 T.C. 437 (1965).
28. *James D. Dunn et al.,* 42 T.C. 490 (1964).

29. *Celluloid Company*, 9 B.T.A. 989 (1927).

30. *Coors Porcelain Company v. Commissioner*, 429 F.2d 1 (10th Cir., 1970).

31. *Riss & Company, Inc. et al.*, T.C. Memo. 1964-190 (filed July 14, 1964).

32. I.R.C. Section 274(e)(1).

33. *Henry G. LaForge et al.*, 53 T.C. 41 (1969), *rev'd and rem'd'd on another issue,* 434 F.2d 370 (2d Cir., 1970).

34. *Acacia Mutual Life Insurance Company v. United States*, 272 F. Supp. 188 (D.C., Md., 1967).

35. *Tripp v. Commissioner*, 337 F.2d 432 (7th Cir., 1964).

36. *Samuel Silverman et al.*, T.C. Memo. 1968-216 (filed September 26, 1968).

37. *Vernon S. Prentice Estate*, T.C. Memo. 1956-3 (filed January 10, 1956).

38. *Trolla v. United States*, 390 F.2d 951 (Ct. Cl., 1968).

39. *United States v. Keig*, 320 F.2d 634 (7th Cir., 1963).

40. *Bonneville Locks Towing Co., Inc. et al. v. United States*, 343 F.2d 790 (9th Cir., 1965).

41. *Lichter et al. v. Charles*, D.C., S.D. Ohio, 1969.

42. *Sandy Estate Company*, 43 T.C. 361 (1964).

43. I.R.C. Section 341.

44. *Guy A. Van Heusen*, 44 T.C. 491 (1965).

45. *Lawrence v. United States*, 299 F. Supp. 187 (D.C., N.D. Texas, 1969).

46. 18 U.S.C. 4 (1969).

47. *See United States v. Goldberg et al.*, 349 F.2d 633 (3d Cir., 1964).

48. *Johnson et al. v. Bingler*, 396 F.2d 258 (3d Cir., 1968).

49. *Bingler v. Johnson et al.*, 394 U.S. 741 (1969).

50. *Leo P. Kaufman Estate et al.*, 35 T.C. 663 (1961).

51. *Nathan Milgroom et al.*, T.C. Memo. 1960-285 (filed December 30, 1960).

52. *Willis D. Owens et al.*, T.C. Memo., Docket Nos. 14390-1 (entered March 30, 1950).

53. *N. W. Ayer & Son, Inc.*, 17 T.C. 631 (1951).

CHAPTER 25

Corporate Minutes: Their Offensive and Defensive Use

Significance

Corporate minutes may furnish the taxpayer with proof that an action is what it purports to be. Contrariwise, the Internal Revenue Service may be able to establish with the help of the corporate minutes that a particular action could not have been what it was labeled as. Thus, many tax cases are won or lost largely on the basis of the minutes. So a regular examination of a corporate income tax return may include the minute books.

The minutes may have tax significance at the very start of a corporation's life. The incorporators may claim they gave their company certain assets in return for corporate stock and notes. But if an Internal Revenue agent reads in the minutes of the organizational meeting that the assets were transferred to the corporation solely in return for corporate stock, the notes will not be deemed to have been a part of the transaction at all and the receipt of the notes may be taxed as a dividend.[1]

The minutes may help to determine whether the organization actually is a corporation. In deciding that a business entity really was a corporation for tax purposes, a court noted that it maintained records comparable to a corporate minute book.[2]

A new corporation's initial choice of a fiscal year for accounting purposes was honored even though the first tax return which reflected the accounting period was not filed on time where the minutes reflected management's intention from the start to use this fiscal period.[3] But minutes showing the adoption of a particular fiscal year will be ignored if, in fact, the books are kept on a different basis. The minutes may establish a presumption; but the fact can be determined only by what was done.[4]

Stockholder Advances

When a stockholder advances money to his corporation, the question often arises as to whether the transaction represents an investment of capital or a loan.

327

Where the corporate minutes do not indicate that a loan which the corporation was obligated to repay was made, the Service may be justified in treating the transaction as a capital contribution.[5] On the other hand, the minutes may clearly indicate that a loan rather than a capital contribution was made to the corporation. Thus, a finding of a loan rather than a capital contribution by stockholder may be supported by a succession of stockholders' resolutions in the minute book of the company, those resolutions referring to the sums as "capital loans" and indicating that they were to be paid out of future earnings when and if such funds were available.[6] Similarly, loans were recognized where the minutes so characterized the transactions and plainly showed the parties' intention to create an unconditional and legally enforceable obligation for the payment of money.[7] Loans were also found where the minutes clearly disclosed that two of the advances questioned by the Service had been expressly authorized by the directors as loans prior to the time they were made.[8]

In another case, shareholder advances to a corporation were not regarded as loans where no mention was made in the minutes concerning the repayment of these amounts.[9]

Intercompany advances were treated as dividends where no resolution was passed by either company authorizing the "loan." [10]

Compensation for Services

Corporate minutes refer in various ways to matters dealing with compensation for services. Sometimes, a corporation will authorize compensation in one year to make up for what was not paid in an earlier year. The question then arises as to the taxable year in which the deduction may be taken. The corporation may claim the deduction in the year of authorization rather than in the year to which the payment applies if no liability existed in the earlier year. One of the most effective ways of establishing this is by reference to the minutes. If the resolution as shown by the minutes discloses no prior agreement or legal obligation to pay the compensation being voted, the deduction may be allowed in the year when payment is approved.[11] Where the minutes fail to recognize that compensation really was for prior years, testimony long after the event may be deemed to be "not convincing." [12]

The minutes should show reasons for a corporation's increasing or decreasing executive or employee-stockholder compensation, and these reasons should be based on individual performance, lest fluctuating salaries be characterized by the Service as dividends and not be deductible by the corporation. Where minutes refer to authorization of salary increases without giving reasons therefor in years of rising profits, and then, the compensation of officer-stockholders is reduced without explanation in a year of poor earnings, the payments may be treated by the Service as equivalent to dividends, with similar loss of deduction.[13]

If the minutes reveal that the directors had considered the compensation of executives, the board action ordinarily carries a presumption of reasonableness of the compensation paid—even in the case of a closely held corporation.[14] But this fact need not necessarily be determinative.[15]

Where compensation is paid in excess of the amount which the directors had authorized, the full amount may be deductible if in fact it was reasonable.[16]

In general, an accrual-basis corporation must accrue compensation in the year that the liability to make payment becomes fixed.[17] But before it can be said that the liability has become fixed, there must be present during the taxable year some proof of corporate action authorizing the payment of an ascertainable amount.[18]

In the case of bonuses to officer-stockholders, it is particularly important that the resolution of authorization appear in the minutes relatively early in the taxable year. If the bonuses are not authorized until late in the year, such "bonuses" are likely to be regarded as dividends or a distribution of profits.

Belatedly-authorized bonuses may be regarded as compensation and not dividends where the corporate minutes show that the bonuses were approved not only after a detailed review of financial statements, but also after consideration of the services performed by each executive.[19]

Where the minutes show a resolution made at the start of a taxable year which clearly sets forth what the compensation scale will be in the event that sales attain a specified figure, the corporate liability is automatic if the conditions are fulfilled so that a formal declaration of payment in the subsequent year would not affect the deductibility of the amount in the earlier year.[20]

The importance of corporate minutes in establishing the reasonableness of compensation was shown in one jury case involving allegedly unreasonable compensation deductions. A copy of the minutes was sent into the jury room for consideration by the jurors.[21]

Repayment of "Unreasonable" Compensation

If an employee receives compensation subject to an obligation to repay part of it under stipulated conditions and he is required to repay any amount in excess of $3000, he may elect to make the adjustment as of the year of receipt or as of the year of the repayment.[22] The existence of the necessary binding obligation to make repayment may be shown by the corporate minutes.[23] Thus, deductions by officers were allowed in the year that amounts of unreasonable compensation were repaid by the officers where they were bound by this entry in the minutes: "Salary payments made to an officer of the corporation that shall be disallowed in whole or in part as a deductible expense for Federal income tax purposes shall be reimbursed by such officer to the corporation to the full extent of the disallowance. It shall be the duty of the board of directors to enforce payment of each such amount disallowed." [24]

Gifts

Any economic benefit which flows from a corporation to an employee is deemed to be compensation unless the contrary can be proven. A so-called "gift" was held to be clearly compensatory where the minutes declared that the employee "for many years rendered valuable services to the corporation at an inadequate salary." [25] Likewise, a resolution that a check be given to an executive at the time of his wedding, "in recognition of the very efficient manner in which he had for years 'handled the company's affairs,' " was held to show compensation, not a gift.[26]

Where a corporation makes payments to the widow of an officer or other employee, the payments may be considered compensation where they are authorized in the minutes "as additional compensation and in consideration of services heretofore rendered to this corporation . . . ." [27] But a gift was recognized where the minutes indicated that payment was made because of "the situation of" the widow.[28]

The corporation can deduct payments made to an employee's widow only if made as compensation (in which case it would be taxable to the widow) or as a payment for business purposes, such as to improve employee morale or to acquire community good will. No deduction was permitted where several directors testified that although they had considered the possibility of business benefits when authorizing the payment, nothing was formally presented to the directorate.[29]

Economic Benefits

The minutes may establish whether other financial arrangements are intended as compensation to employees. If an economic benefit (such as the payment of an officer's life insurance premiums) is meant to be compensation, the minutes should so indicate; for in the absence of such a notation, the amount may be disallowed as a deduction to the corporation on the theory that the company was merely acting as an agent for the officer.[30]

A corporation's assumption of the payment of the personal income taxes of its officers may be regarded as additional compensation; that will certainly be the case if the terms of the resolution indicate that the corporate action was in recognition of services performed by the executives.[31]

Fringe Benefits

If an employee would take advantage of any exclusion of sick pay from his gross income to the extent provided by the Internal Revenue Code, there should be a corporate record, as in the minutes, that a sick pay plan existed.[32] A sick pay plan was found to have existed where the corporate minutes made reference to the plan before any payments were actually made.[33] But a sick pay plan was not recognized where the minutes stated that there should be accident and health plans for such employees as the officers considered should be covered. This was not deemed to be a *plan,* but something which was operated on an *ad hoc* basis.[34]

Officer-stockholders of a corporation were permitted to exclude from income payments pursuant to a medical reimbursement plan although 12 non-officers were not covered by the plan. The portion of the minutes which set up the plan stated that only employees who are officers shall be "qualified" employees for purposes of reimbursement under the plan.[35]

Corporate minutes in themselves do not create pension liability and, hence, a basis for an allowable deduction. If a board of directors resolves to establish a pension fund for the benefit of employees in substantial compliance with the terms and provisions of a trust instrument attached to the resolution, no deduction will be allowed if the trust agreement is not actually executed until the following taxable year.[36] But if the directors appropriate funds for a pension plan whose establishment they have ordered, a deduction will be permitted even though the implementing trust is not created until the following taxable year, for the money would have been set aside, as directors' intentions had been made apparent from the minutes.[37]

**Corporate Minutes:
Their Offensive and
Defensive Use**

The Accumulated Earnings Tax

There is no better place than the corporate minutes to record a corporation's reasons for retaining its earnings. The minutes are a contemporaneous record reflecting the company's activities and the reasons therefor. They are the diary of the directors' thoughts which resulted in the dividend policy that was adopted at the meeting. They show the motives and the objectives sought by the decision to retain earnings. Thus, minutes setting forth the business reasons for retention of earnings may prevail over evidence of circumstances from which might be drawn inferences to the opposite effect.[38]

The absence of any notation in the minutes may be regarded as indicative of the fact that there was no plan for retention during the year of accumulation. Retention will be recognized as valid if based upon the exercise of good business judgment. But if the minutes fail to show that retention was based upon good judgment, the accumulated earnings tax may be imposed even where mere carelessness was the cause.[39]

Minutes showing that no dividend was declared because the corporation would need money to consummate a deal it was negotiating were held effective[40] as were minutes showing that accrued earnings were retained to cover expansion costs.[41]

Where the minutes are relied on to show the reason for retaining earnings, they must contain more than vague recitals of objectives.[42] They must state substantial and material facts showing valid reasons for retaining the earnings.[43] That the minutes prepared by the directors and their counsel were deliberately utilized to emphasize the solid basis for retention is not fatal. An aura of tax consciousness does not destroy the fact that minutes contain evidence of plans to expand or to otherwise effectuate some need of the business.[44]

Arm's Length Transactions

If there are several corporations under common control, the Internal Revenue Service may seek to reallocate all of the income to a single corporation on the ground that there was no valid non-tax reason for channeling income to several companies.[45] In one case where the Service was permitted to disregard several corporate entities by reallocating all income and expenses to a single corporation, the court pointed out that there was no proof of the existence of any arrangement to assign different functions to different companies such as would justify the utilization of several corporations for business reasons. The court specifically commented that no corporate minute books were presented at the trial.[46]

Reallocation by the Service of a subsidiary's income to the parent company was not permitted where the minutes showed that the maintenance of a high-volume business required that the business be divided among several separate corporate entities and that the key employees of each be given stock ownership in the corporation.[47]

Write-Offs

Write-off of inventory as obsolete or worthless requires affirmative proof that the officers considered these items to be such during the taxable year. This kind of proof can be supplied by the corporate minutes.[48]

A corporation was not permitted to take a deduction for obsolescence on its old plant when equipment was transferred to a new plant. The change had been made pursuant to a resolution adopted by the board of directors. Significantly, however, no mention was made anywhere in the resolution that obsolescence was a reason for the action.[49]

Timeliness of Payments

An accrual-basis corporation can take no deduction for unpaid expenses it owes to a cash-basis individual owning more than 50 percent of the stock if payments are not made within two and one-half months after the close of the taxable year.[50] The question of constructive payment is vital: Was the amount available to the intended payee without substantial limitation so that payment could be *deemed* to have been made within the permissible time? The minutes may be decisive in establishing whether the intended payee received on time what was equivalent to payment. If the minutes award specific amounts to named persons, placing the amount to their credit subject to payment upon demand, constructive payment has taken place even if actual payment is not made until a subsequent taxable year.[51] But even though the minutes recite that a certain person is to be paid a specific sum and that amount is accrued on the books, this is not necessarily proof of an allowable deduction, for the corporation may not have sufficient funds to permit a constructive payment.[52]

Contributions

An accrual-basis taxpayer and a cash-basis taxpayer are on the same footing in the case of contributions. Deductions are taken in the year of actual payment. But an exception may be made in the case of an accrual-basis corporation. If the directors authorize a contribution in one taxable year and payment is made in the first two and one-half months of the following taxable year, an election may be made to take the deduction in the year of authorization.[53] (See chapter 16, What Can Be Done with Contributions.) The authorization of the directors need not be in writing.[54] But a written declaration that the resolution was adopted must accompany the tax return of the year to which the election applies.

Tax-Exempt Foundation

A charitable foundation lost its tax-exempt status because income was deemed to have accumulated in unreasonable amounts. The court pointed out that neither the minutes nor any other part of the record indicated any particular use to which either the accumulated income or the then current income would be put.[55]

Sale of Property

The fact that the stockholders rather than the corporation sold property, which they received from the corporation as a distribution in kind so that the corporation is not subject to a tax on the sale, may be shown by the corporate minutes.[56] But if the minutes are so carelessly prepared that it cannot be ascertained whether the property was distributed to the stockholders before or after the sale, those minutes will not be effective.[57]

Dividends

For tax purposes, it is not necessary that there be any record of the declaration of a dividend in the corporate minutes. A distribution will be taxed as a dividend if the facts indicate that it is essentially equivalent to one, regardless of the formalities.[58] In order for a corporate distribution to a shareholder to constitute a dividend, it need not be formally declared a dividend by the board of directors.[59]

Minutes may establish the time of a dividend payment. The minutes of one corporation provided that a dividend of a stipulated amount be declared and paid as of December 31, and that the appropriate dividend checks be mailed or handed to the stockholders not later than January 1. The Service maintained that the shareholders, who were on the cash basis, had constructively received the dividends on December 31. The court held that, under the dividend resolution as recorded in the minutes, the stockholders did not have unfettered command over the dividend proceeds on that date, for the checks were not written by the corporation until January.[60]

The Limited Effect of Corporate Minutes

The language of corporate minutes is not necessarily controlling. A court can go behind the formal resolution and delve into the conduct of the directors in formulating their official act.[61] Minutes do not always reflect everything that occurred or was said at a meeting.[62]

The fact that minutes purport to document a particular situation may be ignored where they are the minutes of a controlled board of directors, or where they are self-serving and amount to "window-dressing." [63] Even though the minutes declare that the corporation's distributions to stockholders are repayments of loans, the payments may be held to be dividend payments.[64]

A company's resolution that its president was obliged to use the corporation's facilities did not create a condition of employment so that occupancy of a company house would be tax-free where, in fact, the president controlled the directors who had voted this action.[65]

Minutes Can Be Harmful to a Corporation

A corporation was assessed a negligence penalty where the minutes revealed that its accountant had recommended that a request for a ruling from the Service be made in the case of purportedly exempt income. The corporation did nothing about the request, and the income was not reported. Inasmuch as this income should have been reported, the entry in the minutes made it impossible for the corporation to plead ignorance as to the taxability of the item.[66]

Retention of earnings for the alleged purpose of acquiring a competitor was rejected where the minutes merely indicated that discussions had been conducted, that neither price nor terms were considered, and that the directors did not consider that any serious offer had been made.[67] Where a corporation argued that its retention of earnings was for the purpose of expansion, its minutes revealed that the directors were seriously considering the liquidation, rather than the expansion, of the corporation at the time.[68]

Stockholder advances to their corporation were held to be stock investments rather than loans as claimed by the corporation when seeking an interest deduction on certain payments to shareholders. The minutes stated that the shareholder advances were to be left "as permanent working capital for the company," which negated the force of the argument that they were loans.[69]

Right of the Internal Revenue Service
to Subpoena Minutes

Where the corporate minutes are invoked to establish documentation for some action or nonaction, it is usually the corporation which appeals to what the minutes set forth. But the Service may apply for a court order compelling the production of corporate minutes. In one case, the Service demanded production of the minutes of a parent corporation and its 17 affiliated corporations which had participated in a consolidated Federal income tax return. The taxpayers offered to produce instead "action minutes" dealing with resolutions, approvals, and the like. But the companies maintained that forward planning projects, reports on economic conditions, reviews of financial conditions, and proposals which never were implemented clearly constituted matters beyond the reach of the Service. The court disagreed. The Service is not constrained to accept a taxpayer's word as to the relevancy or materiality of any records. The companies' certified public accountants looked at the minutes in order to review contingent liabilities and compliance with internal accounting procedures. As that made good sense to the accountants, it made equally good sense for the Service to examine the minutes. Even if the examination of the minutes was merely a fishing expedition, there was nothing wrong with that.[70]

NOTES

1. *Joseph T. Coyle et al.*, T.C. Memo., Docket Nos. 19409-10 (entered January 25, 1950).
2. *Perry R. Bass et al.*, 50 T.C. 595 (1968).
3. Revenue Ruling 68-125, 1968-1 CB 189.
4. *Iron Mountain Oil Co. v. Alexander*, 37 F.2d 231 (10th Cir., 1930).
5. *Powers Photoengraving Co.*, 17 T.C. 393 (1951).
6. *Ortmayer et al. v. Commissioner*, 265 F.2d 848 (7th Cir., 1959).
7. *The 1661 Corporation v. Tomlinson*, 247 F. Supp. 936 (D.C., M.D. Fla., 1965).
8. *Edwards Motor Transit Company*, T.C. Memo. 1964-317 (filed December 10, 1964).
9. *Henderson et al. v. United States*, 245 F. Supp. 782 (D.C., M.D. Ala., 1965).
10. *Chared Corp. v. United States*, D.C., N.D. Texas, 1969.
11. *Lucas v. Ox Fibre Brush Company*, 281 U.S. 115 (1930).
12. *Compeco Dye Works, Inc.*, T.C. Memo., Docket No. 3066 (entered July 19, 1949).
13. *Builders Steel Company*, T.C. Memo., Docket No. 17796 (entered March 25, 1949).
14. *Palmetto Pump and Irrigation Company v. Tomlinson*, D.C., S.D. Fla., 1962, *aff'd*, 313 F.2d 220 (5th Cir., 1963).
15. *Ray Guzowski et al.*, T.C. Memo. 1967-145 (filed June 30, 1967).
16. *L. R. Schmaus Co., Inc. v. Commissioner*, 406 F.2d 1044 (7th Cir., 1969).
17. Regulations Section 1.446-1(c)(1)(ii).
18. *John T. Savage et al.*, T.C. Memo. 1970-158 (filed June 18, 1970).
19. *James J. Glenn et al.*, T.C. Memo. 1970-184 (filed June 30, 1970).
20. *Mobile Drug Company v. United States*, (D.C., S.D. Ala., 1930).
21. *Coca-Cola Bottling Company of Mitchell, South Dakota v. United States*, D.C., S.D., 1958.
22. I.R.C. Section 1341(a).
23. *Vincent E. Oswald*, 49 T.C. 645 (1968).
24. Revenue Ruling 69-115, 1969-1 CB 50.
25. *Taylor-Logan Company v. White*, 62 F.2d 336 (1st Cir., 1932).

336

Corporate Minutes:
Their Offensive and
Defensive Use

26. *Nickelsburg v. Commissioner*, 154 F.2d 70 (2d Cir., 1946).
27. *Martin Kuntz, Sr. Estate et al.*, T.C. Memo. 1960-247 (filed November 22, 1960).
28. *Corasaniti et al. v. United States*, 212 F. Supp. 229 (D.C., Md., 1962).
29. *Allen Industries, Inc. v. Commissioner*, 414 F.2d 983 (6th Cir., 1969).
30. *Hubert Transfer & Storage Company*, T.C. Memo., Docket Nos. 12078 and 13229 (entered March 31, 1948).
31. *Old Colony Trust Company v. Commissioner*, 284 U.S. 552 (1929).
32. *E. W. Chism Estate v. Commissioner*, 322 F.2d 956 (9th Cir., 1963).
33. *Bogene, Incorporated et al.*, T.C. Memo. 1968-147 (filed July 11, 1968).
34. *Larkin et al. v. Commissioner*, 394 F.2d 494 (1st Cir., 1968).
35. *E. B. Smith et al.*, T.C. Memo. 1970-243 (filed August 26, 1970).
36. *Abingdon Potteries, Inc.*, 19 T.C. 23 (1952).
37. *Crow-Burlingame Company*, 15 T.C. 738 (1950).
38. *Cecil B. DeMille Productions, Inc.*, 31 B.T.A. 1161 (1935), *aff'd*, 90 F.2d 12 (9th Cir., 1937).
39. *E. L. Bride et al.*, T.C. Memo., Docket Nos. 34598-9 (entered October 30, 1953), *aff'd*, 224 F.2d 39 (5th Cir., 1955).
40. *Thomas W. Briggs et al.*, T.C. Memo. 1956-86 (filed April 16, 1956).
41. *Magic Mart, Inc.*, 51 T.C. 775 (1969).
42. *In re W. T. Ray et al.*, D.C., M.D. Tenn., 1967, *aff'd*, 409 F.2d 1322 (6th Cir., 1969).
43. *American Metal Products Corporation et al.*, 34 T.C. 89 (1960), *aff'd*, 287 F.2d 860 (2d Cir., 1961).
44. *Faber Cement Block Co., Inc.*, 50 T.C. 317 (1968).
45. I.R.C. Section 482.
46. *Shaker Apartments, Inc. et al. v. United States*, D.C., N.D. Ohio, 1966.
47. *V. H. Monette and Company, Inc. et al.*, 45 T.C. 15 (1965), *aff'd*, 374 F.2d 116 (4th Cir., 1967).
48. *Dunn Manufacturing Co.*, 14 B.T.A. 225 (1928).
49. *S. S. White Dental Manufacturing Company v. United States*, 38 F. Supp. 301 (Ct. Cl., 1941).
50. I.R.C. Section 267(a).
51. *Michael Flynn Manufacturing Company*, 3 T.C. 932 (1944).
52. *H & H Drilling Co., Inc.*, 15 T.C. 961 (1950).
53. I.R.C. Section 170(a)(2).
54. *Faucette Co., Inc.*, 17 T.C. 187 (1951).
55. *Stevens Bros. Foundation, Inc.*, 39 T.C. 93 (1962), *aff'd*, 324 F.2d 633 (8th Cir., 1963).
56. *Ripy Bros. Distillers, Inc.*, 11 T.C. 326 (1948).
57. *Wichita Terminal Elevator Co. v. Commissioner*, 162 F.2d 513 (10th Cir., 1947).
58. *Beretta v. Commissioner*, 141 F.2d 452 (5th Cir., 1944).
59. *Nasser et al. v. United States*, 257 F. Supp. 443 (D.C., N.D. Cal., 1966).
60. *Alvin Hill et al.*, T.C. Memo. 1962-239 (filed October 9, 1962).
61. *Childers et al. v. United States*, D.C., M.D. Tenn., 1969.
62. *Alan B. Larkin et al.*, 48 T.C. 629 (1967), *aff'd*, 394 F.2d 494 (1st Cir., 1968).
63. *Robert R. Walker, Inc. et al.*, T.C. Memo. 1965-28 (filed February 16, 1954), *aff'd* 362 F.2d 140 (7th Cir., 1966).
64. *Cornelius C. Noble et al.*, T.C. Memo. 1965-84 (filed April 7, 1965).
65. *Lloyd E. Peterson et al.*, T.C. Memo. 1965-255 (filed September 21, 1965).
66. *Colombo Club, Inc.*, 54 T.C. 355 (1970).
67. *Coastal Casting Service, Inc. v. Phinney*, D.C., S.D. Texas, 1970.
68. *In re W. T. Ray et al. v. United States*, D.C., M.D. Tenn., 1967, *aff'd*, 409 F.2d 1322 (6th Cir., 1969).
69. *Oak Hill Finance Company*, 40 T.C. 419 (1963).
70. *United States et al. v. Acker*, 325 F. Supp. 857 (D.C., S.D. N.Y., 1971).

CHAPTER 26

Procedure and Practice Guide

Treasury Regulations

The regulations issued by the Treasury Department are intended to help a taxpayer understand the tax law or the manner in which the Internal Revenue Service will interpret it. But frequently, a taxpayer is trapped by these regulations.

A course of action may be planned (or not undertaken) on the basis of the language of regulations which may have been held, for example, to be unconstitutional, or beyond the authority conferred on the Treasury. For instance, the regulations provide that a tax-free corporate separation (see chapter 28, Corporate Reorganizations and Estate Planning) is possible only where two or more existing businesses are operated by a single corporation. But it has been held that this requirement is improper as beyond the scope of the Internal Revenue Code provision on the subject.[1] After several other courts had handed down decisions to the same effect, the Internal Revenue Service announced that it would follow the findings of these courts.[2] But the language of the regulations has not been changed.

Sometimes, Treasury Regulations are promulgated with retroactive effect. Then, a taxpayer is bound by ground rules which did not exist when he planned and executed his transaction.[3]

Rulings and other Internal Revenue Service releases may be too brief or too simplified to cover all of the exceptions and fine print. The mischief in relying totally upon Revenue Rulings, official tax return instructions, and the like is that, for the most part, they speak to the limited fact patterns that the Internal Revenue Service considered when it heard those particular cases. They cannot be regarded as comprehensive statements of the tax law and, thus, are dubious reeds upon which a taxpayer may lean.[4]

Private Rulings

Sometimes a taxpayer or his counsel is able to obtain a personalized ruling from the Internal Revenue Service upon a specific question. But it is not an abuse of discretion for the Service to revoke retroactively a ruling issued in response to a particular request by a particular taxpayer.[5]

In addition, a private letter ruling to one taxpayer is not binding upon the Internal Revenue Service in the case of another taxpayer with an identical situation.[6] Where a ruling is obtained on behalf of one corporation, it is not controlling in the case of other companies owned by this corporation even though the point involved is identical.[7] Private letter rulings are issued to the private party requesting them and it is not intended that they should be relied on by the general public.[8]

Assistance by the Internal Revenue Service

If a taxpayer receives aid from an employee of the Internal Revenue Service, he has no assurance that the Service will accept the result as correct. Each year the Service provides information and assistance to millions of taxpayers. Its employees cannot be expected to be correct as to every question, nor are they held to a standard of infallibility, especially when all of the facts may not have been fully presented, perhaps because the taxpayer did not understand the full implications of the particular problem.[9]

The government is not bound by an erroneous interpretation of the law made by a subordinate agent.[10] Misrepresentations by a government agent cannot have the effect of making legal that which the law declares to be illegal.[11] Even where a taxpayer was sufficiently important (a United States Senator) to obtain a written ruling as to the effect of a proposed transaction directly from the Commissioner of Internal Revenue himself, the Internal Revenue Service (under the administration of a subsequent Commissioner) could ignore that favorable ruling and assess additional tax on the transaction in question.[12]

Judge Learned Hand declared that "harsh as it may be, one accepts the advice of a revenue official at his peril," [13]

Reliance upon the official instructions issued with government tax forms is misplaced. These instructions are merely explanatory; they are not meant to be all-inclusive. For a full explanation of the tax requirements, the Internal Revenue Code and the Treasury Regulations must be referred to, as well as additions and modifications which are published in the *Federal Register*.[14] Anything less is likely to be characterized by the Service or a court as insufficient, which means that even official Internal Revenue Service explanations are of limited value.

Agreements with the Internal Revenue Service

In the case of a controversy with a Revenue agent, a taxpayer may attempt to settle the dispute by making substantial concessions, even as to issues on which he believes that he is correct. Should a higher Internal Revenue Service official refuse to accept the settlement, this places the taxpayer in a very awkward situation, for he already has thrown in his hand on matters so that he now must argue against his own concessions. Agreement reached with, and recommended by, an Internal Revenue Service conferee in the case of a dispute is not binding and has no effect.[15]

Anyone entering into an arrangement with the government must risk having accurately ascertained that the official who purports to act for the government has kept within the bounds of his authority. This is so even though the agent may have been unaware of the limitations upon his authority.[16] One court pointed out sadly that it does not create a satisfactory, reassuring atmosphere for the government to repudiate the act one of its own agents performed in the course of his duties.[17] But it happens.

Rulings of Different Federal Authorities

The fact that a taxpayer has received a ruling or a directive from one governmental agency does not mean that the Internal Revenue Service will accept this for tax purposes. The ruling of one governmental agency made under one statute does not control the ruling of another governmental agency made under a different statute for a different purpose.[18] This may be likened to what is referred to in labor relations as a jurisdictional dispute; the person in the middle is likely to get burnt.

Where a corporation was required to maintain its books and records in accordance with the rules of the Federal Communications Commission and the Rural Electrification Administration, the accounting rules of these administrative agencies were not controlling on Federal income tax questions.[19] The fact that a depreciation method is prescribed by the Federal Power Commission does not mean that the method is acceptable to the Internal Revenue Service.[20] Obsolescence was not allowed for tax purposes although a 15-year write-off was permitted by the Interstate Commerce Commission.[21] And the order of a referee in bankruptcy that a certain advance was a loan did not determine the nature of the transaction for income tax purposes.[22]

Dividend Distributions

The board of directors needs to be familiar with practice and procedure as to dividend distributions. Any distributions by a corporation to its shareholders when there are earnings and profits accumulated since February 28, 1913 are presumed to be dividends in the absence of proof to the contrary or a statutory exception specified in the Internal Revenue Code.[23] A distribution is deemed to be from the most recent earnings. Thus, a dividend was found where, in one year, a corporation made a distribution of its earnings for that year, even though they were insufficient to wipe out the accumulated deficit with which the corporation had started the year.[24]

Distributions which a shareholder received from a corporation that had never had earnings and profits may be taxed as a dividend. Earnings and profits are imputed to a corporation which is a successor in a tax-free reorganization to a predecessor corporation which did have earnings and profits even though the shareholder was completely unaware of this reorganization, which may have taken place many years previously.[25]

Where a corporation's facilities are used by stockholders without charge, dividends may be found to have been constructively received.[26] Reimbursed travel expenses of an officer-shareholder were treated as dividends in the absence of proof that they involved business travel.[27] Withdrawals from a corporation by a stockholder were treated as dividends where there was no evidence of any agreement as to the time of repayment of these moneys.[28]

If corporate contributions to an employee benefit plan are made by a corporation under circumstances such that the chief stockholders are the principal beneficiaries, these payments may be regarded as dividends.[29]

Where stock of a retiring employee had to be sold back to the surviving shareholder, and it was the corporation that actually bought the retiring shareholder's stock, this was regarded as a dividend to the survivor.[30] Corporate moneys had been used for his benefit to discharge his obligation.

The proceeds of a sale of stock to a controlled corporation may be treated as a dividend for tax purposes.[31]

A corporate tax deficiency may have the dual result of being expensive both to the corporation and to a shareholder. Where the Internal Revenue Service disallowed corporate deductions for the chief stockholder's travel and entertainment by reason of failure of proof that it was the corporation which benefited, he was deemed to have received a constructive dividend in the amount of the expenses disallowed.[32] After a corporation was found to have unreported income, a constructive dividend of this unreported amount was deemed to have been received by the stockholders who had knowledge of the transaction on the theory that if the corporation *had* reported additional income of that amount, it would have paid out the exact amount as dividends.[33] Where the sole stockholder of a corporation withdrew money from a wholly-owned subsidiary corporation when the latter had earnings and profits, he was deemed to have received a constructive dividend from the *parent* company, which in turn was regarded as having received a dividend in this amount from its subsidiary.[34]

A corporation made a payment to the widow of a deceased officer. The executive approving this payment did so because he regarded it as a moral duty to make up to the widow for the fact that her deceased husband had cut her off in his will. The payment was not the result of a corporate motivation, but rather the result of a desire of the executive who had authorized the payment to right what he considered a moral wrong. There was testimony that he frequently gave his children moral lessons. The payment to the widow was taxed to him as a dividend as it represented the satisfaction of his personal desires.[35]

A distribution or other economic benefit may be taxed as a dividend even where the beneficiary is not a shareholder. If a person derives an economic advantage from dealing with a corporation, he may be taxed on the benefit's value as a dividend even if he was not a shareholder at the time, provided that he had beneficial ownership and control of the stock.[36]

Social Security Benefits

An individual eligible for Federal Old Age benefits under the Social Security Act may earn up to $2400 a year without losing tax-exempt Social Security benefits. If earnings exceed that amount, $1 of benefits are lost for each $2 earned above $2400. When the individual attains age 72, however, these forfeitures no longer apply.[37]

Unavailable Forms

If a Federal income tax return or other form must be filed by a specified date, failure to file is not excused by the fact that the Internal Revenue Service ran out of forms.[38]

Certain tax forms may be reproduced by a taxpayer or purchased from a commercial printer; but the type of paper, color of the form, nature of the ink, etc., must meet the specifications issued by the Internal Revenue Service.[39]

Refund Claims

The filing of a refund claim with the Internal Revenue Service may amount to the opening of Pandora's box. Once a taxable year is reopened for one purpose, it is validly reopened for all purposes.[40]

In one case, a Revenue agent disallowed deductions in the amount of $1200.60, and a deficiency notice of $972.48 in tax resulted. Subsequently, the taxpayer sought a review of this matter, as a result of which other disallowances of $22,168.96 were made. With interest, this brought about a deficiency of $27,569.15.[41]

Relations with Professional Advisors

The privileged nature of communication between a taxpayer and his attorney may be lost if a third party is present, even if that third party is the taxpayer's regular accountant.[42] The Internal Revenue Service may use as a witness against a taxpayer the attorney who had prepared his income tax return if the attorney had acted not as a lawyer, but merely as a scrivener for the taxpayer. Under these circumstances, the attorney-client relationship is not established, and any communication to the lawyer or other documents in his custody are not protected by the privilege.[43]

The right to associate with others of one's choice at any time is one of the liberties protected by the First Amendment.[44] But frequently, a transaction is disregarded for tax purposes as lacking in business or economic reality if a taxpayer undertook a course of action after receiving advice from his tax consultant.[45] One of the factors which led a court to conclude that a certain transaction was a tax sham was evidence that the taxpayer had consulted with a named tax attorney. From a consideration of all of the evidence the court concluded that there was good cause to support an inference that the transaction was principally motivated by tax savings.[46]

In finding for the taxpayer in one case, the court pointed out that he had not consulted a tax advisor as to the most advantageous method from an income tax standpoint.[47] Another court was inclined to accept a taxpayer's explanation that a certain transaction had business motivation and was not a tax dodge because he had not consulted in advance with counsel or anyone else as to the income tax consequences of the transaction.[48] Improper tax avoidance was not found where a taxpayer had followed the advice of an attorney who testified that he was not a tax lawyer.[49]

But it may be unrealistic to argue tax unawareness. It is difficult to believe that sophisticated businessmen arranging a major transaction fraught with tax potentials would remain innocent of the tax implications.[50] Pretended tax indifference can be a trap. One cannot better the words of one decision: "I think he would have placed himself where the Court at least would have opened his eyes if he had said that he did not give some consideration to the tax problem, the Court would have known that that was not a fact. People look after their own interest, that's the reason America is great. . . ."[51]

Reliance upon Experts

A taxpayer may buttress his case with the testimony of expert professionals. But if the Internal Revenue Service position in a controversy is supported by the equally persuasive testimony of experts of comparable stature, there is a stand-off. The taxpayer loses because he has not met his burden of proof.[52]

One's reliance upon an expert is misplaced if his adversary's expert has even more imposing qualifications or fewer chinks in his armor. One taxpayer's valuation expert was bypassed by a court when it was shown that he had failed to pass an examination of the American Institute of Real Estate Appraisers, whereas the Internal Revenue Service's expert had passed the examination.[53]

Tips on Preparation of Tax Returns

Omission of income may be deemed to be fraud and not negligence when a taxpayer fails to let his accountant know about the transaction.[54] Omitted income is surrounded by the aura of willful failure to report where even the accountant is kept out of the secret. In another case, a corporation was assessed a fraud penalty where income of uncertain character had been omitted, despite the accountant's recommendation to his client that a formal ruling be requested. The ruling was not requested.[55]

Where a taxpayer failed to include certain income on his tax return, the omission could not be characterized as simple negligence, for he must have known that his income was larger than reflected on the tax return; credit applications he had filed contained statements of much higher income.[56]

One frequently hears the gratuitous advice that something should be left on the Federal income tax return for the Revenue agent to disallow so that he will not dig around too much and thereby unearth something far more serious. It is more likely that if the Revenue agent easily finds the crumbs which have been tossed out for him to discover, he will be encouraged to delve more deeply; for such items create doubts as to the accuracy of the entire return.[57]

Taxpayers get irritated just as other people do—assuming there are other people. But if anger shows on the tax return, it may prejudice one's case in more important areas. One taxpayer had been engaged in a controversy with the Internal Revenue Service about a certain deduction. In rejecting the taxpayer's position, the court pointed out that the return presented substantial, obvious doubts about taxable income, specifically referring to a claimed deduction of $250 for "Harassment I.R.S." The taxpayer got his editorial comment about the Internal Revenue Service into the record. But that was all that he got.[58]

In the case of a questionable deduction, it is easy to conclude that one should claim it since the worst that can happen is a disallowance which would leave the taxpayer in exactly the same position as if he had not deducted that item in the first place. But a disallowance may be accompanied by a negligence penalty, as where the point had been covered by the Treasury Regulations.[59] And if the court is convinced that the taxpayer's knowledge of taxation was so great that he *must* have known the item was not deductible, there could be a fraud penalty for willful understatement of income.

NOTES

1. *Coady v. Commissioner*, 289 F.2d 490 (6th Cir., 1961).
2. Revenue Ruling 64-147, 1964-1 CB (Part 1) 136.
3. *United States et al. v. California Portland Cement Company et al.*, 413 F.2d 161 (9th Cir., 1969).
4. *Vulcan Materials Company v. United States*, 446 F.2d 690 (5th Cir., 1971).
5. *Automobile Club of Michigan v. Commissioner*, 353 U.S. 180 (1957).
6. *McLane et al. v. Commissioner*, 377 F.2d 557 (9th Cir., 1967).
7. *Bornstein et al. v. United States*, 345 F.2d 558 (Ct. Cl., 1965).
8. *Bookwalter v. Brecklein et al.*, 357 F.2d 78 (8th Cir., 1966).
9. *Jacqueline Stokes*, T.C. Memo. 1970-200 (filed July 16, 1970).
10. *Bookwalter v. Mayer et al.*, 345 F.2d 476 (8th Cir., 1965).
11. *Smale & Robinson, Inc. v. United States*, 123 F. Supp. 457 (D.C., S.D. Cal., 1954).
12. *James Couzens*, 11 B.T.A. 1040 (1928).
13. *United Block Company, Inc. v. Helvering*, 123 F.2d 704 (2d Cir., 1941).
14. *Arthur William Peterson et al.*, T.C. Memo. 1970-181 (filed June 29, 1970).
15. *Sampson et al. v. Commissioner*, 444 F.2d 530 (6th Cir., 1971).
16. *Federal Crop Insurance Corp. v. Merrill*, 332 U.S. 380 (1947).
17. *Walker-Hill Co. v. United States*, 162 F.2d 259 (7th Cir., 1947).
18. *Times-World Corporation v. United States*, 250 F. Supp. 43 (D.C., W.D. Va., 1966).
19. *WEG Dial Telephone, Inc.*, T.C. Memo. 1966-41 (filed February 25, 1966).
20. *Gulf Power Company*, 10 T.C. 852 (1948).

21. *Kansas City Southern Railway Company et al. v. Commissioner*, 52 F.2d 372 (8th Cir., 1931).

22. *Haber et al. v. Commissioner*, 422 F.2d 198 (5th Cir., 1970).

23. I.R.C. Section 316(a).

24. *Linton A. Mollath et al.*, T.C. Memo. 1965-290 (filed November 2, 1965).

25. *Commissioner v. Sansome*, 60 F.2d 931 (2d Cir., 1932).

26. *Lloyd E. Peterson et al.*, T.C. Memo. 1965-196 (filed December 13, 1965).

27. *George W. Knipe et al.*, T.C. Memo. 1965-131 (filed May 17, 1965).

28. *Clarence L. Bibb*, T.C. Memo. 1965-296 (filed November 8, 1965).

29. Regulations Section 1.404(a)-1(b).

30. *Sullivan v. United States*, 363 F.2d 724 (8th Cir., 1966).

31. *Ole Bardahl et al.*, T.C. Memo. 1965-116 (filed April 29, 1965).

32. *Robert R. Walker, Inc. et al.*, T.C. Memo. 1965-28 (filed February 16, 1965), *aff'd*, 362 F.2d 140 (7th Cir., 1966).

33. *Ruderman v. United States*, 355 F.2d 995 (2d Cir., 1966).

34. *George R. Tollefson et al.*, 52 T.C. 671 (1969), *aff'd*, 431 F.2d 511 (2d Cir., 1970).

35. *Montgomery Engineering Company v. United States*, D.C., N.J., 1964, *aff'd*, 334 F.2d 996 (3d Cir., 1965).

36. *Lacy et al. v. Commissioner*, 341 F.2d 54 (10th Cir., 1965).

37. Regulation 4, Section 404, 432.

38. *Gregg v. Phinney*, D.C., W.D. Texas, 1962.

39. Revenue Procedure 70-26, 1970-2 CB 507.

40. *Rife et al. v. Commissioner*, 356 F.2d 883 (5th Cir., 1966).

41. *Jockmus et al. v. United States*, 222 F. Supp. 781 (D.C., Conn., 1963).

42. *Himmelfarb et al. v. United States*, 175 F.2d 924 (9th Cir., 1949).

43. *Canaday v. United States*, 354 F.2d 849 (8th Cir., 1966).

44. *United States v. Tarlowski*, 305 F. Supp. 112 (D.C., E.D. N.Y., 1969).

45. *Borge et al. v. Commissioner*, 405 F.2d 673 (2d Cir., 1968).

46. *Gyro Engineering Corporation v. United States*, 276 F. Supp. 454 (D.C., C.D. Cal., 1967).

47. *Edmund F. Ball et al.*, 54 T.C. 1200 (1970).

48. *Henry McK. Haserot*, 41 T.C. 562 (1964), *rem'd'd*, 355 F.2d 200 (6th Cir., 1966), *on remand*, 46 T.C. 864 (1966), *aff'd*, 399 F.2d 828 (6th Cir., 1968).

49. *Sam Siegel*, 45 T.C. 566 (1966).

50. *King Enterprises, Inc. v. United States*, 418 F.2d 511 (Ct. Cl., 1969).

51. *Feldman v. Thomas*, D.C., N.D. Texas, 1945, *aff'd*, 156 F.2d 488 (5th Cir., 1946).

52. *United States v. Miriani*, 310 F. Supp. 217 (D.C., E.D. Mich., 1967).

53. *Chichester et al. v. United States*, 185 Ct. Cl. 591 (1968).

54. *Burrell et al. v. Commissioner*, 400 F.2d 682 (10th Cir., 1968).

55. *Colombo Club, Inc.*, 54 T.C. 355 (1970).

56. *Benjamin Sandler et al.*, T.C. Memo. 1970-55 (filed March 3, 1970).

57. *James Schulz*, 16 T.C. 401 (1951).

58. *Edward T. Wayland*, T.C. Memo. 1970-140 (filed June 3, 1970).

59. *Barton et al. v. Commissioner*, 424 F.2d 1295 (7th Cir., 1970).

CHAPTER 27

State Law: Its Effect
on Federal Taxes

Tax factors affect almost every move we make in our business and personal lives. Tax factors are, in turn, affected by many nontax factors.

In this chapter we shall deal with the effect of state law on Federal taxation and, in the next chapter, the integration of corporate tax planning and an individual's estate planning.

The effects of the Federal income tax may vary from state to state as the result of differences in state law. Such variations do not, however, violate the constitutional prohibitions against delegation of the taxing power and denial of equal protection of the laws.[1]

At the same time, it must be recognized that Federal income tax laws are to be construed in the light of their general purpose—to establish a nationwide scheme of taxation uniform in its application. Hence, their provisions are not to be taken as subject to state control or limitation unless the language or necessary implication of the section involved makes their application dependent on state laws.[2] But, as has already been indicated, such dependency on state laws is sometimes required. For example, the existence of property rights or rights to property is determined solely by state law. The Internal Revenue Code creates no property rights, but merely attaches federally defined consequences to rights created under state law.[3]

Property Rights

State law generally determines the character of the interest or property right, and Federal law determines the application of Federal tax to that right or interest.[4] Thus, whether leasehold improvements belong to, and are taxed to, the lessor or the lessee is a matter of state law.[5] Whether the Federal income tax applies to the original owner of income-producing property or to a transferee may depend upon whether an effective transfer had taken place under state law. A transferor of a stock certificate was subject to Federal income tax upon dividends where, under applicable state law, title could be transferred only by delivery of the certificate along with an appropriate endorsement or power of attorney.[6] So, where an oral conveyance of realty is invalid under state law, the transferor remained liable for the Federal income tax on the rent therefrom.[7]

While Federal law determines whether insurance proceeds are to be included in a decedent's gross estate for Federal estate tax purposes, it is necessary to look to the applicable state law to ascertain the nature of his rights under the policies.[8]

On the other hand, contrary to the general rule giving ascendancy to state law, where the property involved is subject to rights created by Federal law, Federal law, not state law, is controlling. Thus, a valid gift during the donor's lifetime of Series E Treasury bonds cannot be accomplished by manual delivery to a donee unless the bonds are also surrendered and reissued in the name of the donee in accordance with Treasury Regulations. Regardless of what state law may say about the requirements for gifts, Series E bonds may not be transferred in any manner except that authorized by the Treasury Regulations.[9]

Once a state-created property interest is found by reference to state law, one enters the province of Federal law. State-created exemptions and limitations are inoperative in preventing the attachment of Federal tax liens.[10]

Form of Organization

Generally, the classes into which organizations are to be placed for purposes of Federal taxation are determined under the Federal tax laws.[11] Thus, Federal law determines what is meant by a personal holding company for Federal tax purposes so that the fact that the corporation in question may not be a holding company under state law is irrelevant for Federal tax purposes.[12]

A corporation may be subject to the Federal tax on accumulated earnings even if state law prohibits a corporation with impaired earnings from paying a dividend.[13]

A trust may be ignored for Federal tax purposes by the Internal Revenue Service even though the trust had complied fully with the formalities of state law.[14] On the other hand, wheteher or not a particular trust is deemed to be revocable for Federal tax purposes is a matter of state law.[15] State law may provide, for example, that unless a trust is specifically made irrevocable, it is revocable.[16] State law may permit a corporation to be a partner in a partnership (as is the case in California).[17]

Corporate Existence

Whether a corporation exists as an entity for Federal tax purposes depends upon state law. A corporation's status, factually or legally, is determined by state law when the corporation fails to comply with certain state statutory conditions which affect the corporation's right to do business.[18] The length of the period of time that a corporation continues to exist as a body corporate depends upon the law of the state in which the corporation was created.[19]

But if a corporation actually continues to function without regard to its status under the laws of the state of incorporation, the resultant activities may trigger Federal income taxes. A corporation is subject to Federal income tax liability as long as it continues to do business in a corporate manner, despite the fact that its legal corporate status under state law has been voluntarily or involuntarily terminated. A liquidating corporation continues its Federal tax existence so long as it retains valuable assets.[20]

Sales

When or even whether a sale has taken place for Federal income tax purposes may depend upon state law.[21] But reality must prevail over mere formalism. The principles and concepts which the courts apply in the application of the Federal income tax law are not governed solely by state criteria. The question of whether there was in truth and reality the sale of a capital asset within the meaning of the Federal tax laws must be considered where the issue involves capital assets.[22]

Form of the Instrument

The form of the instrument or its validity under state law does not control its treatment for Federal tax purposes.[23]

It is not decisive that notes are executed in accordance with state law and are described by the parties as "loans" if they have the characteristics of equity for Federal income tax purposes.[24] In one case, it was noted that although an investor's advancing funds at the risk of success of a business may be a criterion for bad debt treatment in Maryland, just the opposite is true for Federal income tax purposes, which purposes cannot be circumscribed by state law.[25]

Reallocation of Income and Expenses

If two corporations are under common control, the Internal Revenue Service may reallocate income from one company to another where the transactions are at less than arm's length even if this results in the reallocation to one of the companies of a type of income which under state law that company is not permitted to receive. Such was the case where Indiana law forbade a finance company from receiving any income except interest; insurance functions were carried on by an affiliate, but the insurance income was reallocated by the Service to the finance company. The court stated that the criteria for what constitutes income and the appropriateness of a reallocation of less than arm's length transactions are a matter of Federal law.[26] But in a later case under rather similar facts, the United States Supreme Court held to the contrary.[27]

In a case involving an intercompany lease, the taxpayer argued that the requisite common control for the purpose of the arm's length provision, more than 50 percent, did not exist, for under state law, 80 percent of the stockholders had to approve a lease of substantially all of a corporation's assets. True, there was not 80 percent control there, but the court held that for Federal income tax purposes the 50 percent rule of the statute[28] must apply.[29]

Embezzlement Losses

An embezzlement loss is taken in the year of discovery unless at year-end there is a reasonable prospect of reimbursement from another party. The extent of the other party's liability, and hence the year of deduction for Federal income tax purposes, may depend upon state law, as where a state statute declared that a bank had no liability if a depositor had failed to exercise due diligence.[30]

Privileged Communications

A taxpayer cannot invoke the sanctity of the attorney-client privilege unless the party to whom communication was made was an attorney. Each state determines, within constitutional limitations, who may or may not practice law in its courts.[31] But once that is established, state statutes are irrelevant inasmuch as the question of privilege in a Federal income tax investigation is determined by Federal law.[32]

A physician-patient privilege is not recognized for Federal income tax purposes, except if it is set out in a state statute. But such a state law will not bar the Internal Revenue Service from examining any records pertaining to a taxpayer.[33]

If, under state law, the workpapers of a public accountant are his property, his client cannot invoke the Fifth Amendment by claiming that the production of this material under subpoena might amount to self-incrimination.[34]

Whether evidence obtained by police can be used in a Federal tax case may depend upon whether the police had followed procedures which were legal under state law.[35]

Bad Debts

For Federal income tax purposes, a debt cannot be written off unless it represents an enforceable obligation. State law may determine that. Where a state law declared that any obligation with annual interest in excess of six percent was void, the holder of a note with 20 percent semi-annual interest could not write off the debt when it became bad.[36]

Decisions by State Courts

If Federal income tax is dependent upon interpretation of rights under state law, decisions as to the meaning of that law by state courts other than the supreme tribunal of that state are not binding upon Federal authorities. The Federal court considering the tax issue will supply its own interpretation of what the state law means after giving proper regard to relevant rulings of other courts of the state.[37]

NOTES

1. *Phillips et al. v. Commissioner*, 283 U.S. 589 (1931).
2. *United States v. Pelzer*, 312 U.S. 339 (1941).
3. *United States v. Bess*, 357 U.S. 51 (1958).
4. *Norton, Jr. et al. v. United States*, 217 F. Supp. 474 (D.C., W.D. Ky., 1963).
5. *O'Malley et al. v. United States*, 220 F. Supp. 30 (D.C., N.D. Ill., 1963).
6. *Edward H. Russell et al.*, 40 T.C. 810 (1963), *aff'd*, 345 F.2d 534 (5th Cir., 1965).
7. *C. O. Bibby et al.*, 44 T.C. 638 (1965).
8. *Max J. Gorby Estate*, 53 T.C. 80 (1969).
9. *Lyla C. Curry Estate v. United States*, 409 F.2d 671 (6th Cir., 1969).
10. *United States v. Taylor et al.*, 254 F. Supp. 752 (D.C., N.D. Cal., 1966).
11. Regulations Section 301.7701-1(c).
12. *Olean Times Publishing Company*, 42 B.T.A. 1277 (1940).
13. *Cooperative Publishing Company et al. v. Commissioner*, 115 F.2d 1017 (9th Cir., 1940).
14. *Moskin v. Johnson*, 217 F.2d 278 (2d Cir., 1954).
15. *Moore et al. v. Campbell, Jr.*, 267 F. Supp. 126 (D.C., N.D. Texas, 1967).
16. *Harold E. Casey Estate*, 55 T.C. 737 (1971).
17. See *Charles Turner*, T.C. Memo. 1965-101 (filed April 15, 1965).
18. *M. H. McDonnell et al.*, T.C. Memo. 1965-125 (filed May 11, 1965).
19. *Title Company v. Wilcox Building Corporation*, 302 U.S. 120 (1937).
20. *Messer et al. v. Commissioner*, 438 F.2d 774 (3d Cir., 1971).
21. *The Jefferson Mills, Inc. v. United States*, 259 F. Supp. 305 (D.C., N.D. Ga., 1965), *aff'd*, 377 F.2d 392 (5th Cir., 1966).
22. *Trousdale et al. v. Commissioner*, 219 F.2d 563 (9th Cir., 1955).
23. *W. O. Covey, Inc.*, T.C. Memo. 1969-273 (filed December 15, 1969).
24. *Berkowitz et al. v. United States*, 411 F.2d 818 (5th Cir., 1969).
25. *Sherwood Memorial Gardens, Inc.*, 42 T.C. 211 (1964), *aff'd*, 350 2d 225 (7th Cir., 1965).
26. *Local Finance Corporation et al. v. Commissioner*, 407 F.2d 629 (7th Cir., 1969).
27. *Commissioner v. First Security Bank of Utah, N.A. et al.*, 405 U.S. 394 (1972).
28. I.R.C. Section 482.
29. *South Texas Rice Warehouse Co. v. Commissioner*, 366 F.2d 890 (5th Cir., 1966).
30. *Rainbow Inn, Inc. v. Commissioner*, 433 F.2d 640 (3d Cir., 1970).
31. *Baird et al. v. Koerner et al.*, 279 F.2d 623 (9th Cir., 1963).
32. *In re Samuel W. Kearney*, 227 F. Supp. 174 (D.C., S.D. N.Y., 1964).
33. *United States et al. v. Kansas City Lutheran Home and Hospital Association et al.*, 297 F. Supp. 239 (D.C., W.D. Mo., 1969).
34. *Deck et al. v. United States et al.*, 339 F.2d 739 (D.C., D.C., 1964).
35. *Miller v. United States*, 354 F.2d 801 (8th Cir., 1966).
36. *William K. Harriman et al.*, T.C. Memo. 1967-190 (filed October 4, 1967).
37. *Second National Bank of New Haven et al. v. United States et al.*, 357 U.S. 456 (1967).

CHAPTER 28

Corporate Reorganizations and Estate Planning

Corporate Reorganizations

Tax planning should consider the many uses and the flexibility of the tax-free corporate reorganization.[1] Although the Internal Revenue Code generally requires immediate recognition of gain or loss upon the sale or exchange of property, certain of the reorganization sections permit consummation of formal business readjustments without immediate taxation of the participating businesses or of their shareholders.[2] The premise of the tax-free corporate reorganization provisions is that certain transactions constitute corporate readjustments and are not the proper occasion for the incidence of taxation. Congressional policy is to free from immediate tax consequences those corporate reorganizations involving a continuity of business enterprises under modified corporate form and a continuity of interest on the part of the owners before and after, where there is no basic change in relationships and not a sufficient "cashing in" of proprietary interests to justify contemporaneous taxation.[3]

Congress realized that the splitting up of a corporation and the merging of two corporations were not events that normally justified the imposition of a tax. Thus, if a stockholder merely traded one stock certificate for another, he would have no cash or liquid assets with which to pay a tax. To Congress, these reorganizations represented essentially a change in form. As a general rule, however, an exchange of stock is taxed.[4] Only six types of corporate reorganization can be characterized as tax-free. These are defined in Section 368 of the Internal Revenue Code by the letters "A" through "F." All are equally sanctioned.[5]

The six types of tax-free reorganization, with their identifying letters, are:

(A) A statutory merger or consolidation.

(B) The acquisition by one corporation, in exchange solely for all or part of its voting stock (or that of its parent corporation where the parent owns at least 80 percent of the acquiring company's stock), of stock of another corporation, provided that the acquiring corporation owns at least 80 percent of the acquired company's stock immediately after the transaction.

(C) The acquisition by one corporation, in exchange solely for all or part of its voting stock (or that of its parent corporation where the parent owns at least 80 percent of the acquiring company's stock), of substantially all of the properties of another corporation. In determining whether the exchange is solely for stock, one disregards the acquiring company's assumption of a liability of the other corporation, or the fact that the property is subject to a liability.

(D) A transfer by a corporation of all or part of its assets to another corporation if immediately after the transfer, the transferor or one or more of its shareholders is in control of the corporation to which the assets are transferred. This applies only if, in pursuance of the plan of reorganization, stock or securities of the corporation to which the assets are transferred are distributed in an approved manner. Requirements are: (1) the distributing corporation and the controlled corporation, immediately after the transaction, must be engaged in the active conduct of a trade or business; (2) the distributing corporation must have been actively conducting that trade or business for at least five years; (3) the transaction cannot have been used principally as a device for the distribution of the earnings and profits of the distributing corporation or the controlled corporation or both.

(E) A recapitalization.

(F) A mere change in identity, form, or place of organization, however effected.[6]

If a transaction qualifies as a tax-free reorganization, there is no recognition of gain or loss upon the disposition of assets or upon the receipt of stock or other property under stipulated circumstances. The theory is that if a corporation changes in a manner which is more formal than substantial, there is no gain or loss because, in effect, it is the same corporation as before. The same is deemed to be true where an investor does not really close out his investment even though it now is expressed in a different way; that is, with different pieces of paper. Inasmuch as the corporation or the investment is really the same before and after the tax-free reorganization, the basis of properties usually is unchanged. A corollary to non-recognition of gain or loss under this theory requires the carry-over of the basis of corporate assets. This insures that any gain or loss realized, but not recognized, will not escape taxation; it will simply be deferred.[7]

The reorganization sections are automatic in their application. Accordingly, a taxpayer may be affected adversely by what was intended to be a relief provision.[8] If a corporation which owns 80 percent or more of the stock in a subsidiary corporation liquidates the latter within three years, there is no gain or loss for tax purposes; if an actual loss is indicated, the corporation should consider having the transaction cast in a manner that does not meet the definition of a tax-free reorganization. If the transaction does not meet the requirements of a tax-free reorganization, then loss otherwise unrecognized will be taken into account for tax purposes. This applies, in general, to all of the tax attributes where one corporation is deemed to have stepped into the tax shoes of another corporation. A net operating loss, an unused capital loss carry-over, an accounting method, etc., of a predecessor corporation will be taken into account by the successor corporation under most forms of tax-free reorganization.[9] But if the principal purpose of a taxpayer's acquisition of a corporation is utilization of an allowance, credit, loss, or other tax benefit not otherwise available, the Internal Revenue Service is authorized to refuse to recognize such a tax benefit.[10] Under specified circumstances, a net operating loss carry-over is automatically reduced or disallowed.[11]

Essential to a tax-free reorganization is the existence of a *sound business purpose*. Congress was trying to give business enterprises leeway in readjusting their corporate enterprises to better suit their business purposes. If the rearrangement had that purpose, Congress was willing to concede them some possible tax advantages. If the rearrangement had no business purpose, the tax-free reorganization was not to be available.[12]

Examples of tax-free reorganizations with a sound business purpose are:

(1) The continuation of two or more enterprises by statutory merger or consolidation to achieve greater financial strength or to eliminate duplicating expenses.

(2) The acquisition of control of another corporation, or substantially all of its properties, for stock instead of for cash. This permits the acquiring corporation to expand, diversify, and strengthen its financial posture without immediate effect upon the acquirer's liquidity. In addition to acquiring the type of asset which appears upon the balance sheet, a corporation may acquire the services of experienced executives or other key personnel by obtaining control of the company for which these persons work, perhaps under contract.

(3) The division of a corporate business into two or more separate corporations for marketing, diversification, risk compartmentalization, decentralization, state tax minimization, and other reasons relating to the operation of the business. This procedure may be used where certain stockholders no longer can work in harmony; each group may proceed in its own way with a portion of the corporate activity. Where key employees refuse to remain unless they are given the opportunity to buy stock, a spin-off may be used to bring down the price of the stock to a price which the employee can afford or to remove from the stock ownership of the employees certain assets which the corporation desires to retain under their original control.[13]

(4) A corporation's elimination of its bond issue through replacement with some form of stock so that onerous fixed charges can be eliminated. The replacement of one-class voting stock with voting and nonvoting shares so that the voting control of a corporation can remain with the active shareholders who are actually running the enterprise. Such a procedure is useful where an active shareholder dies and his stock goes to his widow or some other persons who do not intend to be active participants in management. A recapitalization can place the voting stock in the hands of persons who will bear responsibility.

(5) The reincorporation of a corporation in a different state where laws or decisions in the state which had granted the original charter are deemed to be too restrictive.

The area of tax-free reorganizations is so studded with exceptions, special rules, technicalities, and formalities that retaining competent counsel is absolutely indispensable.

Estate Planning

Estate planning is customarily regarded as a technique for an individual's orderly disposition of his properties in line with his objectives and with minimum income tax, estate tax, and gift tax cost.[14] But corporate tax planning frequently can be integrated with an individual's estate planning. Sometimes this is essential from the corporation's point of view.

One of the most desirable objectives of estate planning is reduction of the ultimate gross estate which an individual will own at the time of his death. If a substantial part of his estate consists of stock in a family or other closely-held corporation, these procedures are available:

(1) If the corporation has but one class of stock outstanding, an individual will be disinclined to part with stock, for that would lessen his proportionate interest in control of the business. A tax-free recapitalization could replace the one-class voting stock with voting common and either nonvoting common or preferred stock. Then he could give away as much of the nonvoting stock as he desired to relatives or to charitable organizations (tax deductions being created by the latter form of disposition). His ultimate gross estate would be reduced, while his proportionate voting power in the corporation would remain unchanged.

(2) A buy-sell agreement could provide an arm's length valuation for the stock, a market for it, and even the financing of the plan, as where the plan is funded by life insurance or otherwise. (See chapter 21, What Happens When a Major Stockholder Dies.) This would supply liquidity to the estate and a valuation procedure which would minimize disputes with the Internal Revenue Service about the size of the taxable estate. Without a buy-sell agreement and the necessary funding, a corporation may be torn hopelessly by dissension as to what course of action to pursue in the case of the shares of a deceased stockholder: to pay excessive dividends demanded by relatives of a decedent who could not possibly qualify for the high salary which had been paid to him, to let the stock get into the hands of outside parties who may prove to be incompetent or hostile, or to liquidate the corporation.[15]

(3) Keyman insurance could reimburse the corporation for loss upon the death of a valuable executive or other employee.

(4) A trust could be provided to acquire the stock of a decedent upon his death. Ordinarily, an executor might be inclined to dump the decedent's stock as rapidly as possible, even without taking proper time to find the best possible price, to avoid the personal nuisance of operating an enterprise with which he might be completely unfamiliar. Actually, it might be to the best interest of the decedent's family to continue ownership, in whatever degree, of the going business. If a trust is created for the purpose of continuation of business, the trustees could be company executives or other knowledgeable employees of ability, or the corporation's accountant and attorney, or business consultants who would have the know-how and, if practical, the desire to keep the business functioning. Unlike individuals, most businesses are worth more alive than dead.

(5) If a decedent's stock in a closely-held corporation amounted to

more than 35 percent of his gross estate or 50 percent of his taxable estate, the corporation could redeem as much of his stock as is necessary to pay death taxes and administration expenses without the dividend implications which generally exist where a corporation redeems shares of a major stockholder at a time when there are earnings and profits.[16]

(6) To the extent that a corporation's accumulated earnings are used to buy back stock for a redemption of the type mentioned in (5), immediately above, these earnings will be deemed to have been reasonably retained for the needs of the business, thus not being vulnerable to the accumulated earnings tax.[17]

(7) If an individual has a number of business and investment interests which are not converted to cash by the executor, there is a problem of how to give to plural beneficiaries their respective fractional interests in undivided property. The individual could transfer all of his properties, or any portion of them, to a newly formed corporation in return for at least 80 percent of its stock. This is a tax-free transfer under one of the reorganization provisions.[18] Then, shares of the corporation could be distributed by the executor in whatever amounts the arithmetic called for to the beneficiaries; the assets would not have to be disposed of (perhaps at a particularly unfortunate time) to pay off the beneficiaries.[19]

(8) Generally, it is realized that if an individual at the time of his death holds any significant "incident of ownership" of insurance on his life, the insurance proceeds are includable in his estate. The right to change the names of beneficiaries and to borrow against the policy are "incidents of ownership" in this connection. An individual might seek to avoid this result by "letting" a corporation own policies of insurance on his life; he, as a corporate officer, could then cause the corporation to exercise any rights under the policy, such as change of beneficiaries. But if an individual owns all of the stock of a corporation, a power reserved to the corporation to change the names of beneficiaries will be regarded as an incident of ownership held by the decedent, and the proceeds will be part of his estate.[20] Whether or not ownership of something less than 100 percent of the stock will serve to avoid this result is not free from doubt—at least, in cases where the shareholder exercises full control.

When one disposes of property before his death, this property will be taken out of his ultimate estate; but if assets are given away within three years of death, this is presumed to be a transaction "in contemplation of death" and the property will be included in the decedent's estate for Federal estate tax purposes, even though practically and legally the property had long since ceased to be his.[21] The executor has the opportunity to prove, if he can, that the decedent's motivation for the transfer was associated with thoughts of life rather than death, that the transaction was not effected when the transferor was so conscious of thoughts of impending death that he had made the transfer in lieu of a testamentary disposition.

But motivation associated with one's business or his business activities is associated with life; transactions for such reasons are not regarded as in contemplation of death. A gift of one's stock to his son to stimulate his interest in a family corporation was associated with life.[22] There was a similar finding where a gift was for the purpose of permitting the donor's children to participate in the business.[23] "Contemplation" was not involved where stock was given to the donor's sons as a reward for working in the family business.[24]

Desire of the donor to relieve himself of management of his own property was a motive associated with life.[25] Such also was the case where a decedent had explained to her daughters in a letter, "In this way, you will see, the burden of responsibility on my shoulders will be considerably eased." [26]

Transactions in contemplation of death are not confined to gifts or other transfers. A major stockholder and his corporation entered into a contract, allegedly as an inducement for him to remain with the company. Under the contract, the corporation would pay a sum equal to twice his annual salary to his surviving wife or issue if he were still employed there at the time of his death. Three weeks later, he died. The commuted value of the payments called for in his contract was includable in his gross estate as a transaction in contemplation of death. His illness had existed for about four months prior to his death, and the agreement was made at a time when he had already made an appointment for surgery.[27]

Other transfers which an individual had made during his lifetime may fail to take property out of his ultimate gross estate. These include transfers with retained life estates,[28] transfers taking effect at death,[29] and revocable transfers.[30]

A major stockholder in a closely-held corporation may be disturbed at the lack of any known value for his shares, which could lead the Internal Revenue Service to impose an astronomical valuation for Federal estate tax purposes in the absence of taxpayer proof to the contrary. To avoid heavy estate tax resulting from his executor's inability to prove a value lower than one utilized by a Revenue agent with delusions of corporate grandeur, the stockholder might cause his little-known corporation to be merged with a better-known one; alternatively, he might arrange to have his corporation taken over by another corporation, the shares of which enjoyed a regular market, in a tax-free reorganization. The shares he thus obtained for the stock of his unknown corporation would be far more susceptible to a valuation he could regard as acceptable: actual sales as opposed to theoretical, sometimes fantastic projections or comparisons.

NOTES

1. *See* Robert S. Holzman, *Tax-Free Reorganizations after the Tax Reform Act of 1969*, Lynbrook, N.Y.: The Farnsworth Publishing Company, 1970.
2. *J. O. Willett Estate et al. v. Commissioner*, 365 F.2d 760 (5th Cir., 1966).
3. *King Enterprises, Inc. v. United States*, 418 F.2d 511 (Ct. Cl., 1969).
4. *Davant et al. v. Commissioner*, 366 F.2d 874 (5th Cir., 1966).
5. *Commissioner v. Mary Archer W. Morris Trust*, 367 F.2d 794 (4th Cir., 1966).
6. I.R.C. Section 368(a)(1).
7. *Reef et al. v. Commissioner et al.*, 368 F.2d 125 (5th Cir., 1966).
8. *Prentis et al. v. United States*, 273 F. Supp. 400 (D.C., S.D. N.Y., 1967).
9. I.R.C. Section 381.
10. I.R.C. Section 269.
11. I.R.C. Section 382.

12. *Commissioner v. Wilson et al.*, 353 F.2d 184 (9th Cir., 1965).

13. Revenue Ruling 69-460, 1969-2 CB 51.

14. *See* Robert S. Holzman, *Holzman on Estate Planning*, Englewood Cliffs, N.J.: Prentice-Hall, Inc. 1967.

15. *See Mountain State Steel Foundries, Inc. et al. v. Commissioner et al.*, 284 F.2d 737 (4th Cir., 1960).

16. I.R.C. Section 303.

17. I.R.C. Section 537.

18. I.R.C. Section 351.

19. *See United States v. Mills, Jr. et al.*, 399 F.2d 944 (5th Cir., 1968).

20. Regulations Section 20.2042-1(c)(2).

21. I.R.C. Section 2035.

22. *D. I. Cooper Estate*, 7 T.C. 1236 (1945).

23. *Greer v. Glenn*, 64 F. Supp. 1002 (D.C., E.D. Ky., 1946).

24. *Off v. United States*, 35 F.2d 227 (D.C., S.D. Ill., 1929). .

25. *Bankers Trust Company v. Higgins*, 50 F. Supp. 188 (D.C., S.D. N.Y., 1946).

26. *The Colorado National Bank of Denver v. Nicholas*, 127 F. Supp. 498 (D.C., Colo., 1954).

27. *Bernard L. Porter Estate v. Commissioner*, 442 F.2d 915 (1st Cir., 1971).

28. I.R.C. Section 2036.

29. I.R.C. Section 2037.

30. I.R.C. Section 2038.

Index

burden of proof (*cont.*)

    taxpayer credibility and, 223

    in timely filing of returns and documents, 227

    in travel and entertainment deductions, 217–218

    use of expert witness and, 222–223

    in write-off for abnormal obsolescence, 221

business bad debt deductions, *see* bad debts

business expenditures:

    advertising as, 79–80, 270

    as business-oriented, 76

    buy-out agreements and, 286

    as capital in nature, nondeductibility of, 76, 286

    vs. charitable contributions, 80–81

    commuting expenses as, 82

    entertainment as, 82–83

    fines and penalties as, 77

    gifts as, 83–84

    in going business, 77

    intent and purpose in, 264–274

    kickbacks, rebates or bribes as, 77–78

    liability insurance of directors and officers as, 85

    life insurance premiums as, 84

    lobbying and political contributions as, 80, 270

    medical reimbursement plan as, 84

    "necessary," 75–76

    "ordinary," 75

    vs. personal expenses, 78–79

    pre-business, 77, 295

    repairs as, 81, 269

    requirement of reasonableness in, 78

    in research and development, 295

    travel as, conditions of, 82, 270

    unreimbursed expenses as, 85

    as unrelated to profit, disclosures of, 319

    wife's travel as, 82

business forms, 11–30

    selection of, 290

    significance of, 11

    in state vs. Federal tax laws, 346

business purpose (*see also* purpose), 265

    morality of, 271

buy-and-sell agreements, 278, 279, 282

    and estate planning, 353

    nonvoting stock in, 285

buy-out agreements:

    anticipating implementation of, 282

    capital status in, 286

buy-out agreements (*cont.*)

    "in contemplation of death," 282–283

    disability insurance and, 285

    forms of, 278–279

    funding of, 279–280

    stock values supported with pay-outs of, 285

    valuation of stock in, 280–282

capital, thinness of, 38, 40

capital assets:

    buy-out agreements and, 286

    definition of, 65–66, 266

    disposition of, as capital, 68

    holding period of, 68–69, 260

    vs. ordinary expenses, 71, 264

    and property "held primarily for sale," 66, 266

    right to future income as, 243

    Section 1231, 66–67, 68

capital asset treatment:

    holding period in, 68–69

    in pension trust contributions, 127

    significance of, 64–65

capital expenditures, 69–70

    in collecting insurance claims, 198–199

    cost of insurance as, 197

    legal expenses as, 70

    loss prevention as, 198

    medical expenses as, 70

    vs. operating income, role of purpose in, 264

    protection of earnings as, 70–71

capital gains:

    casualty gains as, 195

    loss of treatment as, 235

    purpose of stock acquisition and, 270–271

    short term vs. long-term, 68–69

capital gains dividends, 26

capital gains tax, 16

    alternative, 64–65

    in electing not to be taxed as corporation, 18–20

    real estate investment trusts and, 25–26

    on regulated investment company dividends, 24–25

"capital loans," 328

capital losses, 18, 19–20, 26, 33

    carry-over provisions for, 259

    involuntary conversions and, 195

    vs. ordinary loss deduction, 21, 270–271